Literary Biographies in *The Lives of Remarkable People* Series in Russia

Crosscurrents: Russia's Literature in Context

Series Editor: Marcia Morris, Georgetown University

Embodying what is specific to a single culture as well as what is common to all humankind, literature has always been a privileged mode of discourse in Russia. *Crosscurrents* takes cognizance of Russian literature's simultaneous particularity and universality by exploring the aesthetic, cultural, political, temporal, and geographical contexts in which it has been written. Monographs and edited collections in the series focus on literature written across cultural periods, geographical divides, and intellectual disciplines. We welcome proposals and manuscripts focused on the intersections between literature and law, religion, philosophy, science, film, the arts, and other disciplines as well as on Russian émigré literature, literature written in Russian by non-Russians, and comparisons of different cultural periods.

Advisory Board

Eliot Borenstein, New York University
Lioudmila Fedorova, Georgetown University
Deborah A. Martinsen, Columbia University
Amy D. Ronner, St. Thomas University
Ilya Vinitsky, Princeton University
Peter Rollberg, George Washington University

Titles in the Series

Literary Biographies in The Lives of Remarkable People Series in Russia: Biography for the Masses, Volume 1, edited by Ludmilla A. Trigos & Carol Ueland
Dostoevsky as Suicidologist: Self-Destruction and the Creative Process, by Amy D. Ronner
Wingless Desire in Modernist Russia: Envy and Authorship in the 1920s, by Yelena Zotova
Babel in Russian and Other Literatures and Topographies: The Tower, the State, and the Chaos of Language, by Martin Meisel
Russian Symbolism in Search of Transcendental Liquescence: Iconizing Emotion by Blending Time, Media, and the Senses, by Anastasia Kostetskaya
Chekhov's Letters: Biography, Context, Poetics, edited by Carol Apollonio and Radislav Lapushin
Physical Pain and Justice: Greek Tragedy and the Russian Novel, by Gary Rosenshield

Literary Biographies in *The Lives of Remarkable People* Series in Russia

Biography for the Masses

Edited by

Ludmilla A. Trigos and Carol Ueland

LEXINGTON BOOKS
Lanham • Boulder • New York • London

Published by Lexington Books
An imprint of The Rowman & Littlefield Publishing Group, Inc.
4501 Forbes Boulevard, Suite 200, Lanham, Maryland 20706
www.rowman.com

86-90 Paul Street, London EC2A 4NE

Copyright © 2022 by The Rowman & Littlefield Publishing Group, Inc.

All rights reserved. No part of this book may be reproduced in any form or by any electronic or mechanical means, including information storage and retrieval systems, without written permission from the publisher, except by a reviewer who may quote passages in a review.

British Library Cataloguing in Publication Information Available

Library of Congress Cataloging-in-Publication Data

Names: Ueland, Carol, editor. | Trigos, Ludmilla A., editor.
Title: Literary biographies in the Lives of Remarkable People Series in Russia : biography for the masses / edited by Carol Ueland and Ludmilla A. Trigos.
Other titles: Crosscurrents--Russia's literature in context.
Description: Lanham : Lexington Books : The Rowman & Littlefield Publishing Group, Inc., 2022. | Series: Crosscurrents: Russia's literature in context | Includes bibliographical references and index. | Summary: "This book examines the role that the legendary Russian biography series, The Lives of Remarkable People, plays in Russian culture. The contributors examine the interplay of research and imagination in biographical narratives, the changing perceptions of what constitutes literary greatness, and the subversive possibilities of biography during eras of censorship"-- Provided by publisher.
Identifiers: LCCN 2021059714 (print) | LCCN 2021059715 (ebook) | ISBN 9781793618290 (cloth) | ISBN 9781793618313 (paperback) | ISBN 9781793618306 (epub)
Subjects: LCSH: 880-01 Zhizn' zamiechatel'nykh" liudeĭ. | 880-02 Zhizn' zamechatel'nykh liudeĭ (Molodaia gvardiia (Firm)) | Authors, Russian--19th century--Biography--History and criticism. | Authors, Russian--20th century--Biography--History and criticism. | Biography as a literary form. | Monographic series--Russia--History--19th century. | Monographic series--Soviet Union.
Classification: LCC PG2991 .L578 2022 (print) | LCC PG2991 (ebook) | DDC 891.709--dc23/eng/20220204
LC record available at https://lccn.loc.gov/2021059714
LC ebook record available at https://lccn.loc.gov/2021059715

A Note on Transliteration

The system of Russian transliteration that we use is that of the Library of Congress, with the following exceptions. Russian first names with common English equivalents will use the latter, for example, Lydia, Alexei, Sergei and Yuri. Masculine family names ending in -skii -ii/yi are spelled with -sky or -y. The vowels ia, io, iu are spelled ya, yo, and yu. The soft and hard signs are not marked. If there is a standard spelling in English of a particular writer's name, such as Alexander Pushkin, Nikolai Gogol or Maxim Gorky, we observe that form. We spell Molodaya gvardiya the way that the press identifies itself in English. All other titles are in LC transliteration.

In the notes and bibliography, we observe strict Library of Congress transliteration, with Russian place names in their English form. In the bibliography, the names of non-Russian authors whose works were published in Russian appear in their original form, not in Russian translation. Unless otherwise noted, all translations from the Russian are done by the individual contributors.

Contents

A Note on Transliteration   v

Acknowledgments   ix

Introduction: Writing and Rewriting the Literary Canon: A History of Russian Biography in the *Lives of Remarkable People* Series   1
Ludmilla A. Trigos and Carol Ueland

Chapter 1: The *Remarkable* Pushkin   45
Angela Brintlinger

Chapter 2: Larger than Life: The Meaning of A. S. Griboedov in Russian National Biography   69
Catherine O'Neil

Chapter 3: N. V. Gogol, Biographer's Conundrum   91
Ludmilla A. Trigos

Chapter 4: Remarkable Tolstoy, from the Age of the Tsars to the Putin Era   117
Caryl Emerson

Chapter 5: Per Aspera Ad Astra: The Remarkable Lives of Fyodor Dostoevsky   143
Alexander Spektor

Chapter 6: In Search of the "True" Chekhov: Approaches and Appropriations   169
Radislav Lapushin

Chapter 7: From Idol to Villain and (Almost) Back: Gorky as Editor and Subject of *Lives of Remarkable People*   189
Irene Masing-Delic

Chapter 8: Alexander Blok as the Model Modernist 215
 Jonathan Stone

Chapter 9: Narrating Eccentricity: The ZhZL Biographies of Anna
 Akhmatova and Marina Tsvetaeva 231
 Alexandra Smith

Chapter 10: Mikhail Bulgakov: Refractions of a Writer's Life 253
 J. A. E. Curtis

Chapter 11: Between Biography and Mythology: The Russian and
 American Lives of Joseph Brodsky 271
 Carol Ueland

Bibliography 299

Index 313

About the Contributors 335

Acknowledgments

Completing a long-term project with many authors is formidable in most times but during a pandemic it becomes next to impossible without the extraordinary help of many people. Librarians are the gatekeeper of scholarship and we benefited from the help of wonderful colleagues and their valiant efforts to further our research, especially when libraries were closed: Robert H. Davis, the Slavic Librarian at Columbia University; Natalia Ermolaeva, Associate Director, Center for Digital Humanities, Firestone Library at Princeton University; Tatiana Chebotareva of the Bakhmeteff Archive in the Rare Books and Manuscripts Library at Columbia University; Diana Greene, Slavic Librarian Emerita, Bobst Library at New York University; and Natalia Nikolaevna Yaroslavtseva of the Herzen Library in Kirov (Vyatka).

This book arose out of a series of panels at various conferences of the Modern Language Association, the American Teachers of Slavic and East European Languages, and the Association for Slavic East European and Eurasian Studies as a result of which the first parts of this manuscript were crafted. We also would like to acknowledge the contribution of three late colleagues who participated in conferences at the earliest stages of our project: Robert Belknap, Catharine Theimer Nepomnyashchy and Nina Perlina.

We would like to thank our authors for *remarkable* contributions as well as their patience and encouragement: Angela Brintlinger, Julie Curtis, Caryl Emerson, Radislav Lapushin, Irene Masing-Delic, Catherine O'Neil, Alexandra Smith, Alexander Spektor, and Jonathan Stone. Irene encouraged us to publish the first versions of several of the articles in the Forum "Lives of Remarkable People" in the *Slavic and East European Journal* (vol. 60, no. 2, Summer–Fall 2016), of which she was the editor at that time. We thank the *Slavic and East European Journal* for their permission to use excerpts of our article "Literary Biography in the *Lives of Remarkable People Series (Zhizn' zamechatel'nykh Liudei)*" in our current introduction as well as excerpts from earlier versions of articles by Angela Brintlinger, "The Remarkable Pushkin," and Caryl Emerson, "Remarkable Tolstoy, from the Age of Empire to the

Putin Era (1894–2006)." Carol Apollonio generously agreed to complete Robert Belknap's unfinished work on Dostoevsky in *ZhZL,* which was also published as "Dostoevsky in the Lives of Remarkable People." Carol's support and advice was instrumental in assisting us in completing the volume. We are grateful to Paula R. Backscheider for her commentary to the Forum, "Opportunities in Comparative Biography," which expanded upon how this material related to Western models and Andrew Baruch Wachtel for his contextualization of the importance of writers' lives in the Russian cultural imagination.

We greatly benefited from participating in the first working conference devoted to Russian life writing organized by Polly Jones in March 2014, "Writing and Reading Russian Biography in the Nineteenth and Twentieth Centuries" at the University College, University of Oxford. Discussions with Nathaniel Knight, Ben Ekloff, Tatiana Saburova, Gerald Stanton Smith, Barbara Heldt and other colleagues stimulated us to think about biography and life writing in new ways. Selected papers were recrafted and published as "Writing Russian Lives: The Poetics and Politics of Biography in Modern Russian Culture," a special issue of the *Slavonic and Eastern European Review*, vol 96, no.1 (January 2018), and then issued as a book under the same title. We thank the Modern Humanities Association for permission to use material from our article, "Creating a National Biographical Series: F. F. Pavlenkov's 'Lives of Remarkable People,' 1890–1924," published in that volume.

Colleagues at the Harriman Institute have been especially supportive of this project. Ronald Meyer, Publications Director, provided invaluable advice throughout. Our initial interest was stimulated by conversations with Edward Kasinec who encouraged us to expand our purview beyond the reception of individual authors to the history of reading and print culture in Russia.

Marcia Morris and Lexington Books were early supporters of our project. Finally, we greatly thank our editor, Eric Kuntzman, for his diligence and efforts to see this book through to completion during difficult times.

Introduction

Writing and Rewriting the Literary Canon

A History of Russian Biography in the Lives of Remarkable People Series

Ludmilla A. Trigos and Carol Ueland

The genre of biography has long been extremely popular among readers and authors but has been dismissed as a serious endeavor by scholars partly due to its hybrid nature, appropriating features of both literature and history. And yet, as Alisa Akimova states: "Approaching history, humanizing it, the biography of a remarkable person teaches the reader to think historically, fostering in him an accountability for the fate of humankind." She offers as illustrations that "the biography of a composer reveals the magic of music, of an artist the wonders of the combination of colors and helps [us] see the world in a new way."[1] Although biography has been historically undervalued as both a literary and historical genre, its larger dimensions are reconceived and its popularity surges in time of cultural and political paradigm shifts. The idea of the sociocultural significance of biography is now becoming central to studies of the genre. Discussing this larger cultural and political purpose, Paula R. Backscheider has observed, "No genre is more important to a nation than biography."[2] Biography can serve as an indicator of cultural currents and particular social practices "whereby the reader, on the one hand 'learns to think narratively . . . , to imagine himself in the role of an active participant or personage' . . . and on the other hand, receives knowledge about society and the processes taking place there."[3] Our methodology of comparative biography allows us to see the important functions that biography can fulfill in society: readers "discover how reputations developed, how fashions changed, how social and moral attitudes moved, how standards of judgment altered, as each generation, one after another, continuously reconsidered and idealized or condemned its forebears in the writing and rewriting of biography."[4] Moreover, comparative biography highlights the poetics of biographical texts across generations by revealing the inner mechanisms by which biographers reconstruct the personality or "living face" of the subject in relationship to the historical context of the subject's as well as the biographer's own times.

There are dozens of biographies for each major writer in Russian literature and many repeated lives within *The Lives of Remarkable People* (*Zhizn' zamechatel'nykh liudei*, or *ZhZL*) series. This volume examines canonical literary biographies within the series and the central role in Russian culture played by the series as a whole from its inception in 1890 through the Soviet period until today.[5] Under this single title, there were three different iterations of the series: the original series, spanning from 1890 to the mid-1920s; its revival under Maxim Gorky from 1933 through the end of the Soviet era; and a return to a private publishing enterprise in the 1990s until today. We investigate the ways in which the treatment of biographical figures in the series over time comprises a case study for continuities and changes in Russian national identity. Florenty Fyodorovich Pavlenkov (1839–1900), a progressively minded St. Petersburg publisher of educational books for the masses, founded the series in 1890 to provide positive models from world history to the youth of his era.[6] Pavlenkov focused on a wide variety of figures from the "world intelligentsia" and sought to provide newly emergent readers with the broadest array of information. Influenced by Pavlenkov's series, Gorky became determined to revive it when he returned to the Soviet Union in the early 1930s. Gorky's continuation became especially important to inculcate Soviet values. By the late Soviet era, *ZhZL* was a mainstay of Soviet publishing. Moreover, the possession of *ZhZL* volumes were an illustration of *kultur'nost'* (education and proper upbringing) and marked their owner as an *intelligent* (a member of the intelligentsia) or at the very least as someone who strove to be perceived as educated and cultured, or upwardly mobile. After the collapse of the Soviet Union and despite the end of state-subsidized publishing, the series survived the transition to a market economy. The series remains a global phenomenon today, not only as the longest-running Russian series, but, as claimed by the publisher, also as the longest-running biography series of any kind anywhere. This longevity allows us to focus on the way that the series and the cultural values it espoused evolved during three very different eras and regimes.

Over the course of the series' history, it has produced more than two thousand individual titles. Given the dominant place of literature in Russian culture, it is not surprising that writers' lives would become some of the most popular and sought-after volumes across all three iterations of the series. The twelve essays in this volume focus on the outstanding figures in the Russian literary canon within the changing historical context of the series. As Michael Benton reminds us:

> Both our knowledge and interpretations of history and individual lives are not fossilized exhibits in some time-exempt museum arranged for the benefit of literary critics. They are changing constructs created from the discipline of research into primary sources and represented according to the predilections of their times. Looked at this way, the rewriting of a literary life in different periods offers a multifaceted portrait of the subject, a historicized view of the genre, and an insight into how particular cultures and societies saw themselves. (131)

The authors of the articles in this volume examine the construction of writers' lives to reveal the changing conceptions of the authorial image according to the impact of the times in which these biographies were written. Attuned to the narrative strategies of the biographers themselves, our contributors turn to questions of the evolving poetics of biography as a genre.[7]

PRECURSORS TO PAVLENKOV'S SERIES

In studying *Lives of Remarkable People*, historians of Pavlenkov's series point to the traditional models for the lives of great men, often citing the most famous classical biographer Plutarch's *Parallel Lives*[8] and the revival of this genre in Thomas Carlyle's lectures published as a collection in *On Heroes, Hero-Worship and The Heroic in History* (1841).[9] Our discussion situates Pavlenkov's series and writers' biographies within the genre of biography in the Western European and the Russian traditions. The origins of biography go back to preliterate times. Far from being only histories of great men, as Anna Makolkin notes, oral biographical forms in both Western and non-Western traditions suggest that "the first biographers may have been women mourning the dead. . . . a person of any occupation and an ordinary person as well."[10] The earliest and shortest written form of biography appears to be the tombstone, commonly noting the dates of a person's birth (if known) and death.[11] In order to tell a life story, there has to be accessible source material: "biography is a fact-dependent genre, which constructs its plot after the original model is completed; a real *life* serves as a matrix for the biography."[12] Many narrative elements remain consistent in different types of biography: the origins (family background and birth), upbringing and education, major accomplishments (often seen as an illustration of virtues), and the death of the subject.[13] Only later did biography become what modern readers consider a "coherent chronological narrative."[14]

Sergei Averintsev discusses the etymology of the term "biography" by noting that *bio* or *vita* were classical terms for the writing of a life used interchangeably by Greek and Latin speaking peoples. Though the genre was ancient, the term *biographia* came about not earlier than the sixth century AD.[15] The genre evolved from an epitaph or eulogy to an expanded description of a person's character, whether positive or negative. Plutarch himself distinguished his genre by stating: "It is not Histories that I am writing, but Lives; and in the most illustrious deeds there is not always a manifestation of virtue or vice, nay, a slight thing like a phrase or a jest often makes a greater revelation of character than battles where thousands fall, or the greatest armaments, or sieges of cities."[16] Makolkin suggests: "Greek and Roman life provided biographical history with plots that had been drawn from the life of the polis or empire. Christianity added another competing institution to the State—the Church."[17] As Christian narrators replaced classical biographers, martyrs and saints became the primary subjects of biography but the narrative structure of the life "did not differ from the most common time-honored forms of biographical narration."[18] In Russia, these figures, such as Boris and Gleb or Alexander Nevsky, were both political and religious.[19] Hence the predominant Russian biographical form from the tenth to the seventeenth century was the hagiographical biography (*zhitie*) as the Orthodox Church continued to influence cultural and political institutions long after the church's role in Western Europe had diminished. As Dmitry Kalugin notes, the term *biografiia* appeared only in the eighteenth century in Russia and was used interchangeably with the words *zhizneopisanie* or *zhitie*.[20] The model of saints' lives persisted throughout the eighteenth century and well into the nineteenth century even in secular circles and strongly impacted the path that secular biography would take in Russia.[21] The lack of secular institutions until the eighteenth century was a significant factor in the late development of biographies of figures whose lives were not suited to a hagiographic model.

Starting in the eighteenth century, the establishment of academic institutions and learned societies provided a broader arena for societal involvement beyond the church and the military which could then be memorialized. As a consequence, the source material needed for secular biographies began to be produced, including the academic vitae and éloges of various learned and professional associations. In addition, the growth of Masonic lodges in Russia served to propagate the ideas of self-improvement and the importance of the individual Christian life. Russian translations and publications of texts such as John Mason's *Self Knowledge* and Alexander Pope's *Essay on Man* "prepared the mental atmosphere for the understanding of a written life."[22] In his discussion of life writing in the eighteenth century, W. Gareth Jones observes that the writing of memoirs by members of the elite came about initially in Russia as a private genre and only later began to be seen as having public significance. The Russian state used biography to boost its status as a European power by disseminating information abroad about its own outstanding personages in the mid-eighteenth century. Discussing the biography of Kantemir published in 1749, Jones suggests that this first publication of an individual Russian writer's biography in Holland, written in French, was meant to "foster the international standing of Russian culture" and was published again the next year in Paris at the "behest of the Ministry of Foreign Affairs with the collaboration of the St. Petersburg Academy of Sciences."[23] Brief sketches of writers' lives were appended to a writer's works but were not yet stand-alone biographies.

The Russian translation and publication of classical collective biographies, the most important of which was Plutarch's *Lives* in 1765,[24] established a connection between classical works and modern biographies.[25] The compilation of dictionaries and encyclopedias of "great men," much of which was translated from other European languages, provided Russia with models for its own collective biography. Notably, the first of them was devoted to writers, N. I. Novikov's *Historical Dictionary of Russian Writers* (*Opyt istoricheskogo slovariia o rossiskikh pisatelei*, St. Petersburg, 1772). Novikov provided brief entries including a writer's rank, position and list of works, thus promoting them as "honored public figure(s)," as equals to other notables.[26] It was followed by the first Russian biographical dictionary of noteworthy political, military and religious personages (*Slovar' istoricheskogo ili sokrashchennoi biblioteki zaliuchaiushchei v sebe: zhitie i deianie patriarkhov, tsarei, imperatorov i korolei, velikikh polkovodets, i t.d.*, 14 parts, 1790–1798, republished 1807–1811) and D. N. Bantysh-Kamensky's *Dictionary of Memorable People of Russia* (*Slovariia dostopamiatnykh liudei russkoi zemli*, 5 vols., Moscow, 1836–1847).[27] By mid-century, a broader range of great men from Russian society were included in two Russian publications—A. E. Münster's *Portrait Gallery of Russian Personages* (*Portretnaia gallereia russkikh deiatelei*, 1865–1869) and M. Volf's *Russian People, Life Stories of Compatriots Famous in the Fields of Science, Welfare and Social Progress* (*Russkie liudi, zhizneopisaniia sootechestvennikov, proslavivshikhsia na poprishche nauki, dobra i obshchestvennoi pol'zy*, 2 vols, 1866). However, from the late 1860s there was no significant development in the expansion of collective biographies or series until the appearance of *ZhZL* in 1890.[28]

Catherine Neale Parke posits that at the turn of the nineteenth century an increased interest in biography across Europe was motivated by technological, cultural, and imperial expansion. Collective biography and other multi-volume works of biography thus play an important role in the formation of national identity by narrating "national history through the lives of its major participants."[29] Keith Thomas differentiates three types of collective biography: group biography, universal biography and national biography.[30] The genre proliferated throughout modern Europe and was frequently motivated by the desire of a particular group to assert its importance in a given culture. Thomas indicates that group biographies are part of a process of developing a national biographical tradition but are limited in terms of audience appeal to select elites. Their primary motive was to bolster the group identity of particular segments of upper-class society and they are frequently oriented toward specific professions and associations (for example, Masonic lodges or geographical societies). The universal biography, in contrast, draws on heroes from many different cultures and backgrounds. The national biography came to the fore in the late eighteenth and early nineteenth century in Western Europe as a vehicle for the establishment of national identity. This process explicitly occurred with the establishment of Russia's first biography series as well.

In Russia a significant dimension of the genre's development involves a discussion of censorship. Although there was also an interest in individual biographies in the eighteenth century, biographical texts from abroad and in Russian were available in a very limited fashion only to elite readers. Those individual biographies coming into Russia were still mainly of political figures and philosophers with a few exceptions. There were multiple foreign biographies of Russian rulers, especially Peter I.[31] The only biographies of recent foreign writers were of Voltaire and Rousseau in the last decades of the eighteenth century.[32] Marianna Tax Choldin discusses the first Russian law (1796) restricting "harmful" foreign publications and the importation of forbidden books. Some of these restricted books were available to select individuals by special request, and as Choldin notes, most requests were for books "containing minute details about famous people, both Russian and foreigners, active in politics in the last decade."[33] Censorship greatly impacted the necessary conditions for the writing of biographies depending on the times, because in order to write a biography accurately, one must have access to facts: "In Russia, one knows nothing. Everything is either a private or state protected secret, and evidence circulating in the public, even in the highest circles, is superficial, inexact, untrustworthy, based only on the vacillations of rumors and stories, often the fruit of one idle imagination."[34] The first task at hand was to collect verifiable evidence to use as the basis of the narrative of a person's life. For a notable example, Pavel Annenkov recognized the necessity to gather and preserve all available reminiscences and biographical data about Alexander Pushkin before the death of his contemporaries. Annenkov's *Materials for the Biography of Pushkin* (*Materialy k biografii Aleksandra Sergeevicha Pushkina*, 1859) became a foundational source and model for later biographers. The works that resulted from this kind of collection, though seemingly unfiltered, still had some sort of guiding principle in the determination of what to include and what to exclude from the final document.[35]

Nathaniel Knight points out that the scarcity of individual biographical texts in Russia prior to the mid-nineteenth century is noteworthy.[36] Nikolai Gogol's first biographer, P. A. Kulish, stated as late as 1854:

> It is a shame that we have still not ... entered into the spirit of biography and somehow coldly collect materials for this kind of work, when, meanwhile, in hardly any other genre is it possible to combine a serious interest in history, profound psychological research, and the most luxurious romanticism. For that reason, perhaps, good biography appears only in the literatures of nations standing on a high level of social development. There it finds many connoisseurs.[37]

This dearth has to do with the conceptualization of ideas of personality that predominated in the public sphere in Russia at the time. But by the mid-nineteenth century, there was a "radical democratization" of biographical discourse when the "right to biography was given to those who, as seen from the perspective of 'representative publicity,' had no achievements to boast of. The emphasis is transferred to the life of the individual and away from his deeds."[38] Kalugin draws attention to the fact that the changing definition of *lichnost'* (which can be translated as the unique personality or personhood) impacts the subsequent focus of biography: "the new kind of biographical writing, which came into existence as a result of the general slackening of state control following the death of Nicholas I in 1855, presented a self-conscious antithesis to 'official biography' and was based on the liberal ideal of individual autonomy, belief in social progress and a commitment to a Westernized model of society which, as it appeared, was to make the development of human personality possible"[39] and had political implications in terms of who would become appropriate biographical subjects. The changing conceptualization of *lichnost'* will recur periodically, particularly in regard to literary biography, over the course of the series' history.[40]

Both Novikov's earlier attention to writers and Carlyle's inclusion of writers as a category of "great men" added figures in the literary field to the panorama of worthy biographical subjects. However, the notion of "deeds" as a marker of "greatness" added a difficulty to their depiction. How does one depict a person whose "deeds" in terms of writings are largely the result of internal emotional and psychological experiences which are hard to access or depict? The case of A. N. Radishchev's depiction of his friend F. V. Ushakov (1789) presents an early example—here the justification for biography rests on the memories of the subject's impact on his contemporaries, and "by its tasks, authorial intentions and radicalism surpassed everything that had been created before in the biographical genre in the Russian language."[41] Several scholars have noted that the more definitive example of this shift in understanding the "right to a biography" occurs in the nineteenth century with the biography of Nikolai Stankevich, written by Annenkov in 1857. Like Radishchev before him, Annenkov could not focus on his hero's activities or writings, but nonetheless produced a striking work, as evidenced by Leo Tolstoy's reaction to reading it: "No book has ever produced such an impression on me. I have never so loved anyone as this person, whom I have never seen. What purity, what tenderness, what love with which he is entirely suffused."[42] Annenkov's work marks a major turn in nineteenth-century Russian biography, although for the most part large compilations of factual materials predominated until the turn of the twentieth century.

Having read Plutarch in his youth, Pavlenkov—as a publisher—recognized the importance of role models in biography for the development of an enlightened population. He had published Gaston Tissandier's *Les Martyrs de la science* (1879), writing in the introduction: "the lives of great scientists must awake in us a striving for work, presenting us examples of perseverance and unwavering energy which make up the secret of success and sometimes the secret of genius."[43] As a product of the 1850–1860s, Pavlenkov was deeply influenced by the liberal and radical figures of the era, such as Pyotr Lavrov (his mathematics and mechanics instructor in his youth), and by his friendship with radical critic Dmitry Pisarev, whose works he published at great personal risk. He similarly believed that a monopoly on knowledge endangered human progress and sought a role in society to promote enlightenment by making books accessible to the masses. Throughout his career, he published texts that aimed at providing the most current and topical scientific information, pedagogical practices and philosophical theory.[44] The target audience for this series, as well as for Pavlenkov's other publications, was the largely newly literate Russian reading public. The overarching concept behind Pavlenkov's biographical series was that individuals, rather than abstract ideas, served as the prime movers in history.

Pavlenkov's biographical library was a multivolume publication of short, readable individual biographies that were different from scholarly or dense, lengthy and decorous "Victorian" biographies intended for upper-class readers. Pavlenkov also diverged from the earlier Russian models presented by collective dictionaries of Russian heroes. Instead, he invented a format for his collective biographical series which combined short but substantive individual biographies into a library. The series overcame some of the limitations of the dictionary or encyclopedic form since the biographies could be published without regard to chronology. From 1890 to 1924, his enterprise published more than two hundred volumes in this series devoted to important individuals in world history, many of whose biographies were unfamiliar to the Russian reading public, such as Ignatius Loyola or Buddha. Not all subjects were exemplars of virtue, for example, Torquemada or Savonarola, but rather were outstanding in their field. Pavlenkov advertised the series as both universal and national, comprised of a foreign and a Russian division.[45] Among the series' heroes were 140 non-Russians and sixty Russians. Though the series featured only four women's biographies, Pavlenkov was ahead of his time in employing women writers and translators in his publishing house.[46] The individual volumes could be easily republished according to market demand and were financially accessible to all readers regardless of class or educational background. Readers could select who was interesting to them from ten general categories: 1) representatives of world religions; 2) political and national heroes; 3) scientists; 4) philosophers; 5) philanthropists and enlighteners/educational activists; 6) explorers; inventors, and people with broad social initiatives; 7) writers; 8) artists; 9) musicians; and 10) actors.[47] While most biographical subjects were deceased, Pavlenkov included two heroes who were still living, the Russian pedagogue Nikolai Korf and Leo Tolstoy.

The main task of the biographer was to relate the major facts of the subject's life and activities, as indicated in the biographies' subtitles. The common form was "Life and—Activity" (*Zhizn' i—deiatel'nost'*) depending on the subject's field. Most biographies followed a conventional chronological format, narrating a life from birth and childhood through the subject's most productive period of activity and ending with his/her death. This exposition did not vary significantly from one type of biography to another, although Pavlenkov sometimes included illustrations for biographies of artists and excerpted musical transcriptions of composers' most famous works. In the writers' biographies, the literary works were presented as facts of the author's life and not given extensive literary analysis. The biographies were usually seventy to ninety pages in length. On occasion, two similar figures would be published together in the same book, while certain biographies were collective in nature, such as those of the Demidovs, the Rothschilds, the Aksakovs, and the Vorontsovs. The longer biographies frequently were counted as two issues within a subscription.[48] The books were produced in softback covers, in 8,100-copy print runs and amounted to more than 1.5 million copies. The volumes were inexpensive, priced at twenty-five kopeks each, which indicated their orientation toward the developing mass market.[49] Pavlenkov's brand recognition was important because in the early nineteenth century, mass readers often asked for books at the library not by title but by the publisher's name. These features made them recognizable, accessible and popular with all classes of readers. Though the intended audience was the newly literate Russian reading public, the biographies' appeal extended far beyond to others, including the intelligentsia. In their youth, Nikolai Berdyaev, Vladimir Vernadsky, Ivan Bunin, and Alexei Tolstoy all read them, and, most notably, Gorky.[50] Both Nikolai Leskov and Ilya Repin commented with enthusiasm about the biographies of Buddha and Aristotle, respectively, and Vladimir Solovyov expressed his expectation to be included in the series upon his death. Noted bibliophile Nikolai Rubakin wrote in his memoirs of the significance of Pavlenkov's series: "Not one of Pavlenkov's works, in my observance can compare with the enormous influence that was shown on readers of all Russian strata, classes and ranks as the 'Biographical library' or *Zhizn' zamechatel'nykhi liudei*.'"[51]

PAVLENKOV AND HIS BIOGRAPHERS

Seventy-eight biographers participated in Pavlenkov's series, the majority of whom were Russians who knew multiple foreign languages. The largest group were *raznochintsy*, and included teachers, literary critics, translators, lawyers and bureaucrats, who were generally categorized as the "democratic intelligentsia."[52] One group of biographers were generalists who worked in any genre, others were subject specialists who were willing to become popularizers (the most famous of these was Vladimir Solovyov, who wrote the biography of Mohammed for the series) and a third group was made up of memoirists who wrote on the basis of their own personal relationships, or memoirs of their subjects.[53] Many of the biographers were people whom Pavlenkov met when he was exiled in Vyatka and Siberia or serving time in the Vyshnevolotsk transit prison, and constituted what the government would call the "untrustworthy element," according to Rubakin.[54] Several, such as Vera Zasulich and Pyotr Yakubovich, wrote biographies under pseudonyms. Pavlenkov thus established a cooperative of working biographers for the series, many of whom wrote five or more individual biographies, with the literary critic Evgeny Solovyov authoring fifteen.

Recent publications of Pavlenkov's correspondence indicate the struggle that he undertook every time he attempted to publish a biography. Pavlenkov's battles with the censorship started at the very beginning of his publishing career and continued through his periods of arrest and exile.[55] His skills in dealing with the vagaries of Tsarist censorship were crucial to the series' inclusion of biographies of figures with a wide range of political and social ideas. Pavlenkov had devised several methods of getting around the censorship. For example, he snuck political figures into the series by marking their activities as literary rather than political; he used the subtitles to label political activists such as Herzen, Pisarev, and Dobrolyubov as primarily "literary" figures. He avoided the advance censorship that mass literature was subject to by increasing the length of the biography. Thus, he commissioned the biographies of Pisarev, Herzen, Tolstoy, LaSalle, and Renan to be longer than ten printers' sheets. The greater length exempted them from having to be submitted to the censorship prior to their printing.

The series blossomed in its early years, releasing ninety-five biographies by the end of 1893, but thereafter increased surveillance by the censorship, especially of Pavlenkov personally, caused difficulties even after the biographies' publication. In a letter from 1893, Pavlenkov expressed apprehension regarding the actions of the Petersburg Censorship Committee, noting: "they are threatening to forbid the continuation of the biographical library" as well as showing hostility to him personally. A later letter also mentions that the biography of Tolstoy had been "arrested" by the committee due to its discussion of his religious philosophy.[56] Pavlenkov had to combat the postpublication "arrest" through further appeals to the authorities, a process that he engaged in for several other biographies. Pavlenkov frequently and successfully pleaded with the committee not to destroy the copies, but to preserve them in the vaults of the Main Directory of the Press in hopes of a possible future release from their "Babylonian captivity."[57] One such biography was that of Mikhail Katkov, authored by Rostislav Sementkovsky.[58] In 1895, when Katkov's biography was arrested due to the objections of the family, who believed it would damage his reputation, Pavlenkov discovered that not all bans were political in nature. Noted biographer Hermione Lee reminds us: "for the biographized and for their friends and family, there is a fight from the death over facts, between the participants in a life and the writers of it."[59] After Pavlenkov's death in 1900, his executors continued the fight to release the Katkov biography, which occurred only in 1910 after Nicholas II took off the prohibition by edict and Stolypin, as Minister of Interior, rescinded the "arrest." However, they were stymied in attempts to publish biographies of certain political figures, such as Karl Marx or recent Russian rulers. Pavlenkov hoped to publish a biography of Alexander II in fall of 1897 and asked Sementkovsky to write it. A biography of Alexander II, had it been realized, would have challenged the long-standing prohibition on biographies of Russian rulers, which remained unchallenged to the end of the Soviet era.

Though documents attest to Pavlenkov's tireless labor and involvement in all aspects of his publishing enterprise, he did delegate editorial and translation tasks to other trusted members of his artel, especially as his health declined.[60] Pavlenkov's practice of having translators and editors of collected editions later become biographers and editors within a series increased their engagement in the common task and their loyalty to the press. The close bonds that were forged by their sense of collective purpose allowed the enterprise to continue successfully after Pavlenkov's death under the direction of his executors, Vladimir Cherkasov, Valentin Yakovenko, and N. A. Rozental. His working collective continued to release the volumes that he had commissioned for the series, along with some reissues of earlier volumes until the publishing house was formally closed in 1915. Writers' biographies proved to be the most enduring and frequently republished; the last reissued volume was Alexander Skabichevsky's biography of Pushkin in 1924. Following Pavlenkov's final wishes, his executors used the profits of his enterprise to create two thousand reading rooms for underserved populations in the Russian provinces.[61]

GORKY'S ZhZL: A NEW SERIES OR A CONTINUATION?

Concurrent with the waning years of the original series, Maxim Gorky, who would become known as the father of Soviet literature, was formulating his ideas on the usefulness of the biographical genre as a tool for making a new type of man. The ethos of the Pavlenkov series easily meshed with Gorky's own utopian vision in its basic educational premise. Galina Pomerantseva, longtime *ZhZL* editor,[62] argues that the series is a continuous one since Gorky initially thought of reinstating Pavlenkov's series as early as 1916, only one year after the formal liquidation of Pavlenkov's firm. Gorky originally conceptualized his series for young readers as an antidote to the spiritual devastations of World War I and as a source for heroic role models. His plans to produce a biographical series for youth at Parus publishers (1916–1917) remained unrealized, as did his later intention to issue a "massive" biography series in cooperation with Z. Grzhebin's publishing house abroad (1919–1923).[63] But the events of war and revolution postponed the accomplishment of his task,[64] which he continued to pursue in his exile in Italy. These years were a period of continual upheaval as the new Soviet state was absorbing private publishers into newly created state enterprises. Gorky continued to think of his series in the scope of world history and was not alone in privileging the importance of biography at that time.

In Europe, the modernist literary experimentation occurring in the 1910–1920s crossed national boundaries and radically altered the development of the genre of biography. Remarking on the emergence of a "new biography," one contemporary commentator observed: "No feature of the literary history of Europe in the last few years is more remarkable than the simultaneous appearance in Germany, France and England of a new conception of biography."[65] Outstanding examples of the "new biography" were written by Lytton Strachey (1918), Virginia Woolf (1927), and André Maurois (1929), who all played a significant role in how biographies would be written henceforth, reacting against the established Victorian biographical tradition. Characteristic features of "new biography" include iconoclastic approaches of the biographer to the subject, use of writing strategies more closely aligned with fiction, and a more selective approach to the material which not only shortened the work, but also allowed for a distillation of key elements of personality. In effect, one feature or detail could serve as emblematic to explain the personality of the biographical subject.⁶⁶ Due to his long experience in literary circles in Western Europe, Gorky was well acquainted with those newer models of Western biography and theory. During that time, Gorky wrote letters to his European colleagues H. G. Wells, Romain Rolland, and Fridjtof Nansen, whom he hoped to recruit as authors for his yet-unnamed series. Gorky suggested that Wells should write on Edison, Rolland should write about Beethoven, Nansen about Columbus, and Gorky himself about Garibaldi. He asked Wells to assist him in finding an appropriate British author to pen biographies of Dickens, Byron, and Shelley.⁶⁷ Gorky highly esteemed biographies that were written in the styles of Maurois, Woolf, Stefan Zweig, and Emil Ludwig. Gorky himself experimented with the form of biographical sketches and received praise from Romain Rolland, who suggested that they should be translated into French.⁶⁸

Parallel to the developments in life writing in Western Europe in the first two decades of the twentieth century, Russian biographers also continued to experiment with a variety of biographical approaches. Ironically, while the scholar and bibliographer Semyon Vengerov (1855–1920) persisted in the nineteenth-century approach by collecting biographical facts in his unfinished biobibliographical critical dictionary of Russian writers, his students rejected that approach and became innovators in biographical theory and practice.⁶⁹ In their exploration of factographic versus fictional forms, formalist critics such as Boris Tomashevsky, Yuri Tynyanov, and Boris Eikhenbaum all found themselves drawn to the genre. The formalists had already concluded that the text itself was paramount to any expression of the author's personality or sociohistorical context. In the essay, "Literature and Biography" (*Literatura i biografiia*, 1923), Tomashevsky gives a more nuanced expression of the role of the writer's biography in the understanding of a literary text. He discusses the "literary functions" of biography, that is, how "the poet's biography operates in the reader's consciousness."⁷⁰ "Biographical legend" is the term he developed to acknowledge that there are specific circumstances when an author's biography can be relevant to the understanding of a literary work, for example, in situations of the author's self-fashioning and its relationship to a particular text. Tomashevsky, using Mayakovsky and Gorky to illustrate his point, insists that "Only such a legend is a *literary* fact" while asserting that the notion of biographical legend is not applicable to authors' lives that do not display an equal level of literariness.⁷¹ In current Western biography theory, this notion is referred to as a "biomyth."⁷² Several contributors to this volume also refer to the concept of the biographical legend in their analyses of literary biographies and discuss the idea of writers "with" and "without" biographies.⁷³

Though influential in the West, formalist biography theory in and of itself was not a productive model for Gorky's series. However, biographies written by formalist critics Tynyanov and Eikhenbaum, who subsequently fleshed out their ideas about the genre, served as prime examples for many subsequent Russian biographers. Tynyanov's biographical novels written from the mid-1920s to the early 1940s about the writers Kiukhelbeker, Griboedov, and Pushkin came up over the course of the series' history multiple times either as models for emulation or as examples against which the series' genre defined itself.[74] In contrast to the formalists, their contemporary Grigory Vinokur reinstated a cultural and sociohistorical context into the writing of biography in his *Biography and Culture* (*Biografiia i kul'tura*, 1927), employing a deliberately polemical title. Vinokur argued for the significance and reintegration of historical events into the narrative of an individual's life as long as those events shaped the subject's personality. Introducing the ideas of Ferdinand de Saussure into Russia, Vinokur posited a structural framework for the understanding of personality and the telling of a life story.[75] Although never translated and thus not influential in Western biographical theory, Vinokur provided a productive biographical methodology for later practitioners of biography in the Soviet context.[76]

After the Bolshevik revolution, collective biography remained an instrument for the construction of national identity and the revision of past history and its principal figures. In the early 1920s, other Russian publishers attempted to found biography series: the Sabashnikov brothers began to issue the *Historical Portraits* series (*Istoricheskie portrety*, 1921), the cooperative press Sheaf (*Kolos*) started the *Biographical Library* series, in 1923 Brokhaus and Efron published the *Images of Humanity* (*Obrazy chelovechestva*) series, and in 1925 the State Publishing House (*Gosizdat*) established its own *Biographical Library* series. In 1928, the publisher Moscow Worker (*Moskovskii rabochii*), prepared a series with the exact title *Lives of Remarkable People* (*Zhizn' zamechatel'nykh liudei*). But none of these presses managed to release more than half a dozen books.[77] Given the lack of success of other publishers, Gorky increasingly saw the need for an updated version of the Pavlenkov series to support the new Bolshevik project. In 1927, he had even proposed that the magazine *Little Fire* (*Ogonek*) should republish Pavlenkov's biographies in shortened versions.[78] Upon his final return from exile to the Soviet Union in 1932 at Stalin's request, Gorky championed the revival of the series to Soviet authorities. Gorky saw an opportunity to further his own vision of a biography series using the foundation that Pavlenkov had established.

In the Soviet Union of the 1930s there was a strong impetus to create a new biography series specifically because of the cultural and political demands of the time. Paraphrasing Evgeny Dobrenko, "the nature and function of biography in the Stalinist political-aesthetic project" needs to be examined further to see how biography responded to the pressures of Socialist Realism.[79]

Elaborating on Gorky's "biographical anthology" which also included *History of the Factories* (1931), The *History of the Russian Civil War* (1931), and *The History of Young Men in the Nineteenth Century* (1932), Katerina Clark remarks that by the mid-1930s, official rhetoric shifted from an emphasis on the "little man" to a focus on leaders or "fathers": "an entire series of 'remarkable people' was singled out as official harbingers of a revolution in human anthropology soon to affect every Soviet man."[80] Gorky's *ZhZL* series became especially important not only for the inculcation of Soviet values but also for the transformation of the Soviet man. Moreover, Jochen Hellbeck suggests that the biographical mold was at the core of the presentation of a personality "as an unfolding subject of revolutionary consciousness,"[81] thus Gorky's idea for the formation of a "new Soviet man" dovetailed perfectly with the teleological goals of Socialist Realism. Gorky wrote:

> To me, any crowd is a gathering of heroic candidates . . . Therefore each hero is a social phenomenon, whose pedagogical significance is entirely valuable. To want to be a hero means to want to be more of a person than you are. . . . We are all born and live as heroes. And when this is understood by the majority, then life will become completely heroic.[82]

Since in Gorky's conceptualization, each Soviet citizen had inherent in himself or herself the potential to become a hero, if he or she wasn't already, what was necessary was to unlock that capacity. Another component necessary to bridge that gap was an understanding of the historical past, since Gorky insisted: "To know the past is necessary, without that knowledge you can go astray in life and again fall into that dirty, bloody swamp from which the wise teachings of Vladimir Ilich Lenin extracted us and set us on the broad and straight path to the great happy future."[83] Reading biographies would be the inspiration, in the words of Fransiska Thun-Hohenstein:

> The genre of biography of a historical personality . . . corresponded better than anything else to the characteristic tendency towards the personalization of history in the historical narrative of the 1930s. In addition, life-writing—marked by artistry and an interesting form of exposition—achieved the necessary freedom for "historical fantasizing" in accordance with the demands of ideology.[84]

Unlike other nonfiction genres, biography had the intrinsic capacity enabling it to be both creative and ideological.

In 1932, *Literaturnaia gazeta* announced the revival of the series: "the main task of the publication is to give a detailed Marxist analysis of that social milieu in which great people came to live and work, to show their persistent and self-sacrificing labor, to illuminate the difference of perspectives on human personality (*lichnost'*) in the epoch of precapitalist and capitalist relations, and in the period of the building of socialism."[85] The intended audience was the "progressive strata of the workers, students and activists of our development."[86] Gorky and his colleagues finally found a home for the series, under the auspices of the State Journal and Newspaper Publishing Collective (*Zhurnalno-gazetnoe ob"edinenie* or *Zhurgaz*). In an editorial structure similar to Pavlenkov's, there was a triumvirate at the top, with Gorky, A. N. Tikhonov, Gorky's longtime friend and literary collaborator and M. Koltsov, the head of Zhurgaz, as its other primary editors. The editorial board included Anatoly Lunacharsky and the academic Sergei Vavilov as well.[87] The series that resulted in 1933 was thus the third such reworking of Gorky's ideas on what the biography series should be. Gorky's main criticism of the Pavlenkov series was that the material was chosen randomly and the series was lacking in internal connections.[88] Though he initially suggested that the updated series would be produced chronologically, with the brightest examples from each epoch in order to show the development of progress over the span of human history, this plan proved to be impractical and he reverted to a model more like Pavlenkov's, organized by spheres of knowledge. Gorky also proposed that there should be as much everyday realia as possible to give a sense of the historical and cultural context.[89] As in the Pavlenkov series, there was a pronounced emphasis on locating the biographical subjects according to the sphere of their activities and a strong orientation toward scientists and innovators. The largest number of biographies were devoted to writers and poets (21), with scientists in various fields (18) and revolutionaries, reformers, and state and political actors (18) and industrialists and inventors (14) in second and third place. Several subfields (explorers, actors and playwrights, military figures, and others) had fewer than ten biographies each.[90] Gorky proposed that the series include lives of old Bolsheviks and leaders from the Civil War, such as Frunze, Kirov, and Sverdlov. However, Thun-Hohenstein astutely comments:

> it appears that the proposed Bolshevik figures were too close to the present, to the struggle for power in Stalin's immediate circle that the story of their lives within the framework of *ZhZL* could turn into too risky a project for the editors and the authors of biographies. It was a much simpler and less dangerous task to depict the political convictions, contradictions, and passing mistakes of such revolutionaries as Zhelyabov, Baboeuf, and Danton.[91]

During the period from 1933 to 1935, when Gorky was most active in overseeing the series, twenty-eight of the fifty biographies published were of the same individuals who were also biographical subjects in Pavlenkov's series. The first biography issued was by scholar and writer A. I. Deich on Henrich Heine, who was also one of Pavlenkov's earliest subjects and whose works had been under special scrutiny by the censorship for most of the nineteenth century.[92]

At first, Gorky chose his biographers in a manner similar to Pavlenkov, employing generalists, subject specialists, and scholars who had already written on their subjects, such as Deich on Heine and Pavel Shchegolev on Pushkin, a practice which has continued to the present.[93] He wanted "remarkable people to be written about by remarkable writers" and sought out accomplished professionals from every field.[94] After his return to the Soviet Union, Gorky realized that his original plan for having the best Western biographers participate in the series was now impossible. Instead, he recruited old acquaintances and political comrades such as Alexander Voronsky, Lunacharsky, Lev Kamenev, and Grigory Zinoviev, for whom he provided a short-lived haven. He also sought out some of the best writers in the Soviet Union, including Mikhail Bulgakov, Kornei Chukovsky, and Viktor Shklovsky. Even so, he was dissatisfied at first with the overall quality of biographical writing that was produced. In a letter to M. Koltsov on Jan. 30, 1933, Gorky expressed his dissatisfaction with what he perceived as an indifference to their subjects' lives on the part of many authors: "Who are they, these authors? What do they love? What do they want? Why are they so clearly indifferent to the work which they took upon themselves?"[95] Gorky feared that their indifference would jeopardize the success of the series. Yet, when Tikhonov and Gorky were confronted with a biographical novel written for the series by Bulgakov about Molière, they saw difficulties with publishing it within the proposed framework for the series due to both its generic form and its lack of correct political orientation. The incident with Bulgakov's *Molière* helped define the limits of creative invention (*vymysel*) in the series and also drew attention to the political risks of publishing something that did not toe the ideological line. Gorky insisted that the biographer should use artistic intuition (*khudozhestvennyi vymysel*) based on historical documents and evidence but cautioned against the falsification of reality.[96]

Despite Gorky's initial concerns, editors and commentators on the series' history point to the period between 1933 and 1941 as a "laboratory of [Soviet] biography," a notion that continues to be invoked to the present day.[97] From Gorky's editorial comments to his biographers, several requirements become clear. Gorky preferred the biographies to adhere to an internal chronology in order to avoid repetition. He wanted the biographies to be understandable to the masses with lively explanations of and concrete examples for any complicated scientific or theoretical material. He asked for all foreign words to be translated into Russian and required the use of selected documents to "illustrate the epoch."[98] Gorky wanted to combine a lively, creative exposition of a life with pedagogical models to inspire imitation, or, in other words, with a series of examples that would demonstrate "how to become a Human with a capital 'H.'"[99] Gorky's conceptualization was further affirmed at the First Congress of the Union of Soviet Writers by Andrei Zhdanov, who called for "heroization" as the defining characteristic of Soviet literature.[100] Though some reviewers lauded the biographies as "guides to the cultural heritage of the past," one critic noted that the distinguishing characteristic of the biographies produced by Zhurgaz was that the emphasis was placed on the epoch rather than the personality and on the activity rather than the hero.[101] Ultimately, the notion of combining creative elements with ideologically driven narrative proved to be extremely challenging.

While Gorky's health declined, Tikhonov increasingly set editorial policy. According to the transcripts of a 1934 editorial board meeting, Tikhonov discussed the four possible types of biography: montage (an accumulation of facts), psychological essay, biographical novel, and a text combining a creatively ideological and scholarly sketch. Tikhonov posited Kamenev's *Chernyshevsky* (1933) as a generic model for the series because Kamenev provided the image of a person who was ideologically oriented to educating the revolutionary in himself. Following the rhetorical precepts of "the reforging and the education of the new Soviet man," Kamenev depicts the dying Chernyshevsky as passing the torch to the emerging revolutionary organizer Lenin. The biography therefore could "serve as a symbol and the quintessential normative model of Soviet biography." Ironically, this biography, which was lauded in June 1934 was taken out of circulation (both from bookstores and libraries) and completely banned for decades.[102]

Despite the initial orientation toward the education of youth, the subscribers for the series in 1933–1934 turned out to be mainly adult readers: Soviet intelligentsia, students in higher educational institutions as well as city and collective farm workers. While Gorky thought the workers could be brought up to the level of the intelligentsia, Tikhonov felt that the intelligentsia reader should determine the series level.[103] Stalin became the "unseen first reader" of the series, judging from Tikhonov's letter to Gorky regarding E. Tarle's biography of Napoleon (1936): "The book turned out well, in my opinion, but again it's very risky. 'The Leader' (*Khoziain*) said that he would be its first reader. What if he doesn't like it?!"[104] As he was dying and the political atmosphere became increasingly repressive, Gorky asked the authorities to allow the Komsomol to take the series under its wing. Scholars like to point out that Gorky had the first ninety issues of the Soviet *ZhZL* series in his personal library and that Tarle's biography of Napoleon was the last book that Gorky was reading before his death.[105] After Gorky's death, Tikhonov resigned and the editorial board was completely replaced, reorienting the series to the youth reader. Nonetheless, it retained its adult readers, and major figures of the Soviet intelligentsia, such as Eikhenbaum, Tynyanov, and Chukovsky, remained affiliated with the series as contributing authors or editors or on the editorial board. The series also could no longer be a haven for writers who had fallen from grace earlier, such as Kamenev, Zinoviev, and Voronsky. The devastating effect of the Stalinist purges on the series has only recently been acknowledged in the series' history.[106] The third original editor, Koltsov, the head of Zhurgaz, was arrested and shot, and several individual writers were repressed. One of Gorky's close friends from prerevolutionary days, A. P. Pinkevich, who wrote the fifth biography for the series on Pestalozzi in 1933 was purged, as were Voronsky, Kamenev, and Zinoviev. Others were severely criticized for their shortcomings.[107]

TRANSITION AND WARTIME

The change of the editorial board after Gorky's death and the transfer of the series to Molodaya gvardiya from April to May 1938 resulted in the delayed appearance of new and previously commissioned biographies in the late 1930s. Initially, the new editors came to a solution similar to Pavlenkov's to produce the number of volumes needed for a given year by counting the longer biographies as two issues. Like the original *ZhZL* series, the biographies were initially meant to be sold by subscription for a full or partial year. Consequently, Molodaya gvardiya took on the obligation of the subscription since they did not have the time to reorganize it on other terms. The transitional period created a large deficit; judging from the data regarding published books, six issues listed in the catalog under 1938 were sent to the subscribers only in 1939. The press tried in vain to cover the debts that arose but had only three years of issuing the series before the war began. All of these factors explain why the prewar *ZhZL* series at Molodaya gvardiya continued along the lines of the Zhurgaz series although there were attempts to modernize it and make it suitable for the young reader. 107 biographies were issued in 40–50,000 copy print runs from 1933 to 1939. The average length of the biography increased from Pavlenkov's original 80–100 pages to 210 pages.

ZhZL IN WARTIME

The series suffered other hardships as political and economic conditions changed due to the war. Molodaya gvardiya press was evacuated to Ufa in 1941–1942, during which time it concentrated on the publication of a variety of materials to aid the wartime propaganda effort, including poster, fliers, and textbooks on military strategy.[108] As in America, where books were considered "a necessary piece of equipment" by the government for their battle against fascist ideas and for their morale-boosting ability, the Soviet authorities recognized the importance of books. But unlike the American examples shipped overseas to the troops, the predominant genre was not contemporary fiction[109] but mainly the biographies of canonical Russian authors who went off to war. Though the main *ZhZL* series remained dormant, the publication of biographies continued. From 1943–1944, fourteen biographies were released under the imprimatur *Great People of the Russian Nation* (*Velikie liudi russkogo naroda*), four of which were of writers (Zhukovsky, Pushkin, Mayakovsky, and Radishchev). In 1944–1945, fourteen more biographies were released under the title *Great Russian People* (*Velikie russkie liudi*), four of whom were writers (Tolstoy, Lermontov, Belinsky, and Gogol). Therefore, approximately a third of the wartime biographies were devoted to writers in acknowledgment of the power of words as weapons. Restricting its focus to Russians during this time period, Molodaya gvardiya also published biographies of a representative selection of figures by profession, including the most important Russian scientists, artists and military leaders.[110] Subjects were depicted as positive role models and culture heroes, inspiring patriotism and self-sacrifice by their deeds. These soft-cover booklets recalled the size and format of Pavlenkov's series. Most of the booklets were less than 100 pages long and were meant to be carried into battle or read in the barracks. The genre was that of a popular sketch and accessible to any reader. The biographies from the wartime series did not have much staying power not only because of their ideological thrust but also because of their perishable format.[111]

Later, in the 1980s, as veterans of the war remembered their experiences and the reading of these booklets, the press reissued a collection of selected biographies in a single volume, *Great Russian People* (1984) in honor of the fortieth anniversary of World War II and the fiftieth anniversary of the *ZhZL* series. The publisher's goal for republication was to reinforce the idea that as in wartime, the general population now could be inspired by "a spiritual arsenal" of the national heroes of the past,[112] evoking "in the young reader the desire to imitate, to help the formation of strong, bold personalities."[113] The compilers of this volume wrote movingly about the fate of these books: "after all, these little books burned in the fiery embrace of tanks, were soaked in the crossing rivers, and remained in the pockets of overcoats which covered soldiers' bodies lined in a row."[114] To the present day, World War II remains a touchstone whenever national values are called into question and the celebration of important cultural and political anniversaries informs the editorial plans for publication of pertinent biographies. Moreover, the series ritualistically commemorates its own history with celebrations and publications in honor of important historical anniversaries.

POST WAR ZhZL

During the post-World War II period to the end of the Soviet era, who was considered "remarkable" depended upon shifting social and political constraints and requirements. Although the original definition proposed under Gorky's editorship was a person remarkable for his epoch, in the years immediately after World War II, the biographical subject was conceived as "a knight without fear and reproach (*rytsar' bez strakha i uprek*)."[115] The series interrupted by the war resumed publication in 1945 with its first books issued in 1946. *ZhZL* biographies could no longer include any negative figures following the directives of party ideologues who required only positive role models for the youth.[116] The great majority of figures continued to be Russian. There was an increasing conservatism due to the repressive ideological constraints of Zhdanovshchina until the death of Stalin, which in combination with the damages and shortfalls of World War II, resulted in limited numbers of new *ZhZL* biographies. By 1957 new book titles increased to double digits, returning to more normal prewar standards. Stephen Lovell discusses how various series, including *ZhZL*, became the bread and butter of Soviet publishing culture: "Soviet book subscriptions and serial editions had proved a very influential means of synchronizing personal or domestic time with societal time. Inexperienced readers were offered a simple and gratifying entrée into the world of the prestigious written culture."[117] As the series developed, the distinctive branding returned, though in a different manner from Pavlenkov's press. Initially, Gorky's *ZhZL* had some consistent formal features, but it took time before the branding obtained its distinctive cover design, fonts for book titles and authors' names, and a flaming torch on the spine. The geometrically segmented cover design features: a bold black title in capital letters at the top, a sketch or photograph of the hero in the right corner; a geographical setting associated with the hero's life in the left; the author's name in the lower left corner; another contrasting location or picture emblematic of the hero's life; and at the bottom, a banner with the series title. Since the institution of this standard cover and spine by artist Yuri Arndt in 1962, the design remains a defining feature today, setting it apart from all of its competitors. *ZhZL* establishes its visual presence, standing out in bookstores, often in its own separate section. The series' reinvigoration demonstrated the ongoing centrality of biography as a genre for Soviet culture and its reconceptualization of the Soviet man as a cultured person. The series assumed a major role in the creation of the "myth of the Soviet reader," now increasingly educated and literate, and the mythology of the Soviet population as "the most reading nation in the world" (*samyi chitaiushchii v mire narod*).[118]

By the end of the 1950s, the series' editors determined that three principles should inform biography writing. The principles of "scholarly accuracy, a high literary level, and reader engagement" emerged out of a conference on the acceptable use of conjecture (*domysel*) and invention (*vymysel*).[119] Once the process of de-Stalinization began after Khrushchev's secret speech in 1956 and continuing into the 1960s, another reexamination took place regarding the function of biography and the nature of the biographical hero. Society struggled to come to terms with the recent revelations about the purges and the rehabilitations not only of returning political prisoners but also of other historical figures who had been removed from early revolutionary and Soviet history.

As a result, there was a turn to interiority and psychology as a way to grapple with moral questions and to reevaluate history as it had been presented. Pomerantseva charts the trajectory of the series in this period: "Since the middle of the 1950s and in the 1960s, the entire path of the development of the Russian revolutionary movement, stage by stage from the Decembrists on, is revealed through the biographies in the series."[120] This intense scrutiny of canonical figures of the nineteenth-century intelligentsia included the rewriting of many earlier biographies devoted to Russian writers. The editorial board made the conscious decision to return to Gorky's original vision by broadening the understanding of who a remarkable person was, allowing heroes to be depicted in a more nuanced fashion than before. A negative hero could still have a positive moral effect by teaching a person what not to do. In addition, they invoked Gorky's idea of using foreign biographers in the series, and published biographies in the series by Shirley Graham DuBois,[121] André Maurois, Stefan Zweig, Emil Ludwig, Hesketh Pearson, and Irving Stone, who was especially popular in the Soviet Union.[122] Maurois, Zweig, and Ludwig were writers who Gorky himself praised as model biographers but who would only be included when the series sought to claim an international status.[123] The choice of foreign biographers, while reflecting Gorky's initial desire to recruit biographers from the same cultural arena as their subject, also solved the problem of how to quickly and economically produce a larger number of biographies every year to satisfy reader demand.

However, old censorship guidelines still remained in place right to the end of the Soviet period. Looking back at the latter part of the Soviet *ZhZL* series in a roundtable discussion in 2006, Alexander Gladkov noted also not only were certain personages still banned from the series, but that there was even a "taboo" on entire areas of the activities of "approved" figures. The discussion also revealed that sometimes the editors were blamed by authors for cuts that actually originated from the censors, as for example, in the Che Guevara biography.[124] Valentin Yurkin, longtime General Director of Molodaya gvardiya,[125] suggested that in some Soviet *ZhZL* biographies of "resurrected" subjects: "individual episodes in some biographies had to be encoded, in order to hint to the reader about this or that event."[126] Another category of missing biographical subjects was still members of the Romanov dynasty. Even as late as 1988, the firm signed a contract with a French publisher to buy the rights to Henri Troyat's biography of Alexander I, because biographies of the tsars (with the exception of Peter I) were still prohibited so they needed to use a foreign author. (The Troyat biography only was published in 1997, well into the post-Soviet period.)[127]

Throughout the series' history at critical junctures, whenever there was a question of how biography should evolve, the editors went back to Gorky as their original source, as seen in the various stenographic records of editorial roundtables on the genre and on the series.[128] Beyond internal discussions in ZhZL among editors and authors, these ideas became public through the use of literary and educational institutions and prominent periodicals, such as *Literaturnaia gazeta* and *Voprosy literatury*, that generated feedback which informed editorial choices.[129] The continual debate revolved around two central topics: the relationship of the hero to society with a focus on his activities and how to portray the hero's the interior life (that is, the expression of personality or *lichnost'*). This attention to not just the form of biography but also to its focus led to the true rebirth of the series and proliferation of writers' biographies beginning in the 1960s. Scholars again invoke the notion of the series as an experimental laboratory of biography, where "factographic and artistic biography meet and biography becomes "a history of personal life'" (*istoriia lichnoi zhizni*).[130] In addition, Molodaya gvardiya launched the almanac, *Prometheus* (*Prometei*), in the mid-1960s, purportedly addressed to the young reader, in order to expand the purview of the genre into other types of life writing, providing a "laboratory" for *ZhZL* and a venue for small forms such as the literary portrait, documentary sketch, essay, and historical short story. It also sought to make previously unpublished archival documents and lesser-known materials available to the mass reader.[131] Writers' biographies became bestsellers during this period, especially valuable as a "deficit product" among collectors of the series. In fact, writers' biographies became so popular, that a rival series, *Writers on Writers*, was issued by Kniga Publishers (eighty-seven books) from 1984 to 1991 but ended with the demise of the Soviet Union.[132]

Polly Jones observes that the new emphasis on an altered notion of *lichnost'* led to increasing psychological depth in biographies of the post-Stalin era.[133] In her discussion of the biographical genre and another rival series *Fiery Revolutionaries* (*Plamennye revoliutsionery*), begun in 1968 and ending only in 1991, she notes that the "fascination with history and biography ... pervaded late Soviet society," suggesting that the new series' revolutionary heroes provided models for the burgeoning opposition movements of the era as well as the "less engaged 'last Soviet generation.'"[134] This focus on the significance of the individual's inner life and "multifaceted human personality" was spurred by the shift away from collective and toward "individual fulfillment as the central promise of the Soviet project."[135] Attesting to the genre's proliferation, the leading literary journal *Voprosy literatury* noted the "biography boom" in the early 1970s that continued well into the mid-1980s.[136] Despite the fact that the 1970s was considered a period of cultural stagnation, reader interest in and demand for books in the series grew exponentially.[137] *ZhZL* remained the standard by which all other biography series, including *Fiery Revolutionaries*, would define itself and be measured. In fact, *Fiery Revolutionaries* was specifically created to address *ZhZL*'s lack of biographies of revolutionary figures from the Bolshevik era onward.[138] By the mid 1970s, "an undetected shift toward literary scholarship (*literaturovedenie*)" took place under the editorship of Yuri Seleznev, who later wrote a biography on Dostoevsky for the series.[139] Mirroring the ideological debates of the 1860–1870s, the press found itself embroiled in an ideological battle between "Slavophiles" and "Westernizers" that threatened its existence.[140]

By its Soviet heyday in the 1960–1970s, *ZhZL* had revised its original guidelines about what biography could be. While in the initial period, Gorky strove for what was later termed "popular-scholarly" (*nauchno-populiarnaia*) biography as the preferred genre: an engaging life story that has a sociopolitical component, is based on documentary evidence, and provides a positive role model for emulation among the youth readership. Despite Gorky's own early love of biographical novels such as those of Maurois, there was little use of novelistic techniques (*belletrizatsiia*) in earliest biographies in the series, "as if the authors are afraid of using all the possibilities of conjecture (*domysel*) and invention (*vymysel*), and if they do resort to them then with great reservation, fearing to be censured for unreliability or the distortion of historical facts."[141] Already in the late 1950s, the term "artistic-scholarly" biography (*nauchno-khudozhestvennaia biografiia*)[142] increasingly appeared as a generic descriptor in discussions of *ZhZL* biographies. The term implies a synthesis of scholarly research into the history of the period and the personal documents that pertain to the subject and a lively narrative that borrows techniques from fiction. The way in which historical materials and documentary evidence is presented in *ZhZL* biographies can be problematic, because the series does not follow a single set of scholarly guidelines: some biographers use footnotes while others provide only a general overview of their sources. While this term closely resembles the current Western notion of "creative nonfiction," Yurkin has repeatedly stressed that Russian biography now emphasizes cultural and historical materials in greater detail and presupposes a deeper knowledge on the part of the reader than Western biography does.[143]

THE COLLAPSE AND REVIVAL OF MOLODAYA GVARDIYA

In the final years of the Soviet Union, as state subsidies slowly dwindled, Molodaya gvardiya became a joint stock company. Yurkin called this period "the most dramatic time in the entire history of Molodaya gvardiya."[144] The subsequent collapse of the Soviet Union in 1991 had far reaching implications for the publishing industry and for the series as well. Post-Soviet publishing underwent the wrenching turn to market economics, and at first the series faltered, publishing only two books in 1992, one in 1994 and drastically reducing the size of the print runs from the 50–100,000 copies common to the Soviet period to 3–7,000 copies.[145] Not only had all production costs increased for the press, but during the first half of the 1990s, readers had little disposable income to spend on increasingly expensive *ZhZL* biographies.

The legacy of the series was also called into question with challenges to its ownership and history. The collapse of the Soviet Union ushered in a revival of interest in the original Pavlenkov series, with republications of the original series by competing presses. Beginning in 1993, three different publishers issued reprints of the original series. The most notable of them was the Ural Press in Chelyanbinsk, which reprinted the original two hundred biographies from 1994 to 1998. The compiler of that edition, Nikolai Boldyrev, accused Molodaya gvardiya of letting the series "enter into the ideologically monotone, Procrustean bed of the Sots-realist model." He argued that in following Gorky's desire for gigantomania, nothing remained of the "elegant laconicism" and "purity of genre" of the Pavlenkov originals. In an age of information overload, the reader needed precisely the kind of biographies that Pavlenkov originally conceived.[146] Boldyrev saw a freedom for the reader in the kaleidoscope of authorial viewpoints of Pavlenkov's biographers. As a 201st biography, the Ural series included a biography of Pavlenkov himself, which was the first full-length monograph devoted to the remarkable publisher. That this biography came out at a press other than Molodaya gvardiya, the institutional home of *ZhZL* for more than seventy-five years, was surprising. After years of loudly proclaiming Gorky as the series founder, these republications spurred Molodaya gvardiya to acknowledge Pavlenkov publicly as the originator in 2001, with a note on the frontispiece of the thousandth volume of the series. In addition, a former director, Vladimir Desyaterik, authored his own biography of Pavlenkov which was subsequently published in the *ZhZL* series. The invocation and reclamation of Pavlenkov as the founder was not only a savvy marketing tool and a way for the press to distinguish its series from upstarts, but also asserted its historical continuity, spanning three centuries and three regime changes, as the first

Russian biography series and as the longest running biographical series of any type anywhere. Yurkin undertook a campaign to make post-Soviet *ZhZL* biographies a central touchstone for new generations of readers, as they were for the Soviet readers, reaffirming traditional educational and moral values. Yurkin attested to the continued and profound impact of *ZhZL*: "In the consciousness of millions of people, this phenomenon [*ZhZL*] usually resides alongside other national holy places, such as the Tretiakov Gallery and the Russian Museum, the Bolshoi Theater and Pushkin's Mikhailovskoe, as many other sites of national culture, comprising its spiritual treasure house."[147] In fact, the term *ZhZL* has entered into the lexicon with the coinage of an adjective, *"ZhZLovskii,"* to denote the very specific markers of the biographies in the series, and is a phenomenon recognizable just by its abbreviation to any Russian reader, entering "the active vocabulary of the nation, has become an organic part of the intellectual life of many generations and has given birth to a multitude of imitations."[148]

POST-SOVIET *ZhZL*

Responding to the economic pressures of the post-Soviet publishing industry and mass culture, the press has expanded and boosted the *ZhZL* brand while maintaining its prestige. From 2005 to 2009, biographies in the series won multiple Big Book (*Bol'shaia kniga*) awards: Dmitry Bykov's *Boris Pasternak* (2005–2006), Alexei Varlamov's *Alexei Tolstoy* (2006–2007), and Lyudmila Saraskina's *Solzhenitsyn* (2007–2008).[149] Spin-offs of the series have exploded onto the scene. Subseries, such as *Secret Agents* (*Razvedchiki*), were created to appeal to niche groups of readers. Beginning in 2005, Molodaya gvardiya started the series *ZhZL, Biografiia prodolzhaetsia*, producing biographies of people who were still alive and active in their fields, including one on Vladimir Putin.[150] In 2008, the press also began issuing audiobooks of select biographies. In 2009, the *Small series (Malaia seriia)* was created to provide a smaller, more portable book, reminiscent of the shorter biographies issued by Pavlenkov. Its first volume was the first full publication of Voronsky's 1934 biography of Gogol. The first five years of the series featured only literary biographies, but since has expanded to many other fields. The *Small series* provides an alternative view of a previous *ZhZL* biographical hero by a different writer who sometimes polemicizes with the main series' biography or finds an overlooked aspect of the hero's life and works.[151] *Universal ZhZL* (*Vselennaia ZhZL*), a newspaper issued since 2009 in two-thousand-copy print runs, has been available, "for lovers of history and literature in the biographical genre."[152] The newspaper allows for direct communication between the publishers and readers, providing more details and previously unknown information about the biographers and biographies while also giving readers the opportunity to weigh in on new subjects for future biographies. Thus, it serves not just as a marketing tool, but also as a gauge of reader response. New forms of media—online sites with interviews of authors, a Facebook reading group, discussions with critics as well as videos based on the biographies and a specialized YouTube channel with topical playlists—have further expanded *ZhZL*'s reach.

Capitalizing on the brand name recognition of *ZhZL* and the long-standing popularity of the series, several unauthorized spin-offs briefly came onto the market without Molodaya gvardiya's consent. The *Lives of Remarkable Children* series (originally published by Oniks press) focuses on the formative stages of development of important national and international historical figures.[153] The *Lives of Remarkable Creatures* series, published by "AST" press, has been made into a cartoon series available online and on the TV channel "Carousel."[154] Another unauthorized spin-off was released by the counterculture press "Ultra.Kultura," entitled *The Lives of Repressed People* (*Zhizn' zapreshchennykh liudei*, also using the acronym "ZhZL," but with a slightly different graphic) beginning in 2001 and continuing until 2005. The series included books on Eduard Limonov, Charles Manson, Alexander Shulgin, Huey Newton, Timothy Leary, Alistair Crowley, Dzhokar Dudaev, Anton Szandor Lavey (b. Howard Stanton Levey, founder of the Church of Satan), Pol Pot, Subcomandante Marcos, and Louis-Ferdinand Céline. This new series amply demonstrated the sensationalist and demythologizing elements in post-Soviet book publishing; the website's slogan announces: "Everything that you know is a lie!" This parody of the original series embodies the idea that the life of an infamous person can be a valuable source of information, either as a desired subversion of the norm (as suggested by Ultra culture) or as a model of what "not to do," as seen in Pavlenkov's series.[155] After 2013, *ZhZL* became a major presence on the internet, expanding beyond the boundaries of the Molodaya gvardiya website, with the creation of a YouTube channel devoted to biographies, with a variety of formats available to the viewer.[156] But because of these innovations and expansions, Molodaya gvardiya may be spreading its resources too thin.

REDESIGNING LITERARY BIOGRAPHY

Kalugin suggests that Russian-Soviet approaches to life writing have "a distinct historical continuity," and that *lichnost'* is "the principal object of biography."[157] New approaches allowed for a more nuanced understanding of creative individuality and a new expansion of how to access *lichnost'*. This central task remained common to all theoreticians of biography who wanted to create a "whole image of the personality" (*tselnoi obraz lichnosti*).[158] Beyond locating the worldview of the subject through their actions and other external details, the biographer seeks to disclose the secrets of the individual's inner world. The scholarly apparatus of the biography (through a documentary reconstruction of the life into a narrative) convinces the reader of the truthfulness of the account, but it is the biographer's sympathy for their subject and creativity of expression that enables the reader to co-experience the life through an emotional engagement with the hero's story. A large degree of the artistic element in biography, not characteristic of scholarly prose, is explained by this extra dimension, going beyond the boundaries of possible scholarly knowledge in the creation of a reconstructed image of a person.[159]

In the post-Soviet era, when the prohibitive aspects of censorship were curtailed and more academics began to enter into the series as biographers there was a new thinking about the genre of biography by writers and literary critics. While earlier official Soviet literary scholarship stressed the social determinability of the creative person, newer approaches, coming mainly from semiotic and structuralist theories, resulted in new concepts of how to write both scholarly and popular biographies. Earlier in the 1960s, renewed interest in formalist biographical methodology and Vinokur's 1927 work, as well as novel approaches to the writer's personality proposed by Mikhail Bakhtin, Yuri Lotman, Lydia Ginzburg, and others, impacted biographers' methods and offered innovative ways of understanding the genre of literary biography.[160] Although their scholarly writing began in the 1920s, their major theoretical contributions only became more widely available and influential beginning in the 1960s and remain so to the present. Building on Vinokur's earlier idea that personality is not a constant, but a "dynamic,"[161] these scholars find new ways of describing how personality is expressed through both verbal and nonverbal means. Caryl Emerson has demarcated the differences in notions of the self as conceived by these thinkers as "dialogic" (Bakhtin), "semiotic" (Lotman), and "societally conditioned" (Ginzburg).[162] How to describe the boundaries of the artist's human personality (*lichnost'*) is the biographer's dilemma. The life of a writer or other creative person consists of both an outer and inner world that are not separated but that actually borrow, cross over, merge and overcome the boundaries between them.[163] Bakhtin remarked in relation to the biography of a writer:

> Dostoevsky in his works, like any writer, is one person but in his life is another. And how these two people (creator and a person in life) are combined is for us still unclear . . . The life and the works are united by what we call the depth of the human personality. Each person is a whole, although he still does not encompass everything. In the works this person, if you will, violates his unity, he is able to reincarnate himself into other people. It is impossible to both separate

and to blend the life and the works, however, it is necessary to distinguish them, to mark the boundary between them.[164]

Though not focused primarily on biography as a genre, Bakhtin's notions of the dialogic self and polyphony provide a theoretical model for biographers to conceptualize the boundaries. While Bakhtin concentrates on linguistic expressions of personality, Lotman expands his purview to include nonverbal modes of self-expression including socially conditioned forms of behavior, gestures and rituals:

> The simple truths about the fact that the human personality presents itself as a complicated psychological and intellectual structure, arising from the intersectionality of epoch-making, class, group and uniquely individual models of consciousness and behavior, that any historical and social process realizes itself through this mechanism and not parallel to it (that is, through human thought and human behavior), that the social process manifests itself also in the structure of linkages and that, subsequently, any humanistic research cannot not take into account the achievements of scholarship in these arenas, all the same have not come into the scholarly consciousness of the literary researcher.[165]

Having previous practical experience as the biographer of Pushkin and Karamzin, Lotman urges other writers to not only draw on models of behavior or semiotic codes but also to plot the moments of deviation from those codes in order to get at the complexity of individual personality. David Bethea observes that for Lotman: "Pushkin and Karamzin were creative precisely because the literary roles/masks they routinely donned . . . allowed them freedom in the privacy of their own thoughts to develop personalities that had little to do with those masks and indeed could be seen in retrospect to actually oppose them."[166] Yet another dimension to this discussion of the creative personality is brought by Ginzburg, whose earlier literary criticism led to new concepts of the self, "personalism," in her later experiments in various forms of life writing. She combines psychological and linguistic approaches to view the manner in which a personality is constructed in human documents such as letters, diaries and memoirs as well as more peripheral memorabilia. Ginzburg sees the self as "inescapably conditioned, *obuslovlennyi*, pressured from the outside in."[167]

Due to the new social and political conceptualizations of society and the self over the last twenty-five years, changes have been afoot in the pragmatics of literary biographies in the series. Earlier, Pomerantseva noted that readers already come to the biography knowing the literary works and want to see a more complex interaction between the writer's life and the work, not just an explication of the writer's personality through the characters they create. Since readers can be expected to know the major writings of a classic Russian author, the biographer can abandon using the titles of the works as chapter headings, and instead can experiment with new organizational principles.[168] Structuring the writer's life around places, dispensing with traditional ordering principle of the life from birth to death, reversing chronology, or focusing only on one significant period or thematic within a life were all new innovations to get at that unique spark of creative genius and window into the author's inner world.

Throughout the history of the series, the formal elements of *ZhZL* biographies remained remarkably consistent, but as Andrei Petrov has suggested, the series is not wedded to "a certain frozen form which was once and for all an accepted canon" and that in recent years it has departed from stereotypes: "We don't have, thank God, a single algorithm for the creation of books in the series."[169] Yurkin compares the choosing of new subjects for *ZhZL* biographies to filling out Mendeleev's periodic table: "the empty squares indicate untouched fields of activity and we fill them with new publications . . . depending on the authors and the completion of manuscripts in correspondence with the canons of the biographical genre."[170] It's clear that series editors try to maintain a balance between figures from popular culture such as biographies of film stars and directors and new national biographies which are in line with the political imperialism of the Putin administration, such as those of the Ruriks, heroes of the Time of Troubles and the Romanovs available in a special boxed set entitled *Tsarist Russia*.

Finding biographers who are both experts in the subjects and skilled at creating an engaging narrative for *ZhZL*'s particular genre of creative nonfiction poses challenges. The series now draws heavily on academics, particularly historians, often affiliated with the leading universities, as well as tapping foreign academics who have already written biographies of desired subjects. In the expanding international market, not only is *ZhZL* entering into agreements with foreign writers, but authors of *ZhZL* biographies are also being tapped by Western publishers.[171] The pragmatics that emerged was the notion that the subject more often chooses the biographer, that there has to be an emotional investment in the biographical subject so that the work can be successful.[172] Molodaya gvardiya also features multiple publications by its most prestigious, "star" biographers, such as Bykov, Pavel Basinsky, and Vladimir Novikov, who while still publishing in the *ZhZL* series, experiment with different formats and approaches on their subject in other parts of the publishing house or even with other publishers.[173]

Critics have recently suggested that the series' quality has declined, that the series lacks sufficient editorial control, accurate fact-checking, and even reliable proofreading.[174] In all fairness, *ZhZL* is not the only biographical imprint criticized for these shortcomings. Nikolai Bogomolov also criticizes the lack of traditional scholarly research in other contemporary literary biographies, specifically pointing to renowned critic and biographer Alla Marchenko's biography of Anna Akhmatova (published by another major press) as an example of poor biographical practice, despite the fact that it won the Big Book Prize for 2009. Given the wealth of scholarship available on Akhmatova's life, Marchenko's inaccurate and sloppy use of dates and facts, such as the insertion of Alexei Tolstoy in a scene that occurs when in fact he was already deceased, is unacceptable. Bogomolov sees much of the deficiencies as a symptom of the voyeuristic tendencies of current popular culture and its focus on scandals and prurient details of everyday life rather than accomplishments. He especially takes to task the mass romance literature by such writers as Elena Arseneva, written for a greedy "addicted" readership on which the virtual experience of the lives of others acts like a narcotic.[175] Bogomolov still praises a number of recent writers' biographies published in the *ZhZL* series such as Bykov's *Pasternak* and Oleg Lekmanov and Mikhail Sverdlov's *Esenin*. Given the increased competition for readership and revenue, what *ZhZL* can offer is its historical reputation, in the words of Petrov, "Our reputation is worth more than sensationalism."[176] In contrast, Bulkina remarks that the current version of *ZhZL* has reformulated notions about the genre, which no longer adheres to Plutarchian precepts but instead fixates on notions of celebrity and scandal: "In this assemblage of libertines and tyrants, then, the writers' series constitutes the last 'lofty genre.' It is in part a nostalgic gift from 'our bookish days,' a reincarnation of the esteemed 'Writers on Writers' series of Soviet times. Its protagonists are now writers from the now-defunct land that once complacently dubbed itself the world's best-read country."[177] A new subgenre within literary biographies in *ZhZL* is the biography of biographers such as Shklovsky, Bakhtin, and Lotman, which, according to critic Oleg Osovsky, uses "excessive and aggressive literariness at the expense of documentation."[178] This is yet another manifestation of self-referentiality in the series, which on a regular basis celebrates itself and significant moments in its history as well as marking other commemorations with the publications of pertinent biographies. The most recent example is Molodaya gvardiya's republication of Pavlenkov's *Biographical Library: The Lives of Remarkable People* in celebration of the 130th anniversary of the series in five separate volumes, hailing it as a "return to its roots."[179]

As the authors of our chapters discuss, new biographies providing different perspectives on Russia's most famous writers still do elicit interest and debate in the cultural arena as well as heightened interest on the part of biographers. Our contributors problematize the challenges of fully knowing or understanding the biographical subject and the specific difficulties of representing and distinguishing between the writers' internal and external worlds. In this connection, our contributors examine the way in which the biographer envisions the relationship between the author's creations and the narrative of his/her life, tracing the major themes of a given writer in his/her works. The articles also explore the theoretical premises and larger historical context underlying the biographer's approach to his/her subject. In their comparative studies, our contributors discuss the poetics of biography, delineating specific formal aspects, including novelistic techniques, the narrative arc of the biographer's text and the way that subsequent biographies either build on or polemicize with earlier examples but always present some sort of innovative portrait of these most famous Russian writers. Aleksei Kholikov observes that "for the sophisticated reader, the life stories in the Lives of Remarkable People series have little in common with . . . 'tabloid' journalism. There are other, more serious reasons [for new biographiia of major Russian writers], which would include a need to rethink the role played by eminent writers in Russian events, a desire to make the acquaintance of once-prohibited writers, and a search for a hero who is not, alas, of our times."[180]

NOTES

1. Alisa Akimova, "Istoriia i biografiia," *Prometei* I (1966):348. Akimova is a biographer in the series, authoring biographies of Voltaire and Diderot.

2. Paula R. Backscheider, "Opportunities for Comparative Biography," *Slavic and East European Journal* 60, no. 2 (2016):272. See also her *Reflections on Biography* (2013).

3. Dmitrii Kalugin, *Proza zhizni: russkie biografii v XVIII I XIX vv.* (St. Petersburg: European University in St. Petersburg, 2015), 13.

4. Richard Holmes, "The Proper Study?" in *Mapping Lives: The Uses of Biography*, ed. Peter France and William St. Clair (Oxford: Oxford University Press, 2002), 15–16.

5. We should note here that we translate the series title into English as "The Lives of Remarkable People" though in the Russian original, the word life is singular which suggests that all remarkable people share certain traits of a "life" and it is those traits or practices that justify the appellation "remarkable."

6. For an overview of Pavlenkov's career and this series in the context of his other publishing projects, see Carol Ueland and Ludmilla A. Trigos, "F. F. Pavlenkov's Literacy Project: Popular Serials and Reading Rooms for the Russian Masses," in *The Edinburgh History of Reading: Common Readers*, Vol. 3, ed. Jonathan Rose (Edinburgh: University of Edinburgh Press, 2020), 157–179.

7. Commenting on earlier published versions of three articles in this volume, Backscheider states: "it was immediately clear to me that the authors who examined these three 'greatest' writers of Russian literature, share a deep commitment to advancing the theory and history of biography through analysis of the texts within the periods of time that the series existed. Always intensely aware of biographical decisions, especially issues of voice and the impact of the time in which a biography is

written, they make substantial contributions to comparative biography studies" ("On Opportunities in Comparative Biography," 273).

8. Inna Bulkina states, "Plutarch rendered that genre [of comparative biography] exemplary, in the literal sense of the word. His technique was the respectful idealization, his watchword was 'to a young man pondering how best to live,' and this monumental gallery of 'great men was expected to serve as an object lesson for his readers and their descendants." (cf. "The Lives of Remarkable People. Between Plutarch and Triapichkin," *Russian Studies in Literature* 49, no. 2 (Spring 2013): 87–95, esp. 90.

9. In a letter to N. K. Mikhailovskii, Pavlenkov sketched out his visionary idea for a new publishing project: "a biographical library, [Thomas] Carlyle and [Gabriel] Tarde, taken in aggregate, must evoke faith in humankind in the hearts of the reading youth," cited in Rassudovskaia, *Izdatel' F. F. Palvenkov,* 47–48. Gorbunov points out that Pavlenkov had published Russian translations of Carlyle's *On Heroes, Hero-Worship and the Heroic in History* (1891) and Tarde's *Laws of Imitation* (1892) and thus saw the pedagogical uses of biography.

10. Anna Makolkin, "Probing the Origins of Literary Biography: English and Russian Versions," *Biography* 19, no. 1 (1996): 87–104, quote from 89.

11. For the ongoing use of the tombstone as a recurring image in Maxim Gorky's philosophy, see the article by Irene Masing-Delic in this volume.

12. Makolkin, 93.

13. Kalugin, 42. A longer list of narrative components in biography can be found in: Michael Rewa, *Reborn as Meaning: Panegyrical biography from Isocrates to Walton* (Washington: University Press of America, 1983), 12.

14. Sergei Averintsev, "From Biography to Hagiography: Some Stable Patterns in the Greek and Latin Tradition of Lives, including Lives of the Saints" in *Mapping Lives*, 22. He suggests that narratives were secondary to the general depiction of moral character and not always presented in chronological order, so that the deeds were "subordinated to the categories of ethical and psychological thought" (25).

15. Averinstev, 19.

16. *Plutarch's Lives,* tr. Bernadotte Perrin, 11 vols, Loeb Classical Library (London and New York, 1914–1919), 3:225, cited in Averinstev, 25.

17. Makolkin, 94.

18. Makolkin, 98.

19. See Anna Navrotskaya, "Aleksandr Nevskii: Hagiography and National Biography," *Cahiers du Monde russe* 46, no. 1–2, La Russie vers 1550: Monarchie nationale ou empire en formation? (January–June 2003): 297–304.

20. Kalugin, 17.

21. Margaret Ziolkowski, *Hagiography and Modern Russian Literature* (Princeton: Princeton Univeristy Press, 1988), 18–19.

22. W. Gareth Jones, "Biography in Eighteenth-Century Russia," *Oxford Slavonic Papers* 22 (1989):62. Our summary of eighteenth-century trends relies upon his description.

23. Jones states that it was undertaken without the expectation of Russian readership. The work was entitled *Satyres de Monsieur le Prince Cantemire avec l'histoire de sa vie.* See W. G. Jones, 64–65 (quote from 65).

24. For the importance of Plutarch in Russia, see V. I. Vatsuro, *Pisateli-dekabristy v vospominaniiakh sovremennikov. V dvukh tomakh.* (Moscow: Khudozhestvennaia literatura, 1980), 1:16, Andrew Kahn, "Readings of Imperial Rome from Lomonosov to Pushkin," *Slavic Review* 53.4 (Winter 1993): 745–68, and S.S. Volk, *Istoricheskie vzgliady dekabristov* (Moscow-Leningrad: Izdatel'stvo Akademii nauk SSSR, 1958). Lynn Ellen Patyk also discusses the far-reaching influence of Plutarch, either through Rousseau or other popularizers, "'The Double-Edged Sword of Word and Deed': Revolutionary Terrorism and Russian Literary Culture," (Diss. Stanford University, 2005), 74–75.

25. See W. G. Jones, 58–81 and Nathaniel Knight, "Biography as Archive: Writing the Lives of Scholars in Imperial Russia," in *Writing Russian Lives: The Politics and Poetics of Biography in Modern Russian Culture*, ed. Polly Jones (Modern Humanities Research Association, 2018), 16–40.

26. W. G. Jones, 65. For a list of both individual and collective biographies that were published from 1740–1800, see 71–80.

27. For a more detailed discussion of nineteenth-century Russian biography, see Knight, passim, Kalugin, passim and Ludmilla A. Trigos and Carol Ueland, "Creating a National Biographical Series: F. F. Pavlenkov's *Lives of Remarkable People*, 1820–1924," in *Writing Russian Lives*, 41–66.

28. In the same year, the Brockhaus and Efron Encylopedic Dictionary (1890–1907) began to be published which demonstrates the topicality of these kinds of projects. Pavlenkov himself issued a popular version, *Entsiklopedicheskii slovar'* (St. Petersburg, 1899).

29. C. N. Parke, *Biography: Writing Lives* (New York: Twayne Publishers, 1996), 9.

30. Keith Thomas, *Changing Conceptions of National Biography: The Oxford DNB in Historical Perspective* (Cambridge, 2005), 2–11.

31. For a survey of negative portrayals of tsars' lives, especially Catherine the Great, in foreign publications, see Marianne Tax Choldin, *A Fence Around the Empire: Russian Censorship of Western Ideas* (Durham, NC: Duke University Press, 1985), 137–61.

32. See the list of published biographies from 1740–1799 in W. G. Jones, 71–80.

33. Choldin, *A Fence Around the Empire,* 18, 28.

34. E. V. Dolgikh, *K probleme mentaliteta rossiiskoi administrativnoi elity pervoi poloviny XIX: M.N. A. Korf, D. N. Bludov* (Moscow: Indrik, 2006), 54.

35. The "materialy k biografii" format becomes almost its own genre in itself during contentious times, since it avoids explicit commentary and value judgments on the contents.

36. For a thorough discussion of the earliest secular biographies in Russia from the late eighteenth through the mid-nineteenth century, see Kalugin, *Proza zhizni.*

37. P. A. Kulish, *Opyt biografii N. V. Gogol'ia so vkliucheniem do soroka ego pisem* (St. Petersburg, 1854), 172.

38. Dmitrii Kalugin, "Soviet Theories of Biography," *Biography* 38, no. 3 (Summer 2015):347. Also see Kalugin's *Proza zhizni* for more detail on biographies from the mid-nineteenth century that emphasize the inner world rather than experience and deeds.

39. Kalugin, "Soviet Theories of Biography," 347.

40. We will mark the use of the term *lichnost'* throughout, since many Russian-speaking scholars do not feel that the word "personality" adequately conveys the essence and nuances of the term in English translation.

41. Kalugin, *Proza zhizni,* 80. Radishchev introduces an ignoble character, uses "piquant details" about the subject including his sexual experience and death by syphilis and ends with political invective. See Kalugin, *Proza zhizni,* 80–111.

42. L. N. Tolstoi, *Polnoe sobranie sochinenii,* t. 60, s. 274 cited in Galina Pomerantseva, *Biografiia v potoke vremeni. ZhZL: zamysli i voploshcheniia seriia* (Moscow: Kniga, 1987), 274. Annenkov's *Life of Stankevich* was written as an introductory article to a volume of Stankevich's letters.

43. Cited in Rassudovskaia, *Izdatel' F. F. Pavlenkov,* 48.

44. Pavlenkov subsidized his publication of Pisarev's works due to the success of his earlier translation and publication of popular physics textbooks by F. Ganot. His later persecution by the authorities was for his personal and professional ties to Pisarev and his family. See Trigos and Ueland, "Creating a National Biographical Tradition," and Ueland and Trigos, "F. F. Pavlenkov's Literacy Project."

45. For a reproduction of one of Pavlenkov's advertisements, see Trigos and Ueland, "Creating a National Biographical Tradition," 53. As Hilde Hoogenboom has noted, Russia imported more literature than it produced through the first half of the nineteenth century, so many of the foreign names on Pavlenkov's list would be familiar to the readers even if they had never read specifically about the subject or his/her works (cf. her "Sentimental Novels and Pushkin: European Literary Markets and Russian Readers," *Slavic Review* 74, no. 3 (Fall 2015): 553–74.

46. They were Sofia Kovalevskaia, George Sand, George Eliot and Princess Dashkova. Of Pavlenkov's seventy-eight biographers, ten were women. On the whole, however, there is a paucity of women in the later history of the *ZhZL* series; only three biographies (of Kovalevskaia, Maria Ermolova, Klara Tsetkin and Marie Curie) were produced prior to 1960. More recently, in the last five years, women's biographies have increased though not substantially and focus mainly on royalty, actresses and religious figures.

47. Assumedly, Pavlenkov took the idea of grouping heroes by their profession or area of activities (*deiatel'nost'*) from Carlyle. This basic structure holds for all three iterations of the series.

48. This accounts for the seeming irregularity of the numbering system within Pavlenkov's and later, Gorky's, catalog. In Pavlenkov's iteration, 198 biographies actually came out in 193 booklets. See *Katalog ZhZL 1890–2010*, ed. E. Gorelik, P. Alexandrova, R. A. Evseeva (Moscow: Molodaia gvardiia, 2010), 46.

49. Jeffrey Brooks, "Readers and Reading at the End of the Tsarist Era," in William Mills Todd, *Literature and Society in Imperial Russia, 1800–1924* (Stanford, CA: Stanford University Press, 1978), 105, 145. For more details on the marketability and popularity of the series, see Trigos and Ueland, passim.

50. *Katalog ZhZL: 1890–2010*, 5.

51. N. A. Rubakin, "Iz istorii bor'by za prava knigi (Rukopis)." Gosudarstvennaia biblioteka im. Lenina. Otdel rukopisei, f. 358 (N. A. Rubakin), published in *Kniga.*

Issledovaniia i materialy, sb. 9 (1964):235. See Trigos and Ueland, "Creating a National Biographical Tradition," 58–61, for contemporary reactions to the series.

52. Iu. Gorbunov, *F. F. Pavlenkov: Ego zhizn' i izdatel'skaia deiatel'nost'* (Cheliabinsk: Ural Ltd., 1999), 153.

53. A list of Pavlenkov's biographers, including their pseudonyms, can be found in *Katalog ZhZL*. Gorbunov provides biographical detail and categorizes them (*F. F. Pavlenkov*, 145–67).

54. Rubakin, "Iz istorii," 211.

55. See A. Blium, *F. F. Pavlenkov v Viatke* (Kirov, 1976). For more on Pavlenkov's relationship to the censorship see N. A. Grinchenko, "K izdatel'skoi deiatel'nosti F. F. Pavlenkova. Pis'ma F. F. Pavlenkova k P. I. Sementkovskomu (1890–1899)," 12–62, and N. G. Patrusheva, "F. F. Pavlenkov i tsenzura," 63–75, in *Knizhnoe delo v Rossii v nachale XIX–XX vv.,*, no. 20 (2019).

56. Books were said to be "arrested" if after their printing they were confiscated by the censorship due to further scrutiny. See Grinchenko, "K istorii izdatel'skoi deiatel'nosti F. F. Pavlenkova," 26. For more information on the Tolstoy biography, see Caryl Emerson's article in this volume.

57. Grinchenko, 53.

58. Rostislav Ivanovich Sementovskii (1845–1919), lawyer, editor (of *Niva*) and translator, wrote five biographies that appeared in the series—Bismarck, Diderot, Krankin, Kantemir and Katkov. Noting Sementovskii's exceptional skills in writing and editing, Pavlenkov gave him a choice of biographies to write and asked him to continually participate in his enterprise. Sementovskii initially agreed to write on Alexander II but only under a pseudonym. It appears that the biography was never attempted.

59. Hermione Lee, *Virginia Woolf's Nose: Essays on Biography* (Princeton and Oxford: Princeton University Press, 2005), 38.

60. See Grinchenko, passim.

61. For a history of the reading rooms, see Ueland and Trigos, "F.F. Pavlenkov's Literacy Project."

62. Our primary sources for materials on the Soviet period until today are scholars and editors affiliated with the series and Molodaia gvardiia. They include Tatiana Nepomniashchaia, Galina Pomerantseva, Valentin Iurkin and Andrei Petrov. To our knowledge, Nepomniashchaia completed the first dissertation on the series in 1968, "Knigi o zamechatel'nykh liudiakh kak tip izdaniia: Seriia ZhZL izdatel'stva "Molodaia gvardiia" (Moscow: Fakul'tet zhurnalistiki. Kafedra redaktsionnogo dela i knigovedeniia. Gosudarstvennyi Universitet imeni Lomonosova). See also her article, "A. M. Gorkii i 'Zhizn' zamechatel'nykh liudei' (K istorii zamysla)," *Vestnik Moskovskogo Universiteta. Seriia XI. Zhurnalistika*, no. 3 (1966): 47–56. Pomerantseva worked in the editorial offices of *ZhZL* for 30 years, rising to the position of section editor for biographies of artists and writers until the mid-1980s. Her articles include: "K istorii stanovleniia i razvitiia serii 'Zhizn' zamechatel'nykh liudei' (1933–1941), *Kniga: Issledovania i materialy* (Moscow: Kniga), 27 (1973): 92–118 and "Seriia 'Zhizn zamechatel'nykh liudei' i zamysel A. M. Gor'kogo," *Kniga: Issledovania i materialy* (Moscow: Kniga) 32 (1976): 36–64, and her book,

Biografiia v potoke vremeni. ZhZL: zamysli i voploshcheniia serii, remains the definitive source on the series' Soviet history. Her experience as an editor who taught and supervised theses also demonstrates how closely the series has been tied as an institution with Moscow's graduate programs in book studies at Moscow State University and the Polygraphic Institute, and in the post-Soviet period, the Russian State Humanities University. We also frequently cite Valentin Iurkin (b. 1940), who has served as executive director of Molodaia gvardiia for decades and written voluminously on the press and series and Andrei Petrov (1959–2021), who had been the head editor of *ZhZL* prior to becoming the director of the press. As with Pavlenkov's enterprise, *ZhZL* has long employed people who work interchangeably as editors, authors of biographies and scholars.

63. Pomerantseva, "Seriia 'Zhizn zamechatel'nykh liudei,'" 36.

64. See Jeffrey Brooks, "The Breakdown in Production and Distribution of Printed Material, 1917–1927" in *Bolshevik Culture,* ed. Abbot Gleason (Bloomington: Indiana University Press, 1985), 151–74.

65. George Alexander Johnston, "The New Biography: Ludwig, Maurois and Strachey," *The Atlantic Monthly* CSLIII (March 1929), 133, cited in Laura Marcus, "The Newness of the 'New Biography,'" in *Mapping Lives*, 195. Marcus draws attention to the wide range of authors of critical and theoretical works, including William Thayer's *The Art of Biography* (1920), James Johnston's *Biography: The Literature of Personality* (1927), Harold Nicolson's *The Development of English Biography (*1927), André Maurois's *Aspects of Biography* (1929), Mark Longaker's *Contemporary Biography* (1934) and Emil Ludwig's *Die Kunst der Biographie* (1936) (195).

66. Our summary of the features of "new biography" relies upon Marcus, "The Newness of 'New Biography',″ 196.

67. A. M. Gor'kii, *Perepiska A. M. Gor'kogo s zarubezhnymi literatorami* (M: Izdatel'stvo Akademii Nauk SSSR, 1960), 64.

68. Pomerantseva, "Seriia *ZhZL*," 37. After's Gorky's death in 1936, the remaining editors decided to publish these sketches in the series as *Portrety zamechatel'nykh liudei* (1936) and republished select sketches in *Literaturnye portrety* (1963, 1967, 1983). The series continued the practice of publishing an occasional volume of sketches by prominent authors such as Kornei Chukovskii and Konstantin Paustovskii.

69. See Mark Gamsa, "Two Million Filing Cards: The Empirical-Biographical Method of Semen Vengerov," *History of the Humanities* 1, no. 1 (2016): 129–53.

70. Boris Tomashevsky, "Literature and Biography," in *Biography in Theory: Key Texts with Commentaries*, ed. Wilhelm Hemecker and Edward Saunders (Berlin/Boston, Walter deGruyter, 2017), 82.

71. Tomashkevsky, 90. For a useful gloss on the essay, see Edward Saunders, "In Search of the Literary Fact, Boris Tomashevsky and the Limits of the Biographical Approach," in *Biography in Theory*, 91–96.

72. See Parke, *Biography: Writing Lives* and Michael J. Benton, *Literary Biography: An Introduction* (New York: Wiley Blackwell, 2015) for more on biomythography.

73. See Tomashevsky, "Literature and Biography," 88, and the chapters by Brintlinger, Trigos, Emerson, and Smith in this volume.

74. See Pomerantseva, *Biografiia v potoke zhizni*.

75. Angela Brintlinger, "Lives and Facts: Biography in Russia in the 1920s," in *Writing Russian Lives*, 100, and Kalugin, "Soviet Theories," 352–53.

76. Kalugin suggests that Vinokur "did not sprout a scholarly tradition and thus remained an isolated intellectual experiment" ("Soviet Theories," 352). However, *ZhZL* editor Pomerantseva spends a great deal of ink discussing the importance of Vinokur's approach in her history of the series, *Biografiia v potoke vremeni* (passim) and in "Seriia ZhZL," 42.

77. *Katalog*, 8. See also Iu. I. Vishniakova, "Vospitanie na obratse: 80 let biographicheskoi serii "Zhizn' zamechatel'nikh liudei" izdatel'stva Molodaia gvardiia" in *Nashe Nasledie, Vestnik PSTGU, Seriia IV: Pedagogika. Psikhologiia*, vyp. 53 (2019): 120–32.

78. Pomerantseva, "K istorii stanovlenii . . . ," 105. Nepomniashchaia states that Tikhonov also told Gorky that the publishing house "Krug" (founded and directed by a number of "fellow-travelers" including Voronsky and Pilnyak) was intending to publish a biography series entitled "Zhizn' zamechatel'nykh liudei" however, she does not provide a specific date or say under whose initiative. See Nepomniashchaia, "A. M. 'Gor'kii i Zhizn' zamechatel'nykh liudei,'" 51.

79. Evgeny Dobrenko, *Stalinist Cinema and the Production of History. Museum of the Revolution* (New Haven: Yale University Press, 2008), 66.

80. Katerina Clark, *The Soviet Novel History as Ritual* (Chicago: University of Chicago Press, 1985), 118, 119. See also her "Little Heroes and Big Deeds: Literature Responds to the First Five Year Plan" in *Cultural Revolution in Russia, 1928–1931*, ed. Sheila Fitzpatrick (Bloomington: Indiana University Press, 1978), "The History of the Factories" as a Factory of History: a Case Study on the Role of Soviet Literature in Subject Formation" in Jochen Hellbeck and Klaus Heller (eds.), *Autobiographical Practices in Russia—Autobiographische Praktiken in Russland* (Goettingen: V&R Unipress, 2004), 251–77. Irene Masing-Delic discusses Gorky's interest in biography as part of his desire to form a new Soviet man in her article in this volume.

81. Jochen Hellbeck, "Galaxy of Black Stars: The Power of Soviet Biography," *American Historical Review* 114, no. 3 (June 2009):618.

82. A. M. Gor'kii, "O tolpe i geroe," *Arkhiv A. M. Gor'kogo* (Moscow, 1969), t. XII, 113–14 as cited in Thun-Hohenstein, 448.

83. A. M. Gor'kii, *Polnoe sobranie sochinenii v 30-tomakh* (Moscow: Goslitizdat, 1955), t. 27, 475.

84. Franziszka Thun-Hohenstein, "V laboratorii sovetskoi biografii: Seriia 'Zhizn' zamechatel'nykh liudei,' 1933–1941," 447 available at: https://histrf.ru/uploads/media/default/0001/09/78f889e5e7e1a7f1f3fd45fa64d429baf620c8b8.pdf Last accessed 3/6/2021.

85. As cited in Sergei Semanov, "Samaia znamenitaia v svete," in V. Iurkin, *Zhizn' zamechatel'nogo izdatel'stva: Molodaia gvardiia—75 let* (Moscow: Molodaia gvardiia, 1997), 193.

86. *Literaturnaia gazeta*, June 5, 1932, cited in Nepomniashchaia, "A. M. 'Gor'kii i Zhizn' zamechatel'nykh liudei',", 51.

87. Other editorial board members were I. Grabar, N. Semashko, A. Frumkin. Regarding the changing composition of the editorial board, see Pomerantseva, "K istorii stanovlenii . . . ," 92–118, Nepomniashchaia, "A.M. Gor'kii i 'Zhizn' zamechatel'nykh liudei,'" 47–56 and *40 let ZhZL: Katalog 1933–1973,* ed. E. I. Gorelik and S. N. Semanov (Moscow: Molodaia gvardiia, 1974), 5.

88. Pomerantseva, "Seriia ZhZL," 37–38.

89. Ibid., 37.

90. See Vishniakova for a more detailed list by category. She provides the total number of biographies produced from 1933–1939 as 107 biographies with an approximate average of 210 pages and a general print run of 40,000–50,000 copies (123–25).

91. Thun-Hohenstein, 447.

92. Choldin, *A Fence Around the Empire,* 43–47,78–84 and A. Fedorova, "Genrickh Geine v tsarskoi tsenzure," *Literaturnoe nasledstvo* (Moscow: Zhurnalno-gazetnoe ob"edinenie, 1935), 635–78.

93. See Angela Brintlinger's article on Pushkin in this volume.

94. Vishniakova, 124.

95. See *M. Gor'kii i sovetskaia pechat',* kn. 2, 244, cited in Pomerantseva, "Seriia ZhZL," 39.

96. Nepomniashchaia, "Knigi o zamechtel'nykh liudiakh," 145–51.

97. See Nepomniashchaia, "A.M. Gor'kii i 'Zhizn' zamechatel'nykh liudei,'" 56, and Thun-Hohenstein, 442. Thun-Hohenstein explicitly notes that in order to get a full picture of the functioning of *ZhZL* in the 1930s as a "unique biographical library" a full analysis of the archival materials, much of which remain unavailable, would be necessary. The disclaimer he provides gets at the crux of the matter which is the lack of open access to the correspondence of the editorial board as well as of editors' correspondence with authors. Regarding the continued use of the term "creative laboratory of the biographical genre," see "Laboratoriia biograficheskogo zhanra," Evgenii Trostin's interview of Andrei Petrov, the series editor: https://историк.рф/journal/лаборатория-биорафического-жанра/ Last accessed 1/24/2019.

98. Summary taken from Nepomniashchaia, "Knigi o zamechatel'nykh liudiakh,"150–53.

99. Vishniakova, 122.

100. A. Zhdanov, *Pervyi s"ezd pistaelei. Stenogramma* (Moscow, 1934), 4, cited in Clark, "Little Heroes and Big Deeds," 206.

101. Quoted in Nepomniashchaia, "Knigi o zamechatel'nykh liudiakh," 179.

102. Thun-Hohenstein, 452.

103. Pomerantseva, "Seriia ZhZL," 50.

104. Thun-Hohenstein, 451.

105. See S. M. Demkina, "M. Gor'kii i seriia 'Zhizn' zamechatel'nykh liudei,'" *Voprosy kul'turologii* 4 (Feb. 2014): 67–72.

106. Writing in the 1970–1980s, Pomerantseva could only give veiled references to these events. Vishniakova's more recent account speaks frankly about the purges and their effect on the series' history (cf. 126).

107. We have found several mistakes even in the latest version of the *ZhZL* catalog (*Katalog, 1890–2010*) where inaccurate death dates of purged biographers are listed. In earlier catalogs, some of the writers and their works are not listed.

108. Examples were: "The Art of War" (*Iskusstvo voevat'*), "Conversations about Military Education" (*Besedy o voinskom vospitanii*), "The Young Partisan's Library" (*Biblioteka molodogo partizana*) and others. See Iurkin, *Zhizn' zamechatel'nogo izdatel'stva*, 35.

109. Molly Guptill Manning, *When Books Went to War: The Stories that Helped Us Win WWII* (Boston: Mariner Books, 2014), 75. See chapter 5 for a detailed discussion of the logistical problems of production and distribution during wartime and for an elaboration on the popularity of different genres, 75–91. Similarly, in China in the 1940s, translated Soviet Socialist Realist novels were distributed as inspirational models to the soldiers who carried them into battle in their backpacks. Mark Gamsa dissects the myth of these activities in his book, *The Reading of Russian Literature in China. A Moral Example and Manual of Practice* (New York: Palgrave Macmillan, 2010).

110. See Trigos' article on the wartime biography of Nikolai Gogol, who was Ukrainian by origin.

111. The editor of the later compilation of wartime biographies, *Velikie Russkie liudi* (Moscow: Molodaia gvardiia, 1984), suggested that any of the heroes in this biographical grouping today could be spoken about differently (407).

112. See the two introductory pieces, "Knigi-soldaty" and "Arsenal dukhnovnyi tsennosstei," in *Velikie Russkie liudi*.

113. "Ot sostavitelia," *Velikie russkie liudi*, 406.

114. Ibid., 407.

115. Pomeransteva, *Biografiia v potoke vremeni*, 144.

116. *Materialy k dokladu redaktsii serii 'Zhizn' zamechatel'nykh"* (Moscow, 1947) as cited in Pomerantseva, "Seriia ZhZL," 50.

117. Stephen Lovell, *The Russian Reading Revolution: Print Culture in the Soviet and Post-Soviet Eras* (Basingstoke: Macmillan and St. Martin's Press, 2000), 92 and passim.

118. For a discussion of the creation of the Soviet reading public and the mythology of the Soviet reader, see Lovell, *The Russian Reading Revolution*, Evgeny Dobrenko, *The Making of the State Writer: Social and Aesthetic Origins of Soviet Literary Culture* (Stanford, CA: Stanford University Press, 2001) and Kathleen F. Parthe, *Russia's Dangerous Texts. Politics between the Lines* (New Haven, Ct: Yale University Press, 2004).

119. Pomerantseva, *Biografiia v potoke vremeni*, 193.

120. Ibid., 207.

121. Shirley Graham Du Bois (1896–1977) was an African American playwright, author and composer who along with her second husband, W. E. B. Du Bois, was an activist for African American and women's rights and a member of the American Communist party. Writer of acclaimed biographies for children, she also wrote an award-winning historical novel about Frederick Douglass, *There Once was a Slave*, which was translated into Russian for the series and published in 1959. Graham and

her husband had been on an extended tour through Europe, Eastern Europe, and China, stopping in Moscow from 1958 to 1959.

122. *ZhZL* published Irving Stone's biography of Jack London in 1960 and his essay on biography ("Biograficheskaia povest'") was translated and published in *Prometei,* Molodaia gvardiia's journal devoted to providing source materials on biography and Russian literature (1966, vol. 1).

123. Interestingly, it became expedient to use foreign biographers for several reasons, some political, some economic, to keep up a steady flow of titles for publication in years when the press was struggling to get a steady flow of volumes out per year. This strategy was employed in the 1960s and afterward. Curiously, the first and only biography of Lenin (*Lenin: Zhizn' i smert'*) in the series was published in 2002 and was written by an American, Robert Payne (in English, *The Life and Death of Lenin*, 1964).

124. V. Iurkin, *Vremia i knigi: Molodaia gvardiia v epokhu peremen* (Moscow: Molodaia gvardiia, 2010), 239.

125. Iurkin was first affiliated with Molodaia gvardiia in 1975 and was appointed as the executive director of the publishing house in 1985, a position he holds to the present.

126. Iurkin, *Vremiia i knigi*, 103.

127. "Zhizn' zamechatel'nykh tsarei," review from *Literaturnaia gazeta*, 2003, republished in Iurkin, *Vremiia i knigi*, 159. Eight years later, *ZhZL* published a new *Aleksandr I* (2005) by a Russian writer, A. N. Arkhangel'skii, which was published in a second edition in 2006.

128. See Pomerantseva's discussion of the conference Penkin convened to discuss the series' orientation in 1946–1947, *Materialy k dokladu redaktsii serii "Zhizn' zamechatel'nykh liudei"* (Moscow, 1947), and other roundtables subsequently published in *Istoriia SSSR, Voprosy literatury,* and other journals, in "Seriia ZhZL," 50–55.

129. Many of these discussions from 1985 on are collected in Iurkin, *Vremia i knigi.*

130. Pomerantseva, *Biografiia v potoke vremeni*, 311.

131. See "Ot redaktsii," *Prometei*, vol. I, 1966, n.p.

132. The series inclined toward a greater use of biographical novels as well as more conventional biographies. A few were first published in the *ZhZL* series, for example, Shchegolev's *Duel and Death of Pushkin* (1933) and Irving Stone's *Sailor in the Saddle* (1960) on Jack London.

133. In addition to Molodaia gvardiia, other publishers developed biography series, especially Gospolitizdat, which were more narrowly focused on a particular era or societal group (for example, "Heroes and Feats" and "Tales of the Actions and People of the Party"). According to Polly Jones, Gospolitizdat was publishing more than 40 biographical series by 1962, of which the two aforementioned series received acclaim. See her *Revolution Rekindled: The Writers and Readers of Late Soviet Biography* (Oxford: Oxford University Press, 2019), 49.

134. Jones, *Revolution Rekindled,* 2, 15. Dmitrii Zhukov, literary critic and biographer, also remarks on the popularity of biography series in *Biografiia biografii: razmyshlenie o zhanre* (Moscow: Sovetskaia Rossiia, 1980).

135. Jones, *Revolution Rekindled*, 17.

136. See the roundtable, "Zhizn' i deiatel'nost'. Nereshennye problem biograficheskogo zhanra," *Voprosy Literatury* 10 (1973), 16–93. The biography series *Life in Art* (Iskusstvo, 1967–1993) also commenced during the same time period and made an emotional appeal to its readers, as did the series *Pioneer-Heroes* (Malysh, 1974/9–1982), geared toward the Soviet youth.

137. See S. Semanov, "Samaia znamenitaia na svete," 200. Semanov was editor of the series from 1969–1976, when he was fired for "Russophilia" (*rusism*). See Petr Palamarchuk, "Staraia 'Molodaia gvardiia,'" in Iurkin, *Zhizn' zamechatel'nogo isdatel'stva*, 158.

138. Jones discusses how the new series strove to correct *ZhZL*'s "mistakes": its ideological oversights, lack of coverage of Bolsheviks and other revolutionaries, its uneven aesthetic quality (*Revolution Rekindled*, 48). This avoidance of tackling the major Soviet political figures of the twentieth century continued in the series even after the fall of the Soviet Union, until Robert Payne's 1964 biography of Lenin was translated into Russian (*Lenin: Zhizn' i smert'*, 2002) and American historian William Taubman's 1990 biography of Khrushchev (*Khrushchev: The Man and His Era*) was translated for the series in 2005. Only in 2009 was Stanislav Rybas's *Stalin* published. None of these biographies have yet gone through more than two editions.

139. Pomerantseva, *Biografiia v potoke vremeni*, 315. See Alexander Spektor's chapter in this volume on Dostoevsky biographies.

140. Iurkin and others allude to these polemics in their essays in *Zhizn' zamechatel'nogo izdatel'stva*.

141. Nepomniashchaia, "Knigi o zamechatel'nykh liudiakh," 181–82.

142. For a detailed examination of the evolution of the term, see I. Ia. Losievskii, *Nauchnaia biografiia pisatel'ia. Problemy interpretatsii i typologii* (Kharkiv: "Krok," 1998).

143. Iurkin, *Vremia i knigi*, 237.

144. Ibid., 93.

145. Some of the last biographies released in print runs of 10,000 were those guaranteed to be bestsellers: Ariadna Tyrkova-Williams's two-volume biography of Pushkin for the bicentennial of Pushkin's birth and the biography of John Lennon (a joint venture with an American publisher) in 2000. See *Katalog*, 198, 203.

146. N.F. Boldyrev ed., *Biograficheskaia biblioteka F.F. Pavlenkova* vol. 1, (Cheliabinsk: Ural Press, 1994), 6–7.

147. V. Iurkin, *ZhZL: Letopis' tsivilizatsii: 120 let serii <Zhizn' zamechatel'nykh liudei>* (Moscow: Molodaia gvardiia, 2010), 5.

148. Iurkin, "Dukhovnoe zaveshchanie" from *Literaturnaia gazeta*, 2005 in *Vremia i knigi*, 112.

149. From 2010 on, biographies no longer competed in the main categories of the Big Book Prize.

150. The first volume in the series was dedicated to Boris Gromov.

151. For example, the *ZhZL* biographies of Joseph Brodsky by Lev Losev and by Vladimir Bondarenko engage in such a polemic. Vladimir Novikov's *Malaia seriia* biography of Pushkin limits his discussion to Pushkin's prose. See Carol Ueland's article on Brodsky biographies in this volume.

152. It can also be downloaded for free on the Molodaia gvardiia website: www.gvardiya.ru.

153. There were twenty books in the series, all written by V. M. Voskoboinikov. In the late Soviet period, Molodaia gvardiia had a series for children, *A Pioneer Means Number One* (*Pioner—znachit pervyi*), which published ninety-two biographies for children from 1967 to 1987. Voskoboinikov published five biographies in the earlier Molodaia gvardiia series.

154. 88 episodes of the cartoon series have been released so far.

155. UltraKultura had published books on LSD use and the essays of Eduard Limonov while he was imprisoned. The UltraKultura version of "ZhZL" did not continue, though this may be due to the death its founder, Ilya Kormiltsev, in 2007 and not to the government's accusations (beginning in 2004) that the press was disseminating propaganda on drug use and terrorism.

156. For an example of a biography "talk-show" featuring a writer's biography, see Angela Brintlinger's article in this volume.

157. Kalugin, "Soviet Theories," 345, 347.

158. Losievskii, 6–10.

159. Ibid., 15.

160. Several contributors refer specifically to Lotman's scholarship in their chapters in this volume, including Angela Brintlinger, Caryl Emerson, Ludmilla Trigos, Alexandra Smith, and Carol Ueland. Alexander Spektor uses the work of Bakhtin to illuminate his discussion of Dostoevsky's biographies. Lotman's biography of Karamzin was published posthumously in the series in 1998.

161. Vinokur, *Biografiia i kul'tura*, 32.

162. Caryl Emerson, "Bakhtin, Lotman, Vygotsky, and Lydia Ginzburg on Types of Selves: A Tribute," in *Self and Story in Russian History*, ed. Laura Engelstein and Stephanie Sandler (Ithaca: Cornell University Press, 2000), 23.

163. Losievskii, 30.

164. M. M. Bakhtin, "O polifonichnosti romanov Dostoevskogo," *Sobranie sochinenii v-6-ti tomakh* (Moscow: Russkie slovari. Iasyki slavianskikh kul'tur, 1996–2012), t. 6, 462–63.

165. Yurii Lotman, "Biografiia—zhivoe litso," *Novyi mir* 2 (1985):230.

166. David Bethea, "Bakhtinian Prosaics Versus Lotmanian 'Poetic Thinking,'" *Slavic and East European Journal* 41, no. 1 (Spring 1997):9.

167. Emerson, "Bakhtin, Lotman," 33. For more about Lydia Ginzburg, see Emily Van Buskirk, *Lydia Ginzburg's Prose: Reality in Search of Literature* (Princeton and Oxford: Princeton University Press, 2016).

168. Pomerantseva, *Biografiia v potoke vremeni*, 289–90.

169. Quoted in "ZhZL—Kniga na vse vremena," a roundtable from *Literaturnaia gazeta* (2003) in Iurkin, *Vremia i knigi,* 105. Each author appears to have some degree of leeway in their use of documentation, but formal academic citation is rarely used. Consistent elements include titled chapter divisions, a list of sources and chronological timeline of the subject's life at the end of the biography.

170. Ibid., 258.

171. Whereas earlier *ZhZL* bought the rights to translate existing biographies by foreign authors, recently, it has commissioned new works, such as in the biography of Joseph Brodsky (2008) by Lev Loseff or the biography of Dmitrii Sviatopolk-Mirskii (2021) by Mikhail Efimov and Gerald Smith. Yale University Press published the English translation of Loseff's work in 2011. One of the Tolstoy biographies written by Pavel Basinskii has been published in English by Glagoslav Publishers.

172. Noted Western and Russian biographers comment on the necessity of an internal connection between the biographer and his hero, an understanding of being "chosen." For a discussion of the affinity between biographers and their subjects, see A. Gladkov, "Na poliakh knigi Andre Morua," *Prometei: Istoriko-biograficheskii almanakh serii ZhZL* 5 (1968): 394–413, Richard Holmes, *Footsteps: Adventures of a Romantic Biographer* (New York: Vintage Books, 1985), and James Atlas, *The Shadow in the Garden: A Biographer's Tale* (New York: Pantheon Books, 2017), among others.

173. For example, Bykov published a *Malaia seriia* biography of Gorky based on a screenplay he had written. After winning the *Bol'shaia kniga* prize for an earlier work on Tolstoy (*Lev Tolstoi: Begstvo iz raia*, 2010), Pavel Basinskii published his *Lev Tolstoi: Svobodnyi chelovek* in 2016 which then was republished in 2017 within the *ZhZL* series. For more on Basinskii's biographies of Tolstoy and of Gorky, see the articles, respectively, by Emerson and Masing-Delic in this volume.

174. See Oleg Osovskii, "'Literaturnost' protiv documental'nosti kak avtorskaia strategia v sovremennoi biografii (Na materiale poslednikh izdanii serii ZhZL)," *Filologiia i kul'tura* 53, no. 3 (2018): 194–98, and "Nou-khau biograficheskogo zhanra," *Voprosy literatury* no. 3 (mai-iun' 2018): 62–83.

175. N. Bogomolov, "Biograficheskoe povestvovanie kak symptom," *Znamia* no. 9 (2009). https://magazines.gorky.media/znamia/2009/9/biograficheskoe-povestvovanie-kak-simptom.html Last accessed 5/18/2021.

176. "Zhizn' zamechetel'nykh tsarei," *VTB—Rossii*, 1 Nov. 2013. https://vtbrussia.ru/education/zhizn-zamechatelnykh-tsarey/ Last accessed 5/18/2021.

177. Bulkina, "The Lives of Remarkable People," 95.

178. O. Osovskii, "Literaturnost'' protiv dokumental'nosti," 194. To date, there is no biography of Lydia Ginzburg in the series, perhaps due to her gender and sexual orientation.

179. "Biblioteka Florentiia Pavlenkova: Vozvrashchenie k istokam," October 2019, https://gvardiya.ru/pub/news/biblioteka-florentiya-pavlenkova-vozvraschenie-k-istokam. Last accessed 5/11/2021.

180. Aleksei Kholikov, "The Writer's Biography: A Genre Without Rules," *Russian Studies in Literature* 46, no. 1 (Winter 2009–2010): 49.

Chapter 1

The *Remarkable* Pushkin

Angela Brintlinger

As Galina Pomerantseva writes "a hundred different authors will write a hundred different Pushkins." That is how the longtime editor of the *Lives of Remarkable People* series characterizes the genre of biography: "Otherwise everything they do would be simply a compilation. But there is only one Pushkin, and thus one of the 100 biographers will come closer to the original than the others. But who? Obviously the one who understands him best. But even if a biographer does not get everything exactly right, he will discover the protagonist for us from some new aspect."[1] To creatively reconstruct a life in writing means to choose a narrative path; otherwise, as Pomerantseva points out, the writer is not a biographer, but merely a compiler. The fact that she uses Alexander Pushkin as an example of this truism about the genre is indicative of the central role the nineteenth-century poet continues to play in Russian biography writ large. "Pushkin is our all," the common saying goes, and given that cliché—which was embraced by the Soviet establishment throughout much of its existence—the popular *ZhZL* series had to include one or more biographies of Alexander Pushkin. Even when subjects like Pushkin and other canonical writers did not embody the values that were being modeled for young Soviet readers, the *ZhZL* series felt pressure—social, educational, cultural, and perhaps even state pressure—to represent these lives.

It is not surprising, then, that over the years Pushkin has been present in, but not central to, the *ZhZL* series. In this chapter I describe ways of approaching Pushkin's biography, taking several detours into questions of genre and of biographies outside the *ZhZL* canon before exploring in more detail the reasons why *ZhZL* efforts to present Pushkin have been fraught with peril. Pushkin, it turns out, is a fairly difficult subject for a biography, and though there have been repeated attempts to include him in *ZhZL*, these have not been particularly interesting or successful.

APPROACHES TO BIOGRAPHY AS A GENRE

The "compilation approach" Pomerantseva mentioned implies bringing together many facts and documents into one big document. And a document, by definition, omits interpretation, which can be a rather tempting solution to the problem of biography. Biographers struggle with their chosen genre, because to organize the life material of any subject—let alone Pushkin—requires emphasizing certain aspects and downplaying others, imposing a narrative on the life, crafting one's own vision of the subject. Particularly with the biographies of writers in a literature-centric culture like Russia's, the desire for completeness, for all-inclusiveness, leads to a lack of selection and to very long tomes—in other words, to uninteresting biographies. As we try to understand how Pushkin has been represented in Russian biography, it is worth keeping in mind that two traditions coexist in Russia: the scholarly encyclopedic approach and the sense that there should be biographies of great men (and women) designed for the "mass reader." The latter cause was taken up by *ZhZL* across its 125-year history, but the former also spawned volumes, and as a result the spectrum of works in print is broad indeed. Before focusing on the *ZhZL* approach it will be instructive to survey some approaches to the genre of biography, using Pushkin biographies as exemplars.

The most widely known "compilation" effort was made in the 1930s by novelist and medical doctor Vikenty Veresaev, who attempted to render Pushkin (and later Gogol) "in life" (*v zhizni*), as he called it—a term that he included in his book titles. His method was pseudo-scientific as he strove for minimal authorial and editorial intervention, creating an all-inclusive document from various historical sources. But his work ended up highlighting the true meaning of a document—words on a page, the veracity of which remains untested, material with no interpretation. Without offering any opinion as to reliability, Veresaev simply copied out the judgments of his subjects' contemporaries. In Pushkin's case, the "systematic compilation of authentic testimony by contemporaries with illustrations" by its sixth edition ran to 488 pages, not including the index. But every edition after the very first placed on display a failure of the concept itself, as Veresaev felt compelled to add asterisks to those documents he found to be less reliable than others. In other words, the compiler felt he had to intervene as editor to shape the Pushkin being presented in his work.[2] Pushkin "in life" needed an intervention.

Veresaev's compilations came to be deemed useful by many scholars, not least émigrés who had no access to Russian archives and libraries after their departure from Soviet Russia. For them, on the one hand, *Pushkin in Life* was a kind of movable archive, a reprinting or repackaging of documents from Russia which the exiled Russians could never actually put their hands on. Nevertheless, the compilations were also almost universally criticized.[3] "Pushkin in this book arises, not 'exactly as if alive,' but just the opposite—exactly as if dead," argued Vladislav Khodasevich. He fumed: "Pushkin without his work is a living corpse." In the preface to the first edition of his *Pushkin in Life*, Veresaev described his biographical concept thus: "for every poet and for Pushkin especially, *Dichtung* differs greatly from *Wahrheit* (fiction from fact) and the poetic work is never the naked diary of the poet."[4] The conflict between the two writers was methodological; Khodasevich believed that Pushkin without an analysis and interpretation of his work was not Pushkin at all, while Veresaev openly and deliberately resisted reading the life of the poet through the work. In focusing on the life, his compilation occupied a position that many believed eviscerated the creative biographical subject.

A compromise position is the *life-and-works* type of biography (in Russian, literally, works and days, *trudy i dni*), which also strives for completeness but which deliberately connects, or at least integrates, the poet's work with the details of his lived biography.[5] Drawing on the fiction, letters, and other writings of the subject, such biographies of necessity make selections in order to present an integrated personality. In some cases, as with Khodasevich's frustrated biographical efforts that he published piecemeal in émigré periodicals, the task was too difficult: to organize, explain, and create a life of Pushkin which would be accessible to the imaginations of the readers and fulfill his own expectations was beyond his abilities.[6] This was not only an émigré problem, and it affected fictionalized biographies as well. Hybridity, perhaps, was too much of a compromise. For example, back in the Soviet Union, Boris Eikhenbaum called Tynianov's drawn-out three-volume *Pushkin* "not so much a novel as a research monograph written in an artistic form."[7] It seems that this comprehensive approach, like Veresaev's hands-off method, is doomed to failure.

Included in the spectrum that I am positing, biographical works—both fiction and nonfiction—frequently are selective, focusing on a particular aspect of Pushkin's life rather than its entire scope. Examples from across the twentieth century include Pavel Shchegolev's *Pushkin's Duel and Death* (1916), P. K. Guber's *Pushkin's Don Juan List* (1923), a book about the women in Pushkin's life, and Ivan Novikov's *Pushkin in Exile* (1982). Faced with a vast amount of material, these biographers chose a specific angle and/or time frame in order to focus on a part of the life, hoping to illuminate through that lens the whole image of the enigmatic and elusive Pushkin.

Many of these biographies, explicitly or implicitly, struggle with Boris Tomashevsky's 1923 notion of the *biographical legend*. As Tomashevsky contended in his famous essay "Literature and Biography" ("Literatura i biografiia," 1923), the *biographical legend* is not coterminous with the lay definition of biography. Instead, he defines a "writer with a biography" as one who highlights facts from his own life to enhance his creations.[8] Tomashevsky argued:

> For a writer with a biography, the facts of the author's life must be taken into consideration. Indeed, in the works themselves the juxtaposition of the texts and the author's biography plays a structural role. The literary work plays on the potential reality of the author's subjective outpourings and confessions. Thus the biography that is useful to the literary historian is not the author's curriculum vitae or the investigator's account of his life. What the literary historian really needs is the biographical legend created by the author himself. Only such a legend is a literary fact. (47)

Biographers struggle with portraying literary figures precisely because of the literature the subjects have produced from their own "life material": if you are too focused on everyday details of life, you run the risk of tarnishing the image the poet himself so carefully created, if he is a writer "with a biography." The author who foregrounds his own biography, in other words, needs a biographer who does not ruin "a created legend," to quote Sologub. Fortunately, he does not always find one who follows his directives.

In an American academic recasting of Tomashevsky's binary, David Bethea translates the idea of "biographical legend" into something perhaps more useful to scholars, namely, the "nonliterary" and "literary" biographies. In his *Realizing Metaphors: Alexander Pushkin and the Life of the Poet* he chooses to look at Pushkin through his poetic relationship with his predecessor Derzhavin, explaining that "the cardinal principle of Pushkin's personality would seem to be... *its resistance to definition from the outside.*"[9] Instead, he tries to look *from within*, from within the poetry. Lev Loseff, in his biography of Joseph Brodsky, did something similar, insisting that he was writing a *literary life*. These approaches avoid the pitfalls of Veresaev's method while also remaining selective enough to keep them from collapsing upon themselves in the way Tynianov and Khodasevich's biographies did in the first half of the twentieth century.

PUSHKIN AND THE GENRE OF BIOGRAPHY

As Pushkin scholar Igor Nemirovsky mused, for some reason, everyday Russians seem to be convinced that there "is no biography of Pushkin," where in fact there are many, dozens even, written by Russian and foreign biographers alike, in every generation, for every new jubilee or anniversary date, from virtually every angle.[10] Pushkin has been the subject of biography, biographical fiction, plays, and films; his *Complete Collected Works* include scholarly commentaries that not only identify for us when each work was written and published, but often explain the life contexts and biographical connections we may need or want to facilitate our understanding of the works. The literature on and about Pushkin and his contemporaries can fill whole libraries. Even devising a clear systematic approach to it is beyond my abilities and certainly beyond the scope of this article. In the British Library alone there are 1,587 titles with the subject "Pushkin." His biography *has* been written—not one hundred different Pushkins, but thousands.

The joint topic of Pushkin and biography is additionally important, though, because here we find ourselves at a telling crossroads of the history of Russian literature and the history of genre in Russian literature, particularly the genre of "life writing." It is one thing to explore biography, but the biography of a writer must include his works, and many have argued Pushkin is not just *a* writer but *the* writer in Russian cultural myth, which complicates any effort to write his biography.

For this reason, it is useful to consider Pushkin's own thoughts on the genre of biography, of life writing, of which we can find several well-known examples. For example, in *Journey to Arzrum* (1830), Pushkin famously contended that someone should write the biography of Alexander Griboedov—who had just been martyred in Tehran—but, as he claimed, "we are lazy and incurious" (*My lenivy i neliubopytny*): "What a pity that Griboedov did not leave memoirs! To write his biography would be the duty of his friends; but in our country remarkable people disappear without leaving a trace. We are lazy and incurious."[11] This statement reads like a clear challenge, and that challenge has certainly been taken up by biographers of Griboedov. The reference to "remarkable people" in Pushkin's statement above may in fact have been in the back of the mind of ZhZL progenitor Pavlenkov when he founded his series and gave it its name.[12]

Pushkin was of course not only appealing to Griboedov biographers to meet this challenge but also making a general statement about Russian responses to their contemporaries. This suggests that he considered the idea of *memorializing* the lives of poets in biography and memoir to be a serious and significant one. We find evidence of this in Pushkin's own correspondence. When his lycée friend Anton Delvig died, Pushkin wrote in a letter to Pletnyov that with Baratynsky the three of them—friends who knew him, who had witnessed the "development [. . .and maturation. . .] of his poetic soul and talent,"—should unite the life-and-works into a portrait of their deceased comrade, whose life, Pushkin argued, had been rich "not in the kind of adventures one finds in a novel but in fine sensations, in a bright, clear intelligence, and in hope."[13]

This genre distinction, between a novel "rich in adventure" and a life in which "the poet's soul develops," suggests that Pushkin conceived of an entirely new kind of "life," one he unfortunately did not take up, leaving

Delvig unmemorialized. Instead, Pushkin's own biographical projects were almost always in the genre of *biographie romancée*. Pushkin explored and fictionalized the idea of the individual in history in such works as his *Moor of Peter the Great* (*Arap Petra Velikogo*, 1828), based on the life of his great-grandfather, and his novel *Captain's Daughter* (*Kapitanskaia dochka*, 1836) billed as "family notes" in the subtitle ("semeinye zapiski"), but resembling nothing so much as novelized memoirs.

The *Captain's Daughter* answers well to the definition of the "life rich in novelistic adventures." Grinev's "family notes"—allegedly written by an eighteenth-century gentleman for posterity—have an uncanny resemblance to a prominent autobiography of eighteenth-century life, namely that of Gavriil Derzhavin, and they present one mode according to which lives can be written.[14] Taking the eighteenth-century concept of *Fortuna*, or Fate, Grinev lays out the pathways that led him to adventure and ultimately family happiness.[15] The *Captain's Daughter* is historical fiction, and that is how we read it.[16] But with a preternaturally versatile author like Pushkin, almost everything we read feels like a commentary on everything else: on romantic personality, on exotic adventures, on genre as such, and on the life of the poet, and thus The *Captain's Daughter*, arguably, was not just a historical novel, but also a commentary on the genre of biography, stylized à la the eighteenth century.

PUSHKIN: THE LIFE

Pushkin's actual life includes more exotic moments and fantastic adventures than any Byronic verse poem or eighteenth-century novel: great-grandson of an *arap*, the so-called "moor" of Peter the Great; member of the first class of the famed *Lycée* at Tsarskoe Selo which was founded to educate the tsar's children but which, in its early years at least, harbored an anti-monarchical liberal spirit that nurtured the poetic and rebellious souls of its young students; a skittish adolescent "crowned" while still at school by the aging Derzhavin as his poetic successor; a poet who published early and was welcomed into the literary brotherhood of *Arzamas* (a group of poets wishing to modernize Russian verse) at a tender age; a carouser and womanizer exiled to the South for his freedom-loving poetry; an atheist and blasphemer who was exiled still further, into the Russian countryside, to live in solitude at a small family estate, spied on by his father and kept company by his old Russian nanny; a friend of Decembrist leaders who missed their revolt in part due to superstition (he famously returned home when a hare ran across the road, which he interpreted as a warning); a chronicler of his times, and innovator in numerous poetic forms and literary genres, who investigated ideas of talent, inspiration, and genius; an aspiring historian who consented to have the tsar as his "first reader" and then chafed under the watchful eye of the third section; a pioneering journalist and professional *literator* whose financial woes spurred on his ambition; a *kammerjunker* who viewed his court uniform as a deliberately imposed humiliation; the jealous husband of a beautiful young wife; a duelist who wrote editorial correspondence on the eve of his fatal duel and seemingly had no thoughts of death as he rode off to face his opponent, cornet Georges D'Anthès.

In Russian literary tradition, Alexander Pushkin is the writer who introduced from abroad numerous genres of both prose and poetry while providing them a uniquely Russian character, and he put his mark on the genre of literary criticism as well. The inventor of the Onegin stanza (based on the sonnet form) and the Russian novel in verse (his *roman v stikhakh*), a consummate poet as well as prose writer who wrote narrative poems, fairy tales, lyric poetry, innovative fiction, history plays, novels, letters, and travelogues, Pushkin not only *wrote* in every genre, but also, within those genres, interspersed his own literary commentary. When the Countess, in his novella "Queen of Spades," asks her nephew Tomsky, "*are* there any Russian novels?," readers of Pushkin's time and readers today recognize this as a tongue-in-cheek comment on the state of prose in Russia at the time when the story takes place—the countess's surprise represents in part the author's frustration that Russian novels were underappreciated and the genre was underdeveloped. When Pushkin's poet declares "I have erected a monument to myself, not made by human hand," readers of Pushkin's time, and we today, know that we are reading one iteration of that "monument." Pushkin was prolific, famously so during the two exceptionally productive Boldino autumns, and importantly he built literary and generic criticism into his poetry and prose. With a life, and a life in literature, like that, it is not surprising that Pushkin should become the subject of numerous biographies.

PUSHKIN IN *ZhZL*

The *Lives of Remarkable People* series—a series that has continued in various iterations now for well over a century—treated Pushkin numerous times and in numerous ways.[17] I embarked upon this chapter thinking that in this series Pushkin would stand before us *at least* threefold, and I hoped to explore a threefold Pushkin (prerevolutionary, émigré, and Soviet).[18] My hopes were fulfilled only partially.

Although there are numerous Pushkin titles in the series, there might have been more; not all planned *ZhZL* biographies actually came to fruition. In the space remaining I review several of those *ZhZL* biographies, but I also strive to explain why *ZhZL* was not the ideal venue for biographies of Alexander

Pushkin, and why in the end better biographies exist outside this biographical series. Of course, given the prominence of Pushkin and the Russian love of biography, there are many other biographies of the poet. For example, a four-volume *Life of Pushkin* by Marianna Basina, originally published by the Leningrad house Children's Literature (Detskaia literatura) in 1969, is so beloved by Soviet and post-Soviet children that it was republished by St. Petersburg publisher Pushkin Fund (Pushkinskii Fond) in 1996 with a foreword by famed academician Dmitry Likhachev—despite nearly a million copies already being in circulation. Likhachev wrote:

> I know from my grandchildren and the grandchildren of friends how much these books interest schoolchildren. Entertaining, beautifully illustrated, they have great aesthetic and moral significance in the edification of today's youth.[19]

The genre designation of Basina's book, "documentary fictional tales," is also fascinating. For this reason alone the books were better suited to the Children's Literature publishing list than to *ZhZL*.

However, across its 125-year history the *ZhZL* series in its several permutations did publish and republish biographies of Alexander Pushkin. Biographies include those written by A. M. Skabichevsky (1891, 1897, 1899, 1909, and 1924), P. E. Shchegolev (1916, *ZhZL* publication 1936), Leonid Grossman (1939, 1958), and émigrée Ariadna Tyrkova-Williams (1928/1948, *ZhZL* publication 1998). *ZhZL* even mobilized Pushkin to help build patriotic fervor; in the series *Great Russian People* (*Velikie russkie liudi*, published during World War II), A. Miasnikov wrote a Pushkin biography that runs to about fifty pages, presenting the poet as a patriot who would have supported Soviet defense efforts.[20] Along with regular *ZhZL* biographies, the publishing house Molodaya gvardiya also issued *Prometei* (*Prometheus*), an occasional series of "historico-biographical almanacs." Volume 10, edited by Pushkin scholar Tatiana G. Tsiavlovskaia and published in 1974 for the 175th anniversary of the poet's birth, was devoted entirely to articles, essays, and new materials about Pushkin and "fills out" the *ZhZL* portrait of Pushkin as patriot. And finally, a new biography in the "small series" (*Malaia seriia*) of *ZhZL* was published in 2014, bringing Pushkin into post-Soviet space. Vladimir Novikov—who had written *ZhZL* biographies of Vladimir Vysotsky and Alexander Blok—turned his attention to Pushkin as well, bringing Pushkin's biography, in his own words, "up-to-date."[21] Pushkin fourfold? Or perhaps simply a multidimensional Pushkin.

Nobel Prize–winning Turkish novelist Orhan Pamuk, writing about the poet C. P. Cavafy, examined why we are so intrigued by the life of a great poet:

> We love poets for the things their poems lead us to imagine; but equally, we love them for how we imagine their lives to be. Confusing poets' lives with their work is an illusion as old as the tradition of confusing words with objects. But in fact it is for the sake of this illusion that we feel such a strong need for poetry, for novels, for literature.
>
> There are some poets whose work we read with their lives in mind, and what we know of those lives ensures that their poetry leaves a more enduring impression.[22]

Recasting Tomashevsky's contrast here, Pamuk presents an issue that is directly relevant for the Russian, Soviet and post-Soviet *ZhZL* series. Indeed, in some ways this is the main question for every different iteration of the "life of the poet": do we as readers imagine the life of the poet *because* of his or her works, or do we care about the "life of a remarkable person" beyond the specifics of his or her oeuvre? Is the subject of a *ZhZL* biography "remarkable" for being famous? creative? imaginative? for producing works of genius in a particular linguistic, cultural, and political context?

There are at least two different audiences for a biography: the amateur audience, readers who are curious about a "remarkable" person and long to lose themselves in another life, another time, to learn some interesting facts and some piquant details, and then to move on to the next biography, or history, or novel. The professional, or scholarly, audience differs greatly from this first. Likely to check sources, have opinions about footnotes, and even know the manuscripts and primary documents firsthand, the professional audience requires a scholarly biography—and may not even mind the occasional dense or unreadable passage. Scholars seek in biography entirely different experiences than those sought by the average Russian reader of the *ZhZL* series, and the series was born of this difference. When Pushkin bemoaned the fact that "in our country remarkable people disappear without leaving a trace" (see above), he was in a sense calling for Russian biography to emerge in the future, and Pavlenkov answered that call. The very opposite of "disappearing without a trace" is a series of publications aimed at a broad and general audience.

To clarify who that audience might be within the Russian context, let us turn to an early *ZhZL* Pushkin biography. A twenty-first-century e-book version of Alexander Skabichevsky's *Pushkin: His Life and Literary Activity* (*Pushkin. Ego zhizn' i literaturnaia deiatel'nost'*) includes an "annotation" that defines both the genre and audience:

> Written in the new-at-the-time genre of poetic chronicle and historical-cultural study, these texts remain valuable today. Written "for simple people," for the Russian provinces, today they might be recommended not only for bibliophiles,

but for the broadest possible public: those who are newcomers to the history and psychology of great people, as well as those whose profession includes these subjects.[23]

But can those audiences be one and the same? Do the same biographies appeal to the professional and the "simple people," or to be more generous, the "broadest possible public?" I remain doubtful.

The Pavlenkov series was not founded for that professional audience, and neither the early volumes on Pushkin (such as Skabichevsky's) nor the most recent publications find favor with a scholarly audience. In terms of presenting Pushkin, as far as I can determine only the *Prometheus* (*Prometei*) volume aimed to unite the two audiences:

> The Pushkin issue of *Prometheus* is a kind of experiment: the edition is intended for a broad readership and its print run is extremely large in comparison to the usual specialized literature, but at the same time . . . it is a new, serious scholarly edition. There is no doubt it will be cited by scholars, and, we hope, also be read by hundreds of thousands of "non-specialists." [24]

So wrote the editor, who concluded by expressing the hope that the volume would be a "new gift for everyone to whom, to use Alexander Blok's felicitous image, 'the cheerful name of Pushkin' is dear."

PREREVOLUTIONARY PUSHKIN

Pavlenkov's series—unlike the later Soviet series—kept its volumes small and cheap. As a *ZhZL* author, Skabichevsky became a resource for Pavlenkov, and his biographical efforts were eminently excerptable. For example, in *Compositions of A. S. Pushkin: the Complete Collection in One Volume* (*Sochineniia A. S. Pushkina: Polnoe sobranie v odnom tome*), which A. Skabichevsky edited, he contributed a biographical essay in which he spoke directly to his intended audience.[25] In his introduction to that volume, Skabichevsky noted that general readers could not enjoy Russian classical works as conventionally published because although the chronological arrangement of literary works is valuable for those who want to study the author in a systematic way with scholarly goals, for the majority, "who have a rather vague understanding of what year this or the other work of a favorite author was penned," this can be "extremely inconvenient" (n.p.).

Trying to avoid too many details in his excerpted biography, Skabichevsky managed to tell Pushkin's life in just sixty columns, starting with his ancestors and ending with the 1880 unveiling of his statue (by Opekushin) that became the occasion for Dostoevsky's famous "Pushkin speech" and many other manifestations of veneration for the "national poet" par excellence. He wrote: "this popular literary celebration, which brought the whole Russian intelligentsia to the poet's feet, will doubtless comprise one of the best pages of Russia's history" (lx).[26] Such early essays into Pushkin's biography remained short, introductory descriptions of the life of the poet and were supposed to familiarize the reader with the poet and set the scene for his collected works to follow in the same volume. In content, these introductions were built on tropes made famous by Alexander Odoevsky's and Fyodor Dostoevsky's brief descriptions of Pushkin's life. In the obituary published in 1837 Odoevsky stressed that "Pushkin is our all, in him are united East and West, he is the best of Russians, and he fell at the hands of a foreign enemy," while Dostoevsky emphasized Pushkin's charge to inspire the creation of the "universal man" who would reconcile all nations under Russian spiritual leadership. For popular and popularizing biographies, within and outside the *ZhZL* series, these clichés fit the bill.

This does not mean that other authors exploring Pushkin's life did not have aspirations to conveying that life more fully, each in his or her own way, and *ZhZL* took advantage of these aspirations. For example, Shchegolev's 1916 *Pushkin's Duel and Death* was the first monograph to be published about Pushkin's fatal final duel; though not written for *ZhZL* originally, a version of that book was absorbed into the *ZhZL* series in 1936. Before that the book underwent several reprintings, and each time Shchegolev took into account new information that was coming to light.[27] In the introduction to the first edition, Shchegolev described his own searches for archival materials, documents, and sources about the last months of Pushkin's life and identified those documents he had failed to obtain, but which he deemed essential for creating a complete picture of this portion of Pushkin's life.[28] Pointing out (and thus attempting to diminish) the "weak" aspects of one's own work is a time-honored tradition, and in this Shchegolev followed his subject, who had incorporated critics' potential reactions into his narrator's musings in *Evgenii Onegin*, effectively offsetting that criticism in advance.

Shchegolev's book consists of two parts: the first is about 120 pages of "biography," where the author strives to lay out the order of events leading to Pushkin's death, and the second part of over three hundred pages consists of a description and publication of the documents related to the biography: interpretation and source material between the covers of one volume.[29] The biographical novelist Anna Kalma—who later published several books with the publishing house Molodaya gvardiya—identified Shchegolev's *Duel and Death of Pushkin* as exemplary, because while built on documents, it "read like a novel." Like many *ZhZL* authors (and readers) who favored the *biographie romancée* style of biography, Kalma nonetheless believed that the dynamics or tension of Shchegolev's book came from its scholarly nature (Pomerantseva 164).[30]

In contrast, Leonid Grossman (1888–1965), also a Pushkin scholar and biographer, found that the more biographers believed in their own genre as a real, legitimate genre, the less they would tend toward "novelized" biographies. In Grossman's opinion, for example, works like Tynianov's *Death of the Vazir-Mukhtar*—a novelized biography about Griboedov—had no business in the *ZhZL* series.[31] This complexity as to value runs through all discussions of Pushkin biographies; fictionalized biographies, like Basina's "documentary fictional tales," were more readable, but published primarily with houses such as Children's Literature, while biographers like Shchegolev, or even Veresaev, felt they needed to include real documents to show their scholarly chops and in order to elevate themselves above the *biographies romancées*.

THE SOVIET PUSHKIN

The new version of the *ZhZL* series, revived in 1933 by Maxim Gorky, was supposed to bridge the gap between readers and world history. Gorky's original idea, based on Pavlenkov's prerevolutionary series, arose in response to the horrors of World War I; his letters to H. G. Wells and Romain Rolland, written in January 1917, emphasize the need to inspire new generations to feats of greatness through examples from the past. As he wrote:

> We adults, who are fated to abandon this world in due time—we will leave our children a pathetic inheritance, bequeathing them a very sad life. This absurd war is a stunning proof of our moral weakness, of the decline of culture. Let's remind our children that people were not always as weak and wicked as— alas!—we are now; let's remind them that all nations had—and still have—great people and noble hearts! It is essential that we do this precisely in our days of victorious cruelty and brutality.[32]

This series, like its predecessor, was written in language comprehensible to school-age children as well as to a nonspecialist general public.[33] And as the 1930s progressed, it became clear that the series of biographies was the perfect institutional home for the Soviet enterprise of monumental hero-worship. Indeed, even after World War II the series continued to consider "the life as feat" (*zhizn'—podvig*) to be its subject (Pomerantseva 96). In Pomerantseva's telling, the vagaries of Soviet history caused a number of shifts in *ZhZL* editorial policy, and every time the editors would return for inspiration to Gorky, founder and font of belief in the concept of "life as feat" (105).

Though the first Soviet *ZhZL* edition of Pushkin was a reprint of a pre-Soviet book, Shchegolev's *Duel and Death*, Gorky and his staff were actively recruiting other authors to write about the nineteenth-century poet. Unfortunately, the biography commissioned in the series from Pushkin scholar Boris Tomashevsky was not completed in time for the centennial.[34] But not long after the Shchegolev reprint, *ZhZL* published a new, full biography of Pushkin written by the outstanding scholar Leonid Grossman (first edition 1939). In his work, Grossman made clear that he had attempted to consider the findings of "all of his predecessors" while still striking out on his own biographical "path," "constructing a description of Pushkin's life as a biographical chronicle using political annals and the literary history of his time."[35] As Grossman had noted about the genre in 1933, "the biographical novel of the new type required that the author, like an architect, be both artist and scholar."[36] Here we see Grossman confronting the complexity we mentioned above: the new era required both readability and authenticity.

The use of the words chronicle (*khronika*) and annals (*letopis'*) suggests that Grossman took his task as a historian seriously, but we know that he considered himself to be a *literary* historian. Indeed, in his ten-page epilogue in honor of the centennial of Pushkin's death, dated appropriately 1837–1937, Grossman took the opportunity to connect the threads from Pushkin and his life and works to the subsequent history of classical Russian literature. He argued that not only should we note the reactions of contemporary poets and writers to Pushkin's death, but we should also examine Pushkin's influence on their works, as well as on the works of later writers. Turgenev, for example, according to Grossman, constructed his protagonists while drawing on the "deep psychological veracity of Pushkin's novelistic heroes" (631); Tolstoy's *Cossacks* emerged from Pushkin's "The Gypsies," while his *War and Peace* was inspired by *The Captain's Daughter* and *Anna Karenina* by *Egyptian Nights*. Dostoevsky, too, built on "The Stationmaster," "Mozart and Salieri," "The Miserly Knight" and "The Poor Knight" (631–32).

Further, according to Grossman, Ivan Goncharov—who remembered Pushkin's visit to his lecture room when he was a student at Moscow University—was indebted to Pushkin for the clarity and precision of the way he drew nature, everyday life (*byt*), and the traits of his characters (632–33). In other words, for Grossman Pushkin was quite literally Russian literature's "all" as he had influenced virtually every worthy subsequent writer including Grossman's contemporaries Gorky, Mayakovsky and Bagritsky (636–37). In understanding Pushkin's life through the *ZhZL* volume, readers were to walk away with the resonance of Pushkin's work for the history of Russian literature and for Soviet literature as well. Written in the wake of the centennial anniversary of Pushkin's death, this volume emerged from Pushkin's legacy.

Like many in his day, Grossman felt the weight of that legacy and a desire to save Pushkin for Soviet culture and conveyed to his readers the paramount need to experience the poet's life.

By the second, 1958, edition of his book, Grossman had decided to expand the sections of his biography devoted to Pushkin's creative work. After all, Grossman argued, Pushkin's literary activity was the "living foundation of his literary legacy" (5). Now Grossman had rethought the very purpose of a biography of the poet: "the task of the scholar, biographer, teacher is to reveal the source of warmth and light in Pushkin's great creations" (5). Here, too, Grossman redefined his own role as a biographer: "our book," he wrote, "is an attempt to take part to the fullest extent of our ability in a collective effort—thoroughly revealing the sources of great creativity" (6). And to underscore the reasoning behind his book, Grossman drew on the master:

> Pushkin himself acknowledged the main material for the biography of a poet to be his thoughts and words: that is precisely how he wanted to construct the life of his dear friend Delvig—on the basis of the "exposition of his thoughts," the "analysis of his poetry." We have tried to follow the poet's own instruction to his future biographers in our work. (6)

A third edition of Grossman's book was published in 1960.

PUSHKIN AT WAR

Between the first two editions of Grossman's "full" biography, Pushkin was pressed into service in another brief format by A. S. Miasnikov. As mentioned above, when World War II broke out, Soviet leader Joseph Stalin employed Russian culture as a part of the mobilization campaign. During the war Molodaya gvardiya published pamphlet-like biographies reminiscent of Pavlenkov's original series in a set entitled *Great Russian People*, and the first of these was devoted to Pushkin.

Miasnikov's parents had perhaps deliberately chosen the name Alexander to match his patronymic, Sergeevich, and in honor of the great Russian poet. In his version, Pushkin's life emerged in its usual periodization (Childhood, Lycée, Petersburg, Southern Exile, etc.), and along the way Miasnikov took every opportunity to highlight the political and patriotic aspects of Pushkin's biography. He noted the poet's place among the "progressive youth of his day" and the "atmosphere of patriotism and love of freedom" in which he matured (17); the "crucible of political passions" that was Petersburg (21); and how he cherished his native land and its natural features. Narrating Pushkin's exile in the south, for example, Miasnikov expostulated, "Crimea's nature captivated

Pushkin" (25). This love of country and of countryside had made Pushkin the favorite poet of generations of Russians; Miasnikov informed his reader that Vladimir Lenin himself had treasured his volume of Pushkin poems when N. K. Krupskaya had brought it to him in Siberia, ultimately giving it pride of place at his bedside "along with his volume of Hegel" (58). In conclusion, Miasnikov quoted Stalin in reminding his readers in 1943 just what they were defending during the Great Fatherland War: "the great Russian nation, the nation of Plekhanov and Lenin, Belinsky and Chernyshevsky, Pushkin and Tolstoy, Gorky and Chekhov, Sechenov and Pavlov, Repin and Surikov, Suvorov and Kutuzov" (57). The Soviet Pushkin at war ranked alongside scientists, artists, politicians, political theorists, and generals.

Given Pushkin's place in Russian literary culture, it may seem surprising that for years after the 1960 republication of Grossman's biography there was no other biography in the series until the post-Soviet era. This may be explained by the fact that there had been an explosion of Pushkin studies starting with the preparation in 1933 (under Gorky's editorship) of the definitive edition of Pushkin's collected works (published from 1937–1959) and the *Dictionary of Pushkin's Language* (*Slovar' iazyka Pushkina*).[37] *ZhZL*'s sole contribution to that enterprise was published in an issue of its sporadic almanac, *Prometheus* (*Prometei*, 1966–1990) with "materials" for biographies, including one devoted to Pushkin in 1974.[38]

THE ÉMIGRÉ PUSHKIN BECOMES THE POST-SOVIET PUSHKIN

The first post-Soviet Pushkin biography in the *ZhZL* series, *The Life of Pushkin* (*Zhizn' Pushkina*), was published in Russia in 1998.[39] But it was not a new publication. This biography was penned by the émigré journalist, politician, and political activist Ariadna Tyrkova-Williams (1869–1962), a good belletristic writer, a Russian patriot and a lover of Pushkin, who devoted over twenty years of her life to its writing. In that sense it represents the ideal biography of Pushkin for *ZhZL*: engaged and passionate, but clearly written, without too many scholarly details; equally interested in life events and in bringing the oeuvre into the biography. Tyrkova-Williams, a former schoolmate of Nadezhda Krupskaya, knew the Bolsheviks as they were finding their ideological feet. A member of an old landowning family from the region around Novgorod, she was a Kadet representative in the post-1906 Duma (like Vladimir Nabokov's father). However, by the time she wrote this biography from 1923 to 1939, Tyrkova-Williams was living in London, and she saw it published in its entirety in Paris only after World War II, in 1948.[40] Unlike the writers of the politicized and patriotic *Great Russian People* version of Pushkin, Tyrkova-Williams had enough distance from Russian imperial politics, Russian politics post-1905, and Soviet politics, to write a fairly dispassionate version of the life of the beloved poet.

Tyrkova-Williams receives praise from the *ZhZL* editors as a person who had good knowledge of the materials, wrote in a beautiful Russian—which they parenthetically claim has been lost to contemporary Russian authors—but more importantly felt "an enormous love for her hero, a love the author transfers to us, her readers" (I: 472). Such an assessment about authors of Pushkin biographies is not unusual; in writing about Marianna Basina, Dmitry Likhachev calls Pushkin "the primary . . . meaning of the author's intellectual life" (I: 5). Tyrkova-Williams herself felt pride that her work did not fall into the trap of the Soviet cult of Pushkin, but rather—as scholar Alexandra Smith puts it—emphasized instead the "semiotics of behavior," details of everyday life, and "paradoxical nature of Pushkin's talent," all of which distinguished her book from the Russian and Soviet materials she used to create it.[41]

Looking at Tyrkova-Williams's *Life of Pushkin* in its *ZhZL* publication, we can say that she marches through the life as one might expect—no particularly innovative techniques of timeline or plot manipulations—but in narrating it gives a few new interpretations. For example, in a chapter entitled "The First Decembrist," Tyrkova-Williams focuses on Alexander I and his speeches about the possibilities of a constitution, but then pivots to describe Pushkin's infatuation with Chaadaev, for him an *arbiter elegantiarum*, and the poetry Pushkin dedicated to him. Relating political events and speeches, the relationships of tsar, intellectuals, and Pushkin's entourage, Tyrkova-Williams never circles back to the assertion she has made in the chapter title, but it makes its point all the same: Chaadaev, Pushkin's youthful crush, had revolutionary tendencies. Tying Chaadaev to Pushkin at this juncture and in this way is enough for her to launch the next chapter, devoted to the youthful "Ode to Liberty."[42] When she ends this first volume with a description of Eliza Vorontsova's lifelong dedication to the poet, the reader feels the author's own admiration, both for the enduring love and the fidelity that outlasted the "Talisman" Pushkin received from his friend (I: 462–68). In these last two examples we see explicitly how Tyrkova-Williams follows the life-in-art model of biography: while narrating Pushkin's experiences, she headlines them with titles from his famous poems and other works.

Over fifteen years passed between the writing of the first and second volumes of Tyrkova-Williams's *Life of Pushkin*—years that were significant for Pushkin studies and for the Soviet Union. In the preface to her second volume, Tyrkova-Williams explains that she wrote both parts in London and published them both in Paris, but she highlights what she calls the "sharp change in attitude toward Pushkin" that happened in the Soviet Union between 1923 and 1939. Almost in shock, she proclaims: "He was officially recognized as a national genius" (II: 5). A glance at the additional bibliographic materials she used in volume two makes it clear that her sources continued to be broadly gathered. Though it includes new post-1923 publications of Soviet origin, such as the *Vremennik Pushkinskoi Komissii* from 1936 and works by Boris Modzalevsky from 1924 and 1928 as well as the volumes of "Pushkin's Manuscripts" his son compiled with Boris Tomashevsky in 1937, the list also features new émigré publications, such as Metropolitan Anastasy's *Pushkin's Relationship to Religion and the Orthodox Church* in Belgrad, 1937, and Modest Gofman's book about Pushkin as a Don Juan (*Pushkin—Don-Zhuan*, Paris 1935), as well as many nineteenth-century Russian publications. We might sum up by saying that Tyrkova-Williams appreciated the new Soviet perspective on Pushkin, but she did not let it overwhelm her view of the poet.

As Nemirovsky noted, there were plenty of great scholars in the late eighties and early nineties who were already writing biographies of Pushkin and could have been commissioned to create a fresh look for *ZhZL*.[43] To name just two, Vadim Vatsuro was alive and working at the Institute of Russian Literature; a consummate specialist in Pushkin and his era, Vatsuro was also a wonderful writer and if asked could have produced a clear and vivid version of Pushkin for *ZhZL*. Yuri Lotman's biography of Pushkin—written for teachers and first published in 1981—is also very readable and would have made an excellent addition to the *ZhZL* library. In point of fact, the first two editions of Lotman's biography had a press run of one million copies, so anyone who wanted to read this scholarly but accessible biography could. Still, *ZhZL* chose to publish Tyrkova-Williams who was, in Caryl Emerson's words, "an amateur."[44] The introduction to Tyrkova-Williams's Pushkin biography as republished by *ZhZL* highlights the reverence she had for her subject and for all that was "Pushkinian" with a capital P. This attitude—lost entirely during the Soviet period, when nothing "capitalized" was permitted, and thus no sense of "religiosity, respect, romanticism"—was one the editors hoped to revive in their post-Soviet audience (I:6).[45] This *ZhZL* edition brought the émigré writer home, and the reprinting marked "the welcome return of a prominent anti-Bolshevik to post-communist Russian culture."[46]

By the 1990s, *ZhZL* was continuing to put out long biographies of remarkable people, often in two volumes. They were specializing in the "fat" biography. But their audience was only partially made up of people who wanted to "improve their lives" by experiencing the lives of others. A significant portion of *ZhZL* buyers were collectors, whose primary interest was in having a complete set to have on their bookshelves. This was true in the Soviet period, and it remained true even in the immediate post-Soviet period, when financial considerations became more of an issue for most Russians. And by republishing Tyrkova-Williams, *ZhZL* scored yet another hefty two-volume addition, using its iconic design for this sturdy hardback publication. Collectors are happy: yet another Pushkin for their shelves.

THE POST-POST-SOVIET PUSHKIN

Vladimir Novikov, a veteran *ZhZL* author, knows that not everyone reads books anymore—not even in Russia. But that does not stop him from reading and writing them, and he is both a fan and an author of *ZhZL*. In an extensive 2014 interview, he included Tyrkova-Williams's biography in a list of books about Pushkin that he deemed of excellent quality, along with: P. N. Miliukov's volume *The Living Pushkin*, published in Paris in 1937;[47] Lotman's Pushkin biography; Tynyanov's unfinished novel; and Irina Surat and Sergei Bocharov's scholarly biography of the poet.[48] Indeed, when Novikov thought about the vast bibliography of works about the poet, he realized that one type was still missing: "a simple and clear little biographical book which would serve as basic nutrition for an underprepared reader, one who was not particularly well-read."[49] Novikov's *Pushkin*—which he claims is "not a biography"—aims to give that kind of reader a story, a way to get to know the poet through the interesting life he lived.[50] "By genre," he writes, "it's a novella."[51]

With so many good books on Pushkin, it was still worthwhile for *ZhZL* to publish yet another by their veteran author: Novikov wrote about Pushkin after completing two *ZhZL* biographies, on Vladimir Vysotsky and Alexander Blok. Three poets, three different time periods, all united, as he argues, by a "muse of poetic democracy." From a methodological perspective Novikov also found the project interesting. Because he wrote it for the "small series" of *ZhZL*, Novikov had to work within a "compact format": "Shorter, even shorter. Can I describe this episode in one sentence? No? How about two? No retardation, no retrospection—forward!" Finally, he drew his slogan from something he overheard Viktor Shklovsky say in 1982: "We are writing for people, not for the scholar at the next desk."[52]

And so, the most recent Pushkin biography for *ZhZL* unites the reasons literary biography has been so popular for so many years, in Russia and elsewhere. Despite Tomashevsky and his theory, people tend to believe that poets lead interesting lives, and the nexus of their lives and creative impulses will always draw readers (even in the internet age). For writers, getting inside another writer is a fascinating project, but more importantly, a challenge: how best to tell the story, how to craft the life journey into a narrative? Finally, keeping in mind both the subject and the reader allows a writer to bridge the past and the present. With *ZhZL*, an author knows that an audience is out there; these books continue to sell on brand reputation alone. At 253 pages, this "short" biography is advertised as a "compass" for the contemporary reader: not "concepts and hypotheses, but the most necessary information."[53] The two-volume "fat" biography has its place, but so does the shorter "novella."

POST SCRIPTUM

For those who no longer read anything . . . The headline shouts from the screen: "Our all, and the sun of Russian poetry. The slave of honor who died for love. Alexander Pushkin—in the program *ZhZL*." In addition to the print empire, *ZhZL* has come to the small screen with a televised talk-show variant. Pushkin's biography was broadcast on 12 November 2013 on the television channel *Vremia* (1). In a way, the summary says it all:

> Nightmare of unhappy schoolchildren and joy of Pushkinists. Descendent of Peter the Great's moor, raised by his nanny. Genius hermit of Boldino who celebrated autumn. Great cuckold and tireless Don Juan who drew feet in the margins [of his manuscripts]. Little freak, drugged with equine stimulant in order to get him married. Unrestrained drunkard, rebel and gambler who ran off with a band of gypsies. First and last professional Russian writer. Spiritual apex of his era, revolutionary and mason. Founder of Russian rap. Fearless duelist who never shot a single person. Underground politician, encoding all world history in his poetry. Good-for-nothing *kammerjunker* whom the tsar hated and feared.[54]

These are the facts, legends, and stereotypes associated with Alexander Pushkin in Russian culture. The talk show, hosted by Pavel Sanaev, vividly demonstrates the bifurcated nature of biography in Russia, its scholarly and popular sides: the Pushkin experts (Natalia Mikhailova, Associate Director of the Pushkin Museum and writer Alexander Epuferev) speak carefully and at length, with historical facts and quotes from documents to support their arguments, while host Sanaev—a slave to his genre and to the "live studio" format, with calls from viewers requiring his attention and a clock ticking—at one point suggests that his guests cannot answer the questions as posed and that viewers should seek the answers on the internet. "Why the internet?" asks Epuferev. "The answers are all in this book," he says, indicating the *ZhZL* volume by Ariadna Tyrkova-Williams. The last words of the initial "scholarly" portion of the show ring: "Not a bad little book, by the way" ("Kstati neplokhaia knizhka"). But at that point, Sanaev turns to his partner, who has summoned Pushkin himself in a séance to answer questions in what will surely be a more authoritative fashion.

NOTES

1. Pomerantseva, 252.
2. See Angela Brintlinger, *Writing a Usable Past: Russian Literary Culture, 1917–1937* (Evanston, IL: Northwestern University Press, 2000, 2008), 12–14.
3. An exception here is Vladimir Nabokov, who in writing his *Nikolai Gogol* (Norfolk, CT: New Directions, 1944) in the United States, referred to Veresaev's 1933 publication about Gogol as an invaluable and "delightful biography" from which much of his own material was drawn. See his *Nikolai Gogol,* 155.
4. V. Veresaev, *Pushkin v zhizni: sistematicheskii svod podlinnykh svidetel'stv sovremennikov s illiustratsiiami na otdel'nikh listakh.* Izd. shestoe, znachitel'no dopolnennoe (Moscow: Sovetskii pisatel', 1936), 9.
5. This is a Russian translation of Hesiod's Latin title, which privileges works over days.
6. For more on types of biography, and on biographies of Pushkin in particular, see Brintlinger, esp. ch. 1.
7. B. M. Eikhenbaum, "Tvorchestvo Iu. Tynianova," 222 in V. A. Kaverin, *Vospominaniia o Iu. Tynianove: Portrety i vstrechi* (Moscow: Sovetskii pisatel', 1983), 210–223.
8. B. Tomashevsky, "Literature and biography," trans. Herbert Eagle, *Readings in Russian Poetics: Formalist and Structuralist Views,* ed. Ladislav Matejka and Krystyna Pomorska (Ann Arbor, MI: Michigan Slavic Publications, 1978), 47–55.
9. David Bethea, *Realizing Metaphors: Alexander Pushkin and the Life of the Poet* (Madison: University of Wisconsin Press, 1998), 153; 137–38.
10. Igor Nemirovsky, Personal communication, March 2, 2014.
11. Aleksandr Pushkin, *PSS* 6: 452. On Pushkin and concepts of biography, see Pomerantseva, 239–43.
12. In a fairly recent scholarly biography of Griboedov, Sergei Fomichev opens his preface by acknowledging this very challenge. See Fomichev, *Aleksandr Griboedov: Biografiia* (St. Petersburg: Vita Nova, 2012), 7. On Pavlenkov and the history of *ZhZL,* see the introduction to this book.
13. "Napishem zhe vtroem zhizn' nashego druga, zhizn' bogatuiu ne romanicheskim prikliucheniiam no prekrasnymi chuvstvami, svetlym chistym razumom i nadezhdam—otvechai mne na eto (. . .)" A. S. Pushkin, Pis'mo Pletnevu P. A., 31 ianv. 1831 g. Moskva**,** in A. S. Pushkin, *Pis'ma,* t. 3. 1831–1833. Pod red. i s primech. L. B. Modzalevskogo. (M.-L.: Academia. 1935), 10–11.
14. Derzhavin, like Pushkin's Grinev, had close encounters with Pugachev during the 1770s. Both Derzhavin and the fictional Grinev wrote up their adventures as autobiography, despite Grinev's generic claims. See Brintlinger, 206, notes 8–10, as well as Samuel Schwarzband, "Les *Carnets* de Derjavine et *La Fille du capitaine* de Pouchkine (Hypothèses)," in *Derjavine: un poète russe dans l'Europe des Lumières,* ed. Anita Davidenkoff (Paris: Institute d'ètudes slaves, 1994), 149–58.
15. Though Pushkin presents Catherine the Great acting as deus ex machina, readers know that Grinev, like Derzhavin, and like his creator Pushkin, lives in the interstices of *will* and *fate,* what Bethea has called the "ontological rhyme" of *volia* and

dolia. See David Bethea, "How Black was Pushkin," in *Under the Sky of My Africa: Pushkin and Blackness,* ed. Catharine Theimer Nepomnyashchy, Nicole Svobodny and Ludmilla A. Trigos (Evanston, IL: Northwestern University Press, 2006), 128.

16. See Dan Ungurianu, *Plotting History: The Russian Historical Novel in the Imperial Age* (Madison: University of Wisconsin Press, 2007). As Andrew Wachtel and others have shown, in Pushkin's hands the novel also enters into an intergeneric dialogue with his own *History of Pugachev*. History, like fiction, must be shaped in order to be understood, and in participating in these competing genres Pushkin demonstrates his knowledge of that narrative fact. See Wachtel, *An Obsession with History: Russian Writers Confront the Past* (Stanford, CA: Stanford University Press, 1994), ch. 4.

17. For the history of the series, see the introduction to this volume.

18. In 1972 Walter Arndt brought Pushkin to the United States in his classic volume *Pushkin Threefold*. I presented the first version of this chapter as "Pushkin Three-Fold in the Pages of *ZhZL*" at the AATSEEL Convention in Chicago in January 2014.

19. D.S. Likhachev in M. Ia. Basina, *Zhizn' Pushkina: Dokumental'no-khudozhestvennye povesti. Kniga pervaia. V sadakh Litseia* (St. Petersburg: Pushkinskii fond, 1996) 6.

20. A. Miasnikov, *Pushkin* (Moscow: Molodaia gvardiia, 1943). In the 1984 republication of these wartime titles, Pushkin appears in both newly written prefaces as a touchstone for Russian biography and as representative of the very idea of the great or remarkable person. Artillery Marshal V. Tolubko, for example, sees these little books as having inspired Soviet soldiers to perform great wartime feats and as presenting even in 1984 "a moral, heroic and patriotic lesson that is particularly valuable for the young generation of our great socialist Motherland" (*Velikie russkie liudi: sbornik,* 6). Compare with the Likhachev quote about "the edification of today's youth" above.

21. Vladimir Novikov, *Pushkin* (Moscow: Molodaia gvardiia, 2014), 2.

22. Orhan Pamuk, "Other Countries, Other Shores," *New York Times Magazine,* Dec. 19, 2013, 2.

23. http://www.litres.ru/pages/biblio_book/?art=175420 accessed 16 May 2016.

24. T. Tsiavlovskaia, Editor's introduction, *Prometei* 10 (1974): 11. Printed in 100,000 copies, the almanac listed for 1 ruble, 24 kopecks.

25. This book came out in 1894 and 1899 via the St. Petersburg typography "Obshchestvennaia pol'za," which Pavlenkov sometimes used, and in 1907 with *Lives of Remarkable People* on the title page. In fact, as early as 1888 Skabichevskii did a biography of Pushkin (entitled *Biografiia A. S. Pushkina*) for Pavlenkov, prior to the advent of the *ZhZL* series, as part of the forty-book "Illustrated Pushkin Library" that Pavlenkov issued that year.

26. Today's scholarly audience, both English and Russian readers, have the benefit of a view from 1880 in Marcus Levitt's *Russian Literary Politics and the Pushkin Celebration of 1880* (Ithaca, NY: Cornell University Press, 1989) to help us understand that page of Russian history more fully.

27. For example, in the introduction to the 3rd edition in 1927, Shchegolev writes: "[N]ew materials and new opportunities to develop them created by the liberation

from censorial and conventional entanglements, prompted me to reexamine the history of the duel" (22). All further references will be included in the text.

28. To the latter belonged Natalia Nikolaevna's letters to her husband, which Shchegolev felt would help characterize her and which he believed to be in the Rumiantsev Museum, as well as the letters of Nikolai Karamzin's wife and daughters to their son and brother Andrei, who was at the time in Paris and thus received written explanations of the events transpiring in Pushkin's family life (25). The Karamzin letters have since been found and published, but it seems that Pushkin's wife may have destroyed her letters. They have not been discovered.

29. I have not seen the *ZhZL* edition of this book, but since its description lists it at four hundred pages, it is the same length as the one I have examined and is likely to be similar.

30. Kal'ma (Anna Iosifovna Kal'manok) also wrote adventure fiction for young adults, such as *The Bookshop near Étoile Square: A Novel* (*Knizhnaia lavka bliz ploshchadi Etual': roman*) (Moscow: Detskaia literatura, 1964), about the French resistance. In 1940 she published *Dzhon Braun* with *ZhZL*, about the American abolitionist John Brown (1800–1859).

31. Pomerantseva, 164–165. She points out that in the prewar years the very meaning of biography was under debate (167). Note that in the end although he never wrote biography for *ZhZL*, Tynianov did enter the canon as a subject (179).

32. M. Gor'kii, *Sobranie sochinenii v tridtsati tomakh* (Moscow: Gosudarstvennoe izdatel'stvo khudozhestvennoi literatury, 1955), t. 29: 374–75.

33. Indeed, Kal'ma thought that school-aged children were the ideal audience for *ZhZL* biographies.

34. Pomerantseva, 136–37. I do not know the specific reason that Tomashevsky's book was not published by *ZhZL*. Pomerantseva explains: "[T]he usual picture: plans are created and changed, in practice everything turns out to be much more modest. Plus, the difficulties of the genre, its lack of clarity, the need to orient oneself to scholarship and art simultaneously. . . . All of this turned out to be an obstacle in the path of many" (137). Tomashevsky's two-volume *Pushkin* was published instead by the Moscow publisher Akademiia Nauk from 1956 to 1961.

35. L. Grossman, *Pushkin* (Moscow: Molodaia gvardiia, 1939), 64. All further references will be included in the text.

36. Quoted from the introduction to his biography of Mikhail Loris-Melikov, *The Velvet Dictator* (1933), in Pomerantseva, 135.

37.Tomashevsky was on the editorial board of the collected edition, *Polnoe sobraniie sochinenii v 16 t.* (Moscow: Izdatel'stvo Akademii Nauk SSSR, 1933–1959) as well as of the *Slovar'* (4 vols, Moscow: Gosudarstvennoe izdatel'stvo inostrannykh i national'nykh slovarei, 1956).

38. T.G. Tsiavlovskaia, ed. *Prometei* 10, 1974, 422 pp, with illustrations, was printed in 100,000 copies.

39. Ariadna Tyrkova-Williams, *Zhizn' Pushkina* 2 vols. (Moscow: Molodaia gvardiia, vyp. 749–750, 1998). All further page references will be included in the text.

40. The original publication was *Zhizn' Pushkina*, vol. 1, 1799–1824 (Paris: Sklad izd. Knizhnyi magazin Vozrozhdeniia, 1929) and vol. 2, 1824–1837 (Paris: Sklad izd. Knizhnyi magazin Vozrozhdeniia, 1948).

41. Alexandra Smith, "Formirovanie literaturnogo kanona v knige Ariadny Tyrkovoi-Vil'iams *Zhizn' Pushkina*," in *Pushkinskie chteniia v Tartu: 2*, ed. L. Kiseleva (Tartu: University of Tartu 2000), 267–81. Quotes drawn from 273, 278, 268.

42. The chapter runs 207–217 in volume 1.

43. Igor Nemirovsky, Personal communication, January 2014.

44. Caryl Emerson, "Our Everything," *Slavic and East European Journal* 48, no. 1 (2004): 88.

45. Volume 1 is 468 pages; volume 2 is 511, with bibliography. They are numbered separately as *ZhZL* biographies, number 749 and 750.

46. Emerson, 88.

47. This volume was put together from a speech the Constitutional Democrat Miliukov gave at one of the *Sovremennye Zapiski* (*Contemporary Notes*) commemorative evenings during the émigré centennial commemorations of Pushkin's death.

48. Vladimir Novikov, "Vyshe Pushkina tol'ko Isus Khristos," *Vselenaia ZhZL* 3.13 (November 2014): 2. For an analysis of Surat and Bocharov, see Emerson.

49. Vladimir Novikov, "*Pushkin*: Opyt dostupnogo povestvovaniia. Fragmenty," *Novyi mir* 3, 2014. https://magazines.gorky.media/novyi_mi/2014/3/pushkin-3.html. Accessed May 7, 2020.

50. Novikov, *Pushkin* (Moscow: Molodaia gvardiia, 2014). Quote from interview at the Moscow International Book Exhibit and Market, November 3, 2019: https://www.youtube.com/watch?time_continue=6&v=84JYcrtORWg&feature=emb_logo.

51. Novikov, "*Pushkin*: Opyt dostupnogo povestvovaniia."

52. *Vselennaia ZhZL*, 2.

53. http://gvardiya.ru/shop/books/zhzl_malaya/808. Last accessed 16 May 2016.

54. The talk show can be accessed on YouTube at http://www.youtube.com/watch?v=b1xK4FqKtw8.

Chapter 2

Larger than Life

The Meaning of A. S. Griboedov in Russian National Biography

Catherine O'Neil

In the preface to her 2003 *ZhZL* biography of Alexander Sergeevich Griboedov, Ekaterina Tsimbaeva claims her book is a corrective to a strange gap in the corpus: there has been no full-length biography of Griboedov in the series until her own.[1] This is "strange" for several reasons and, in fact, not accurate, since the first biography in the series was actually published in 1893 by literary critic Alexander Skabichevsky.[2] Numerous biographies about Griboedov appeared throughout the twentieth century from other presses, including ones by S. M. Petrov (1950), V. N. Orlov (1952), N. A. Popov (1957), A. A. Lebedev (1980), and V. P. Meshcheryakov (1989).[3] The biography of Griboedov in English by British historian Laurence Kelly (2002) and the biography by literary scholar Sergei Fomichev (2012) are the major biographies written after 2000.[4] Many fictional accounts of Griboedov's life have come out since his death, most famously, *The Death of Vazir Mukhtar* (*Smert' Vazir-Mukhtara*, 1929) by Yuri Tynyanov. Indeed, so canonical is Tynyanov's novel, and so well-known its author as a literary theorist and historian, that it has become a parallel biography despite its fictional genre.[5]

Yet it is certainly surprising that after Gorky revived the series in 1933 that there was no other biography until Tsimbaeva's post-Soviet version. Griboedov's comedy *Woe from Wit* (*Gore ot uma*) is a popular staple in the national theatrical repertoire and, perhaps more important, is taught in every school in the Russian-speaking world. Moreover, its author was a major figure in the most important literary and political circles. Beyond his literary fame and friendship with heroic revolutionaries, Griboedov was a major political player in Russia's "great game" diplomacy in the Caucasus and Persia. Many other Russian writers were also government officials, but in Griboedov's case this aspect comprises a more central part of his biography and legacy: his murder as an official representative of the Empire in a foreign land looms large in political and cultural discourse to the present.[6] Beyond these three major aspects of Griboedov's biography—as a man of letters, a would-be Decembrist, an officer of Empire—his other impressive but understudied accomplishments include his linguistic talent as a polyglot, his economic and entrepreneurial efforts and his musical gifts. Each category has its own set of students and enthusiasts who produce both scholarly and amateur works. Yet the paucity of full biographies in *ZhZL,* the Russian national biography series, is unusual given Griboedov's cultural and political importance.

THE BIOGRAPHICAL SUBJECT: WHO WAS ALEXANDER GRIBOEDOV?

As Griboedov scholar Nadezhda Tarkhova points out, mystification and conflicting accounts of "simple facts" abound in the case of Griboedov. Even the material that does exist does not help complete the portrait of the man himself:

> There is no writer in Russian literature whose biography over a span of two centuries preserves as many riddles and dark spots. Even today, 200 years after Griboedov's birth, despite the fact that no small number of documents have been discovered that shed light on events from various parts of his life, we have not made much progress in studying it.[7]

Alexander Griboedov was born in 1790 or 1795—or, possibly, in 1794—into an illustrious but not wealthy family.[8] Raised in Moscow, he studied law at Moscow University and served during the Napoleonic campaign but did not see much action due to illness. On leave in Petersburg, he befriended prominent writers and actors and joined literary and theatrical circles. In 1818, he applied for government service in the Ministry of Foreign Affairs and was appointed to the Russian Mission to Persia, headquartered in Tbilisi, Georgia. During his first stay in Georgia, he began his comedy *Woe from Wit*, completing it during leave in Moscow in 1824. The comedy was widely disseminated and admired but did not pass the censor because its satire was considered politically dangerous. The comedy was published in its entirety only in 1862, twenty-three years after its author's death. Griboedov served General Ermolov in Georgia and Persia until 1825, when he was arrested for suspected involvement in the Decembrist Uprising. No evidence was found against him, and he returned to Georgia, where he served General Paskevich, a distant relation on his mother's side, who replaced Ermolov after the Decembrist Uprising.

Under Paskevich, Griboedov's diplomatic work became much more extensive than it had been previously. He participated in the Russia-Persian wars that resulted in the defeat of the Shah's army and produced substantial territorial gains for Russia, notably Yerevan and parts of Azerbaijan. He was a major contributor to the Treaty of Turkmanchai in 1828 and returned to Petersburg in triumph with the signed treaty in March of that year. For the next three months he passed his time in Petersburg with literary and theatrical friends, meeting frequently with Alexander Pushkin and the exiled Polish poet Adam Mickiewicz, among others, before returning to the Caucasus in June. He was promoted to the position of Minister Plenipotentiary of the Russian Mission in Tehran, a weighty title designed to help his task of collecting the substantial war reparations from the Shah's government. In Tbilisi, before going to Persia, he married the sixteen-year-old Nino Chavchavadze, the daughter of his friend, Alexander Chavchavadze,[9] a Georgian nobleman, Russian officer, and fellow poet.

In December 1828, Griboedov arrived in Tehran during a time of religious and political unrest, when there was great resentment toward the Russians due to the devastating terms of the Turkmanchai treaty. One of the articles of the treaty granted all citizens of the Russian Empire on Persian territory (now including Armenia) safe repatriation to Russia if they so desired. When Mirza-Yakub, the head eunuch of the Shah's harem, and two Armenian women who were wives of a high-ranking Persian requested and were granted asylum in the Russian mission, the prevailing anti-Russian sentiment came to a head and triggered an uprising in Tehran. The event culminated in the brutal massacre of the entire Russian mission on January 30, 1829. Griboedov's dead body could only be recognized by fragments of his uniform and a scar on his finger that resulted from his participation in an infamous duel in 1818. The Persian court, terrified of retaliation from the Russian government, sent Khosrow Mirza, the Shah's grandson, on a Mission of Apology, which was received graciously and with relief by the Tsar's court in Petersburg.[10] Griboedov was buried in Tbilisi, on the slope of Mount Mtatsminda. His was the first grave of what later became the "Pantheon" of illustrious Georgian artists and poets in 1929.

The shadowy legacy of Griboedov resonates beyond Russian literary history due to his involvement in international affairs, which at points intersected with the history of England, Iran, and France. Russian researchers such as Sergei Shostakovich, Militsa Nechkina, Sergei Fomichev and Nadezhda Tarkhova have fully explored Russian archives for original sources. Over the past century scholars have quite reasonably hoped that new material would someday be discovered, because records of his life might be preserved outside the borders of the Russian empire. However, the thorough work of British and Middle Eastern historians suggests that all the documents that can be found have been. Although a few letters and other sources about the events surrounding Griboedov's work and, particularly, his death have been unearthed, it seems now that much that we hoped would shed light on his life outside Russia is likely to have been destroyed or lost forever.[11] We are left with a maddeningly incomplete body of his correspondence and short original works that have survived only in partial or draft versions.

Unraveling the true nature of Griboedov's career in the political and diplomatic spheres remains challenging as well because of conflicting reports of his character and behavior. On the one hand, it is an oft-repeated cliché that Griboedov was an example of "the best" of his nation: brilliant, talented, sensitive, knowledgeable about the languages and places he was assigned to. Yet his attitude toward Persia was very narrow and negative, a reflection of other well-documented aspects of his personality: arrogance and cynicism. As he himself wrote in 1820: Persia is a "sorrowful kingdom in which you not only will not learn anything but you will also forget what you knew before."[12] In his defense, the "strong arm" display of power was standard Russian diplomacy, and Griboedov was, at least at first, an improvement over his predecessor, Ermolov, who demonstrated Russian strength by ignoring local customs and etiquette.[13]

Recent scholarship reveals that Griboedov was a primary drafter of the 1828 Treaty of Turkmanchai,[14] a diplomatic coup for Russia, which, in the grand scheme was the reason for lingering antagonism toward Russia on Iran's part. By Griboedov's final and fatal trip to Tehran, however, much had changed: he was now Minister Plenipotentiary of the Russian Mission in Tehran in charge of what he thought was an agreed-to formality to collect war reparations. But his mind was focused on his future: he had hopes of settling in Tbilisi with his new wife and of founding a profitable "Transcaucasia Company" in Georgia, modeled on the British East India Company. At this point, he seems to have let his guard down with disastrous consequences. Or, perhaps, he had not studied Persia quite enough to understand the mood when he returned: accounts of his entrance to Tehran and of the days leading up to his death abound in episodes that suggest bad will on his part, a misreading of the local customs and situations, and plain bad luck. The abundance of these stories, however, are based on two primary accounts, themselves not entirely reliable but, unfortunately, all that remains of eyewitness reporting. The fact that they are all that we have and the sheer drama they contain have resulted in their being included in every version of Griboedov's death, often closely paraphrased or even quoted verbatim.

"AN INSTANTANEOUS AND BEAUTIFUL DEATH": GRIBOEDOV'S DEATH AND ITS AFTERMATH

The announcements of Griboedov's death in the official press immediately after it occurred were versions of a statement found in the correspondence between Count Nesselrode and Tsar Nicholas I, a politically expedient assessment that exonerated the Persian government of involvement in the massacre and launched the tradition of ascribing blame for the deaths to a fanatic and impersonal mob—and to Griboedov's own failings: "the Persian Shah and the Royal Heir had nothing to do with this vile and inhuman plot and the event should be explained by the excessive zeal of the late Griboedov, who did not fully understand the coarse customs and mentality of the Tehran mob."[15]

The tsar and Nesselrode received reports via Paskevich from the only Russian survivor of the massacre, Ivan Maltsov, the Russian mission's First Secretary. He was able to escape by hiding in a distant room that was occupied primarily by Persian servants, dressing up as a Persian, and bribing the guards who recognized him.[16] He was not an eyewitness to Griboedov's death but his account up to the point he went into hiding can be believed in general terms. The second "eyewitness" was the Persian secretary assigned to the mission, who was fighting on the side of the Russians until Griboedov was forced to retreat further into the compound and the secretary was able to blend in with the crowd and escape. This account, "Mehmendar's Narrative," was published in French and English in 1830 but only appeared in Russian in 1858, and then only in partial translation.[17] Both accounts include action-packed descriptions of the crowd's rage and violence, as well as a dramatic buildup to the ominous event. For these reasons, most biographers incorporate them verbatim into their narratives, having little need to embellish them further.

The mythologization of Griboedov's death began almost immediately after it happened. Of the two main accounts by Griboedov's friends (who were hostile to each other), Faddei Bulgarin and Alexander Pushkin, it was Pushkin's *Journey to Arzrum* (1836) that propagated several legends surrounding Griboedov that cannot *not* be mentioned, even if they are apocryphal: Pushkin's extraordinary and poetic meeting, while traveling on a lonely road in Armenia, with the unmarked box carrying Griboedov's corpse, and the story that Griboedov's corpse could only be recognized by a scar on his finger from a duel. In fact, Pushkin's meeting was most likely imagined,[18] but so important is the cultural bond between the two poets in Russian literature that one cannot present Griboedov without it.

MATERIALS TOWARD A BIOGRAPHY

Short pieces on Griboedov's life had been published in the decades after his death, but none openly addressed all aspects of a "life" as called for in modern biography: psychological and personal qualities, politically sensitive events such as the Decembrist Uprising and the wars with Persia, or socially scandalous events, such as duels, which could only "safely" be referred to after the participants were dead. The closest thing to an early biography was an article by Bulgarin, whose "Reminiscences of the Unforgettable Alexander Sergeevich Griboedov" (1830) in *Son of the Fatherland* (*Syn otechestva*), were published about a year after Griboedov's death,[19] followed a few years later by Pushkin's note in *Journey to Arzrum* (1836). Bulgarin published an (uncredited) letter as an appendix to his "Reminiscences," by V. N. Grigorev, a low-level official working in the Caucasus at the time of Griboedov's death and burial.[20] The letter describes Griboedov's funeral and the reaction to his death in Georgia in detail. This account serves as the basis for the biographical trope of emphasizing Nino Griboedova's grief. It was the first of many accounts that quotes the epitaph chiseled on Griboedov's monument, a grandiose marble construction with a statue of a bereft kneeling woman: "Your spirit and your deeds remain eternally in the memory of Russians; why did my love for you have to outlive you?"; and on the left side of the tomb, "To the unforgotten from his Nina."[21] Bulgarin's memoirs alternate between straightforward information about facts of Griboedov's life and sentimental digressions about how painful it was to recall his friend. It omits Griboedov's political and social difficulties: his participation in a four-way duel in 1818, his arrest after the Decembrist uprising (which was forbidden to be mentioned in any case) and rather emphasizes Griboedov's talent as a writer and diplomat and his affection for the author, Bulgarin himself. He was mocked for this self-serving account, but the fact remains: Griboedov did leave the manuscript of *Woe from Wit* with the note "I entrust my 'woe' to Bulgarin. His faithful friend, Griboedov."[22] In addition, he was the person Griboedov relied on for financial help and who took the most trouble to settle his legacy on behalf of his widow and mother.[23] Despite Bulgarin's unsavory reputation, Griboedov clearly did think of him as a friend.

As for Pushkin, his account despite its brevity is worth including here because of its resonance for the history of Russian biography: "It's too bad Griboedov didn't leave us his notes. The task of writing his biography should fall to his friends, but remarkable people disappear in our country, leaving no trace. We are lazy and incurious."[24] Pushkin's account popularized the biographical myths regarding Griboedov's forebodings of his death as he left for Persia and his corpse being recognized only by the scar on his finger from the four-party duel (451). Pushkin here (and elsewhere) describes Griboedov's life as "enviable" because he accomplished a work of genius and was recognized as a leading writer on his time, he married the woman he loved and, finally, he died a hero's death: "His very death, taking him in a brave and unequal battle, held nothing terrible for Griboedov, nothing agonizing. It was instantaneous and beautiful" (452). Pushkin early on exemplifies the biographical tradition of assessing the death in terms of the life, as in biographer Hermione Lee's formulation.[25] It says more about Pushkin's notion of a heroic death than about Griboedov's actual last moments that such a death could be declared either "instantaneous" or "beautiful"!

The fact that no detailed overview of Griboedov's life was published earlier is not surprising, given the political and literary circumstances of the time. First, the nature of Griboedov's mission to and death in Persia were, if not classified, not widespread information. The tsar's acceptance of the "Apology Mission" from the Shah precluded vocal indignation about his death in public. Second, as a poet, Griboedov's renown was limited due to the fact that, although written in 1824, *Woe from Wit* was not published until 1862. Only certain scenes that had passed the censorship could be performed and were staged only in the two capitals. Proof that Griboedov could have written much more than this play and the handful of poems published in his lifetime only came to light in 1859, with the publication of his rough notebook (*chernovaia tetrad'*) that he had left with Stepan Begichev in 1828. This notebook contained the first acts of the drama *Georgian Night*, as well as other planned works and travel notes.

Personal memoirs about Griboedov began to come out in the late nineteenth century, after the death of Nicholas I, when the censorship about events during his reign was loosened. Formerly, it was forbidden to mention the Decembrist Uprising publicly, which precluded discussion of Griboedov's arrest in 1826 and the testimonies of some of his best-known contemporaries who were themselves involved in the uprising. Thus their reminiscences were only published after 1855.[26] The mid-1850's also became a watershed period for the "release" of material pertaining to Griboedov due to the deaths of persons who might obstruct the "truth" of his story (that is, possibly negative or complicated aspects): his widow, Nino Chavchavadze (1854), Tsar Nicholas I (1855), Griboedov's sister Maria (1856), and Griboedov's closest friends Begichev and Bulgarin (both 1859). By the late nineteenth century, there was a wealth of material at a biographer's disposal: biographical reminiscences, a slew of important articles about Griboedov as diplomat and his work in the Caucasus by A. P. Berzhe,[27] an increasingly open assessment of the Decembrists and the construction of an unassailable "myth" surrounding them,[28] and most importantly, Griboedov's own voice through publication of his notebooks, travel notes, and personal letters.[29]

GRIBOEDOV'S BIOGRAPHY IN PAVLENKOV'S ZhZL

The first Griboedov biography in *ZhZL* was by literary critic and historian Alexander Skabichevsky in 1893[30] and was more complete than what had been published before. Before he began writing for Pavlenkov's press, Skabichevsky worked with Nekrasov's journal *Notes from the Fatherland (Otechestvennye zapiski)* from 1868 until it was shut down in 1884. Many of the aforementioned materials on Griboedov were published in his own main venue.[31] By the time Pavlenkov began *ZhZL* in 1890, Skabichevsky was a leading literary critic who was much aligned with the values of Pavlenkov's circle and bridged the gap between high culture and a more popular readership.

The literary reviews and biographical sketches he wrote for Pavlenkov were aimed at a broad public. Skabichevsky's prominence was such that Pavlenkov entrusted him with the biographies of the three "founding fathers" of Russian literature, Pushkin (1891), Lermontov (1891), and Griboedov (1893), whose main heroes (Onegin, Pechorin, and Chatsky, respectively) were seen in the second half of the nineteenth century as the spiritual fathers of literary heroes. The later biographies, of Pisemsky (1894) and Dobrolyubov (1894), reflect the intellectual milieu in which Skabichevsky lived and worked, albeit as a secondary figure.

Skabichesky attempts a psychological portrait of Griboedov: he was probably the first to write in a biography that Griboedov had a difficult childhood and a tyrannical mother: "This was a haughty woman with a difficult character, who subjected everyone in the household to her powerful will" (8). However, given the dearth of information about Griboedov's childhood, his evidence for this depiction consists of direct quotations from *Woe from Wit* (in quotation marks, but without reference), thus equating Chatsky with his creator, as was typical in nineteenth-century biographical practice. He describes Griboedov's mother and uncle as direct prototypes for Maria Alekseevna and Famusov from the play.

When discussing later periods of Griboedov's life, for which he had documentary evidence, Skabichevky quotes directly from his sources, relying most heavily on the accounts of a handful of important contemporaries—notably Bulgarin, Begichev, Kyukhelbeker, and Maltsov.[32] For his account of the massacre in Tehran, Skabichevsky does not change anything from the official version of Griboedov's death, but by quoting extensively from Maltsov's account he presents this dramatic scene to a public to whom it was previously unknown. He stops short of the graphic violence in Maltsov's depiction but includes the detail that the body could only be recognized by the scar on the finger (95).[33] After describing the massacre, Skabichevsky concludes with the body's journey to its resting place in Tbilisi, alluding to Pushkin's "meeting" with Griboedov's remains and quoting extensively from the Russian governor of Tabriz's official report. He dedicates his final paragraphs to Nino's grief and her years of solitude at her family estate: "In those infrequent instances that she stayed in Tbilisi, it was a rare week that she did not undertake the steep incline of the mountain of Saint David in order to visit the precious remains. She died of cholera in her forty-fifth year, in 1857, and was buried next to her beloved husband" (100).[34] It became a biographical commonplace to end Griboedov's life story with the two intertwined legends—of Pushkin's encounter with Griboedov's remains and of Nino's grief at his tomb.

In his epilogue, Skabichevsky focuses on Griboedov's poetic legacy, citing the genius of his play and quoting influential literary thinkers such as Belinsky and Goncharov on Griboedov's importance. His final assessment is a detailed review of the play and its significance in Russian literature. His final words on Griboedov are not about the man at all but about his play, and specifically his creation, Chatsky, whom he defends against those who accuse Chatsky of being less "witty" than his author supposes, because he takes on opponents who are unworthy of him. This polemic about Chatsky—begun, typically, by Pushkin—characterized discussions of the play throughout the nineteenth century resulting from the equation of Chatsky in Russian society with the Decembrists after the uprising. Thus, Skabichevsky's version ends with a critical essay on his greatest work and differs from other biographies in its complete absence of a final conclusion about Griboedov's own character or life.

GRIBOEDOV IN THE BIOGRAPHICAL NOVEL

Despite the fact that most other canonical nineteenth-century Russian writers had at least one biography in the Soviet series, there was no other biography of Griboedov. However, it would be a mistake to say Griboedov's life was unknown or unstudied in all those years. There was a turn to a different form of biography in the period from the 1920–1930s, an updated form of fictionalized biography. Yuri Tynyanov produced perhaps the best fictionalized biographies of Russian Romantic poets, about Kyukhelbeker (1925), Griboedov (published on the centennial of his death, 1929) and Pushkin, which he never finished (part 1, on Pushkin's youth, was published in 1935).[35] Tynyanov avoided the biographical conundrum of how much to speculate by writing a novel instead of a biography, as he suggested in his *Avtobiografiya*: "Where the document ends, that's where I begin."[36] He created a noncanonical portrait of Griboedov, whose intelligence and humanity are undermined by a lack of empathy and fearfulness (although he is by no means cowardly). His uncharitable thoughts about and actions toward friend and foe alike make him, arguably, more human, and certainly more nuanced than a straightforward portrait of the hero-poet. In this sense Tynyanov's time parallels our own, where heroes are, if not villainous, extremely morally flawed or psychologically damaged. G. E. Pomerantseva, in her account of the development of *ZhZL*, discusses the fact that though Tynyanov's novels were seminal to the received images of the lives of these poets and provided a vivid portrait of their historical epoch, they were not appropriate models for *ZhZL* biographies because they were fiction.[37] Yet in actuality, Tynyanov was working on his final fictionalized biography at the same time that he was working closely with the *ZhZL* editorial board in his capacity as a literary historian and scholar.[38] The popularity of Tynyanov's fictionalized version of Griboedov in *The Death of Vazir-Mukhtar* may have mitigated the need for another representation of Griboedov's life for much of the twentieth century, at least as far as the series editors were concerned. Tynyanov, it turns out, is Tsimbaeva's main foil in her work on Griboedov, a point not lost on many of her readers and which I will examine more closely below. The tension between the fact-based historical narrative and Tsimbaeva's imaginative additions needs to be examined further.

THE POST-SOVIET *ZhZL* BIOGRAPHER: WHO IS EKATERINA TSIMBAEVA?

Starting in the 1990s, the post-Soviet *ZhZL* took on new life and broader scope, revisiting canonical subjects with the benefit of greater ideological freedom, greater availability of domestic archival materials and greater access to non-Russian sources. These sentiments were reaffirmed in 2013 on Ekho Moskvy's weekly radio show, "Book Bazaar" (*Knizhnoe kazino*). The editor Andrei Petrov describes with humor and enthusiasm the publishing house's orientation: "*ZhZL* is not about warm and fuzzy people, remarkable in the sense of their 'goodness,' but about famous people, symbols of an epoch, about whom one simply enjoys speaking."[39] He discusses new biographies of the Decembrists Pestel and Ryleev and biographies that would reassess traditional "villains" previously unworthy of inclusion in the series, such as Tsar Paul I, Ivan Mazeppa, and, significantly, Faddei Bulgarin.[40] As Petrov explains, "[our books] should be about famous people, about great people, with both a plus and minus side. As a rule, every person is a combination of plusses and minuses." Such statements confirm a post-Soviet divergence from earlier *ZhZL* standards and provide the context in which Ekaterina Tsimbaeva produced her biography of Griboedov. Her work must be fearless in reassessing its subject and his circle and its narrative strategies must be energetic, surprising and fresh.

A professor at Moscow University, Tsimbaeva is both a serious historian and popularizer of cultural topics in a variety of media. Her biography of Griboedov was first published in 2003 and republished in an expanded edition in 2011.[41] It won two awards and much acclaim: "Best Book of the Year" for 2003 (Russian National Library prize) and the prize in honor of the 115-year anniversary of *ZhZL* (2015).[42] She has published two scholarly monographs, one on Catholicism in Russia (2008) and the other on ecumenism in Russia (2015).[43] Her other work focuses on the interconnections of literature and history, most recently a monograph which includes chapters on Griboedov's *Woe from Wit,* Tolstoy's *Anna Karenina* and Charles Dickens' *The Mystery of Edwin Drood.*[44] Tsimbaeva's most recent articles address the fate of the Russian language on the global scene.[45] After her biography of Griboedov, she produced two more biographies for *ZhZL*, also significantly about literary figures: British mystery writer Agatha Christie (2013), and Russian fabulist Ivan Krylov (2014).[46] She is obviously knowledgeable about both English literature and language.

In addition to her articles, she has done interviews on Radio Mayak as an expert on Griboedov and Christie and on nineteenth-century Russian culture in general.[47] She has given a variety of catchy and topical interviews. Judging from the frequency of her appearances on the popular-scholarly program "Kafedra" after the launch of her Agatha Christie biography, Tsimbaeva has become a prominent figure in more "highbrow" popular culture. She is someone who speaks well and colorfully but also with great scholarly authority. Her interviews on Griboedov and Russian ecumenism were aired on the show's subseries "the Great Nineteenth Century," reinforcing the idea of "great" that seems to be the red thread in Tsimbaeva's thinking about Russian culture as a whole. Her literary criticism in tone and content are in tune with the Putin era's ideological tendency to promote—and even revive—Russian imperial culture. In the case of her Griboedov book, she appeals to the anti-British sentiment pervading Russian politics in recent decades.

TSIMBAEVA'S *GRIBOEDOV*: STYLE AND REACTIONS

Few *ZhZL* biographers give the reader insight into their authorial process by providing a preface, however Tsimbaeva's introductory comments provide a preview of her biographical approach: "the author, a professional historian, a specialist in social thought of the nineteenth century, has attempted as much as possible to create a scholarly work within an artistic form" (7). She begins with what turn out to be two signature tropes in her writing: an allusion to

British literature (Sir Arthur Conan Doyle's Professor Challenger) and a grandiose claim: "Up to now there has been neither a scholarly nor even an artistic biography of Alexander Sergeevich Griboedov, encompassing his entire life, works and varied political activity" (5–6). She notes that scholarly works tend to compartmentalize Griboedov according to different aspects of his life and activities. Somewhat to the surprise of educated Russian readers, she states that: "Griboedov has been even less lucky in artistic works," singling out the "false portrait" of Griboedov created by the wrongfully acclaimed Yuri Tynyanov (6). Tsimbaeva recognizes that the image that forms the basis for her readers' ideas is Tynyanov's Griboedov. She forcefully declares that her biography is the first complete biography of Griboedov, at both times "scholarly" and "artistic" (7) which readers will find appealing as well as historically faithful to documents and facts ("Behind the Narrator, the Historian stands looking over his shoulder" [8]). Ultimately, she claims that her work is a truthful account of the missing pieces of Griboedov's life where, for lack of evidence or any record at all, the "facts" must be imagined—and, she declares, her account is no less "truthful" for all that.

As numerous readers and reviewers have noted, she takes more liberties than other biographers by filling in (or inventing) details that are not and cannot be known. To be sure, all biographers have to fill the gap between documented fact and dark spots in the life. Yet no other Griboedov biographers regularly diverge from their carefully objective stance and instead clearly state what can and cannot be known, citing the sources for all their information. For example, in recent works by Fomichev and Kelly, any wandering into the realm of speculation is couched in cautious language and acknowledged up front on the part of the biographer or the source he cites.

As noted earlier, the book received two prizes (for the first edition) and was subsequently "expanded and corrected" in a second edition in 2011. A number of online reviewers praised it on the publisher's website.[48] However, two serious reviews in *New Literary Observer* (*Novoe Literaturnoe Obozrenie*) and *Independent Gazette* (*Nezavisimaya gazeta*) as well as several online reviewers criticized its content and style. One of them sums up the situation more evenhandedly:

> A substantial biography of Griboedov, despite justified criticism and several factual errors, nonetheless has the right to exist as its author's interpretation. Sure, marvelous specialists, who have studied and read a lot about the life of one of the most notable figures of Russian literature and diplomacy of the nineteenth century, will find flaws and no shortage of reasons to express disagreement. Yet for those readers who have nothing to compare it to the book can seem fairly interesting.[49]

Even Tsimbaeva's critics, for the most part, agree with her admirers on the book's strengths: persuasive writing, good knowledge of and description of the period, and in parts—notably the detailed reconstruction of *Woe from Wit*—creative and convincing literary scholarship. Her vivid (if lengthy) descriptions of the historical era evoke the image of a brilliant Russian culture in no way inferior to—and in many ways superior to—the so-called "leaders of world culture," notably England and France. Her patriotic tone, bordering on chauvinism, would have a greater appeal to Russian readers than Russia's image as the barbaric interloper found in European and Iranian histories of this period. The narrator's voice merges with Griboedov's at several instances when providing assessments that border on chauvinistic, not exactly passing them off as Griboedov's thoughts but not clearly distinguishing them. An example of the narrator's ironic tone is the following:

> The country that for brevity's sake was called England—Great Britain, or the United Kingdom—consisted of two unequal parts. The worse part, in terms of sparse population and poor natural resources, comprised what was located on the British Isles (England, Scotland, Wales, Ireland) and all its colonies (Canada, Australia, South Africa and various trifles). The better part was India: a densely populated and immensely wealthy country. At the head of Great Britain stood the king, but it was possible to forget about him, as he was a ruler only in name. And in 1819, one might even say there was no king at all: George III had gone mad and was removed from matters of state, and the regent, the future George IV, only occupied himself with personal matters, first and foremost with contemporary men's fashion, although he was too fat to look good in tight trousers and high-waisted frock coats. In 1820 the English had welcomed his official ascension to the throne, but his first action had been to attempt to divorce his half-insane wife, Caroline. Parliament blocked this (divorce was never permitted in England under any circumstances), the king persisted, newspapers printed cartoons, the people got angry, and things only calmed down upon the death of the queen.
>
> The worse part of the British realm belonged to Parliament.
>
> The best—to the East India Company. (236)

Thus, the power of the East India Company is introduced with heavy-handed irony, dismissing as "the worst part of the United Kingdom" the country most Russian readers know as the glamorous birthplace of Byron, Austen, and Dickens. Her detailed contrast of the Russian and British empires helps set up her explanation for the massacre in her epilogue, laying blame at the feet of the British authorities, a reading favored by many Russian historians, including Fomichev.

The aforementioned reviews point out valid concerns with Tsimbaeva's experimentation with the form of "fictionalized history" as opposed to "historical fiction," a much more common genre in Russia. Re-creating what cannot be known becomes, in the mind of reviewer V. A. Koshelev, the main flaw of the book. Modern "popular" biographers, he writes, do not use the word "probably" and thus mar their whole enterprise by presenting invented scenes as facts.[50] Less charitably, Alexei Filippov calls her work "pretentious" and notes passages he finds absurd:

> Ekaterina Tsimbaeva has embarked on the path of 'bringing to life' the epoch she describes. And in so doing she wanders so far off that she presents the reader with a great abundance not only of 'details of everyday life' in the post-Catherinian estates of Moscow, Petersburg and Tiflis, but she has even penetrated Griboedov's own most intimate thoughts . . . Even if we could believe in a certain plausibility in her rendering of Griboedov's thoughts about his writing on Begichev's estate, her effort to become Griboedov in the last moments of his life, when the mob of Muslim fanatics stormed the mission in Tehran, falls apart completely.[51]

Tsimbaeva's narrative structure follows a conventional, chronological approach. It is more than fifty pages before our hero appears in the first chapter, following a "Prologue" about his family lineage. She conscientiously explains her choice of the year 1795 for Griboedov's birth in a lengthy paragraph set off by italics (57–58). Her reasoning is sociohistorical: the earlier date means Griboedov would have been born out of wedlock but nothing suggests a stain of this sort on his mother's reputation.[52] Subsequent chapters follow the usual life stages, similar to those found in biographies written by Skabichevsky, Kelly, and Fomichev, but labelled with the role Griboedov played in each period: "Student," "Hussar," "Playwright," "Diplomat," "Genius," "Decembrist," "Peace Maker," "Minister," as is frequent practice in *ZhZL* biographies. The thirty-page epilogue is entitled "Heirs" and includes questions about the sources of the massacre, recalling a "Whodunnit" summation in crime fiction. During each of these chapters Tsimbaeva goes into Griboedov's "head," and readers familiar with his letters and notes will recognize verbatim passages quoted without reference. She explained her use of this device in the preface as a way to evoke the authentic language of the man and his times. The most elaborate foray into her hero's thoughts occurs at the moment of his death, as the mob is attacking the Russian embassy, which is the climactic scene for any biography of Griboedov.

The original accounts of the massacre are highly dramatic, including the distant shouts of the mob as it comes closer, the closing of the bazaar on the mullahs' orders, the first attack that resulted in the murder of the Shah's chief eunuch Mirza-Yakub, then the pause while the crowd increases in size and then returns to destroy the rest of the mission. Simply reproducing them provides a riveting narrative in most biographies. For this reason alone, most biographers do not embellish or alter them. Instead, Tsimbaeva's emphasis shifts to the causes of the event and to Griboedov's ruminations on why this is happening to him. Possible explanations have remained baffling and inconclusive to scholars of Griboedov's life and the history of the region as a whole.

In Tsimbaeva's biography, these events take up six pages of narrative, three of which are a faithful rendering of the aforementioned accounts. But she interrupts her depiction of the attack and destruction of the mission and Griboedov's death with a long internal monologue in which Griboedov tries to understand why he is being attacked and who may be behind the disastrous situation in which he and his staff now find themselves. The interruption of the dramatic action has an almost comic effect. First, Griboedov systematically adumbrates who his most likely enemies may be: "Was it the Shah?," then "Alliair-khan [the governor of Tehran and the Shah's son-in-law]?," and finally "The English?" Each possibility is thoroughly weighed in his mind, presumably as he deflects rocks being hurled at his head and slashes heroically at his attackers. What should have been a highly touching scene when he thinks of his pregnant bride in the last moments of his life becomes ludicrous because of the rapid shifting of his thoughts as he puzzles out another possible conspiracy against him:

> Ah, Nina, Nina! Terrible news awaits her. Will she be able to give birth to their child? Will his son survive? Or is he doomed to be the last of his family? It's a good thing that the Macdonalds will take care of her. Macdonald? He too had a reason for disliking him: the idea of the Transcaucasia Company, which he found out about through his own networks, made him very angry. (Tsimbaeva, 2011, 512–13)

To many readers, this representation of Griboedov's thinking was implausible: would these rational thoughts really be going through Griboedov's head at that moment? Tsimbaeva undermines the most poignant and dramatic event of her subject's life story. These are not "flashbacks" or cinematographic elements that increase the drama of the story, but rather stumbling blocks impeding the movement of the scene. Moreover, they are unnecessary here since Tsimbaeva, like other biographers before her, repeats these speculations in her epilogue.

WHOSE GRIBOEDOV GETS THE LAST WORD?: TSIMBAEVA VERSUS TYNYANOV

By the time the *ZhZL* series was revived in the 1930s under Gorky's guidance, the Russian literary world had already been captivated by Tynyanov's nuanced and complex biographical novels. His first historical novel, *Kyukhlya* (1925), included a characterization reflecting the Griboedov portrayed by his friends in their memoirs: he does not participate in intrigues and he is affectionate with his eccentric friend Kyukhelbeker. *Vazir-Mukhtar* was Tynyanov's second historical novel and demonstrates what he had learned in writing the first as well as the external conditions specific to Tynyanov's own time.[53] Maxim Gorky had a great regard for these works; he wrote in his article "On literature" (1930) that they were the best examples of a new genre in Soviet literature: original historical novels of a high artistic quality. Gorky wrote Tynyanov about his impressions of the novel: "Your Griboedov is remarkable, although that is not how I expected to find him. But you have portrayed him so convincingly that it must be how he really was. Or, if not—how he will be from now on."[54] Tynyanov's enduring and successful novel has been reissued more than ten times since its first publication, as recently as 2018, and is firmly established in the Russian literary canon.

What is positive in Tsimbaeva's work is her new perspective on Griboedov's importance to Russian music and his visionary project of founding the Transcaucasia company as a rival to the British East India Company. However, Tsimbaeva fails to achieve her stated purpose to wrest Griboedov from Tynyanov's dominant characterization. Had she toned down her claims, had she not declared herself to be "the first," had she not put herself in the position of being "answerable to Griboedov alone," had she not spoken so dismissively of Tynyanov, who actually accomplished a fusion of history and fiction with complete success, she would have been spared many negative comments from readers. There are not enough reviews to know how the broader reading public reacted to her book or, in fact, how many people read it. But the appearance of a second edition suggests sales of the first edition were strong.

The complexity of Tynyanov's novel and its rich verbal style makes it more vivid and, ultimately, more psychologically convincing than any conventional biography. Tynyanov's authority as a knowledgeable and original thinker about the poetry, poets and epoch he discussed helped forge this sense of the novel's "believability," a quality which has been noted by many readers and critics of the text.[55] Tsimbaeva, however, takes Tynyanov to task for creating an inauthentic depiction of Griboedov: "He drew the image of a man who sacrifices his convictions for the sake of his career, who betrayed his fellow-thinkers, the Decembrists, who is consumed by pangs of conscience and is repulsive both to himself and his author" (6). She claims Tynyanov could not have created such a Griboedov had he acquainted himself with the biographical materials that were already available. No one can question Tynyanov's knowledge of the Golden Age that continues to resonate in Russian literary studies to this day. His close acquaintance with Griboedov's work is evidenced amply in the text of his novel. Yet, even Tynyanov's so-called "negative" portrait of Griboedov, certainly a feature of the novel, does not contradict the impression we get from the biographical material itself, which shows in equal measure his coldness and arrogance alongside his brilliance, and makes him both unlikeable and likeable, a balanced portrait of his character which Tsimbaeva presents as well.

Another complaint of Tsimbaeva relates to the atmosphere of Tynyanov's novel; the action takes place in a dark world of intrigue and envy from which none of the figures in Griboedov's life who are usually viewed as positive– from Kyukhelbeker to Pushkin to Nino Chavchavadze—are exempt. Tynyanov, she continues, "was infused with the ideals of the Silver Age with its exaltation of split personalities, fruitless doubt, unbelief in the future and the destruction of everything of worth. He simply could not understand the people of the Golden Age, for whom indecisiveness, depression and the inclination toward suicide were foreign" (6–7). In this sense, Tsimbaeva is right: Tynyanov produces a Griboedov appropriate to his own era and historical context, which may well have made this portrait resonate even more with a variety of audiences.

Ultimately, Tsimbaeva will have to reconcile herself to ongoing comparisons with Tynyanov, if she has not done so already. In a 2017 interview on Radio Mayak, she was introduced with praise and fanfare by host, Igor' Ruzheinikov, who inadvertently let slip some small gaffes that may have stung his guest. First, he admitted he had not yet read her book, and then he described with great warmth Tynyanov's novel. He even alluded to it in the title of the program, "100 Faces of Vazir-Mukhtar." The novel came up during the course of the interview, as Ruzheinikov was familiar with the 2009 teleseries based on Tynyanov's novel and assumed many of his listeners were too. Tsimbaeva repeated her criticisms of Tynyanov: he was hostile to Griboedov and he created an unsavory and immoral character who was imbued with the sensibilities of the Silver Age rather than the Golden Age. But she conceded finally that the novel was well written and that the Griboedov Tynyanov created is "perfectly fine" as the hero of a novel but should not be confused with the historical Griboedov whom she purportedly depicts. At the end of the interview Ruzheinikov thanked her warmly, telling his audiences to go forth and read Tsimbaeva's book—"And Tynyanov, too!" They should be read, he suggested, side by side.[56]

NOTES

1. Ekaterina Tsimbaeva, *Griboedov* (Moscow: Molodaia Gvardiia, 2003, reprinted 2011). "[F]or mysterious reasons no one has attempted to bring together all the amassed information [on Griboedov] into one volume" (5–6).
2. *A. S. Griboedov: Ego zhizn' i literaturnaia deiatel'nost'* (Moscow: 1893).
3. For a full list of Griboedov biographies, see V. A. Koshelev's review of Tsimbaeva's biography: "Blesk i nishchita 'neprelozhnykh istin,'" *Novoe literaturnoe obozrenie*, no. 6 (2003), https://magazines.gorky.media/nlo/2003/6/blesk-i-nishheta-neprelozhnyh-istin.html [Last accessed 10/6/2020].
4. At least one biography has come out since Fomichev's, by military historian Sergei Dmitriev: *Poslednii god A.S. Griboedova. Triumf. Liubov'. Gibel'. Istoricheskie issledovaniia* (Moscow: Veche, 2017).
5. Other fictional versions of Griboedov's biographies include: Timrot (1965), Gaivoronskii (1998), and Esenkov (2004) (see F. I. Melvill, "Paradoks Griboedova," in *Na pastbishche mysli blagoi. Sbornik statei k iubileiu I.M. Steblin-Kamenskogo*, 304). For a discussion of Griboedov in Russian and Iranian popular culture, see Firuza Melville, "Alexander Sergeevich Griboedov: Russian Imperial James Bond *Malgré Lui*," in Rudy Matthee and Elena Andreeva, eds, *Russians in Iran. Diplomacy and Power in the Qajar Era and Beyond* (London and New York: I.B. Tauris, 2014), 49–74.
6. Griboedov's ongoing presence in Russian culture can be seen in the Russian-language news reports of the 2016 assassination of Andrei Karlov, the Russian ambassador to Turkey, many of which refer to his death as a precedent, and most recently in the 2020 Nagorno-Karabakh conflict. See "Okhota na postal" (*RIA Novosti*, Dec.20, 2016, https://ria.ru/20161220/1484144546.html) and "Ot Griboedova do Karlova" (*AiF*, Dec. 19, 2016 https://aif.ru/society/history/ot_griboedova_do_karlova_posly_rossii_i_sssr_pogibshie_ot_ruk_ubiyc).
7. Nadezhda Tarkhova, "K probleme izucheniia biografii Griboedova segodnia," *Voprosy literatury*, no. 4 (July-August 2013): 130–50, https://voplit.ru/article/k-probleme-izucheniya-biografii-griboedova-segodnya/ [last accessed 10/5/20] I am grateful to Angela Brintlinger for directing me to Tarkhova's most recent work.
8. The fact that even the year of his birth cannot be determined with absolute certainty is representative of the many challenges his biographers face from the start.
9. Alexander Chavchavadze (1786–1846) was a Georgian prince born in St. Petersburg. He rose high in the Russian military service and was known in his native Georgia as a poet, many of whose works became popular songs. His houses in Tbilisi and Tsinondale were centers of social and cultural exchange between educated Russians and Georgians.
10. For more on this mission, see George A. Bournoutian, *From Tabriz to St. Petersburg: Iran's Mission of Apology to Russia in 1829* (Costa Mesta, CA: Mazda Publishers, Inc., 2014).
11. British archives have been mined by D. P. Costello, Evelyn Hardin, Kelly, and others; Iranian, Armenian, and Georgian archives by George Bournoutian and F. I. Melville. In addition to the British diplomatic archives, Kelly researched

the India Office archives and the Ottoman archives (*Diplomacy and Murder in Tehran*, 298–301).

12. Griboedov, letter to unknown addressee, 17 Nov. 1820, in Fomichev and Kotliarova, eds. *Sochineniia* (Moscow: Khudozhestvennaia literatura, 1988).

13. In a letter to V. Kiukhel'beker on November 27, 1825, Griboedov describes his horror after witnessing the execution of a Chechen prince: "I have been so disturbed [lit: interrupted] that I have not been able to describe this bloody event properly to you. It happened a month ago and I have not been able to banish it from my memory" (quoted in Kelly, *Diplomacy and Murder,* 124).

14. N. Ia. Eidel'man, *Byt' mozhet, za khrebtom Kavkaza* (Moscow: Nauka, 1990), 86–90.

15. Quoted in I. S. Siderov, "O gibeli A.S. Griboedova," *Rossiiskii arkhiv: Istoriia otechestva v svidetel'stvakh i dokumentakh XVIII–XX vv*. (Moscow: Studiia TRITE, 1992), 91–97. http://az.lib.ru/g/griboedow_a_s/text_0170-1.shtml This article lists the way Griboedov's death was described in official Russian publications, all of which come down to variants on this quotation. Siderov's brief article recounts the official versions of the massacre in the Russian press in the immediate aftermath of the events. No further details of Griboedov's work and life can be found in them.

16. I. S. Mal'tsov, "Iz donesenii," in *A.S.Griboedov v vospominaniiakh sovremennikov* (Moscow: Khudozhestvennaia literatura, 1980), 292–302.

17. Mehmender, *Reliatsiia proisshestvii, predvariavshikh i soprovozhavshikh ubienie chlenov poslednego rossiiskogo posol'stva v Persii*, in Fomichev, ed., *A.S. Griboedov v vospominaniiakh sovremennikov* (Moscow: Khudozhestvennaia literatura, 1980), 303–29. First published in French, it was soon thereafter published in English as "Narrative of the Proceedings of the Russian Mission, from its Departure from Tabreez for Tehran on 14th Jummade 2D, until its Destruction on Wednesday the 6th of Sha'ban," *Blackwood's Edinburgh Magazine*, no. 171 (September 1830): 496–512.

18. S. Fomichev, "Griboedovskii epizod v 'Puteshestvii v Arzrum'" in *Pushkinskaia Perspektiva* (Moscow: Znak, 2007), 440–54.

19. F. V. Bulgarin, "Vospominaniia o nezabvennom Aleksandre Sergeeviche Griboedove," *Syn otechestva za 1830 god* (no. 1, vol. 9, 3–42), in N. Piksanov, ed. *A.S. Griboedov v vospominaniiakh sovremennikov* (Moscow: Federatsiia, 1929), 21–42.

20. The letter was published as "Pis'mo iz Tiflisa k Bulgarinu" in *Syn Otechestva za 1830 god*, no. 2. See V. N. Grigor'ev, "Zametki iz moei zhizni," in N. Piksanov, ed. *A. S. Griboedov v vospominaiiakh sovremennikov*, 200.

21. The image of Nino Chavchavadze as a disconsolate widow was no doubt born in the elaborate symbolism of this monument. The monument took years to build, during which Nino petitioned the Russian and Georgian governments alike to get funding and permission to build it on the sacred Mount David in Tbilisi. It seems out of character for a young and inexperienced girl, sixteen at the time of her husband's death, to commission a monument that is so centered on herself. In fact, in a letter she wrote to Bulgarin from April 23, 1830, she describes a quite different monument than the one that eventually came to be: "I am certain you will be able to commission an artist who would be able to portray Alexander Sergeevich's merits, his tragic death,

and the sorrow of his friends." See Iurii Khechinov, "Zhizn' i smert' Griboedova" (*Nauka i zhizn'*, no. 9–10, 2003). The path between this original, more modest (on her part) and greater tribute to Griboedov as a whole (not including any word about her own love and loss) and the final heavy-handed tribute to romantic grief, has yet to be discovered. A clue to the origin of the final monument may be in the word "unforgettable" (*nezabvennyi*); cf. the title of Bulgarin's memoirs, "Reminiscences of the Unforgettable Alexander Sergeevich Griboedov."

22. Quoted in Piksanov, ed., *Griboedov v vospominaiiakh sovremennikov*, 21.

23. Opinions about Bulgarin's "helpfulness" in regard to Griboedov's affairs vary wildly, with most coming down to a negative view of Bulgarin. Yet enough evidence has come to light showing the mutual bond between Griboedov and Bulgarin that suggests the friendship was sincere and that Bulgarin was not as cynical in his obsessive evoking of Griboedov after the latter's death to help bolster his reputation in the literary world. See Angela Brintlinger and Benjamin Richards, "Perechityvaia Bulgarina: Byl li Faddei Venediktovich podletsom i naskol'ko nas eto dolzhno volnovat'?," in *A.S. Griboedov: epokha, lichnost', tvorchestvo, sud'ba, Khmelitskii sbornik*, no. 16 (Viaz'ma, 2014), 32–44.

24. Pushkin, *Polnoe sobranie sochinenii v 10-i tomakh*, ed. B.V. Tomashevskii, VI: 452.

25. Hermione Lee, "How to End it All," in *Virginia Woolf's Nose. Essays on Biography* (Princeton and Oxford: Princeton University Press, 2005), pp. 95–122.

26. See Ludmilla A. Trigos, *The Decembrist Myth in Russian Culture* (New York: Palgrave Macmillan, 2009), xxi.

27. See P. Zabolotskii, "Obzor literatury o Griboedove" in Piksanov, ed., *Griboedov, A.S. Polnoe sobranie sochinenii [v 3 t.]*. Saint Petersburg: Izd. Imp. Akad. Nauk, 1913, Volume 2, 283. Zabolotskii also mentions a "biographical outline" (*biograsicheskaia kanva*) published in Griboedov's first collected works in 1889, ed. N.M. Lisovskii, but this was not so much a biography as a "non-systematic listing of events in Griboedov's life according to the year" (279). Presumably Skabichevsky had access to this information as well.

28. See Trigos, *Decembrist Myth*, 12–29.

29. Begichev's memoirs, now canonical for Griboedov biographers, languished in manuscript form until 1890, when they turned up in an antiquarian book shop owned by A. Shliapkin. They were first published in *Russkii vestnik* no. 8 (1892). The fact that Skabichevsky quotes Begichev so often shows he took advantage of this new material. See Piksanov, *Griboedov v vospominaniiakh sovremennikov* (1929), 4.

30. A.S. Skabichevskii, A.S. Griboedov, ego zhizn' i literaturnaia deiatel'nost' (Petersburg: Tip. P. P. Soikina, 1893). Due to the expiration of copyright on Pavlenkov's publications, a reprinted version is available online (Moscow: AiKiu Izdatel'skoe reshenie, 2016), http://az.lib.ru/s/skabichewskij_a_m/text_0100.shtml. Because this edition is not paginated online, references will be made to the original.

31. For background information on Skabichevsky, see B. Smirnov, A.M. Skabichevskii –literaturnyi kritik (Volgograd: Izd. Volgogradskogo universiteta, 1999). 30. A.S. Skabichevskii, A.S. Griboedov, ego zhizn' i literaturnaia deiatel'nost' (Petersburg: Tip. P. P. Soikina, 1893). Due to the expiration of copyright on

Pavlenkov's publications, a reprinted version is available online (Moscow: AiKiu Izdatel'skoe reshenie, 2016), http://az.lib.ru/s/skabichewskij_a_m/text_0100.shtml. Because this edition is not paginated online, references will be made to the original.

32. See L. K. Dolgopolov and A. V. Lavrov, "Griboedov v literature i literaturnoi kritike kontsa XIX—nachala XX v." on the deluge of publications about Griboedov (110) and tendency to equate Griboedov with Chatsky in late 19th c. criticism (111–12) in Fomichev, ed., A. S. Griboedov. Tvorchestvo. Biografiia. Traditsii (Leningrad: Nauka, 1977), 110–12.30. A.S. Skabichevskii, A.S. Griboedov, ego zhizn' i literaturnaia deiatel'nost' (Petersburg: Tip. P. P. Soikina, 1893). Due to the expiration of copyright on Pavlenkov's publications, a reprinted version is available online (Moscow: AiKiu Izdatel'skoe reshenie, 2016), http://az.lib.ru/s/skabichewskij_a_m/text_0100.shtml. Because this edition is not paginated online, references will be made to the original.

33. This detail is neither in Mal'tsov nor in the Mehmendar "Narrative"—indeed the latter claims his corpse was intact: "I recognized his altered features and was fully satisfied that, after death, the corpse had been subjected to no indignities" ("Narrative," 496). It is not clear where the description of the disfigured corpse originated but, certainly, Skabichevsky would have known it at least from Pushkin's Journey to Arzrum.

34. The pathos of these events is surprisingly deflected by details about money: the "generous" pension Griboedov's widow received and the cost of the monument. These details about the funeral and Nino's mourning were likely taken from Grigoriev's letter which Bulgarin published as an appendix to his "Reminiscenses."

35. See Angela Brintlinger's chapter "Science Fiction: Tynianov and *Death of the Vazir-Mukhtar*" in *Writing a Usable Past*, 22–40.

36. Tynianov, *Kak my pishem* (1930), 161. Quoted in Brintlinger, *Writing a Usable Past*, p. 27.

37. See Pomerantseva, *Biografiia v potoke vremeni. ZhZL*, 179.

38. Pomerantseva remarked: "the appearance in the series of Tynianov, who in the readers' consciousness was firmly associated with the biographical novel, at the very moment when the editorial board was searching for possible ways to expand the biographical genre, signified our turning to his expertise—the valuable expertise of both researcher and artist" (179–80).

39. A. Petrov, "Osennye Novosti Molodoi gvardii," 29 sent. 2013, https://echo.msk.ru/programs/kazino/1165784-echo/.

40. The projected biography of Bulgarin by Oksana Kiianskaia has not yet appeared in the series.

41. A page-by-page comparison of the two editions reveals few changes: the addition of three pages and one item in the bibliography. The three added pages are more details about the plan for the Trans-Caucasia Company and its likelihood for commercial success were it to be realized. Tsimbaeva's article on the topic is the only addition to her bibliography: "Gosudarstvennyi proekt A.S. Griboedova," *Vestnik moskovskogo universiteta*, seriia 8, Istoriia, no. 2 (2004).

42. See her CV at MGU: http://www.hist.msu.ru/Departments/CIS/Staff/Tsimbaeva.htm. (Last accessed 12/20/2019).

43. Tsimbaeva, *Russkiĭ katolit͡sizm: zabytoe proshloe rossiĭskogo liberalizma* (Moscow: Editorial URSS, 1999), and *Russkiĭ ėkumenizm: Poisk osnov mezhkonfessional'nogo edinstva v Rossii XIX veka* (Moscow: URSS Lenand, 2015).

44. *Istoricheskii analiz literaturnogo teksta* (Moscow: KomKniga, 2005; second edition 2015).

45. See E. Tsimbaeva, "Russkaia klassicheskaia literatura i problem formirovaniia 'bol'shoi rossiiskoi natsii," *Via Evrasia*, no. 5 (2016): n.p. http://www.viaevrasia.com/bg/almanach-via-evrasia-2016-5-оглавление.html; and "Velikii i moguchii . . .' Ne slishkom li moguchii?," *Rodina*, no. 9: 20–22. Most of her work has been published in MGU journals or thick journals such as *Voprosy literatury* and *Voprosy istorii*.

46. *Agata Kristi* (Moscow: Molodaia Gvardiia, 2013), print run 5,000, series # 44; *Krylov*. (Moscow: Molodaia Gvardiia, 2014), print run 3,000, series # 63.

47. For a list of her interviews on the Kremlin-supported station Radio Mayak, see https://radiomayak.ru/persons/person/id/217743/.

48. Viktoria Milenko: "A huge thank you to the author! It has been a long time since I read a book this way, not hurrying or skimming, yet disappointed that it ended so soon" (http://gvardiya.ru/shop/books/zh_z_l/griboedov); Bagir07: "One of the best books I've read lately" (https://www.livelib.ru/book/1000534191-griboedov-ekaterina-tsimbaeva); Akella Akella: "read his great play in school and reread it quite recently. It made me want to learn more about the author. This book in the *ZhZL* series is the best you could pick" (https://www.labirint.ru/reviews/goods/278867/).

49. "Surikatya," https://www.labirint.ru/reviews/goods/278867/

50. "Having undertaken extensive research, the author of a scholarly article dedicated to the childhood years of Griboedov would offer his hypothesis finally beginning with something like '*We may suppose* the Griboedovs spent 1795 to 1800 in the village of Timirevo.' . . . The author of a popular biography, not allowing any 'suppositions,' simply writes, based on the hypothesis put forth in the scholarly article above: 'In the spring of 1795 the Griboedovs were forced to leave their home. . . . They settled in Timirevo for the summer and there they remained until 1800.'" (Tsimbaeva, 58). All the rest of the biographical narrative is built on this original 'supposition,' presented as an *unconditional fact* (Koshelev, "Blesk i nishcheta").

51. Aleksei Filippov, "Griboedov v teni" (*Nezavisimaia gazeta,* May 15, 2003). http://www.ng.ru/massolit/2003-05-15/7_griboedov.html. Online reviewer "Medulla" writes similarly: "And this very impression that you are reading a fictionalized biography by a writer with a completely personal relationship to her subject, yet who at every line claims to speaking from scholarly fact and that 'this is how it really was and only I know it' – is completely infuriating." https://www.livelib.ru/book/1000534191-griboedov-ekaterina-tsimbaeva

52. Tarkhova, writing after Tsimbaeva's biography was published and advocating the earlier year, 1790, explains her case in equally convincing sociohistorical terms. Readers interested in the whole story should consult her article, "K probleme izucheniia biografii Griboedova segodnia," for the whole argument.

53. See Brintlinger, *Writing a Usable Past* for a discussion of the historical parallels and veiled references in Tynianov's novel.

54. Letter to Tynianov, 24 March 1929 (accessed online, http://www.imli.ru/lit-nasledstvo/Tom%2070/Том%2070-52_Горький-Тынянов.pdf.

55. See G.A. Levinton, "Griboedovskie podteksty v romane 'Smerti' Vazir-Mukhtara," *Tynianovskii sbornik. Chetvertye Tynianovskie chteniia* (1990), 21–34. A nuanced discussion of Tynianov's tampering with historical veracity can be found in Brintlinger, *Writing a Usable Past*, 31–40. Now that this excellent book has appeared in Russian translation, perhaps Tsimbaeva will read it and reconsider her assessment of Tynianov's novel.

56. Interview with Igor' Ruzheinikov, Radio Mayak, Jan. 15, 2015. https://radiomayak.ru/videos/video/id/1618766/

Chapter 3

N. V. Gogol, Biographer's Conundrum

Ludmilla A. Trigos

Near the end of his life, Nikolai Vasilevich Gogol wrote: "It's necessary to leave a surviving testament to posterity that must be dear to us and close to our heart like children are close to their father's heart (otherwise the tie between now and the future is disrupted)."[1] As a genre, biography functions to preserve the tie between present, past, and future, presupposing that the biographical subject will be instructive or useful to future generations. Writing Gogol's life poses many challenges, compelling a biographer to make crucial choices in order to create a coherent representation. S. T. Aksakov observed that understanding Gogol was difficult even for those who knew him because he was: "in perpetual motion, in struggle with human imperfection . . . no one knew Gogol entirely . . . Of course, some friends knew him well, but they knew him, so to speak, in pieces."[2] One hundred years later, Gogol remained an enigma, as Andrei Bely remarked: "We still do not know what Gogol is."[3] Biographers continue today to try to reconcile the different faces of Gogol in order to make him understandable to contemporary readers, as can be seen in the most recent biographies of Gogol in the *Zhizn' zamechatel'nykh liudei* (*ZhZL*) series.

This article surveys how the writers of *ZhZL* biographies in different eras grappled with the challenges posed by Gogol's idiosyncratic and eccentric personality, opposing critical interpretations of his literary output, and ethnic origins.[4] Despite his indisputable artistic genius, Gogol seems an unlikely candidate for inclusion in a series that strove to provide positive role models for the younger generation, especially during times with strict ideological constraints. Yet Gogol's biography went through several iterations, beginning in 1891 by A. N. Annenskaya (republished four more times before

1925), to the texts written in the Soviet era by A. K. Voronsky (completed 1934, finally released in 2009),[5] N. V. Vodovozov (1945, in the wartime series *Velikie Russkie Liudi*), N. L. Stepanov (1961), and I. P. Zolotussky (1979, with expanded and corrected editions in 1984, 1998, 2005, 2007, and 2009), the latter becoming the standard series biography for the late Soviet and post-Soviet eras.[6] The biographies of Gogol thus serve as a reflection of the developmental arc of the series as a whole, mirroring the evolution of approaches to biography as well as the central concerns of their immediate context.

Certainly, for much of the nineteenth and a good part of the twentieth centuries, literary critic V. V. Belinsky's assessments of Gogol greatly informed subsequent analyses of his work and life. Any biographer has to come to terms with Belinsky's insistence on Gogol's realism and social significance of his oeuvre, as well as the critic's reaction to Gogol's polarizing work, *Selected Passages from Correspondence with Friends* (1847). Belinsky charged that Gogol tried to play the role of moral prophet, but that he was not a thinker and should have confined himself to creating his works instinctively rather than philosophizing. He rejected *Selected Passages* outright, but still maintained that Gogol's earlier works had value. Other critics held that the work was the result of a sick mind that had succumbed to religious fanaticism or questioned Gogol's sincerity in his declarations (some seeing Gogol's desire for financial support from the government as a hidden motivation for the work), while the smallest number applauded Gogol's turn to religion in the work as a genuine expression of traditional Orthodox values.[7] Most biographers treat *Selected Passages* as an important turning point in Gogol's life, because its publication created such violent reactions and contradictory reevaluations among Gogol's contemporaries, and because Gogol's health took a decided turn for the worse in response, as he himself commented in his letters.

In crafting Gogol's biography, several questions thus arise: does one view Gogol's personality and his works as an organic whole, which goes through an evolution, or does one see a schism between Gogol's actions and works before his serious turn to Christianity and after, a transition marked by *Selected Passages*? These vexed questions of Gogol's behavior only became slightly more understandable once later psychological approaches become available, though even Belinsky himself sought to ascribe Gogol's lapse to mental illness. Pathographies produced by Russian psychiatrists in the early 1900s discussed Gogol's oeuvre and life in that light.[8] As Irina Sorotkina notes, "'The enigma of Gogol' mystified his contemporaries until they explained it by illness, which supposedly transformed a brilliant writer and ardent patriot into a religious maniac."[9] Later Freudian and other psychological theories allegedly allow access to a deeper understanding of motivations or complexities of his inner life, though there were taboos against "psychologizing" or discussing topics of a sexual nature within the *ZhZL* series (at least until the post-Soviet era).

Another central issue that dogs the biographer is Gogol's ethnicity and national identity. How does the biographer treat Gogol's Ukrainian origins given that the author has been unequivocally granted pride of place in the canon of Russian literature as a writer whose works defined *Russian* national identity? In an obituary, I. S. Turgenev wrote that with Gogol's death, Russia had "the right (the bitter right, given to us by death) to call Gogol 'great.'"[10] Yet even during his life, Gogol's pronouncements on Russia's destiny were taken up by Belinsky and other contemporaries as articulating Russia's future path and assisting in the formation of Russian national identity. Thus, Gogol's inclusion in the canon of classic Russian writers leads us to explore how biographers come to terms with or nullify his ethnic origins and the tension between his place of birth, his complicated national identity as a Ukrainian writer choosing to write his literary works in Russian but also living primarily in Russia and Italy. Stephen Moeller-Sally has suggested that the genre of biography played a pivotal role in integrating Gogol into that canon after his death.[11] Though an in-depth analysis of the Ukraine question is beyond the scope of this article, it should be noted here that all the biographies in question deftly elide Gogol's Ukrainian-ness and his Russianness. Certainly, the biographers make much of his purported Cossack blood, his entree into his literary career as a "Ukrainian" writer who provided colorful pictures of Ukrainian "folk" life (though later those stories were perceived as less historically accurate and authentic than originally thought). Most biographers point to Gogol's unusual hairstyle, one that they describe as a Cossack topknot, sometimes explaining away this feature as an affectation of national pride (he changes his hairstyle after he returns from Rome). Several proclaim that his facial features, especially his long nose, were typically Ukrainian, as a kind of negative cultural stereotyping.[12] On the positive side, many biographers exploit the Ukrainian landscape and ethnographic elements (folk music, local peasant beliefs, and rites) to lend a lyrical quality to descriptions of his homeland and to highlight Gogol's inborn artistry. Yet they do not subscribe to the idea that Ukraine and Russia are two distinct countries with different languages and often overlapping historical and cultural legacies. Edyta Bojanowska treats this cultural disjuncture most eloquently, noting that "Gogol's upbringing and education fostered the identity of a Russian nobleman (who happened to live in Ukraine)," but emphasizes that once Gogol ventured into St. Petersburg he was surprised to find himself perceived as a Ukrainian and at worst as a *khokhol* (hick). She concludes that the experience made him into a "self-conscious Ukrainian."[13] Yuliya Ilchuk, on the other hand, indicates that dual national identities were typical of Gogol's generation as but one "compromise with the empire's demand for national homogenization" and sees Gogol's identity as "hybrid," subject to continual self-revisioning.[14] Though the idea of *malorossiistvo* has recently been discussed by many Postcolonial studies scholars as the "deformation of the Ukrainian psyche under Russian colonial rule,"[15] there has not been significant attention to the topic in his biographies in the popular series. Gogol has been fully claimed as a Russian writer despite his Ukrainian origins.[16]

Finally, literary biography should also address the nature of Gogol's artistic genius and how it intertwines with contemporary notions of authorship. Unlike other predecessors (for example, the Decembrists) or some other contemporaries, who represented themselves in "a Byronic key," Gogol was "not inclined to enact his own biography for the benefit of the reading public."[17] The literary critic Boris Tomashevsky pointed out the necessity of separating the biographical legend created by the author from the author's actual life, yet this equation became more common in the twentieth century as the influence of Belinsky on literary critical approaches toward Gogol began to wane. Many biographers at various times specifically inscribe Gogol's biography into his works, thereby connecting Gogol's heroes' actions with his own. In addition, since Gogol left a rich epistolary record of his relatively short life, biographers frequently use the letters to correlate Gogol's and his characters' behavior. There are several explanations for this approach. First, the Romantic expectation of the direct translation of the poet's life into his works remains a common biographical strategy. Second, in some biographers' texts, this tactic fills in the blanks of Gogol's life experiences, extrapolating Gogol's heroes' anxieties about certain life events as stemming from his own subconscious. Donald Fanger suggested that Gogol was a writer "without a biography"; his life lacks such important milestones as love affairs, marriage, or children: "dedication to the work in progress largely drains the biography (as opposed to the career) of visible content."[18] Hence, for certain biographers, the boundaries between career and life story became porous. Additionally, the literary critic Yuri Lotman posited that Gogol exemplified a new turn in ideas about how biography and authorship interconnect, with Gogol gaining the "right to biography" because he saw his mission as an artist "to speak a higher Truth."[19] This article will demonstrate how Gogol's posthumous reputation and life story was shaped by *ZhZL* biographers even as they also responded to their own contemporary political, ideological, and literary pressures.

GOGOL ON THE CUSP OF THE TWENTIETH CENTURY: A. N. ANNENSKAYA'S *GOGOL: HIS LIFE AND LITERARY ACTIVITY* (1891)

The inclusion of Gogol in the canon of Russian literature and the concomitant reading of his selected works in the standardized curriculum in Russian schools necessitated the creation of an appropriate biography.[20] As Robert Maguire suggests, there was a change in critical evaluations of Gogol after his death, which opened up new perspectives. The critic Nikolai Chernyshevsky perceived Gogol as a typical man of his milieu, education and upbringing, but different in that he had "an energetic desire to minister to social defects and to his own weaknesses," coupled with a "mysterious spark of genius."[21] Chernyshevsky challenged Belinsky's view that there were "two Gogols" and the notion that *Selected Passages* was a deviation or change from Gogol's earlier ideas and works. Insisting that the text grew organically out of Gogol's earlier period, Chernyshevsky attempted to remove Gogol from earlier moralizing approaches by fully analyzing his works and life, to discern a pattern and explanation for his behavior.

In the period from his death into the 1890s, Gogol became "an object of study" with publication of several new (incomplete) editions of Gogol's works and letters published as well as memoirs by his contemporaries. P. A. Kulish began gathering the reminiscences of Gogol's friends and acquaintances almost immediately after Gogol's death, but his first essays in biography were considered "tentative and fragmentary."[22] S. P. Shevyrov's death prevented him from completing his own life of Gogol. Maguire notes that despite the fact that Gogol's popularity did not decline even decades after his death, there was no attempt to shape or synthesize the increasing number of publications related to Gogol's life and work. He speculates that there may have been both political and personal factors at play. Not only may Gogol's personality have been "too puzzling to an age that honored the verities of science and positivism," but some governmental authorities were "disturbed by the demonstration of popular affection for Gogol," fearing that his works would influence the development of revolutionary ideas in Russia.[23]

It was into this atmosphere that the first biography of Gogol was written for Pavlenkov's *Lives of Remarkable People* series, by Alexandra Nikitichna Annenskaya (1840–1915). A pedagogue, translator and author, she wrote five books for the series besides *Gogol: His Life and Literary Activity* (*Gogol: ego zhizn' i literaturnaia deiatel'nost*,' 1891).[24] She was a product of the 1860s in her perspectives on progress and social and political change and was deeply involved in the women's movement. Her biography of Gogol was the eighth book in the *ZhZL* series overall, published in its second year of existence, and was republished in 1894, 1903, 1910, and 1914. She was the sister of noted publicist and revolutionary P. N. Tkachev and the wife of the economist, critic, and populist N. F. Annensky, who met the publisher Pavlenkov in a transit prison while they were both in political exile. She was an accomplished writer of children's literature, and prior to the revolution, her works were considered indispensable to every children's library.[25] Her own educational training as a governess and practical experience as a teacher of children and adults shaped her approach to literature as an important guide for the moral development of future generations.[26]

Annenskaya's text remains the most concise Gogol biography in the series overall, providing a chronologically ordered narrative of Gogol's family life, childhood, and youth, as well as his entry into literary life, travels, and works. In common with other writers' biographies in Pavlenkov's series, the works are touchpoints for the life rather than objects of extended literary criticism. Though she refers to Gogol's letters as well as the memoirs of Gogol's contemporaries Alexandra Smirnova-Rosset, Pyotr Pletnev, and others, and contemporary journals and articles throughout her text, she does not provide a bibliography or list of sources. She evidently consulted the first biographies of Gogol written by P. A. Kulish, which, as Ilchuk suggests, provide a portrait a Gogol "who was preoccupied exclusively with his spiritual quest, with his sinful human nature, and with his unrealized social ideals—the image that the Slavophiles popularized in the 1850s."[27] Annenskaya did not have the benefit of V. I. Shenrok's *Materials for a Biography of Gogol* (1892–1897) in crafting her biography, though all later biographers use this valuable source for their depictions of Gogol.[28] Unlike other contemporary biographers such as Fedor Vitberg, who insisted that the fundamental task of the biographer was to resolve the ongoing debate about Gogol's moral character,[29] Annenskaya remains relatively neutral. She may well have been writing in reaction to the popular brochure *Gogol as a Teacher of Life* (*Gogol kak uchitel'zhizni*, 1888), published by Leo Tolstoy's imprint *The Intermediary* (*Posrednik*), which went through several subsequent editions.[30] Tolstoy's booklet privileges *Selected Passages* over all of Gogol's other texts, realizing Tolstoy's intention to disseminate more about Gogol's life through the prism of that work. As he wrote to Nikolai Strakhov: "I dream of publishing *Selected Passages from Correspondence* in the *Intermediary*. It will be a wonderful life (*zhitie*) for the people."[31] In contrast, Annenskaya does not create a hagiography, eschews superfluous detail, and crafts a text that is appropriate for general readers. She dispenses with the genealogy typical of most Gogol biographies, concentrating instead on Gogol's immediate family and surroundings in *Malorossiia* (present-day Ukraine) as the first formative influences on his character. The work demonstrates the contemporary perception of Ukraine as merely a southern province of Russia, eliding any true "national" differences between the inhabitants of Malorossiia and Russia other than geographical location and some inborn inclinations (for example, Gogol's susceptibility to Ukrainian folk tales and songs).[32]

Annenskaya portrays Gogol as a "dreamy" child and indifferent student, immediately establishing a dichotomy between Gogol's expectations and reality itself which weaves through the rest of the text. She emphasizes that he dreamed of dedicating his life to serving his country. His dreams are tested repeatedly as the biography progresses, first by the cold reception he receives in Petersburg and his difficulty in finding an appropriate position in government service or in the theatrical world, and then in his inability to gain an immediate foothold in the literary world. Annenskaya explains his early failures as the result of Gogol's inability to privilege his own writing over the pedestrian idea of service to state: "But as before, Gogol dreamed of a great cause, of a feat for the good of many, yet he still sought that cause outside of literature" (28). Once Gogol sees himself as serving both goals, does he begin to find fulfillment in his writing: "Practically since childhood searching for a profession in which he could gain fame and bring benefit to others . . . he finally understood that his true calling was literature, that the laughter evoked by his works, had beneath it a deep, educational significance" (47). Thus, following Belinsky's lead, Annenskaya posits *Dead Souls* as the central text in Gogol's oeuvre because of its social significance.

Annenskaya does not provide a particularly flattering picture of Gogol as a child or adult. She mentions that Gogol had difficulty making friends because of his reticence and secrecy; she lays the blame on the poor pedagogical and disciplinary methods of the lycée for his defects in character. She also downplays Gogol's peculiarities of dress and manner, his odd behavior and tendency toward illness (whether real or hypochondriatic) during his adulthood.[33] Indeed, Annenskaya speaks of Gogol's unspecified illnesses only after he contracts malaria while in Rome, and she attributes his turn to religiosity (already present in his childhood) to visions he saw while ill. She links the growing religious fervor that Gogol experienced to his anxiety about the success of his literary works and his financial deprivations. For Annenskaya, Gogol's emotional and spiritual health were intimately tied to his works; his nerves were shattered by the process of writing (and the lack of inspiration he frequently experienced) as well as by the progressively more arduous task of getting works through the censors for publication:

> Perhaps it was the result of his sickly condition, perhaps as the result of his nervous inclination which supported and developed this religious tendency in him, but unmediated creativity now rarely visited him, which in earlier years had created vivid images on the basis of some sort of accidentally heard-of event. However, he could not stop the labor which he considered his holy duty, his feat

for the good of mankind, and he wrote, dissatisfied with himself, continually destroying and reworking what he wrote (64–65).

She makes an apologia, explaining Gogol's publication of *Selected Passages* as his misapprehension during an attack of illness that his letters could have a beneficial influence on mankind.[34] She attributes Gogol's spiritual crisis at the end of his life to several factors, both external and internal: an increase in his religious feelings, which led to his negative assessment of his own literary works and his difficulty in finishing the second volume of *Dead Souls*; the "unexpected wreck" and failure of *Selected Passages* and his split with Belinsky; his worsening illness and fear of death; and finally, his spiritual disenchantment when discovering his lack of faith on his pilgrimage to Jerusalem to purify himself and gain insight into his true path. She focuses on Gogol's struggle for inspiration and his increasing belief in prayer as the means to gain it. Annenskaya posits this combination of struggle and faith in his "higher duty" as the key to Gogol's genius and personality (65). She highlights his last days as ones where there was "a difficult battle in his soul between the artist and the pietist" (86). Annenskaya speculates that Gogol's thoughts at the end of his life centered on fulfilling his duty to mankind through his writing:

> It's not clear what these unending corrections to which he subjected his "Dead Souls" would serve. Would it attest to some more mature artistic sense . . . or maybe, in the throes of religious self-flagellation he renounced the great meaning of his artistic talent and tried to compose pictures of virtuous people who would serve as edifying examples for his contemporaries and his descendants? (86).

For Annenskaya, Gogol's demise occurs due to an increasing fear of death and his need for spiritual purification, an organic evolution of tendencies evident in childhood—not a split between past and present.

Jeffrey Brooks describes Annenskaya's Gogol biography as an example of the "occasionally rather tendentious" presentations in the *ZhZL* series and notes the difficulty a progressive or radical biographer would have with reconciling "Gogol's unwelcome conservative political and religious pronouncements with his social service as a writer."[35] Yet despite the sources that she had access to and her personal political biases, she doesn't take a completely one-sided view of her subject. To provide a positive and more progressive depiction and to defuse the intense religiosity of Gogol's later years, she highlights Gogol's continual civic mission to serve society (in one or another capacity, then finally as a writer) and emphasizes his laborious literary efforts. Though she attempts to remain relatively neutral, Annenskaya echoes Belinsky at the end of the biography:

> As a thinker and a moralist, Gogol stood lower than the foremost people of his time, but from his early years he was animated by a noble striving to benefit society and a lively sympathy for human suffering and found a poetic language, brilliant humor and lively images to express them. In those works in which he devoted himself to the direct force of creativity, his observation and his mighty talent deeply penetrated into life's phenomena and with its clearly truthful pictures of human vulgarity and baseness served to awaken social consciousness. (90)

With Gogol's progressive credentials highlighted, her biography aligns with Pavlenkov's goal to provide enlightenment to the mass reader and to disseminate information about important members of the world's intelligentsia. Tendentious or not, Annenskaya's biography continued to be published up until 1914, indicating that it remained popular and sold well for Pavlenkov's press despite the competition from other presses.[36]

CREATING A MODEL GOGOL FOR SOVIET RUSSIA?

Alexander Konstantinovich Voronsky (1844–1937), Old Bolshevik, leading Marxist literary critic and editor of the journals *Red Virgin Soil* (*Krasnaia nov*,' 1917–1927) and *Projector* (*Prozhektor*, 1922–1927), began writing for the ZhZL series after his fall from political grace, producing two biographies: *Zheliabov* and *Gogol*, most likely undertaken at Gorky's suggestion.[37] His bibliography displays his broad knowledge of the most recent publications on Gogol in the Soviet Union and abroad, including the works of Bely, Merezhkovsky, Lunacharsky, Pereversev and Tynyanov. Voronsky's Gogol biography was scheduled for publication in 1934, in honor of the 125th anniversary of Gogol's birth and only one year after Gorky's reinvigoration of the series in Soviet Russia. But the book never reached readers because of political events. Its entire print run of 50,000 seemingly disappeared (with the exception of the test copy and a few others that later were found in private hands). After the assassination of S. M. Kirov on Dec. 1, 1934, Voronsky again was expelled from the party, arrested on Feb. 1, 1937, and executed at some point thereafter. At some point, the typeset plates of the Gogol biography were destroyed.[38] The text only became known to the public in the mid-1960s. In 1964, Yuri Mann published an abridged version of the last chapter in *Novyi mir* with his own introductory article and individual chapters were later published in collections of the author's articles. The complete text was finally published in 2009 in ZhZL's *Malaia seriia*.

Voronsky opens his narrative with epigraphs from Chernyshevsky and Giorgio Vasari on the nature of artistic genius, which, respectively, emphasize Gogol's importance to Russia and draw the comparison between Gogol and Leonardo da Vinci. The idea of dualism, a central concept for Voronsky's understanding of Gogol's genius, serves as a leitmotif throughout the text. Voronsky stresses that Gogol's dual nature was inherent in him from childhood: "Two Gogols. Two original enemies of each other within one person, even in the youth and adolescent" (50). For Voronsky, the key to understanding Gogol's evolution as a writer and as a person, and to understanding Gogol's works, lies in this essential psychological split and in the progression from lighter to darker tonalities (as also seen in DaVinci's work).[39] Voronsky also manifests the dichotomy between the lofty and the earthy sides of Gogol in his focus on Gogol's body, citing the significance and impact of Gogol's stomach problems and his hemorrhoids on his work and life (69, 223 and passim).

Voronsky's *Gogol* grimly reflects the horror of daily life and the realities of the Stalin era. Voronsky provides detailed literary analyses of all of Gogol's works, focusing in large part on manifestations of evil in the literary works, and ascribes events and emotions experienced by Gogol's characters to Gogol himself. He traces the development of the devilish figures in Gogol's early stories into the incarnations of *poshlost'* and triviality evident in later works. Voronsky sees Gogol's short story "Vii" as an important autobiographical text and the key to understanding the cataclysmic change that Gogol underwent both as an artist and in his personal life even prior to the debacle of *Selected Passages*:

> Something happened to Gogol in 1833 when he was writing 'Vii'... the autobiographical essence of the tales rests, in our view, in the fact that 'unconstrained joy,' healthy sensuality, youthful freshness were defeated by the world of Ivan Ivanoviches, the Mayors, the Khlestakovs, the Chichikovs and other pigheads. And it seems that the old witch is old Russia, having mounted the poor philosopher, she turns living reality into terrifying tormenting visions (121).

Voronsky speculates that Gogol's searing internal "cataclysms" may be related to "some sort of intimate, sexual events" which Gogol then transposed onto the story of the young seminarian, Khoma Brut (121–22). His analysis demonstrates a dual nature as well, touching on lofty/metaphorical as well as sexual/earthly elements in the story. Regarding *Selected Passages,* Voronsky claims that it is penetrated by a fear of death: "In world literature, words can hardly be found that convey with such shattering force the howl right before death as those contained in *Selected Passages*" (321). Voronsky acknowledges that Gogol primarily appeared there as "a prophet, ascetic and reactionary utopian, but he was still not in the condition to suppress the artist in himself. And the artist possessed an unusual gaze and penetration . . . where [he] broke through" (325).

Voronsky considers the nature of Gogol's artistic genius inherent in the storm in his soul: writers "like Gogol endure gigantic internal events, reversals and their most negative characteristics exist as if to show the eternal, tireless and victorious battle of man over everything that he considers base and unworthy in himself. For the triumph of humanity's genius over the inert (*kosnoe*) and the elemental (*stikhiinoe*) it's necessary to speak of the vices and failures of great men" (437). Unfortunately for Voronsky, this sentiment did not coincide with the tenets of Socialist Realism, which demanded positive role models and portrayed not life as it was, but life as it was supposed to be.

Voronsky's biography concludes with a devastating image taken from one of Gogol's unfinished novels. Two captives are imprisoned in a deep dungeon when another figure enters: "It was a man, but without his skin. The skin was ripped from him. He was completely covered in blood. His veins were blue and spread out like branches all over him. Blood flowed from him. A bandura on a leather strap hung on his chest. On his bloody face, his eyes flickered terribly." Voronsky ends his text with the lines: "Gogol was that bloody bandura player and poet, with eyes that had seen too much. It was he who against his will cried out to the new Russia with a darkened voice, 'Don't give in . . . !' For that they skinned him alive" (439). This chilling conclusion reveals as much, if not more, about the biographer and his own time as it does about his subject.

Though Hugh McLean minimizes the biography's emotional impact, especially as a refraction of anxieties due to the Stalinist purges, he rightly calls Voronsky's work "a relic of early Soviet mentalities."[40] As such, it would not have been a viable candidate for inclusion in the series, even if the manuscript hadn't been lost, then found, and then both book and author arrested and executed. For though Mann highly values Voronsky's biography as the first truly Marxian approach: "providing a corrective to earlier studies by Bely (too formalistic) and Pereverzev (vulgarly sociological),"[41] it is surprising to see how out of step its methodology was with its times. In the quote above, Mann speaks from the perspective of the 1960s and not the mid-1930s, when all literary focus was on the creation of the model Socialist Realist biography for the model Socialist Realist reader. At this juncture in 1934, the doctrine of Socialist Realism was being codified and the state demanded heroic portrayals of classic Russian writers, yet Voronsky dwelt upon the all-too-human aspects of Gogol and his idiosyncrasies. He provided an iconoclastic and at times indecorous portrait of Gogol even as he exalted Gogol's works. Evgeny Dobrenko suggests that writers like Pushkin and Gogol were expected to fulfil particular functions to inspire burgeoning Soviet writers and readers and the parameters of their lives would thus be limited, or "canned," having been reduced to figures "who write."[42] From this perspective, there was no need for individual personality or creativity, merely labor.[43] Though Voronsky situates his narrative squarely in Gogol's socioeconomic milieu, he places greater emphasis on the tools of psychology and psychiatric theories to explain Gogol and his inner motivations and goes far beyond showing "how" Gogol worked, straying dangerously (for the time) into the realm of how Gogol felt and thought. Evidently, Gogol's subversive potential far outweighed his benefit as a Soviet role model due to the destabilizing effect of his laughter and social satire. It is telling that a *ZhZL* biography of Gogol did not appear again until 1946, when the Russian classics were mobilized to inspire patriotic fervor during World War II.

GOGOL IN THE *VELIKIE RUSSKIE LIUDI* SERIES

The study of the lives of remarkable people was especially valuable in wartime, as Professor A. Vershinsky pointed out, to nourish patriotism in Soviet youth.[44] Literary critic and historian N. V. Vodovozov's 1945 concise biography conforms to that purpose, specifically written for the inspiration of troops at the front and civilians during World War II.[45] Appropriately, it opens with a lyrical discourse regarding the long-standing history of Ukraine (not *Malorossiia* here) as a contested site, immediately drawing a parallel between past history and current events, and demonstrating the historical importance of Gogol's purported ancestor, Ostap Gogol, a brave Cossack who fought against the Turkish forces in the seventeenth century: "Progressive people understood even then the necessity of Slavic unity before the face of common enemies" (3). This is Gogol for wartime consumption: Gogol becomes a patriot, both because of his family lineage and because of his contributions to Russian culture. From the first lines there is a pronounced emphasis on the solidarity of Ukraine, Poland, and Russia. Further stressing patriotism, the biographer dwells upon the idea of self-sacrifice, shifting from past to present to provide a variety of perspectives on the theme. Because it aims to stir patriotic feelings within the reader and to provide exemplary role models, this text focuses on Gogol's literary works that emphasized pan-Slavic unity and heroic feats, such as *Taras Bulba* and *Dead Souls*.[46] Vodovozov insists that Gogol had become prophetic: "Gogol sensed what great strengths were in the Russian people. The great artist believed that the day would come when the mighty forces of people would go out onto the free, wide road and the entire world would raptly bow before the beauty of the Russian spirit, before the greatness of its heroic feat" (82). This prophetic ability inspired Gogol to conclude *Dead Souls* with the eternal image of Russia as a troika rushing forward to greatness. In Vodovozov's biography, Gogol wanted more than anything to bring great benefit to his [Russian] homeland (17).

Vodovozov does not depict a radical split between Gogol's earlier and later life but rather illustrates an evolution in Gogol's religious views that he attributes to external, foreign influences in Italy (53) and to the death of his close friend, Iosif Vielgorsky. However, unlike other biographers, Vodovozov unearths an unusual literary model for Gogol's *Selected Passages* in Silvio Pellico's *Dei doveri degli uomini* (1834, translated into Russian as *Obiazannosti cheloveka*), which lends Gogol's work a revolutionary credential and credibility it had not yet been granted in Russian criticism and refutes discussions of the work as the product of a religious fanatic.[47] Vodovozov asserts that Gogol bowed to lofty patriotism and a sense of mission to create a morally instructive book which would rectify the ills of mankind. Depicting Gogol at this point as a utopian (91), Vodovozov insists that Gogol's miscalculation was due to his isolation from his homeland, which did not allow him to have a clear idea of his country's situation. In detailing Gogol's deteriorating health and final days, Vodovozov paints Count A. P. Tolstoy and the priest Father Matvei as the scapegoats for his rapid decline. The biography ends with an affirmation of Gogol's importance in Russian literature:

> Nothing can erase the great writer Gogol from the memory of the Russian people or diminish the great significance of his works ... His passionate, undying selfless love for his native people, his limitless faith in its bright future gave Gogol the strength for the creation of his great works ... The immortal images created by Gogol more than once appeared in the speeches of the Great Stalin as terrifying weapons crushing the enemies of our people (118).

Appropriately for a wartime biography, the book reinforces the bond between literature and politics, with Gogol as a weapon in its last line. The conclusion further demonstrates the continued importance of nineteenth-century classic writers as galvanizing culture heroes even during wartime.

A NEW GOGOL FOR A NEW ERA: N. L. STEPANOV'S *GOGOL* (1961)

In the post-Stalin era, there was a demand for increasing psychological depth in literature that aligned with the "broader post-Stalinist reconceptualization of the individual personality or *lichnost'* which came part and parcel as a result de-Stalinization."[48] Galina Pomerantseva, series editor from the 1950s to the 1980s, comments that this new emphasis on the "whole person" and the inner life of the hero resulted from the changing demands of both readers and writers.[49] Polly Jones also suggests the new imperative to present the hero's *lichnost'* in a more complex portrait emerged out of a "growing emphasis on individual fulfillment as the central promise of the Soviet project" given that earlier ideological foundations of Soviet values had been destabilized.[50] However, that personality had to be connected to the most critical feature of the *ZhZL* biography at the time: the emphasis on the subject's guiding principle or cause (*delo*) which was inseparable from the hero's feat (*podvig*): "the life as heroic feat (*zhizn'-podvig*) elevates the soul, awakening our desire to imitate the hero, an astonishing person, whom we aspire to comprehend."[51]

In 1959, literary historian and critic N. L. Stepanov took part in a series of editorial discussions at Molodaya gvardiya revolving around the genre of biography and the proper focus of *ZhZL* biographies. *ZhZL* editors demanded three principles: scholarly authenticity (*nauchnaia dostovernost'*), high literary standards (*vysokii literaturnyi uroven'*), and interest (*zanimatel'nost'*). Stepanov doubted that such lofty requirements would be possible to fulfill in a series that published twenty-four books a year. He added that in creating an engaging work with a focus on the hero's inner world and individuality, an author would write "too subjectively," with the biography resembling a novel (Pomerantseva 194). Stepanov cautioned against novelization; he saw possibilities for the use of literary devices in biography but only within certain parameters.[52] Stepanov's involvement in the discussion occurred two years prior to his own work for the series and gives insight into his thinking about the genre of *ZhZL* biographies.

Stepanov wrote his biography of Gogol after years of critical study of his subject. He had experience as a popularizer, having produced a pamphlet on Gogol, *The Great Russian Writer, N. V. Gogol* (*Velikii russkii pisatel' N. V. Gogol*,' 1952) for the centennial of Gogol's death[53] in addition to a weighty (584+ page), scholarly tome, *N. V. Gogol: The Creative Path* (*N. V. Gogol': tvorcheskii put*,' 1955, 2nd edition, 1959). Having already written other versions of Gogol's life, Stepanov allows himself to explore new narrative techniques in telling Gogol's story. The biography's description promises a focus not on the external events of Gogol's life, but on the how the writer's mission (*delo*) was "inseparably merged with the social and educational role of art and became for him a creative feat (*podvig*)."[54] Following in the footsteps of Yuri Tynyanov, his professor and mentor in Leningrad,[55] Stepanov composes something closer to a *biographie romancée*, taking license to create imaginary dialogues between characters, providing evocative internal monologues to portray Gogol's inner turmoil and setting the mood with lyrical descriptions of the Ukrainian countryside, and later, the picturesque streets of Rome. He depicts young "Nikosha" as an impressionable child, raised in a religious household by loving, gentle parents who somehow could never make ends meet. This setting contrasts with the luxury and richness of the estate of his rich relatives, the Troshchinskys, whose worldly goods enchant Gogol upon his first visit (15) and later engender Gogol's love of material goods, reflected in his focus on fashion and clothing in both life and literature. Stepanov ascribes revolutionary inclinations to Gogol even during his childhood. He portrays Gogol as upset by inequality and the harsh treatment of the peasants and inspired by forbidden verses such as Kapnist's "Ode on Slavery" (21–22). Stepanov fleshes out Gogol and the world around him, creating a vivid portrait of the artist within his contemporary cultural and historical milieu. Unlike other *ZhZL* biographies, Stepanov fully depicts Gogol's childhood, adolescence and his friends as a way of prefiguring the important thematics that would arise in Gogol's literary works. He provides autobiographical details that may have sparked Gogol's interest in Cossack themes (stories from his grandmother [25]), the idea of the long-suffering meek soul or "little person" (the life of St. Akaky [11]), and even at that early stage, the influence of Pushkin's poetry, which created a sensation among the Lycée students (62). He also foreshadows Gogol's later solitary life in his commentary after citing a letter from 1827: "This internal alienation and reserve in his own spiritual world later became the source of the writer's loneliness and the tragic decline of his later life" (67).[56] The biographer intrudes in the text more than once, to comment on a particularly important moment or to clarify something that appears to be unclear (for example, regarding Gogol's flight abroad after the failure of "Hans Kuchelgarten") (86). Unlike Voronsky, who perceived Gogol's dual nature from the beginning, Stepanov portrays the gradual evolution of Gogol's personality, highlighting the traits inherent in him from birth that led to his final crisis. Stepanov similarly grapples with how to explain the roots of Gogol's illness and behavior without resorting to psychological motivations or psychiatric disorders. He blames religion and religious fervor as well as an undefined illness. Under the influence of the nefarious Count A. P. Tolstoy, who Stepanov conflates with a black shadow over Gogol's life, Gogol becomes transformed into a preacher "with a fanatical fire in his eyes" (359) during the compilation and writing of *Selected Passages*. Stepanov dramatizes the controversy that the book provoked, depicting the subsequent downward spiral that Gogol experienced. Further emphasizing Gogol's humanity, Stepanov details the terrible treatments and physical tribulations that Gogol underwent in the last days of his life as the doctors tried to save him from death. This humanizing strategy could be seen by some critics as diminishing Gogol's greatness rather than building him up, despite Stepanov's assessment of Gogol's artistic legacy and seminal influence on later generations of writers. His conclusion echoes Chernyshevsky: "He told us who we are, what we lack, what we should strive for, what to disdain and what to love. And his entire life was a passionate battle with ignorance and vulgarity in himself as well as in others, it was animated by one ardent, unchanging goal—the thought of service for the good of his homeland" (427). Ultimately, if Gogol was to be posited as a role model, those aforementioned qualities validated and distinguished him. This summation sounds surprisingly similar to Annenskaya's prerevolutionary biography but has been infused with greater feeling and empathy. Stepanov thus responded to the 1959 editorial call for *ZhZL* biographers to depict their subject's inner life in an absorbing manner.

Though this work features many aspects of a well-written biography, which should have made it accessible and popular among the mass reader, it was not republished after its first edition in 1961. There are likely several reasons for this decision related to Stepanov's stylistic and creative choices: the editorial distaste for novelistic strategies which made the biography appear less trustworthy; a distrust of overly intimate portrayals which could diminish the subject in the public's eyes; the sense that though Stepanov sought to portray Gogol as an organic whole, he neglected a central aspect of Gogol's personality, his spiritual life.[57] Indeed, on a later roundtable on writers' biographies in *ZhZL*, one commentator specifically noted that Stepanov's work was a "rather listless presentation of Gogol's life and work" despite the biographer's erudition.[58] This critic contrasted Stepanov's work with the next iteration of Gogol's biography, by Igor Zolotussky, which he felt far exceeded Stepanov's efforts in its conceptualization of the arc of Gogol's life.

THE SPIRITUAL PATH: IGOR ZOLOTUSSKY'S *GOGOL* (1979–2009)

Igor Zolotussky's version of Gogol's life falls within guidelines set by *ZhZL* editors, yet also spurred a cultural debate of what was an appropriate representation of Gogol as a culture hero for contemporary times.[59] Zolotussky is the quintessential example of the kind of biographer that the editors wanted: an accomplished journalist and literary critic and typical member of the Soviet intelligentsia. Born in Moscow in 1930, he had a comfortable, even charmed early childhood, since his father was a member of the Soviet military intelligence and the family lived abroad for some time due to his father's work. During the purges, this idyll was destroyed when his parents were arrested (his father in 1937 and his mother in 1941) and he was sent to an orphanage in the Far East. Despite his dismal surroundings, he excelled as a student, graduated from Kazan University and first worked as a teacher, journalist, and correspondent. He was recognized as a talented literary critic by Kornei Chukovsky in 1961, which led to his return to Moscow and work as a literary critic at *Literaturnaia gazeta* and the journal *Ural* in the late 1960s.[60] Both of his parents survived their time in the Gulag, so he was well aware of the hypocrisies of the system and the way it terrorized its citizens, whether committed Communists or not. Remembering his past, Zolotussky attributed his own survival to art and indicated his opinion that Russia's literature and spiritual life had been saved through loyalty to tradition.[61] Zolotussky calls Gogol his guide to the past and to how to live a spiritual life, insisting that he felt he needed to defend Gogol in his work:

> Gogol didn't need that defense, however, people around him only ever discussed how he betrayed himself, taking the wrong path and because of it he perished. But I already knew that Gogol's spirit did not perish, but on the contrary rose loftily. I was convinced of it, even before having gone through the archives, reading his papers, his contemporaries' memoirs and most importantly, his works. Specifically, in his stories, plays and *poema* lay the answer to how and by what willpower he accomplished that ascent.[62]

Zolotussky's biography has since been called a "classic in the genre of biography" though originally it generated controversy.[63] From the first paragraph, Zolotussky clearly signals his new approach to Gogol's life by quoting from the life of St. Stephen of Perm. This work would be a spiritual biography, with a contextualization of Gogol's life within the Orthodox milieu in which Gogol grew up and lived: "Orthodox *Malorossiia*, in which Gogol was born, still preserved the remnants of pagan rites. Everything blended together here: both faith in Christ and the travels of the ancient *vertep* (puppet show) where puppets played the heroes of the Bible and the Cossacks, barkeeps and deacons" (7). It is surprising that attention to the spiritual side of Gogol would be at the forefront of a text written in 1979, in the era of stagnation. What may have provided impetus or at least a tacit assent to this perspective was that the main editor of the *ZhZL* series from 1976–1981 was Yury Seleznev, who was concerned with those issues himself.[64]

Zolotussky's central image is of the path or road (*doroga*) in its literal and metaphorical manifestations in Gogol's life and works. The idea serves as the organizing principle in charting Gogol's evolution from a talented but capricious youth to a writer with an artistic and spiritual mission. Zolotussky highlights the journey motif by detailing how Gogol's experience of being on the road inspired him creatively and saved his health more than once; he also focuses on the image through Gogol's oeuvre (especially in relation to *Dead Souls*, which he considers Gogol's masterpiece).

Zolotussky takes issue with the notion of two Gogols, insisting elsewhere that it is impossible "to tear away Gogol the Prophet from Gogol the Poet, such a separation would result in the destruction of the whole, in the splintering of the twofold genius of Gogol."[65] Providing a corrective to earlier assessments of Gogol's *Selected Passages* and a profound analysis of the text, Zolotussky situates the "storm" that took place as the result of its publication as a battle between Belinsky and Gogol, the two central figures of the era's literary arena. He writes of Belinsky's struggle to preserve a Gogol without *Selected Passages*, completely nullifying the work in the Russian literary imagination (383–92). Moreover, Zolotussky illuminates the changing views of Belinsky toward Gogol in the last few months of his life. Zolutussky depicts Belinsky on his deathbed, using his last breath to say that Gogol was a "genius" (*genii*). Zolotussky insists that Belinsky was trying to give "his last word" on Gogol, that Gogol was indeed "a genius" (392). Zolotussky posits *Selected Passages* as foundational, not just for explaining Gogol's genius but also for mapping Russian literature's future path. He asserts that it, and not Gogol's *Overcoat*, is the generative text for Gogol's literary heirs, most importantly Dostoevsky and Tolstoy, usually seen as two artistic polar opposites.[66]

Zolotussky compellingly explains the nature of Gogol's genius and creativity, depicting Gogol's inner life without excessive psychologizing. He insists that Gogol's indefatigable labor over his literary works, endlessly writing while standing at his desk wasn't "stubbornness, nor a new fad taken to an exorbitant end by a genius, but simply the inability to live otherwise, to exist otherwise" (457). By grounding his discussion of Gogol's deep spiritual orientation in the belief system and culture of the time, Zolotussky illustrates the disaster that occurs when Gogol's faith is tested: "He went with fear [to Jerusalem] of seeing his own lack of faith and was persuaded that he saw it. This shook him. Had he been in a different place (as he often was in different places), it would not have had such an impression on him. But that night he returned to his hotel with a clear understanding, he was devastated" (400). Gogol's thorny path was in a way predetermined by the clash between mind and faith: he had to write, but he couldn't; he had to believe, but he couldn't. Since he did not believe in the righteousness of what he wrote, he had to destroy what he wrote or to endlessly rewrite it.

Zolotussky portrays Gogol's final year very differently from other biographers, who all provide an increasingly dark and inexorable decline. In response to his "godsent confessor," Father Matvei, who in earlier accounts admonished Gogol into giving up writing for a spiritual life, Gogol allegedly replies that the law of Christ "can also be fulfilled in a writer's calling" (461). Rather than portray the choice as an either-or situation, as earlier biographers had, Zolotussky demonstrates that Gogol saw the connection between the two, that his mission was to do something for the benefit of mankind, and that once he fulfilled his mission, he would die (as he told his close friend Alexandra Smirnova in November 1851 and as his mother intuitively sensed). Describing both the ups and downs of Gogol's last year, Zolotussky writes a chronicle of the last terrible days of Gogol's life. Carefully analyzing Gogol's last letter, Zolotussky notes how the handwriting changed, from letters written "like small pearls connected on a strand, to suddenly resembling the letters that a child would write as if someone who couldn't see would be reading them" (474). He details the inevitable decline, from the point at which Gogol lost strength, burned his papers and fell ill, and finally died. Yet despite the close reading, it appears that Gogol remains as much a mystery in death as he was in life, at least to those surrounding him. After describing the significance of Gogol and his works to Russia's cultural legacy, Zolotussky ends with a sad tally of Gogol's remaining physical belongings (a few worn items of clothing, a gold watch, a few hundred books); Gogol had only forty-three rubles and thirty-three kopeks in silver to his name (479). The contrast between Gogol's spiritual and cultural legacy and his material goods appears to be a deflation, while also invoking the spiritual example provided by the lives of the saints and bringing us full circle to the first image of the biography, of the birth of St. Stephen of Perm. Praised for his evangelical activities and as the founder of "Permian writing," St. Stephen of Perm is also credited with spurring the rebirth of Russian spiritual and cultural values in the late fourteenth and fifteenth centuries.[67] Thus as St. Stephen enriched the Russian spiritual and cultural tradition, so did Gogol. Attention to Gogol's spiritual dimension allows the biography to remain relevant in the Putin era, when traditional Orthodox Christianity and imperial values dominate the cultural and historical discourse.[68]

Zolotussky elsewhere remarks that no one has yet solved the enigma of Gogol, who, like his 1909 monument in Moscow on Nikitsky Boulevard sculpted by N. Andreev, "seems to call and then beckon, and when you approach, looks away."[69] Voronsky also was also drawn to the riddle of Gogol's monument: "It seems that I've succeeding in discovering Gogol's secret. But all the same, I have the feeling that he will not allow it."[70] Gogol continues to attract biographers if only because there are no easy explanations for his inner motivations, the nature of his creativity and his tragic death. The Gogol biographies illustrate the changing ideas about biography as a genre in ZhZL from the nineteenth to the twenty-first centuries. Though the notion of providing a positive role model never changed, the biographies' points of emphasis did: civic, patriotic, creative, moral, and/or spiritual lessons were to be adduced from Gogol's biography, depending on the ideological concerns of the biographers' times.

NOTES

1. N. V. Gogol', letter to P. Viazemskii, January 1, 1852, in *Polnoe sobranie sochinenii i pisem v semnadtsati tomakh* (Moscow-Kiev: Izdatel'stvo Moskovskoi Patriarkhii, 2009), t. 15:461.

2. S. T. Aksakov, "Neskol'ko slov o biografii Gogolia," *Moskovskie vedemosti* 35 (1852): 360, 361, as cited in Stephen Moeller-Sally, *Gogol's Afterlife: The Evolution of a Classic in Imperial and Soviet Russia* (Evanston, IL: Northwestern University Press, 2002), 57.

3. A. Belyi, "Gogol'," *Vesy* 4 (1909):70.

4. Though beyond the scope of this article, another contrast would be how biographers deal with Gogol's relations with women (or apparent lack of sexual or love relationships). Each *ZhZL* biographer makes at least a passing remark about the fact that Gogol lived as a bachelor, had some strong friendships with women, and that there were even rumors of a his "hidden love" (as per Annenskaia) for Smirnova (called an "affair" in I. Zolotusskii's biography) and a strange, thwarted romance/proposal to Anna Mikhailovna V'elgorskaia. Speculations of an intimate nature are discussed in both A. Voronskii's and Zolotusskii's biographies. Beyond discussing onanism and the possibility that Gogol visited bordellos, none of the *ZhZL* biographers subscribe to the idea that Gogol may have had homosexual leanings. The classic treatment of Gogol's homosexuality in the West remains Simon Karlinsky's *The Sexual Labyrinth of Nikolai Gogol* (Chicago: University of Chicago Press, 1976).

5. See the introduction to A. V. Voronskii's *Gogol'* (Moscow: Molodaia gvardiia, Malaia seriia, vyp. 1, 2009) which details its cloak and dagger publication history. The biography has been recently republished in two separate printings, one outside of the series in 2019 and again as a part of the primary series in March 2020.

6. I do not discuss A. V. Lunacharskii's sketch on Gogol in *Siluety* (Moscow: Molodaia gvardiia, 1965) because it is a brief literary analysis.

7. For contemporary reactions to *Selected Passages*, see Paul Debreczeny, "Nikolay Gogol and His Critics," *Transactions of the American Philosophical Society* 56 (Philadelphia, The American Philosophical Society) Part 3 (1966): 50–63.

8. Cf. Belinsky's "Letter to N.V. Gogol" (1847): "Either you are ill—and you must hasten to take a cure, or. . .I am afraid to put my thoughts into words!" in *Belinsky, Chernyshevsky, and Dobroliubov: Selected Criticism*, ed. Ralph E. Matlaw (Bloomington: Indiana University Press, 1976), 85. Robert A. Maguire discusses several works of psychological criticism, beginning with N. Bazhenov's *Bolezn' i smert' N. Gogolia* (1902), I. E. Mandel'shtam's *O kharaktere Gogolevskogo stilia. Glava iz istorii russkogo literaturnogo iazyka* (1902), D. N. Ovsianiko-Kulikovskii's *Gogol* (1912), and I. D. Ermakov's *Ocherki po analizu tvorchestva Gogolia* (Moscow-Petrograd, 1923). See Robert A. Maguire, *Gogol from the Twentieth Century: Eleven Essays* (Princeton: Princeton University Press, 1974), 21–27.

9. Irina Sirotkina, *Diagnosing Literary Genius: A Cultural History of Psychiatry in Russia, 1880–1930* (Baltimore and London: The Johns Hopkins University Press, 2002) and Maguire, 14–44.

10. I. S. Turgenev's obituary for Gogol in *Moskovskie vedomosti*, cited in N. Vodovozov, *Gogol'* (Moscow: Molodaia gvardiia, 1944), 117.

11. See Moeller-Sally, *Gogol's Afterlife* for a thorough discussion of biography's role in canon formation.

12. Though Vladimir Nabokov does not make the connection between Gogol's long nose and his national identity (indeed he calls Gogol "the oddest Russian in Russia" [12]), he devotes pages to it at the beginning of his idiosyncratic 'biography' *Nikolai Gogol* (Norfolk, CT: New Directions, 1944). In one of many subversions of convention, Nabokov's biography begins with Gogol's death and ends with his birth. He concludes with a conversation he had with his publisher: "let us have a picture of Gogol's nose. Not his face and shoulders, etc. but only his nose. A big solitary sharp nose—neatly outlined in ink like the enlarged figure of some important part of a curious zoological specimen" (154).

13. Edyta M. Bojanowska, *Nikolai Gogol: Between Ukrainian and Russian Nationalism* (Cambridge, MA: Harvard University Press, 2007), 40.

14. Yuliya Ilchuk, *Nikolai Gogol: Performing Hybrid Identity* (Toronto: University of Toronto Press, 2020), citation from 32, 3–41.

15. See Vitaly Chernetsky, *Mapping Postcommunist Cultures: Russia and Ukraine in the Context of Globalization* (Montreal & Kingston: McGill-Queen's University Press, 2007), 314, fn24.

16. See Bojanowska, *Nikolai Gogol,* especially 170–316, which highlights the ambiguities of Gogol's portrait of Russia.

17. Moeller-Sally, 8.

18. Donald Fanger, *The Creation of Nikolai Gogol* (Cambridge: Harvard University Press, 1979), 14–15.

19. See Caryl Emerson's essay in this volume for a discussion of Lotman's juxtaposition of the two opposite biographical examples of Gogol and Lermontov and how they play out in Tolstoy's biography.

20. Certain works of Gogol became a part of the standard literary curriculum in gymnasia as early as 1844. *Dead Souls* became a part of the centralized literary curriculum introduced by the Ministry of Education in 1872. See Alexey Vdovin, "Dmitry Tolstoy's 'Classicism' and the Formation of the Russian Literary Canon in the High School Curriculum," *Ab Imperio* 4 (2017): 108–37.

21. Maguire, 13–16. The first quote is cited from Chernyshevsky's review of *Sochineniia i pis'ma N. V. Gogolia,* ed. P. A. Kulish, 6 vols, St. Petersburg, 1857, in *Sovremennik*, no. 9, 1857, in *PSS*, IV Moscow, 1948, 610. The second quote is Maguire, 13.

22. See H. D. Wiebe, *Kulish iak Hoholeznavets* (Winnipeg, CA: Dept. of Slavic Studies, University of Manitoba and the Ukrainian Free Academy of Arts and Sciences, 1972) for an assertion of the critical importance of Kulish's biographical work in preserving Gogol's literary legacy immediately after his death. See also Y. Ilchuk's discussion of the similarities between Kulish and Gogol and Kulish's role in preserving (and in some cases, censoring) Gogol's legacy, 34–35 and 152–57. Asserting that Kulish's representation greatly influenced the first Gogol biographies, she suggests that Kulish selected what he felt was appropriate, omitting mundane

topics and obscenities, softening or muting criticism of the empire and replacing "Rus'" and "russkii" with "Rossiia" and rossiiskii or velikorossiiskii to "reflect his own idea of bipartite Rus'" (156).

23. Maguire, 14–15.

24. The others were of Dickens (1892), Rabelais (1892), George Sand (1894) and Balzac (1895). Pavlenkov's press later took advantage of the expiration of copyright on Gogol's works (as of Feb. 21, 1902) and in order to popularize his tales among the masses also published an inexpensive "Illustrated Gogol Library" from 1901–1902. See Carol Ueland and Ludmilla A. Trigos, "F. F. Pavlenkov's Literacy Project: Popular Serials and Reading Rooms for the Russian Masses," for a discussion of Pavlenkov's guiding vision for his press.

25. Annenskaia's inclinations can be seen in her literary works focusing on the plight and limited choices of women and girls of the *raznochintsy* and in her translation of Harriet Beecher Stowe's *Uncle Tom's Cabin* (1908). See the entry on A. Annenskaia in *Literaturnaia entsiklopediia* (Moscow: 1929–1939). She later published *N. V. Gogol, ego zhizn' i proizvedeniia* (in the children's journal *Vskhody*, 15 February 1902, no. 4), which begins with Gogol's arrival at school in 1821 and uses novelistic devices to tell his life story. See Moeller-Sally for a discussion of the shift in emphasis from the *ZhZL* biography to the fictionalized version, 109.

26. For more on Annenskaia's children's stories, see Ben Hellman, *Fairy Tales and True Stories: The History of Russian Literature for Children and Young People (1574–2010)* (Leiden: Brill, 2013), 103–6.

27. Ilchuk, 157. Kulish's three foundational works are: *Neskol'ko chert dlia biografii N. V. Gogolia* (St. Petersburg, 1852); *Opyt biografii N.V. Gogolia: so vkliucheniem do soroka ego pisem* (St. Petersburg: Tip. Eduarda Pratsa,1854); and *Zapiski o zhizni Nikolaia Vasil'evicha Gogolia, sostavlennye iz vospominanii ego druzei i znakomykh i iz ego sobstvennykh pisem v dvukh tomakh* (St. Petersburg: Tip. Iuliusa Shtaufa, 1856). Since Annenskaia's biography of Gogol does not include a bibliography, we cannot be certain of her sources, but she most likely accessed Gogol's letters through Kulish's volumes. Her biography predated the publication of V. I. Shenrok's *Materialy dlia biogafii Gogolia,* 4 vols. (Moscow: Tip. A. I. Mamontova), 1892–1897, a valuable source of primary material (though some of it was paraphrased and put into a narrative form), much cited by later biographers of Gogol. She would have had access to the articles Shenrok published on Gogol's student years in historical journals (which later became one section of his *Materialy*), as well as Shenrok's *Ukazatel' k pis'mam Gogolia: zakliuchaiushchei v sebe ob"iasneniia initsialov i drugikh sokrashchenii v izdanii Kulisha s prilozheniem neizdannykh otryvkov iz pisem materi N. V. i ego sobstvennykh* (Moscow: Tip. T. Ris, 1886). Ilchuk has pointed out that Shenrok published a key to Gogol's letters which Kulish first published without the correspondents' names under pressure from certain friends and family members.

28. Maguire calls Shenrok's thematically oriented materials a landmark in Gogol studies; it "prefigured nearly all the directions" that later critics and biographers would follow (16).

29. See Moeller-Sally for a detailed discussion of other prerevolutionary biographers of Gogol, 55–72.

30. Edited by Vladimir Orlov, its first print run was 12,000 copies; it was republished in 1893, 1896, 1902 and 1910. Zolotusskii treated the topic of Tolstoy's changing opinions of the work directly in his article, "Tolstoi chitaet 'Vybrannye mesta iz perepiski druz'iami'," in *Gogol' i obshchestvo liubitelei rossiiskoi slovestnosti*, comp. R. N. Kleimenova (Moscow: Izdatel'stvo Academia, 2005), 211–22.

31. L. N. Tolstoy, letter to N. Strakhov (16 October 1887).

32. At only one point does Annenskaia use the derogatory term "khokhol" to refer to Gogol, when she discusses the class differences of aristocrats such as Zhukovsky and Pushkin in the Petersburg writers' circles in comparison to Gogol (cf. 26 "witty khokhol"). Bojanowska notes that the word "khokhol" to refer to a Ukrainian is not a neutral term but rather a "Russian ethnonym... with strong overtones of 'hick'" (1–2).

33. An example of an event that other biographers treat as evidence of Gogol's hypersensitivity and selfishness is Gogol's unexpected flight abroad to Lübek after the dismal reviews of "Hans Kiukhelgarten." Gogol used money that his mother entrusted to him for the payment of the taxes on the family estate and squandered it all on his trip, sending plaintive letters home, insinuating that he fled Russia because of a disastrous love affair.

34. Annenskaia may have been aware of the first "medical" biography of Gogol's life, *Genio e follia* (1863) by Cesare Lombroso. See Sirotkina, *Diagnosing Literary Genius*, 14–44.

35. Jeffrey Brooks, *When Russia Learned to Read: Literacy and Popular Literature, 1861–1917* (Princeton, NJ: Princeton University Press, 1985), 344. Brooks quotes the 1910 edition of Annenskaia's *Gogol*, 76.

36. After Pavlenkov's untimely death in 1900, his executors republished Annenskaia's Gogol biography three times. For information about other popular biographies on Gogol from the 1890–1909, see Moeller-Sally, 55–72 and 104–14. Starting in 1909, during the centennial celebration of Gogol's birth, depictions of Gogol's life were strongly influenced by the critical approaches of the symbolists.

37. For more on the relationship between Gorky and Voronsky, see Andy McSmith, *Fear and the Muse Kept Watch: The Russian Masters from Akhmatova and Pasternak to Shostakovich and Esenin under Stalin* (New Press, 2015), 87.

38. Voronsky's exact death date remains uncertain. Vladimir Voropaev, "Zabytaia kniga: Ob Aleksandre Voronskom i ego 'Gogole,'" in A. Voronskii, *Gogol* (Moscow: Molodaia gvardiia, 2009), 6.

39. Bojanowska views Gogol's *dvoedushie* in his struggles to reconcile the various aspects of his identity as a Ukrainian writing in Russian and for Russians. See my point about *malorossiistvo* above.

40. Hugh McLean, "Aleksandr Voronsky. *Gogol'. Zhizn' zamechatel'nykh liudei*. Malaia seriia, vypusk 1. Moscow: Molodaia gvardiia, 2009. Bibliography. Illustrations. 448 pp. Cloth," *Slavic and East European Journal* 54, no. 2 (Summer 2010): 358–60.

41. Iurii Mann, "Predislovie," *Novyi mir*, no. 8 (1964): 228–30, cited in Maguire, *Red Virgin Soil*, 444.

42. Evgeny Dobrenko, *The Making of the State Writer: Social and Aesthetic Origins of Soviet Literary Culture,* trans. Jesse M. Savage (Stanford, CA: Stanford University Press, 2001), 280.

43. Moeller-Sally discusses the ideologically acceptable version of Gogol in Vikentii Veresaev's popular book *How Gogol Worked* (1932 and 1934), which came out two years earlier in a series entitled "How the Classics Worked" at Mir publishers. He suggests the series served as a "training manual" for emerging Soviet writers. The volume on Gogol described Gogol's writing process, emphasizing that Gogol's unceasing labor (*trud*) was the path to artistic genius (cf. 146–49). Voronsky did not include *How Gogol Worked* in his bibliography but cited Veresaev's *Gogol in Life* (1933) as a key source.

44. A. Vershinskii, "K voprosu ob izuchenii biografii zamechatel'nykh liudei," *Istoricheskii zhurnal* 10 (1943):105.

45. N. V. Vodovozov (1902–1977) was a professor of Russian Literature with a specialization in Old Russian Literature. Prior to his Gogol biography, he had written biographies of Malthus (Berlin: Grzhebin Publishers, 1922) and Chernyshevsky (Detgiz, 1939). For Molodaia gvardiia, he also wrote biographies of Mikloukho-Maclay (1938) and Belinsky (1944) in the *Velikie Russkie Liudi* series.

46. According to *Literatura i iskusstvo* (Feb. 23, 1944), one 'typical' soldier read Gogol's *Taras Bul'ba* three times. Cited in Maurice Friedberg, *Russian Classics in Soviet Jackets* (New York: Columbia University Press, 1962), 157.

47. Though Pellico was embroiled in carbonarism earlier in his life, by the time he wrote this pamphlet he concentrated on religious themes. The work addressed young people, using "the language of moral duty, self-control and family virtues." See Arianna Arisi Rota and Roberto Balzani, "Discovering Politics: Action and Recollection in the First Mazzinian Generation," in Silvana Patriarca and Lucy Riall, *The Risorgimento Revisited: Nationalism and Culture in 19th Century Italy* (Palgrave Macmillan, 2012), 79.

48. Polly Jones, *Revolution Rekindled,* 15.

49. Pomerantseva, 187–95.

50. Jones, 15.

51. Pomerantseva, 199.

52. Pomerantseva, 193–95.

53. It was written for the All-Russian Society for the Dissemination of Political and Scholarly Knowledge. Stepanov also contributed to other centennial publications, including *Gogol i teatr* (1952).

54. N. L. Stepanov, *Gogol'* (Moscow: Molodaia gvardiia, 1961), frontispiece. All further references will be included in the text.

55. Stepanov completed his studies at Leningrad State University and the State Institute of the History of the Arts (*Gosudarstvennyi institute istorii iskusstv,* or *GIII*) in 1925, both institutions where Tynianov lectured during those years. For information about their relationship, see Stepanov's memoirs in *Iurii Tynianov* (Moscow: Molodaia gvardiia, 1966).

56. The quote reads: "Isolating myself from everyone, not finding a single person with whom I may share my long-considered meditations, to whom I can reconcile my

thoughts, I am orphaned and have become alien in empty Nezhin. I am a foreigner, wandering in a foreign land to seek that which one finds only in one's homeland, and the secrets of the heart, bursting forth in the open, in greedy revelations, sadly are left in its depths where there is such deadly silence." Though other biographers cite the letter, they do not interpolate their comments as narrators.

57. Pomerantseva retroactively provides this assessment, though it is uncertain that the topic of Gogol's spirituality would have found willing ears in the early 1960s (cf. 208).

58. N. Skatov, "Dvizhenie vpered," *Voprosy literatury* 9 (1980):199.

59. Zolotusskii's biography was originally published in 1979, then expanded and republished in a second edition in 1984 which went through 3 other editions (1998, 2005, 2007). In 2009 it was released in an uncensored, restored form. I have confirmed that the passages I cite are the same in both 1979 and 2009 versions.

60. Interview with I. Zolotusskii, Radio Kul'tura, http://old.cultradio.ru/doc.html?id=28678&cid=46. Last accessed 1/16/2020 and I. Zolotusskii, *Nas bylo troe. Roman-dokument* (St. Petersburg: Fond "200-let Nikolaiu Gogoliu," 2011), available online at: https://zvezdaspb.ru/index.php?nput=1402&page=8.

61. See I. Zolotusskii, *Ispoved' Zoila* (Moscow: Sovetskaia Rossiia, 1989), 3.

62. I. Zolotusskii, *Nas bylo troe*, 155.

63. I. Zolotusskii, *Gogol'* (Moscow: Molodaia gvardiia, 2009), tirazh page. All further references will be included in the text. See below for a discussion of critical views expressed in the biography roundtable published in *Voprosy literatury* no. 9 (1980):179–251.

64. See Alexander Spektor's article in this volume and Robert Belknap and Carol Apollonio, "Dostoevsky in the Lives of Remarkable People," *Slavic and East European Journal* 60, no. 2 (2016): 241–51: Seleznev's biography was "more concerned with nationalism and religion" (245).

65. Zolotusskii, *Ispoved' Zoila*, 193.

66. For a discussion of Gogol's influence on Tolstoy's post-conversion writing, see Irina Reyfman, "Tolstoy and Gogol: Notes of a Madman," in I. Reyfman, *Rank and Style: Russians in State Service, Life and Literature, Selected Essays* (Boston: Academic Studies Press, 2012), 200–11. Reyfman posits that Tolstoy was "following in [Gogol's] footsteps" by publicly declaring that he found his true faith (207).

67. Serge A. Zenkovsky, *Medieval Russia's Epics, Chronicles and Tales* (New York: Dutton, 1974), 259.

68. The biography has been republished three times since 2000: 2005, 2007, 2009.

69. Zolotusskii, *Ispoved' Zoila*, 264.

70. Voronskii, 5.

Chapter 4

Remarkable Tolstoy, from the Age of the Tsars to the Putin Era

Caryl Emerson

In the past century-and-a-quarter, five biographies of Leo Tolstoy (1828–1910) have appeared under the *ZhZL* imprint: in 1894, 1944, 1963, 2006, and 2016. They are very different books. The founding editor of the series, Florenty Pavlenkov, had imposed no ideological or aesthetic norms on his authors. He asked only that their volumes be compact, lucid, accessible to nonspecialists, and, in the loosely progressive nineteenth-century sense, serve the cause of enlightenment.[1] Originally the series was to emphasize popular technology and science. Expanding into the cultural sphere, Pavlenkov preferred the lives of "forbidden authors" whose ideals and works were considered "too dangerous for distribution to the mass reader" (Trigos and Ueland 52). By this standard Leo Tolstoy, rebel and dissident, could only be high priority—even had he not been the world's most famous living writer. But the life of a *literary* person poses a special challenge. Writers come well-armed to do battle with whatever wordsmith is hired to track them. Since biographers of writers work with the same creative material as do the subjects of their research (that is, words), they know from the inside out that their human subjects, dead or alive, command the tools to fight back—the way a dancer, watercolorist, musician, or astronomer might not. Masters of their trade, writers (and especially novelists) can blur and manipulate myths, plant misleading documents, strew the biographer's path with confounding counterwords. The remarkable lives of other eminent subjects—role models in public service or the natural sciences featured in other *ZhZL* volumes—arguably cause less anxiety to their biographers. But writing about writers is always a risky enterprise. This risk reaches unprecedented intensity with Leo Tolstoy.

The paradox here is itself thoroughly Tolstoyan. Even before the task begins, too much already exists in words—and the word is too compromised. In the spirit of John Stuart Mill on enlightened publishing, Pavlenkov's series was intended to educate through the exemplary life.[2] That life could be benevolent or horrific, isolated or socially embedded, but it was related through its deeds. Pride of place was given to the subject's actions and interactions in historical context rather than to later assessments or shifting critical interpretations, whether of masterworks or master ideas. "The images of Pushkin or Socrates or Kierkegaard act on people independent of whether or not these people have read their texts," wrote Nikolai Boldyrev, in his editor's preface to a 1994 reprint of the *ZhZL* biography of Ivan the Terrible.[3] Books in the series were to recuperate, if at all possible, the texture of a lived life.

Noteworthy lives are not always rich in interesting deeds, however, and Tolstoy's long life is remarkable for its paucity of external adventures or cataclysmic events. Few crises were imposed on it from the outside: by fate, by his own body, by the whims of the tsarist state. Nothing in Tolstoy's privileged realm compares with Dostoevsky's litany of deprivations—poverty, traumatic arrest, hard labor, Siberian exile, grand mal epilepsy. On the contrary, Tolstoy always had too much of every good thing: noble rank, fame, financial resources, children, stamina, health, emotional energy. During the second and increasingly controversial half of his life, the way Tolstoy created an "event" for himself was to scrutinize the moral implications of an appetite or a habit and then to take the pleasurable part away—reject it, publicly condemn it, urge the rest of us not to do it. To reject what others coveted was almost a reflex for Tolstoy, from his earliest years. In his own personal behavior, true, Tolstoy frequently failed to honor his denunciations, which triggered further confessions and condemnations. What was absent as a lived event was thus present as an unstoppable flow of words, increasingly judgmental as he grew older. Tolstoy generated more words about himself and his now-crooked, now-cleansed "path of life" than any single outside third person could ever possibly generate about him. And this relative lack of outer adventure, combined with an abundance of inner confessional narratives, was in some tension with the model of an act-based, edificatory life. Tolstoy was by temperament a novelist, not a poet or scientific inventor. His genius resides less in the peak moment, the breakthrough discovery or lapidary lyrical insight, than it does in sheer staying power: in the creation and chronicling of whole persons, whose lengthy lives-in-process embody his own evolving, unresolved quests. But because he was a *confessional* novelist who sought absolute sincerity every time he set pen to paper, he routinely condemned his own writings. One earnest word repeatedly undid another previously uttered earnest word. Can a medium as slippery as this, which can be infinitely done and undone, even qualify as a moral act? Tolstoy struggled over this paradoxical question for as long as he lived and wrote.

THE *ZhZL* LIVES OF TOLSTOY

Each of the five *ZhZL* Lives of Tolstoy served the needs of a different time while resolving the Tolstoyan paradox in its own way. The aim of the present essay is to twofold: to place these Remarkable Tolstoys in some theoretical context, and then to sample Tolstoy's midlife conversion or crisis (*perelom, perevorot*: his turning point) in the first, and then the last two, biographies, tsarist-era (1894) and Putin-era (2006, 2016). The 1894 volume, *L. N. Tolstoy. His Life and Literary Activity*, was the work of a professional biographer, Evgeny Solovyov.[4] A member of Russia's secular intelligentsia at the far end of a century of triumphant positivism, Solovyov was not much interested in Tolstoy's search for God. But on that issue as on many others, Solovyov tracked a contentious, highly publicized moving target. He sought a perspective that could do justice to Tolstoy's spiritual quest and his championship of justice for the people, while not alienating an increasingly sophisticated fin-de-siècle readership more concerned with private aesthetics than with social issues. The final two biographies, 2006 and 2016, display some of the same threshold tensions. In the twenty-first century as in the nineteenth, mainstream older readers had been raised on civic ideals and materialist notions of progress. As that Soviet-era promise proved increasingly hollow, however, and as post-communist thought confronted an ideological void, curiosity revived (and research too) about more transcendent realms. The massive 2006 *Lev Tolstoi* was hailed as "a new Tolstoy for a new Russia."[5] It was the collaborative effort of two respected late-Soviet-era comparativists, Alexei Zverev (1939–2003) and Vladimir Tunimanov (1937–2006), survivors into the post-atheistic academy and heir to a vast Tolstoy industry. These two experienced scholars had no page limit and their pick of public and private documents to mold the writer they needed. This turned out to be a Tolstoy devoted to a life of the spirit. To an extent that would have perplexed their subject, this spiritual quest was portrayed as compatible with the institution of the Russian Orthodox Church.

In 2016, a quarter-century out of communism, the prizewinning scholar and literary journalist Pavel Basinsky published his *Lev Tolstoi. Svobodnyi chelovek* (Leo Tolstoy. A Free Human Being). A year later it was reprinted under the *ZhZL* imprint.[6] At one-third the bulk of Zverev-Tunimanov, Basinsky's book revived the pre-Soviet criteria for the series: reader-friendly and chatty, footnoteless, exemplary rather than encyclopedic. Our focus on the first and last two Lives of Tolstoy, which brackets out the USSR, highlights yet another parameter: Pavlenkov's original concept for *ZhZL* and how it changed under his successor, Maxim Gorky, who revived the series in 1933. The revival was in fact a reconstitution of the series on a new foundation.⁷ Boldyrev, in his 1994 preface cited above, notes that under Gorky's tutelage, despite the "indubitable success of the Soviet *ZhZL* among its readers, internally [the series] lost a great deal: first, because it was fitted to the ideologically uniform procrustean bed of a Socialist Realist template, and second, because it tended toward gigantomania, so that soon nothing at all remained of the elegant laconicism of Pavlenkov's life-stories" (6–7). The case of Tolstoy is exemplary of this oscillation. At a trim 180 pages, Solovyov's 1894 biography resembled a novel by Turgenev. This mold was broken by Viktor Shklovsky's 860-page biography for the revived series in 1963. That remained the model for the first post-Soviet volume, which weighed in at 850 pages of tight type—longer than *Anna Karenina*. In 2016, as I suggest at the end of this essay, Basinsky will reconceive his task for the series by applying another genre altogether, neither a conversation with the reader nor a distanced and detailed epic chronicle. This most recent *ZhZL* Life does not imitate the "gigantomania" of Tolstoy as novelist but honors a different, more intimate side of Tolstoy's genius: his perfect sense of the speaking voice inside a miniaturized dramatic scene.

Length is one obvious quantitative difference between these *ZhZL* lives. Qualitatively, too, the five texts differ in the sorts of dialogue they facilitate between biographer and subject. In 1894, Solovyov could—and did—address Tolstoy as a contemporary, as one public-spirited mortal man to another, both alive and each capable of changing his mind. Solovyov is distraught, for example, at the uncompromising corollary that Tolstoy attaches to his doctrine of nonviolence: that we must "resist not evil"—period, with no qualifiers. After summarizing Tolstoy's position, Solovyov, in a first-person confession stretching over a half dozen pages, respectfully lays out his opposing conviction. Life's innumerable negatives, he argues, can be changed to positives *only* through our willingness to resist evil (with or without violence)—and he calls on Count Tolstoy to respond (130).⁸ But the immortal dead must be handled in another way. By the twenty-first century, Tolstoy's biographers are stage-managing a legacy. Dialogue comes about not by exhorting a living personality (who is, of course, always free not to respond), but rather by featuring an ignored document or defamiliarizing our fixed perception of it. All five biographies make copious use of the written record. But with Solovyov in 1894 we sense an unresolved, often irritated voice under every text. In 2006 the agenda and intonation are more scholarly, the stash of documents bottomless and uncensored. But the edifice is closed, and none of the participants can answer back. In 2016, a dialogue with the living is again opened up—heartbreakingly, as in a Chekhov play—so that responsive persons again exist on both sides of the biographical record. But they exist on different planes, as actors and audiences do, and thus revise the reader's sense of what an interlocutor might be.

A brief note on the two volumes in between. In the exhausted year 1944, a life of Tolstoy by the Soviet medievalist, textologist, and Tolstoy specialist Nikolai Gudzy was published under the rubric *Great Russian People* (*Velikie russkie liudi*), later subsumed under the *ZhZL* imprint as #130, New Series.[9] At eighty pages and a print run of 25,000, it was a cameo-sized Tolstoy for the trenches. Its purpose was to reassure Russian readers that the author of *War and Peace*, had he still been alive in 1941, would surely have modified his categorical pan-pacifism in the face of this heroic defensive war against the new barbarians of Europe. Gudzy's booklet opens on Tolstoy's resistance to all bodily constraint as a swaddled infant—his first experience of coercion—and closes on the desecration of Yasnaya Polyana in late fall, 1941, "criminal actions by the human scum of Hitler's gang" (79). (Tolstoy's estate was occupied for forty-seven days and the manor house set on fire by retreating Nazi troops when the Soviet counteroffensive began.) In between these two acts of violence the conventional life-chronicle unfolds, with emphasis on Tolstoy's "complicated" relation to war (21)—thrilling in the courage it calls forth and horrific in its carnage. The turning point of the early 1880s began as a rejection of "churchly faith" but quickly spread to an overall renunciation of "privileged classes in all civilized countries" (51). Gudzy's frail pamphlet, which eases out of Tolstoy a sort of patriotic communism, is laconic and condensed even by Pavlenkov's standards. Its message, although edifying, is thoroughly ideological.

The third *ZhZL* biography, Viktor Shklovsky's huge volume (864 pages) published in 1963 as #350 [New Series], bears the inimitable marks of that distinguished Soviet writer's critical priorities and provocative, aphoristic literary style.[10] If the demand for a one-dimensional wartime Tolstoy poses risks to the complex lived life, then a biography penned by an author with a distinctive voice and creative gifts of his own can also compromise the autonomy, and even the integrity, of its subject. One need only recall the scandal of Mikhail Bulgakov's biography of Molière, commissioned and then rejected by the *ZhZL* series in 1933, which opened on an invocation to the midwife who safely delivered the sickly infant in 1622; from that point on, the French playwright unabashedly sees, creates, and suffers through Bulgakov's eyes.[11] Shklovsky is more conventional. But he too is deeply concerned with how, and what, his subject sees. Tolstoy and his fictions figure prominently in Shklovsky's own theoretical writings on literature, which feature a Tolstoy preoccupied with clarity, objectification, and the perfectly palpable thing (or image of a thing) that can be manipulated or estranged. Appropriately,

Shklovsky's *Lev Tolstoy* begins with an eccentric detail about its hero's birth, in a chapter titled "About the green divan, which was later reupholstered in black oilcloth." The obligatory chapter devoted to Lenin's 1908 treatise on Tolstoy as "Mirror of the Russian Revolution" is more than politically correct boilerplate; Tolstoy interests Shklovsky precisely as a mimetic realist of genius. Although the spiritual crisis cannot be ignored, it is not pathologized. "A Few Words about Tolstoy and Religion," occurring midway through the book (1963, 506–13 / 1978, 466–72) admits that religious rapture was natural to Tolstoy—but the supernatural was not. True, Tolstoy used words like religion and god, but these words were synonymous with truth, beauty, and his own perception or "sense of the world" (511 / 470). For Tolstoy as for Konstantin Levin, God was best understood as part of the natural landscape, a force bonding the thinking person to the Russian peasant.

Throughout Shklovsky's erudite yet untormented biography we sense the familiar diction, intonation, and focus on props or estranged details associated with this founding formalist critic, informing and at times deforming the dark metaphysical contours of its eminent subject. Shklovsky as biographer raises important questions. How can another's life be protected from an overbearing narrator? It is not enough to cite more of Tolstoy on himself; there is too much material, and it is too cunningly self-condemnatory and solipsistic. The responsible biographer must constantly adjudicate. Here two Russian students of biography come to our aid.

TWO USEFUL FRAMEWORKS
(TOMASHEVSKY AND LOTMAN)

In his 1923 essay "Literature and Biography," Boris Tomashevsky takes up the issue of readerly curiosity about a writer's person. He notes that in some eras "the personality of the artist was of no interest at all to the audience"—and in other eras, readers clamor to see the author's face and actions, willing even to fabricate the missing details.[12] Often, if the personality in question is charismatic and internally contradictory, only the time and space of a lived life can stitch together the subject's many conflicting sides into a single coherent image. Prudently, Tomashevsky aligns Tolstoy not with the Realist writers of the nineteenth century but with those two eighteenth-century auto-mythographers, Rousseau and Voltaire. "The biographies of such authors require a Ferney or a Jasnaja Poljana," he writes, "they require pilgrimages by admirers and condemnations from Sorbonnes or Holy Synods" (49). What Tomashevsky does not address in this mythic genesis, however, and what confronts all biographers of Tolstoy, is that urgent, specifically

Tolstoyan tension between the particular and the universal. Tolstoy obsessed over his own particular life. He compulsively documented his personal experience as a model (positive in its ideals, negative in its acts) for all people everywhere to acknowledge in themselves, to learn from, and if possible to transcend. Naturally Tolstoy feared that the authority of this model would be diminished if it were reduced to the contingent and merely personal.

The task of the Tolstoy biographer is even more complex, however—or more quixotic. By 1894, the time of the first *ZhZL* Life of Tolstoy, this titanic writer was on the brink of becoming the modern world's first multimedia celebrity.[13] In the interests of spreading his word, he had long been complicit in his own mythologization. But after years of sitting for portraits and putting up with being caricatured, Tolstoy was now proclaiming that for the good of the world's moral growth, his biography—together with the most beloved of his ficticiously outsourced quasi-autobiographical alter egos—should be forgotten altogether. Only his distilled Principles of Life deserved to be remembered.

The desire is not outrageous; most writers wish to leave a mark on their society. But when the subject of a biography constantly disputes this mark while challenging everything a society lives by, we depart biography for the larger realm of sociology, or perhaps even social pathology. One guide to this abrasive odyssey is an essay by Yury Lotman from 1986, "Literary biography in its historical-cultural context (on the typological correlation of a text with the personality of the author)."[14] Lotman builds on Tomashevsky's formalist essay from 1923 while moving it into the more technical language of cultural semiotics. There are indeed eras with biographies and eras without them. But in every historical era, Lotman argues, whatever its hierarchy of texts, a subject must *earn the right* to biography. By this Lotman means the right of that subject to enter a community's collective memory (however morally constituted and through whichever social class) by emerging from anonymity, departing from societal norms, becoming freshly audible and visible, all of which establishes its life story as an event (805–6). In Lotman's view, lived experience becomes a "biographical event" only when the subject freely crosses a perceptual boundary, that is, chooses a behavior that obliges others—the background audience—to sit up and take notice.

Lotman then proceeds to build a grammar. In the 1830–1840s (Tolstoy was still a teenager), the status of biography in Russia, like the status of prose itself, was at a crossroads. Salon culture was being replaced by rising literacy and the book market. As in the Romantic era, the creativity of artists and poets was measured against a model biography—but it was no longer acceptable to live like Eugene Onegin, consciously choosing and discarding masks between St. Petersburg ball and manor house. The right to biography was now granted to those with a coherent outer story and a lofty inner mission (812).

Nikolai Gogol set the new norm for this transitional era: by text and deed, the writer must prove his right to speak on behalf of a higher Truth. No longer could the artist create something, stand back, and take pride in it as an autonomous work (over there is my statue, my painting, my poem, separate from myself). Creativity was fused with identity and presumed self-cultivation (*samovospitanie*, 814).

But then Lotman introduces a crucial complication. This Gogolian agony and messianic ambition coexisted with another and earlier Romantic-era model, that of Mikhail Lermontov, a writer who scrutinized the world objectively, cynically, clinically, "experimentally," perceiving human behavior not as a source of guilt but as a source of information (815). We might paraphrase Lotman's point by saying that Lermontov looked back to an eighteenth-century classicism and to Pushkin's sense of honor, privacy, and discretion; Gogol, in turn, looked forward to a more personally fraught expressionism—intimate, voyeuristic, fascinated by the depths of sin and its shameful public exposure. In Russian culture, both models have facilitated the image of the writer as savior or prophet. Lotman ends his essay on the cliff-hanging comment that "all this complex cultural work culminates in the creation of two great biographies: that of Tolstoy and Dostoevsky, biographies which, if we did not have them, all understanding of their creative work would be unthinkable—as would be nineteenth-century culture more generally" (816). Not only do these two titans achieve the "right to biography" that then provides a key to unlock their works, but their personal life experience, so it would appear, supplies the infrastructure for the cultural life of an entire century.

Let us take Lotman's hypothesis one step further, beyond his cutoff point. The two alternatives of his literary spectrum for the 1840s, an ardently repentant Gogol and a cold clinical Lermontov, are fused in Tolstoy and doing battle there. These two poles are not easily reconciled. When the Gogolian principle is dominant (the Great Writer obliged to create a moral exemplar), then whatever the writer really dies of, at one level he dies of guilt. A writer motivated like Gogol is martyred at that point where lived biography and edifying ideal fail to coincide. But to coincide with one's ego-ideal is not the only option, and arguably not the most desirable. When the biographical dominant is modeled on Lermontov and his hero Pechorin rather than on Gogol, the writer can pursue universal Reason—objective and skeptical—with neoclassical austerity, vaulting over the self-deprecating personal confession to arrive at naturalism, disinterested and aloof. Life need not be a prayer when it can be a laboratory.

In this model, reminiscent of Flaubert or Zola, the writer, like the objective scientist or the pragmatic statesman, is a professional who produces goods. If the good is solidly constructed, according to its own rules, and if it succeeds with its users, the lived life that produced the good is as irrelevant to it as are a mathematician's personal habits to the robustness of his theorems. A subject is judged by its wares. The vices of the self are no threat because the task of a writer is to observe and relate, not to suffer, confess, or transform. A "Life of a Remarkable Writer" structured with this priority would resemble *ZhZL* volume #22 on James Watt, #37 on Johannes Kepler, or #61 on Michael Faraday—scientists who preceded Evgeny Solovyov's volume on Tolstoy. "Here's the life, and there's the experiment." Each is equally real, but they are outside each other and evaluated separately.

But what is the situation with Tolstoy? Surely we see where this argument is going. Even if we lay aside the priceless wares (the corpus of his literary masterpieces) and attend solely to the person, Tolstoy is "Gogolian"—Romantic in his feelings of guilt and his high degree of personal answerability—yet at the same time "Lermontovian," committed to the efficacy of reason and rational judgment. The guilty feelings are real, but the sinner is somehow not so psychically wounded by them that the science of objective observation ceases to function. Guilt can be documented with the confidence of a detached and universalizing mind. Thus does Tolstoy mercilessly assault his own sentimentalized, hypersensitized constantly shifting historical self with what he insists are timeless truths deduced from reasonable consciousness (*razumnoe soznanie, razumenie*).

In his 1894 biography, Solovyov assesses the contemporary debates over Tolstoy along precisely this stress line—but he privileges the sensitized emotional self as the more precious part of the contradiction. "It used to be said that Count Tolstoy is a great artist and a poor thinker," he writes. "This is completely unfair. As a thinker, Count Tolstoy is a potent quantity to be reckoned with. He is a brilliant dialectician; his thought is always original and his immense erudition profound beyond any doubt. His contradictions are not those of a person who thinks poorly, but *the contradictions of a living human heart governed by an anguished skeptical mind*" (141, emphasis in original). Solovyov correctly assessed the battlefield. And his quote suggests that Lotman's dual model applies not only to creative subjects but also to their biographers, who will tend to favor one pole over the other.

THE 1894 TOLSTOY: HURTING, INFURIATING, ACCESSIBLE

Evgeny Solovyov (1863–1905) was a St. Petersburg journalist, playwright, and professional writer of lives—and he was prolific. By the time his Tolstoy appeared in 1894 (*ZhZL* #158), he was answering for ten biographies in the series, including Hegel and Dostoevsky (both published in 1891), Osip Senkovsky in 1892, and in 1893 Ivan the Terrible, Oliver Cromwell, and

Dmitry Pisarev. In addition to Tolstoy, the *ZhZL* catalog for 1894 lists biographies by Solovyov of Karamzin, John Milton, the Rothschild Brothers, and Turgenev—with biographies of Buckle and the just-deceased Ivan Goncharov in preparation.[15] In tackling the Bard of Yasnaya Polyana, the sole living subject among his series commissions, Solovyov adopted the sentimentalizing Gogolian route. Tolstoy is caught in a hall of mirrors, in the grip of self-generated guilt and contradiction, a seeker stalled en route to self-perfection. This task brought Solovyov more than the routine biographer's anxiety. In his 2006 *ZhZL* biography of Pavlenkov, Vladimir Desyaterik provides a glimpse into the fraught prehistory of this initial *L. N. Tolstoy*.

Solovyov worried about the book. The whims of the censor, the vagaries of the reading public (which ridiculed as well as revered Tolstoy), and the reaction of the capricious subject himself were all potential headaches. Solovyov wrote to Pavlenkov in December 1894 that his Buckle was stalled at the censor, and "as regards Tolstoy, personally I wager that I'll have to surrender (*stavliu na kapituliatsiiu*)"[16] When in due course the Tolstoy biography was approved and published albeit with excisions of materials related to Tolstoy's religious views, Solovyov braced himself—but, it appeared, all for naught. "Tolstoy has come out," he wrote Pavlenkov, and "to my surprise, the little book was not ripped to shreds. Now I sit and await a 'furor'—if only a little one. After all, it must attract some attention, otherwise it's simply insulting." His next letter to Pavlenkov betrayed some authorial bitterness. "Tolstoy was published in a print run of 2520 copies, but there's not been the slightest 'furor' . . . I personally sent a copy to Lev Nikolaevich, to Soldatov, to Mikhailovsky—but they're all silent, not a word . . . nothing at all. And even among my friends, when you say 'Tolstoy has come out,' the answer is: 'Oh, really? That's interesting!' To hell with it. I no longer know what to hope for, or what to expect."[17]

By 1894 the Russian reading public was hypersaturated with images, and caricatures, of the Bard of Yasnaya Polyana. Tolstoy himself had long been indifferent to the commercial publishing market and was trying to escape his biography, not to reengrave it. In no way could Solovyov be neutral in this ongoing struggle of Tolstoy against his own accreting and discarded selves. As biographer he attempted to tie his narrative tightly to that contradictory human image, honoring its confessional twists and turns. Direct quotes from the master are massive, and fictive characters' utterances are routinely endowed with the authority of Tolstoy's own voice.[18] Solovyov is not embarrassed by the cries of his subject's beating heart, however illogical and inconsistent. On the contrary: he faults the post-1880 Tolstoy for trusting overmuch in the power of reason in human life, "nine-tenths of which is run by the "utterly unconscious processes" of reflex and instinct (133). Fidelity to moral intuition and habit had been a cornerstone of *War and Peace* and the key to Levin's resurrection at the end of *Anna Karenina*, and Tolstoy was wrong to abandon it. As regards the existence of God, Solovyov demurs that proofs for or against are outside his professional competence. But he does highlight Tolstoy's reverence for the paradoxical ethics of the man Jesus. And Solovyov attributes Tolstoy's most crippling conviction—an unqualified nonresistance to evil—to a direct, and faulty, literal reading of Christian love (132).

Stylistic prototypes for Solovyov come from two masters of European Sentimentalism, Jean-Jacques Rousseau and Nikolai Karamzin. After the manner of Karamzin, personal asides to the reader and ecstatic apostrophes are frequent. But that eighteenth-century literary tradition, so compatible with Tolstoy because focused on the impulses of the private subject, is combined (at times incongruously) with the biographer's own populist, progressive intelligentsia worldview. Tolstoy's inner spiritual search and growing moral crisis is identified with the public-spirited conscience of Russia's repentant gentry. Such Radishchev-style civic Sentimentalism ultimately proves inadequate to the complexity of his subject. Repeatedly, Solovyov comments on the sluggish growth of Tolstoy's "love for the common people": it was only in the Caucasus, among soldiers and Cossacks, that "Tolstoy began to love the simple people (*prostoi narod*)—and with his whole heart, not only with his reason" (47). Furthermore, it was easier to love the *narod* in the Caucasus than at Yasnaya Polyana, where serfdom was an economically necessary fact of life. Solovyov is troubled by Tolstoy's wild and wasteful youth—but he pardons it, because "Belinsky had died, and there was no guide to take his place" (64). (An astonishing remark, given that the aristocratic Tolstoy, in all phases of his life, despised crude, common-born polemicists of Belinsky's sort and would never have learned at their feet.) It wasn't until Sevastopol, we read, that Tolstoy had a chance to glimpse the *narodnaya dusha* (people's soul) inherent in the pre-Reform soldier. And even with this love for the people at last securely in place, the spiritual crisis unfolded in all its extremist particulars because of "Count Tolstoy's pessimism and Russophilism" (109). Especially to blame was Tolstoy's insistence (beginning with *War and Peace*) that the heroism of the Russian people lay in their simplicity, modesty, submissiveness to fate, and "the knowledge that they knew nothing." In Solovyov's view, such fatalism, resignation, and glorification of the non-intellectual path could serve neither progress nor human dignity. These traits were simply a sign of the people's "suppression of personality" (*podavlennost' lichnosti*, 115).

By the 1890s, however, both Karamzin's sentimental apostrophes to the reader and the gentry guilt of the Emancipation decade sounded badly out of date. To appeal to a more sober critical audience, and moreover one with a rising intellectual interest in transcendental worlds, Solovyov sums up Tolstoyan truth in the post-*Confession* years in five interlocking but incompatible precepts (Chapter 13, "Tolstoy's teaching," 124–43). These precepts are: that the fundamental idea of life is religious; that this religious idea is practical; that the teaching of the world contradicts the teaching of Christ; that we must not resist evil; and that we must help our neighbor and love him. But how, asks Solovyov, can this internally contradictory doctrine possibly provide practical guidelines for action? Tolstoy seems to suggest that to live by reason is easy, pleasant, without conflict, and yet everywhere in his rules for life the analyzing mind is set against the anguished heart. Once upon a time the overwhelming force in human lives was *necessity*. That was tragic, but it was tolerated because understood as objectively hard-edged and unavoidable. Now, Tolstoy's analytic mind had substituted for this grim and cold law of necessity something that he called love—an emotional quality supposedly warm, subjective, and voluntarily embraced. But this love feels as hard-edged and irrational as necessity, because it is so often blind and non-discriminating (139).

Solovyov distrusts the moral foundation of this new law and would expose its contradictions. For Tolstoy, a man governed sentimentally, the highest priority is to be happy. For him this means: free of guilt, cleansed of sin, at peace with oneself. But since the teachings of the world cannot guarantee us happiness, Tolstoy puts forward in its place the teaching of Christ—ignoring the world's claims for justice and its outcries against evil (129). Solovyov's direct appeals to the reader address Count Tolstoy too, in their shared zone. "Everyone will remember, I think, how Tolstoy, having ended up in the Rzhanov House, that den of terrifying poverty, of hopeless poverty" [134]. In 1894, most of Solovyov's readers would have remembered such well-publicized events as Tolstoy in the Rzhanov Hospice for the Destitute, helping with the 1882 Moscow census and experiencing firsthand how an urban slum breeds beggars and cynics. Solovyov the civic journalist creates a narrative zone where life, text, and readership are still in process.

The impossibility of reconciling mind and heart provides Solovyov with his ending device, which had to be open-ended. Dissatisfaction with oneself and tension with the world becomes itself a positive biographical constant. "Before us is the grandiose picture of eternal restless seeking," he writes (142). Count Tolstoy will never settle on any ready answer for anything, because that would be to live "by formula." And "a formula is salvation . . . a formula keeps us warm, we're in a fur coat or by the stove, it's cheerful, a glass of wine is at hand, it's all easy and pleasant, as if in the company of friends" (142). Since Tolstoy rejects all those familiar intoxicants, happiness, that singular necessity, will always evade him. And thus, without fear of later self-contradiction or superannuation, Solovyov can authoritatively conclude the biography of a subject not yet dead.

THE 2006 TOLSTOY: HONORABLE OPPONENT OF THE CHURCH

If Solovyov portrayed a Tolstoy-in-process, torn by conflicts of economic privilege and gentry guilt, then the Zverev-Tunimanov team confronted a vast and stable canon. The coauthors were free to reassess and even ridicule any part of this canonized record, both its political and hagiographical dimensions. But on balance they favor the "Lermontovian" pole of Lotman's options for literary biography: a writer who subjects the world to corrosive reason and thus, upon seeing an indulgent sentiment take hold, moves like Grigory Pechorin to disenchant it. Distanced in time and space from their subject's nineteenth-century world, the authors are, in good post-Soviet fashion, nostalgic toward many aspects of it: its slower pace, its elegance, wealth, leisure, and presumption of personal agency. They show us an aristocratic Tolstoy seeking out truth as a passionate but ever-dissatisfied observer, an experimenter, a mind of the eighteenth century (or perhaps of the precocious seventeenth) that is skeptical about everything—except, significantly, the existence of God.

Such an image, to be sure, accords with Russian cultural policy under Vladimir Putin, with its aim of shaping and satisfying a re-Christianized twenty-first-century readership. But it is not an untrue reconstruction of Tolstoy. The 2006 biography is crammed with quotes. They are often deployed in an unexpected way, however, inadvertently revealing to us our habitual biases about Tolstoy's life. Among those habits is our tendency not to trust Sofiya Andreyevna, or to dismiss the more strident sides of Nikolai Strakhov, Tolstoy's consultant on spiritual matters in the 1870s, or our desire, no matter what, to see Tolstoy as a nay-saying rebel rather than a consensus-seeker who humbly heard out the arguments of monks. This new team of biographers takes even the out-of-favor eyewitnesses seriously and at their word.

Alexei Zverev began the biography, wrote the Preface and the first two parts, and provided an appendix on Tolstoy's plays. (This freestanding essay, "Tolstoy's Dramaturgy," is a superb survey of Tolstoy's theater, beginning with comedies of public humiliation and ending with Christian spectacles of moral transformation.[19]) When Zverev died in 2003, his colleague and close friend Vladimir Tunimanov continued the work until his own death in 2006. Both sought a stable Tolstoy, one whose "eternal restless seeking" could be resolved and made useful to a nation traumatized by the collapse of the

Soviet regime. Their biography is a conventional, gargantuan fusion of life and works. In 2008, two years after the book came out (and immediately sold out), an article appeared in *Voprosy literatury* by Aleksei Kholikov: "The Writer's biography: A genre without rules" ("Pisatel'skaia biografiia: Zhanr bez pravil"). Kholikov wonders about the sudden hunger for biography in the twenty-first century, and why the *ZhZL* series has been so successful. Surely more is at stake, he insists, than the reason provided by Alexander Herzen, that people are always hungry for gossip and love to pry into others' lives. Today's reason is loftier: the "need to rethink the role that the greatest writers played in the fate of Russia," the "search for a hero who is—alas—not of our time" (Kholikov 42).

So the historical Tolstoy, all the better for being wondrous and strange, would be restored as a model for Russia's more hopeful future. We noted above that the Zverev-Tunimanov biography had been praised as a "New Leo Tolstoy—a book for a new [or for our current] time, a new Russia" ("Novyi Lev Tolstoi—kniga novogo vremeni, novoi Rossii . . ."), one "cleansed of all political asides and misunderstandings" (Yurkin 77). Among these cleansings were the trademark intelligentsia concerns of Solovyov's biography: material progress, optimism, entrepreneurial activity, westernization combined with love for the *narod*. Gone too is the presumption that the twin evils of "tsarist-state-and-serfdom" were the biggest obstacles to Tolstoy "loving the people." The institutional embarrassment that confronts these two post-Soviet biographers is not serfdom, and not Tolstoy's aristocratism or his opposition to autocracy, but his hostile, prideful, stressed relation with the Russian Orthodox Church. In a brief preface to the volume, Valentin Kurbatov tries to fathom the "instinct" that summons all Russian writers to Yasnaya Polyana every autumn—a pilgrimage, a mystery, a gravitation toward the "heart of the clan," the recurring suspicion that "we are the dream, the empty art, and the authentic reality is he" (5). But a *ZhZL* commission alone could not have persuaded Zverev and Tunimanov, at the end of their distinguished careers, to take up the huge labor of re-researching a life already so overexamined. (Kurbatov titled his preface "The mystery at the edge of the 'commission.'") What could possibly be new in it? (7).

The novelty, Kurbatov suggests, is the "personality-ness (*lichnostnost'*) of their reading" (7), a virtue he then glosses at length. The new biography justifies itself by the "calm passion with which the authors 'liberate' the human being in Tolstoy from under the avalanche of 'external life,' from under the burden of interpretations . . . in order to glimpse what is earth-bound, shared in common, what can fortify us in true self-understanding" (7). The 2006 team had addressed two types of "exhausting Tolstoyan question": "what is asked of the human being, and what is asked of the Church" (7). Kurbatov intimates that in the second category especially, Tolstoy's relation to Russian

Orthodoxy, earlier *ZhZL* biographies had fallen short. For the Church is not an institution to be despised like any other. Its teachings and monastic personnel had forced Tolstoy to confront the most stubborn and painful contradiction of his inner life: the problem of *gordynia*, spiritual pride. Such pride is not a private matter. It radiates out into an imperious, even a tyrannical, social relation. And, Kurbatov notes, Zverev and Tunimanov, at last free of Soviet-era taboos against a theologically informed ethics, "patiently seek that boundary beyond which self-condemnation grants to itself the dangerous right to judge others" (7–8). Tolstoy, devoted to the idea of universal love, observes the particulars of the world and cannot refrain from judging them harshly. The Church fathers, monks, and recluses are far more successful at this task—and Tolstoy knows it. Thus does this massive biography enter into implicit dialogue with Solovyov's life-in-process a century earlier. Solovyov, a secular social critic, considered literal Christian doctrine a handicap to his questing subject. For Tolstoy's biographers in 2006, this same doctrine provides Tolstoy with the chance to learn, as all Russians must, from the collective repository of their moral wisdom: the official Church.

Zverev and Tunimanov lay out this lesson in their treatment of the pivotal pre-crisis year 1877 (part 3, "The Turning Point," 325–32). It begins quietly, even hopefully. Focus is on the final part of *Anna Karenina*, not the heroine's self-absorbed tragic end but the inexplicably positive epiphany that restores Konstantin Levin to productive life. Nothing had changed, but everything potentially could change, and for the better—if only "faith could be found and the mystery of creation discovered in union with other believers" (325). Should this peasant-bred communal wisdom prove insufficient, then running like a trickle of sanity through the story is Sofiya Andreyevna's matter-of-fact lack of concern. Her husband having a crisis was such a common occurrence, to upset the household over each eccentricity would be the highest folly. Still, there had been a perceptible shift in behavior: Tolstoy's renewed interest in church ritual during that year, his four visits to Optina Pustyn' monastery, the elders' high opinion of him, and their praise of his humility. "There is no basis for not trusting Sofiya Andreyevna's words" that Tolstoy, in his turn, "acknowledged the wisdom of the elders" (329). These retreats to the monastery were "an almost idyllic page in this far from idyllic period of Tolstoy's life, so fraught with explosions and rebellion" (330). Of course Tolstoy found much to fault with ecclesiastical routine, bureaucracy, hierarchy, and the unseemly accumulation of wealth. But we are reminded that such had always been the case with Tolstoy: the very fact that he is attracted to something, pays attention to it, begins to practice it, comes to need it, means that ultimately it will be rejected. Tolstoy could neither "subdue his reason" and the "rational analytic principle" in himself, nor could he "subordinate himself automatically to ritual" for any length of time (328). That Tolstoy rebels against a value or a practice is not a sign of its unworthiness. Quite the opposite: rejection legitimates a stage in his own spiritual growth.

One detail is foregrounded in their discussion of Tolstoy's religious writings. At some point, most penitents admit their helplessness and seek guidance. But in *The Confession*, the biographers note, "there are no prayers—which would be inappropriate there" (337). Tolstoy's inability to feel prayerful (grateful, fulfilled, graced) is related to his spiritual pride, a charge that Zverev and Tunimanov examine with great care. Opinions are recruited from all sides, coming together only deep in the book, in the chapter on the 1901 Edict of Separation from the Church ("Otluchenie," 563–81). The immediate cause for the Holy Synod's act were some blasphemous scenes in *Resurrection*, a novel implacably hostile to the same Church that had intrigued Tolstoy earlier and earned his cautious respect. Why was this decisive ecclesiastical step taken in response to a work of fiction, rather than the numerous, equally hostile treatises in Tolstoy's own name that had preceded it?

The Separation chapter opens on the family's very negative opinion of Tolstoy's cynical, satirical treatment of the prison church service in *Resurrection*. Sofiya Andreyevna was repelled by it, Tatyana Lvovna embarrassed. Tolstoy's sister Marya Nikolayevna, after an irregular and tempestuous life now living as a nun in the convent of Shamordino near the Optyn monastery, was sorely aggrieved. The didactic scenes in the novel contrasted unfavorably with the more balanced, open-minded recollection of church experiences in his *Confession* two decades earlier (563–64). "In *Confession* we have the living process of a religious quest," the biographers note. "In the novel we have its depressing results, the final result. In *Confession* there is drama, pain, deep sadness. In the novel there is dissatisfaction, caricature, the crude underseam of a ritual ceremony, something resembling the unmediated theatrical performance of a play" (564).

The prison church service offends, then, because Tolstoy—whether or not a poor thinker, which Solovyov had disputed—was indisputably a master novelist, and the prison service falls below the bar for novelistic art. We are reminded that in an earlier version of the scene, Tolstoy had resorted to his favorite device of perception "through the eyes of a child" (565)—so effective when deployed by Natasha Rostova at the Opera and Pierre Bezukhov on the battlefield of Borodino. Those scenes work because there is an individual alive inside the story space, groomed by the author to experience the event. But Tolstoy's fury had grown too large, he could not contain it. In the *Resurrection* church service he excluded all "individualized nuances" and fell into generalization, but "a generalization belonging to a single person, to an all-seeing, all-hearing, all-knowing author striving to expose a lie" (566). This stripped Tolstoy of the compassion that novelistic vision must provide—and that was provided, say, by Dostoevsky, in his description of the Easter service in his semiautobiographical *Notes from the House of the Dead*. Dostoevsky had suffered along with his fellow prisoners and transcended it in his art. But there is "no hint of any repentance, bliss, or religious experience" among the inmates depicted by Tolstoy, who (unlike Dostoevsky) were created not warmly, out of shared communion and personal memory, but coldly, out of intellectual contempt.

For those familiar with Tolstoy's views on incarceration and state punishment, the scandal of the prison church service in *Resurrection* contains nothing new. "But articles and treatises are one thing," the biographers write: wholly different is a church service described in this vein "in a novel by Russia's most eminent and widely read writer" (567–68). Any move against Tolstoy had been out of the question while Tolstoy's devoted reader, Tsar Alexander III, was still alive. However, with the ascension of a new tsar in 1894 and the appearance of *Resurrection* in 1899, the Church finally spoke out. Among us has appeared "a new false teacher . . . Count Tolstoy, seduced by his own proud mind" (568). This verdict was not a formal excommunication or anathema but the far milder sentence of "separation" (*otluchenie*) or "falling-away" (*otpadenie*). Tolstoy could still be pulled back into the fold, the Church remained willing to forgive. It was a brave and independent step for the Holy Synod to take, for everyone in Russia was against it—except, perhaps, Tolstoy himself. The edict was hugely controversial within the Synod, splitting the monasteries and pitting churchmen against one another. These voices are documented in detail. We hear the great wandering schemamonk Ksenofont support Tolstoy against the ravings of John of Kronstadt (576–78); we watch as the government desperately attempts to ban all publicity about the event, which only fanned the flames of Tolstoy's fame. For those accustomed to tracing Tolstoy's more secular foes—the symbolist poets who abhorred his prudishness, or the revolutionaries who regretted his distrust of all politics—this relocation of the Tolstoy Debate within a differentiated, sophisticated Church community is an eye-opener. "A blind ape-like faith is not pleasing to Christ," Ksenofont declared: "faith must be conscious. Tolstoy is a fervent opponent of nihilism and has contributed powerfully to weakening its appeal . . . For this we owe him our grateful thanks" (578).

The theme of spiritual pride runs like an agonized thread throughout the 2006 biography. It is a worthy focus, not least because Tolstoy himself would have eagerly, if unsuccessfully, tried to learn from it. Consider again the hypothesis suggested earlier, that Tolstoy unhappily fused in his one person the Gogolian and Lermontovian routes to self-knowledge. Gogol is all feverish guilt. Lermontov is cold, rational analysis. But the behavioral acts that trigger Tolstoy's guilt—hotly undertaken, coldly cast off—are inextricably woven into what the 2006 biography identifies as the dynamic of *gordynia*, spiritual pride. Its rhythm is one of continual repentance for things past, and a constant projection of perfection in the future. But at any single moment in the present, Tolstoy's uncompromising oppositional stance and continual flood of confessional writings betray his conviction that condemning oneself confers the right to judge others. Such, said the Church, are the seductions of a proud mind.

The 1894 and 2006 biographies arrive at different conclusions, both paradoxical. Solovyov, in his final pages, notes two constant traits of Tolstoy's person (159): first that he was a practical man, focused on active deeds, and second that he was, after his own fashion, a *narodnik* or "man of the people," loving the life and perspective of common folk. Neither is problem-free. "Without a doubt Tolstoy idealized the life of the *narod*, even though its life was already tainted by the factory and soldiering," Solovyov wrote (160). And if Tolstoy considered the path of Christ "practical" for the nineteenth-century person, that was because Tolstoy mistakenly considered Christian teachings to be categorically simple. Such simplicity is nowhere to be seen in the 2006 biography, which everywhere documents the complicated fallout of seemingly simple, principled ethical moves. In his writings on self-discipline in his treatise *On Christian Teaching*, for example, Tolstoy had drastically simplified the eight cardinal sins as designated by the Church fathers.[20] He dropped five of them: melancholy, anger, despair [*unynie*], vanity, and pride. He kept sloth, gluttony, and lust—especially lust; in fact, "fornication" became the single most dangerous failing, more serious than greed, pride, or intolerance. In this reordering of the cardinal sins, the predictable and thus uninteresting part is Tolstoy's obsession with the "out-of-control sensual body," for him the source of all vice. More interesting is Tolstoy's indwelling practicality, which also fascinated Solovyov. Experience had taught Tolstoy that it was impossible to control moods or attitudes (the sins of melancholy, anger, despair). Better not demonize them, then, and develop the good habit of modest minute-by-minute living. But Church doctrine challenged Tolstoy on precisely this "practical" ethics, arguing that it was both possible, and necessary, to change our *attitudes*. To insist on the exclusive rightness of one's own attitude, on the wrongness of other ways of thinking or living, and to withhold love or forgiveness from those wrongdoers, was deeply unchristian spiritual pride.

With this spiritual conundrum in mind, Zverev and Tunimanov end their volume on a bittersweet note. Their afterword opens not on the enraptured pilgrims of Kurbatov's preface but on the disappointed visitors to Yasnaya Polyana during Tolstoy's final years, who left this mecca with their faith in the Master "if not broken, then cracked" (755). They note the remark of Tolstoy's secretary Valentin Bulgakov in 1912, two years after Tolstoy's flight and death, that the household without the Master seemed "simpler, more alive, less contrived," almost "as if a burden had fallen from people's shoulders" (756). That relief was short-lived. The suffering of Sofiya Andreyevna would prove immense and inconsolable. From the rest of the Tolstoy-reading twentieth century, our biographers mention only one name, Leonid Pasternak, citing his judgment (with which they concur) that Tolstoy's enduring contribution to humanity was "a new type of spiritualization (*odukhotvoreniia*) for perceiving the world" (771).

TOLSTOY 2016: PLAYABLE DRAMA
WHERE ALL ARE TRAPPED

Pavel Basinsky's *Lev Tolstoy* avoids many of the pitfalls of its ZhZL predecessors: Solovyov's frustrated attempts at conversation with a living subject, Gudzy's weaponization of *War and Peace*, Shklovsky's distraction by material things, Zverev-Tunimanov's massive thick descriptions that beg to be studied rather than experienced. Basinskii (b. 1961) paces the life differently.[21] He creates a Tolstoy that seeps into the reader from all sides, a balancing act between a stubborn biographical subject and the recalcitrant outside world, with just enough (but no more) documentation to motivate each inspirational or infuriating move. The conceptual pivot of the biography is Tolstoy's quest for freedom. At first this is freedom *from* (those confining swaddling wraps that Gudzhy also invoked), then freedom *to* (perfecting himself in the world), then finally freedom *out of* (institutions, family, the body, personal memory). The opening chapter identifies 'Life as Violence.' But Basinsky is quick to point out that the Tolstoy household was loving and enlightened; neither children nor serfs felt the rod (10). No Dickens or Dostoevsky here. Violence or coercion (*nasilie*) refers, rather, to all constraint that interferes with the joy that is natural to the human condition. Tolstoy's conviction that freedom is natural, simple, and deserved permeates both Basinsky's text and Tolstoy's life. For the obsessively healthy Tolstoy, happiness is a self-evident right, its absence an abomination. His flights to the Caucasus, Crimea, and abroad to Western Europe were not escapes, and not adventures or grand tours, because Tolstoy did not crave the exotic or strange for its own sake. Although passionately curious about the immediate tangible world, the site of discovery was always the inner self. And when he began to create fictional "doubles," they were not those projections of the evil in human nature that so mesmerized the Romantic epigones of his generation, but the morally demanding prompts to self-improvement that filled his own diaries and rule books. Tolstoy was never interested in validating wickedness. He wanted to destroy it.

For a decade, the rhythms and demands of a growing family kept Tolstoy's doubts at bay (the bond of marriage, after all, had been liberation from debauchery). Then came the *perevorot*, the turning point. It is presented alternately from inside Tolstoy's diaries and from the outside, the eyes of the world. Tolstoy's life came to a halt. But this stoppage was not sudden, and (why should his diaries lie?) did not make him unhappy. Even as rumors of his insanity circulated, Tolstoy's happiness, clarity, and freedom grew. Basinsky agrees with Zverev-Tunimanov that Tolstoy, raised by believers whom he trusted and loved, tried hard to find wisdom in the official Church (200–3). But the Orthodox Church was too small and rigid. It was a vision of Christian universality that led to his ecstatic creative work over the Gospels, which in turn led to his renunciations, each made necessary by the one before: clerical rituals, the state, private property, literary rights. At the generative core of these serial rejections is Tolstoy's hovering status as a *religious dissident* (212)—which, Basinsky reminds us, was a criminal offense in late imperial Russia. Sofiya Andreyevna's anxiety over her husband's radical egalitarianism was not merely financial. She feared for her family's freedom and safety. Tolstoy, after all, did not monopolize the meaning of freedom.

None of the persons, values, or institutions that Tolstoy renounced are demonized by Basinsky. Konstantin Pobedonostsev, head of the Holy Synod and implacable foe of Tolstoy, is presented as a highly learned and principled man who did not shrink from criticizing the behavior of tsars (223). He and Tolstoy simply understood Christianity differently. (Tolstoy, it might be said, was the early Gnostic Christian alternative to post-conversion Rome.) Tolstoy's rejection of private property was more complex. Personal wealth had been a coveted positive value in his life for fifty years; he was even something of a money-grubber (*stiazhatel'*) (232). In his 1894 biography, Solovyov too in had noticed this trait in Count Tolstoy, ascribing it to the no-nonsense economic realism of the aristocratic class. Basinsky does not reason along class lines—but he sympathizes with Sofiya Andreyevna's refusal to turn her family into a working commune. For even as the marriage disintegrated, she continued to work hard in habitual and heroic ways: defending her husband to Pobedonostsev, to the newspapers, and in public fundraising efforts during the famine of 1891–1892. What broke the back of their union was the death of their young son Vanechka in 1895, and the intrusion of Vladimir Chertkov, fanatical convert to Tolstoy's person and ideology. But Chertkov also is not demonized. "Freedom is not given for free" is the opening motto of the chapter devoted to him (256). To the aging thirsting Tolstoy, this manipulative disciple, however "spiritually unfree and non-autonomous," was utterly essential as agent, publisher, and spiritual confidant (273). Thus does Tolstoy design his own trap. He does the right thing by his family when he transfers his wealth to his wife—but then continues to live among them, reproaching them, changing no one and (as his eldest daughter Tatyana notes in her diary) embittering them all (244).

The controversial Separation Edict pleased no one, although Tolstoy was happy to have another platform for his views. But Basinsky emphasizes less the issue of spiritual pride and more the wording of the edict itself: intelligently written, devoid of anything "cruel or medieval," free of any hint of reprisals or punishment (319). Tolstoy, of course, wished it were harsher. He had been called a "prodigal son," not a *heretic*. And this, too, attests to the strange, impractical, a-synchronic time-space of the Tolstoy phenomenon. Matters came to a head with the protracted scandal over Tolstoy's six wills between 1895 and 1910, to which Basinsky devotes a lengthy chapter. Despite the growing global fame of Tolstoyanism, despite the urbane sophistication of Chertkov, no one in the family, right up until 1909, had any idea how legal wills worked. It was not in the spirit of Tolstoy to investigate such mundane details of the modern state. And thus resentment, fear, anger, and conspiracy brewed around revisions and codicils that would have been thrown out of court: "everyone was acting blindly" (335).

So too is the flight from home presented as both sighted and blind. Basinsky blames no one, seeing the aims of all parties in frantic flux. Tolstoy, although separated from the Church, had hoped to visit with monastic elders at Optina Pustyn monastery, but bungled communications prevented this from happening (370–72). At the Astapovo train station, as their father lay dying, *all* the Tolstoy children—not just his faithful daughter Alexandra and the triumphant Chertkov—agreed that it was best not to let their mother in to the sickroom (400). For those trapped in Tolstoy's powerful grip, there was no easy way out. By the last page only one person is free, and he has just died.

For a life so shamelessly made public in its own time, Basinsky's biography is impressive in its scrupulous avoidance of graphic scandal. He hints at moments of intense embarrassment or loss of control, but without voyeuristically celebrating them. No single point of view is allowed to dominate for long, and his decentered compassion for all parties makes the biography read like the script for a play—perhaps one that Stanislavsky might have staged. The case could be made that Basinsky accomplishes with his compassionate Life of Tolstoy what Tolstoy himself did in his unfinished dramatization of his own diaries begun in 1896 and titled *And the Light Shineth in Darkness*. In 1900, Tolstoy confided to his disciple Pyotr Sergeyenko that this drama might be the most important thing he ever wrote, the repository of his "most sincere and intimate thoughts."[22] These thoughts, worked out in stage dialogue, contain not only his own convictions but also his knowledge of their painful reverberations, rebuttals, and human cost.

In *The Light Shineth,* Tolstoy gives shape, dignity, and self-understanding to unresolvable biographical dead ends. Everyone acts reasonably out of their own situation. But people Tolstoy loves intimately are improved upon, ennobled in behavior and intent. Masha, the fictive Sofiya Andreyevna, nursing their youngest child while preparing for the wedding of their eldest, cannot share her husband's views—but wants to; she weeps rather than shouts, grieves rather than spies. Tolstoy's alter-ego, the landlord Nikolai Ivanovich Saryntsev, is helpless to refrain from preaching at his family, knowing it is ridiculous. His daughter's fiancé is a convert to nonviolence, and yet Saryntsev cannot prevent the incarceration of this innocent man in a mental hospital and punitive battalion. Although the family priest leaves the Church under Tolstoy's influence, by the end of the play he has rejoined it. One of Saryntsev's hungry peasants chops down his master's tree and Saryntsev cannot protect him from the law. Meanwhile, his peasant carpenter is astonished at his master's lack of skill at planing a simple board—and why try, sir? We carpenters can't get enough work as it is. But (the carpenter sighs) rich folk want to try everything, even though they can't give anything up; they're too used to it.[23] Tolstoy the playwright brings each brief devastating scene to a close at the point where all parties have nothing else to say.

Basinsky does the same. As did his predecessors, his biography occasionally makes use of Tolstoy's fiction as chapter titles: "A Landlord's Morning," "Prisoner of the Caucasus," "Family Happiness," "The Devil." But he does not discuss the major novels. He does, however, devote two compassionate pages to *The Light Shineth* (238–39)—suspecting, perhaps, that this would be Tolstoy's final attempt at self-liberation through art. Basinsky notes which characters are presented as honorable opponents, which as deluded. And then he sums up the marital relation in a judgment that partakes equally of the two authorial models for biography that have structured this essay: ardent and repentant Gogol, clinically observant Lermontov. Tolstoy had always been both, and perhaps only a biography modeled on his own self-dramatization could properly balance the passions involved. Basinsky say this about the light shining in darkness (239): "This is not a conflict of greed against idealism, but the conflict of two serious and principled life positions, in which each person, loving the other, tries lovingly to insist on their own—but unsuccessfully." Every biographer of an autobiographical artist faces this challenge and tries to succeed at it. But the paradoxes of the living Tolstoyan word remain unresolved.

NOTES

1. For the story of the series, see Ludmilla A. Trigos and Carol Ueland, "Creating a National Biographical Series: F. F. Pavlenkov's 'Lives of Remarkable People', 1890–1924," *Slavonic and East European Review*, 96.1 (2018): 41–66, esp. 46–51.

My opening paragraphs are much indebted to their essay, which provides valuable insight into the series founder, both as publisher and as persecuted political dissident. One is struck by the contrast between Pavlenkov, a shrewd businessman willing to compromise to get his texts into print, and Leo Tolstoy, who was equally dissident and populist in his publishing ventures but high-minded, impractical, and contemptuous of market forces—as the famous Count could afford to be.

2. ZhZL lives were classified according to the subject's activity—scientific, state, sociopolitical, musical, etc.—and some biographical subjects had multiple tags (see Trigos and Ueland 53–54). Tolstoy's biography is subtitled only "literary," doubtless to disguise his political activism.

3. Nikolai Boldyrev. "Chelovek v nepreryvno meniaiushchemsia landshafte." *Ivan Groznyi, Petr Velikii, Menshikov. Potemkin. Damidovy. Biograficheskie ocherki.* Chelyabinsk: Ural, 1994. 5–12, here p. 65–12, esp. 6. On the post-Soviet restoration and reprinting of the original Pavlenkov Series, see Trigos and Ueland, 62–63.

4. Evgenii Solovyov, *L. N. Tolstoi. Ego zhizn' i literaturnaia deiatel'nost'*. Zhizn' zamechatel'nykh liudei (St. Peterburg: Biograficheskaia biblioteka F. Pavlenkova, 1894).

5. Aleksei Zverev and Vladimir Tunimanov, *Lev Tolstoi*. Zhizn' zamechatel'nykh liudei (Moscow: Molodaia gvardiia, 2006).

6. Pavel Basinskii, *Lev Tolstoi—Svobodnyi chelovek* (Moscow: Molodaia gvardia, 2016), reissued under the ZhZL imprint and series cover in 2017. The pagination of the original 2016 publication is cited in this essay. Basinskii has written two other books on Tolstoy, focusing on the final decades: the death-centennial book *Lev Tolstoy. Flight from Paradise* (2017, English version 2010), and an account of Tolstoy's clash with his most charismatic opponent within the Church, *The Saint Against the Lion: John of Kronshtadt and Lev Tolstoy* (2015).

7. On this revival and the post-Soviet "rehabilitation of Pavlenkov" after Lenin's disapproval of his publishing enterprise, see Trigos and Ueland, 61–65.

8. Solovyov notes—correctly—that Tolstoy does not soften the precept into: Resist not evil by evil (or by violence or coercion); according to Tolstoy at this stage in his life, *all* resistance is wrong (131). Claiming to be "no optimist" about human nature or history, Solovyov cannot accept this moral stance (130). "I ask myself: what is the good? . . . I know that [my] answer will be unappealing to the followers of Count Tolstoy, but . . ."

9. See N. K. Gudzii, *L. Tolstoi* (Moscow: Molodaia gvardiia, 1944); also p. 67, ZhZL catalog *Katalog "ZhZL." 1890–2010* at http://www.libros.am/book/id/352673/slug/katalog-zhzl.-1, accessed 1/14/2013. N. K. Gudzii (1887–1965) was part of the scholarly team that worked on the Tolstoy Jubilee edition in the 1930–1940s. The 1944 booklet was a topical assignment. In 1953 (with Znanie Publishers) and in 1960 (with Khudozhestvennaia literatura) Gudzii published expanded versions of his life of Tolstoy.

10. V. Shklovskii, *Lev Tolstoi* (Moscow: Molodaia gvardiia, 1963). An English translation was published by Progress Publishers, Moscow, in 1978. See the brief mention of Shklovsky's volume (as well as its 1967 abbreviated sequel) in the Series in Iurkin 177.

11. Bulgakov's *Zhizn' gospodina de Mol'era* was not published until 1962. An English translation by Mirra Ginsburg as *The Life of Monsieur de Molière* appeared in 1986.

12. Boris Tomaševskij. "Literature and Biography" in *Readings in Russian Poetics: Formalist and Structuralist Views*, Ed. Ladislav Matejka and Krystyna Pomorska (Chicago, IL: Dalkey Archive Press, 2002).

13. For the painful story of this irreversible auto-mythologization helped along by communication technology, see William Nickell, *The Death of Tolstoy*, especially ch. 1, "The Family Crisis as a Public Event," and ch. 3, "The Media at Astapovo and the Creation of a Modern Pastoral."

14. Iurii Lotman. "Literaturnaia biografiia v istoriko-kul'turnom kontekste" In Iu. M. Lotman, *O russkoi literature. Stat'i i issledovaniia (1958–1993)* (St. Petersburg: Iskusstvo-SPb, 1997), 804–16.

15. Solovyov's *Ivan the Terrible* is #125, his *Cromwell* #186, his *Pisarev* #127. The year 1894 saw the publication of Solovyov's *Karamzin* (#154), *Milton* (#155), *The Rothschilds* (#157), *Turgenev* (#159), plus a second edition of *Pisarev*. In 1892 Solovyov published on Senkovsky and Russian journalism (#86); in 1895, Buckle (#180) and Goncharov (#181). See *Katalog "ZhZL,"* 22, 25–26, 18, 28, 29. Accessed 14 January 2013.

16. These letters are cited in Vladimir Desiaterik, *Pavlenkov* (Moscow: Molodaia gvardiia, 2006), 314–15.

17. Desiaterik, 315.

18. See, for example, Solovyov's invitation to his reader to "reread [Tolstoy's] 'A Landowner's Morning,' everywhere replacing, with the permission of the author, 'Prince Nekhlyudov' with 'Count Tolstoy'" (Solovyov, 40). In earlier chapters, *Childhood* is cited at length as an account of Tolstoy's own childhood (an interpretation that Tolstoy himself vigorously rejected).

19. Zverev and Tunimanov, "Dramaturgiia Tolstogo," 722–53. Zverev notes that the entire concept of a heterogeneous public was foreign to Tolstoy's understanding of performative success. For him, *obshchenie* was not so much communication, with its presumption of a two-way differentiated response, as it was communion, more like a liturgy.

20. For Tolstoy's astonishing reconfiguration of the most common sins afflicting the human creature, see G. M. Hamburg, "Tolstoy's Spirituality," 153–54.

21. An expert on the post-conversion years, Basinskii authored a big, bestselling death-centennial book (*Leo Tolstoy. Flight from Paradise* (2010 / 2017), also in English, and an account of Tolstoy's clash with his most charismatic foe inside the Church (*The Saint Against the Lion: John of Kronshtadt and Leo Tolstoy. The Story of a Hostility*. 2015). *Flight from Paradise* won the Russian "Big Book" National Literary Prize.

22. Quoted. in Donna Tussing Orwin, "Chronology," for Sept. 1, 1900, in *The Cambridge Companion to Tolstoy*, ed. Donna Tussing Orwin (Cambridge: Cambridge University Press, 2002), 38.

23. Scene 1, Act III, "And the Light Shineth in Darkness," A Drama in Five Acts (1896–1897, 1900). Translated by Marvin Kantor with Tanya Tulchinsky in Leo

Tolstoy, *Plays: Volume Three, 1894–1910* (Evanston: Northwestern University Press, 1998), 15–104, here p. 66.

Chapter 5

Per Aspera Ad Astra
The Remarkable Lives of Fyodor Dostoevsky

Alexander Spektor

SETTING THE PARADIGM

As numerous essays in this volume attest, writing about the lives of Russian nineteenth-century literary giants has never been easy. Critical reception—and the writer's biography as an integral component of its formation—became an especially precarious endeavor during the Soviet period, when most, if not all, cultural values underwent a drastic reappraisal. Yet, there is hardly a figure in the Russian nineteenth-century literary canon whose posthumous life in Soviet Russia has been more troublesome than that of Fyodor Dostoevsky. As the fountainhead of the literary canon, Pushkin was untouchable. Lermontov was an obvious victim of the tsarist regime. Gogol was too closely associated with Pushkin and yet still too distant from the Revolution. The major writers of the later nineteenth century, Turgenev and Chekhov, were liberal enough to be useful, and Tolstoy was given carte blanche by Lenin himself.[1] For the Soviet critical establishment, however, Dostoevsky became a difficult stumbling block. Among the major nineteenth-century authors, Dostoevsky's anxiety about Russia's "hovering over an abyss" was most pronounced; his stance against the liberal movements of the 1860s and 1880s was unequivocally firm; and his warnings against the possibility of social and political cataclysms unless Russia turned away from Western-based ideologies reverberated with a searing intensity.[2] In short, Dostoevsky was a writer with the strongest ideological positions, and he voiced them loudly in both his fiction and journalistic writing.³ Obviously, these positions radically contradicted those adopted by the Soviet ideological machine. At the same time, Dostoevsky's prominence as a major voice of Russian letters and his quickly growing international fame—along with that of Tolstoy—established him as the most recognizable and popular of Russian literary exports. Dostoevsky's growing stature made it impossible for the Soviet critical apparatus to throw the writer off the "ship of socialism," forcing it to develop a proper relationship to the writer. Its task was to help Soviet readers understand Dostoevsky's greatness as an artist, while at the same time explaining his unfortunate shortcomings as an opponent of the socialist heaven on earth.

Importantly, with the exception of a few notable examples like Bakhtin's 1929 *Problems of Dostoevsky's Creative Art* (and its revised 1961 version *Problems of Dostoevsky's Poetics*) or Viktor Shklovsky's *For and Against*, first published in 1957, most Soviet scholarship on Dostoevsky fell into the paradigm of vacillating between admiring Dostoevsky's artistry and condemning his political views. In general, Soviet studies of Dostoevsky correspond to what Evgeny Dobrenko and Galin Tihanov define as "the particularity of the Soviet situation," which "consisted in the special status of the political," in which "the political . . . was all concentrated in the higher echelons of power," transforming literary criticism in the Soviet Union "from a *source* of power into a conductor of power."⁴ Expressing the ideological direction of Soviet culture, Soviet literary critics had to adapt their approach to Dostoevsky so that it would fit into the demands of their current and evolving political situation. As expected, the interpretation of Dostoevsky—both of his works and his life—changed in accordance with the party line. Whether or not Dostoevsky's prose satisfied orthodox Marxist ideology was secondary to what the given moment defined as orthodox Marxism. If Dostoevsky could be useful to garner the patriotic fervor needed for the war effort or if the general ideological atmosphere of the time became more relaxed, the critical establishment would provide the appropriate "Marxist" reading of his works. For example, Valery Kirpotin's address on the 125th anniversary of Dostoevsky's birth in November 1946 argued that Dostoevsky's psychologism was "a special artistic method of penetrating into the objective essence of a contradictory human collective, into the very core of the social relations which troubled him, and a special artistic method of reproducing them in the art of the word."⁵ Such an analysis, as cultural historian Vladimir Seduro argues, made Dostoevsky "doubly acceptable" "from the point of view of Marxism" (268).

However minute they may seem from our present-day perspective, the ideological shifts of the Soviet era were at times quite drastic and frequently required an astonishing amount of agility on the critic's part as the directives from above demanded radical change in the critical reception sometimes even within a short time period. The case of David Zaslavsky, one of the most influential Soviet cultural critics of the 1930s to the 1950s, is instructive here. In 1946 Zaslavsky celebrated Dostoevsky's quasquicentennial with a rather tolerant and laudatory article in *Literaturnaia gazeta*, which, as Seduro states, set the tone for a more flexible attitude toward Dostoevsky.[6] Yet as Zhdanov reintroduced a more orthodox Marxist doctrine in 1947, the same Zaslavsky denounced Dostoevsky as "one of the most passionate enemies of socialism, revolution, and democracy."[7] Finally, in his *Dostoevsky: Critical Biographical Sketch* (*Dostoevskii: kritiko-biograficheskii ocherk*, 1956), Zaslavsky once again softened his view, describing him as a great artist with a regrettable case of extreme ideological myopia.[8] As a rule, the usual variables in such interpretative permutations were the shift in Dostoevsky's worldview before and after his Siberian imprisonment, the difficult balance between the artist and the ideologue, Dostoevsky's affiliation with the petit bourgeois class, his (in)ability to transcend his class origins in his writing, and, finally, his belief in the contradictory nature of human personality which obviously challenged Marxist ideology and, depending on the time, was emphasized or glossed over. In short, Soviet critics could be said to be more careful interpreters of the ideological policies of the state rather than of Dostoevsky's prose.

Hence, critical reception of Dostoevsky during the Soviet era was less of an attempt to provide a fresh interpretation of Dostoevsky's works than a party-bound obligation to neutralize Dostoevsky's invectives against socialism. As such, it can be seen as a barometer of the ideological pressures of a given period during the Soviet era. Since the trajectory of Dostoevsky's critical reception up to the 1970s has been splendidly analyzed by Seduro,[9] in what follows, I examine the transformations of Dostoevsky's late-Soviet and post-Soviet image from the Thaw to the contemporary period. To do so within the scope of a single essay, I focus on Dostoevsky's twentieth- and twenty-first-century biographies, a place where the two poles of Dostoevsky—the artist and the man of the strongest convictions—unite into a holistic if, at times, contradictory vision. In this sense, it is instructive to look at the biographies of Dostoevsky that came out in the *ZhZL* series and were intended for the widest readership.[10]

The paradigm for the critical evaluation of Dostoevsky in the Soviet Union was set by Maxim Gorky, the founder of the Soviet permutation of *ZhZL*. What gradually emerges in Gorky's evaluation of Dostoevsky—and this dichotomy sets the course for most Soviet-era Dostoevsky scholarship—is Dostoevsky's bifurcation into an artistic visionary and an ideological reactionary. Gorky's attempts to recuperate the artist while rejecting the ideologue comes out most prominently in his attitude toward the staging of *Demons* by the Moscow Art Theater in 1913 and his 1935 attempt to defend the publication of Dostoevsky's most political novel by the publishing house Academia.[11]

Arguing against the staging of *Demons* in 1913, Gorky insists that the novel—even more so than *The Brothers Karamazov*, which the theater successfully staged two years earlier—is "a dark spot of malevolent misanthropy against the bright background of Russian literature."[12] In general, Gorky distinguishes between reading the novels and watching them performed on stage. While the reader is able to see past the negative traits of Dostoevsky's characters, the theater audience might not: "reading Dostoevsky, one can correct the thoughts of his heroes and as a result they gain in beauty, depth, and humanity. When one is shown Dostoevsky's creations on the stage, the artists' performance . . . imparts to his characters a sense of a particular significance and larger finality."[13] Moreover, the overwhelming number of negative characters in the novel makes Gorky doubt whether their depiction on stage is "necessary and useful to the interests of social pedagogy."[14] For Gorky, the absence of the authorial presence constitutes one of the main dangers in staging Dostoevsky's texts since it does not allow the audience to dissipate the tension and density of the characters' words and actions: "on the stage, the author's opinions are not as clear as the gestures, and . . . Dostoevsky's novel . . . will take on the character of a constant nervous convulsion."[15]

Stanislavsky and Nemirovich-Danchenko pushed back, arguing that in *Demons* Dostoevsky depicts the inner truth of Russian life and that, contrary to Gorky's argument, the staging of the novel would result in getting rid of "everything that is superficial (and forced)" in the novel, bringing out its inner essence.[16] Whether in Gorky's attempt to distinguish the text from its stage performance, or in Stanislavsky and Nemirovich-Danchenko's insistence that the performance of *Demons* would separate the wheat from the chaff, and reveal "the deep, positive ideas of the novel" (ibid.), we see the manifestations of the Russian cultural establishment's anxiety about Dostoevsky's fiction. This anxiety comes out in the acceptance of the writer's importance, on the one hand, and, on the other, in the acknowledgment that to be effective or useful his prose needs to be neutralized. While the polemic between Gorky and the directors of the MKhAT took place in 1913, the framework it created became a standard for Dostoevsky's critical perception after the Revolution.

Hence, an article in *Literaturnaia gazeta* written in defense of Academia's decision to publish *Demons* in 1935 similarly stated that while *Demons* might paint a superficial caricature of the Revolution, it is, at the same time, a deep work of art, expressing the struggle of the human spirit.[17] Putting forth the party's official position on the matter, Zaslavsky's response in *Pravda*, titled "Literary Rot," ridiculed *Literaturnaia gazeta*'s argument. The top Soviet critic asks: how can the novel "contain an artistic concentration of all the arguments that could be put forth by an artistic genius against the revolution and simultaneously—the downfall of these arguments?"[18] Instead he contends that "*Demons* is the weakest of all Dostoevsky's novels . . . It is the dirtiest libel directed against the revolution . . . , a reactionary screed dressed in the form of a work of fiction" (ibid.).

Academia's decision to publish *Demons* received support from Gorky, who sided with the publishing house and suggested that the ban on the publication of *Demons* would "tempt young people" but also that publishing the novel performed a pedagogical function: "One must know the enemy, his 'ideology,' and it is obvious that reading the book in which this ideology is given clearly and eloquently is the easiest way to do so."[19] Significantly, Gorky affirmed the novel's artistic value and issued a warning about the possible émigré reaction to the news that Dostoevsky had been banned in Russia. Zaslavsky responded that his intent was not to ban Dostoevsky, but only *Demons*, and even then, only as a separate volume, leaving it intact in the collected works. Ironically, arguing against Gorky, Zaslavsky invoked the authority of none other than the Gorky of 1913 who wrote "with convincing force wrote about the depraving effect of *Demons*, a novel which is *sadistic and unhealthy*."[20]

This brief history of the staging of *Demons* in the 1910s (successful) and its publication in the 1930s (unsuccessful) is a good illustration of the tension between the Soviet critical establishment's need to accept Dostoevsky's artistic merit, while at the same time rejecting his political and social views. Gorky's ambivalence about Dostoevsky set the paradigm for the difficult balancing act in which the Soviet literary critics had to carefully shift between giving the green light to Dostoevsky the artist and denouncing Dostoevsky the ideological opponent of the socialists. Dostoevsky's prose then becomes a highly contested space where the author's unprecedented artistic mastery in depicting the depths of the human personality exists in a state of constant tension with his perceived ideological lapses. Navigating between the two becomes the hard task of Dostoevsky's first Soviet *ZhZL* biography by the literary critic Leonid Grossman, which came out as late as 1962. Dostoevsky's second biography in the series was published in 1981 by the Dostoevsky scholar Yuri Seleznev; the most recent one, authored by the renowned contemporary philologist Lyudmila Saraskina, came out in 2011.

A comparative study of these three volumes becomes a useful tool to examine the changes in Dostoevsky scholarship during the growing liberalization of Soviet criticism from the early 1960s to the beginning of the 1980s. It also allows us to trace the cultural shift from the Thaw to the Stagnation to the post-perestroika collapse of socialist ideology in contemporary Russia. In this sense, the two Soviet biographies by Grossman and Seleznev and the post-Soviet one by Saraskina show different stages of the struggle to free Dostoevsky from the bad ideologist/great artist dichotomy put into circulation by Gorky and continued by several generations of Soviet critics.

While Grossman's biography for the most part continues to follow Gorky's paradigm, Seleznev and Saraskina manage to escape it with various degrees of success.

THE ARTIST AND THE IDEOLOGUE

Unlike Tolstoy, who for the most part lived a privileged, uneventful life on his estate, Dostoevsky's life presented his biographers with a treasure trove of material.[21] As with his prose, Dostoevsky's life could be easily broken into a series of threshold moments or pivotal periods, which tempt biographers to ascribe special significance to them. For Grossman, Dostoevsky's love for his mother, his relationship with his difficult, increasingly depressed and alcoholic father, ending with his father's alleged murder by his own serfs, is the first of such periods. Grossman finds the origins of the split between Dostoevsky's artistic sensibilities and his reactionary ideology in the contrasting personalities of his parents. In Dostoevsky's father's surviving photo, he observes "a somewhat proper, aloof face with thin, pursed lips and stern eyes beneath Mephistophelian eyebrows."[22] In contrast, Dostoevsky's mother exerts an unambiguously positive influence on her son. From her Dostoevsky inherits both his literary talents and his love for his fellow men. Using the Bible, which Grossman appropriately calls "a collection of stories from the Old and New Testaments" (15), his mother teaches young Fyodor how to read. Dostoevsky values these "legends" first of all for their "artistic significance," finding them to be "extraordinary works of folk epos, full of drama and lyricism" (ibid.). Grossman locates one of the first major impulses for Dostoevsky as a writer in the tragedy of his mother's life, a woman tortured by her husband's incessant jealousy, yet, whose letters to her husband exhibited undeniable literary talent. For Grossman, the contrasting figures of Dostoevsky's father and mother forever determined both the writer's contradictory character and the nature of his creative output.

The sensitivity and compassion Dostoevsky acquired from his mother engendered his particular brand of realism. As Grossman states, they enabled him to rise above the conventions of the natural school and imbue Dostoevsky's first novel with traits of the "romantic wave" (52). The depth of Dostoevsky's ability to experience the social injustice of Russia's downtrodden and his talent for bringing this experience to his readers separates the young Dostoevsky from his contemporaries and becomes the trademark of his prose: "This was the 'new word' of the beginning author that so dazzled his contemporaries: the strength and the authority of feeling, trampled by reality, yet preserving under the yoke of the despotic regime the meaning of the higher value life" (53).

In Grossman's depiction, Dostoevsky is a man in whom empathy and compassion triumph over rational analysis. Consequently, his superb artistry dominates his inferior philosophizing, which is inadequate in comparison to that of Dostoevsky's most *progressive* contemporaries. This dichotomy feeds Dostoevsky's disagreement with Belinsky, as well as his participation in the Petrashevsky circle. Dostoevsky's writing, in which "social drama transforms into . . . internal tragedy" cannot satisfy the "furious Vissarion," who in the last stage of his life and career insisted on art's strict subordination to social reality (70). The disagreement between the critic Belinsky and the writer Dostoevsky boils down to how each understood art's responsibility to address the pressing demands of the times. Grossman's description of Dostoevsky's attendance at the meetings of the Petrashevsky circle, however, is where the true limitations of Dostoevsky's ideological worldview emerge. What attracts Dostoevsky to the Russian Fourierists is that neither envisions the possibility of change through radical political action. Embracing the idealistic idea of the Golden Age, Dostoevsky does not transcend "philanthropic sermonizing and social dreaming" (103). While Grossman's assertion that "even in the forties we are faced, first of all, with a great artist, a true *poet*" feels like a polemical pushback against a number of Soviet critical denunciations of Dostoevsky's artistic significance, it nevertheless conforms to the already established Soviet critical commonplaces about the author (104, italics in the original).[23]

Only under the influence of another Petrashevsky circle member, Nikolay Speshnev, does Dostoevsky's compassion-based idealism germinate into social action. The charismatic Speshnev brings consciousness to his disciple's spontaneity. Grossman describes their relationship as "the impact of the willful and powerful personality of the revolutionary leader on the contemplative nature of the poet-utopianist" (118). While Speshnev is finally able to stir the young Dostoevsky into action, Grossman makes sure to point out that the source of Dostoevsky's participation in the Speshnev conspiracy is still an "artistic dream about the ideal community" (109) and that the writer's willingness to participate in social upheaval does not extend to taking up arms. As Grossman puts it somewhat awkwardly, Dostoevsky "was ready to serve the rebelling masses with just a printing press" (ibid.).

The tension between Dostoevsky the artist and Dostoevsky the social reformer manifests itself in his reading of Belinsky's letter to Gogol at one of the Petrashevsky circle's Friday gatherings. While the ideologist "endorsed Belinsky's 'minimal program' such as the abolition of slavery, physical punishment, and the strict implementation of the law," the artist "worshipped Gogol and must have been pained by Belinsky's personal angry condemnations of him [Gogol]" (133). In the same vein, Dostoevsky's testimony during his subsequent interrogation was first and foremost the statement of a free artist, who "protests against the violence of censorship upon his artistic designs and openly wages a battle for his own tragic style in Russian literature" (137).

It is hard to avoid the temptation to interpret Dostoevsky's Siberian imprisonment as an absolutely pivotal period in the writer's life. And Grossman does not. In the biography, Dostoevsky's four-year confinement in prison becomes a milestone, marking an experience of katabasis, during which he reformulates his artistic task. His unmediated encounter with the Russian people in the Siberian prison reveals to Dostoevsky the necessity of overcoming the separation between the Russian intelligentsia and the uneducated classes. The costs of such a conversion are rather high, since in order to achieve it, Dostoevsky must reject "his socialist beliefs, which now seem to him directed against the people, cosmopolitan, un-Russian" (174). Grossman's understanding of the changes occurring during Dostoevsky's imprisonment exposes the ultimate unsustainability of the Soviet dichotomy of Dostoevsky as a writer of genius and a backward thinker. Hence, while his arrest, trial, and hard labor clinch Dostoevsky's maturation as a writer, symbolically they also become acts of his "moral execution" (173) and complete his turn "from the Utopian socialism of the forties to the reactionary convictions of the post-prison period" (174). Grossman carefully omits any mention of Dostoevsky's pre-prison religiosity, while at the same time emphasizing the writer's lapsed relationship with the Christian faith after Siberia. Most importantly, Grossman suggests that Dostoevsky experiences a transformative religious crisis during his mock execution in 1849, after which "a 'lack of faith' will forever remain at the foundation of Dostoevsky's worldview" (176).

After his release from prison, Dostoevsky's worldview becomes increasingly conservative. Dostoevsky's definitive switch to "the dark and ominous forces" of history (298) occurs in the mid-1860s with the publication of his journal *The Epoch*, where he undertakes open and irreconcilable polemics with the liberal journal *The Contemporary*. *Notes from the Underground*, published in 1864, during what Grossman calls a personally and politically "terrible" year in Dostoevsky's life, celebrates the victory of Stirner's glorification of the self at the expense of others over Chernyshevsky's rational egoism. At the same time, true to his method, Grossman insists that Dostoevsky's artistic gift helps him overcome his ideological conservatism in his major prose. The artist prevails over the reactionary. Hence, in Grossman's reading, *Crime and Punishment* is first and foremost a social novel, in which Dostoevsky gives a series of vivid and accurate portraits, inseparable from the social context of the times. In the novel, "for the first time in Russian literature, the theme of capital ... assumes ... the character and depth of ... gripping social tragedy" (334). Dostoevsky's attempt to depict the bankruptcy of nihilism ultimately grows into the denunciation of individualism, which in the novel's epilogue "crumbles before the simple laws of wise universal life." In *The Idiot*, Dostoevsky depicts the struggle of "an ideal man" against developing Russian capitalism, but fails to resolve the contradictions that plague Myshkin's character in which "the homeless wanderer" and the "declassé remnant of the dying kin" becomes a millionaire and "delivers speeches in defense and praise of titled nobility and high-ranking strata" (421–22). The true pinnacle of the novel is the contrasting character of Nastasia Fillipovna, who in Grossman's version becomes "an embodiment of moral sensitivity and purity, the drive towards the ideal and love" (422). While Myshkin is doomed to inaction, Nastasia Fillipovna is "a brave character, capable of protest and struggle" (ibid.).

Similarly, Grossman's reading of *Demons*—the most controversial work from the point of view of the Soviet establishment—emphasizes the inadequacy of Dostoevsky's social and political views. Here, Dostoevsky the artist plays a trick on Dostoevsky the political thinker. Under Dostoevsky's pen, Nechaev, "who amazed his contemporaries with his tragic character and hard-tempered will," becomes a petty caricature (451). According to Grossman, Dostoevsky achieves his satiric goals but misses the opportunity to present the true character of the revolutionary movement in contemporary Russia. Once again, accepting the framework of Dostoevsky as the politically narrow-minded artistic genius forces Grossman to put forth interpretations that are hard to piece together. Accordingly, Dostoevsky misunderstands the true significance of the rising political unrest in the country because of his poor political acumen yet discerns its historical truth because of his incredible artistic perception. Grossman notes that in the notebooks to *The Adolescent*, Dostoevsky jots down Versilov's thoughts on the inevitability of the victory of communism. Grossman refuses to engage, however, with Dostoevsky's statement that the historical triumph of communism is also "the most distant point from the kingdom of heaven," and that Dostoevsky's farsightedness is rather of an apocalyptic nature (441).

Dostoevsky's last novel brings him full circle back to his first, and in Grossman's interpretation, he once again produces a social novel. The difference between the beginning and the end of Dostoevsky's creative career is in the scale of these works. In *The Brothers Karamazov*, Dostoevsky depicts a vast—epic—panorama of Russian life. His lack of faith in man's social instincts drives Dostoevsky's critique of socialism in the novel, forcing the writer "to reject truly humanistic, atheistic, revolutionary ethics" (510). Yet, once again, Dostoevsky's artistry sets the record straight by giving Ivan an argument against the cruelty and injustice of the tsarist regime that is hard to refute. But even more than a depiction of any specific character, the *constructive principles* of the novel allow Dostoevsky to transcend his own ideological narrow-mindedness: "if one evaluates *The Brothers Karamazov* from the positions set by the artist himself in accordance to his own constructive laws, Dostoevsky's last novel appears as a true conclusion to his artistic path, a comprehensive synthesis of his creative experience, the expansion of the novel-poem to the novel-epos" (518).

While for Bakhtin, Dostoevsky transcends the social novel to produce a new kind of philosophical novel in which characters engage each other in a dialogue by taking existential rather than social positions, in Grossman's biography, the artist transcends the ideologist. As a result, true social reality shines through Dostoevsky's ideological confusion: "All of his pamphlets against the nihilists are pushed into the background by the wise and sensitive heart of a great artist" (530). To solidify his embrace of Dostoevsky's artistic talent, Grossman concludes the biography by quoting Stepan Trofimovich's argument for the everlasting significance of Shakespeare and Raphael: "The enthusiasm of contemporary youth is just as pure and bright as it was in our time. Only one thing happened: the goals switched; one beauty was substituted with another" (ibid.). Ascribing these words to Dostoevsky himself, Grossman ends by insisting that Dostoevsky accepted the revolution as the new ideal of beauty for the younger generation of Russians. Together with his "unforgettable portrayals and astounding dramas permeated with burning social rebellion," this firmly secures Dostoevsky's place in the Russian literary pantheon: "Despite all his effort to become a proponent of darkness, he continues to be the bearer of light" (502).

THE PHILOSOPHER AND THE PATRIOT

If Grossman's biography, proclaiming the triumph of the artist and the defeat of the ideologist, satisfied the necessities of the Thaw, the late Soviet period, also known as the Stagnation, needed a new approach. Yuri Seleznev, the former head editor of *ZhZL* and a Dostoevsky scholar, solves the problem of Dostoevsky's staunch opposition to the growing socialist movement in Russia in his 1981 biography by suggesting that the difference between the writer and his ideological opponents has been exaggerated and/or misunderstood.[24] Seleznev's Dostoevsky is not altogether an orthodox Soviet writer, but he is not anti-Soviet either. Rather, he is "late Soviet," made wise by the recent experiences of the darkness of Stalinism, and somewhat of a philosophical dissident. What makes the argument for writing Dostoevsky into the late Soviet framework difficult paradoxically also makes it quite possible: the motivating principle behind the writer's work is similar to what moved his revolutionary contemporaries. Both wanted to improve the lot of humanity, both engaged in the same task, hence, Dostoevsky's discord with the radical critics has been exaggerated in earlier Soviet criticism. Dostoevsky's writings help the Socialist cause by rallying the readers against deviations from authentic socialism.

Besides bridging the gap between Dostoevsky and the radical critics, Seleznev's biography embraces Dostoevsky as Russia's most philosophical writer; in fact, corresponding to the rise of reader interest in existential, philosophical questions among the Soviet intelligentsia during the Stagnation era, the biography is congenial to its subject matter. The monograph is structured around two existentially critical experiences in Dostoevsky's life from which the narrative pendulum swings back and forth. The execution scene on December 22, 1849, becomes the point of reference for the first half of the book; Dostoevsky's death on January 28, 1881, is the second. While waiting for his execution on Semenovsky Square, Dostoevsky remembers his childhood, the loss of his mother, his studies at engineering school, his first literary success, etc. For the most part, the narrative lens of Seleznev's biography is Dostoevsky's consciousness, and large chunks of the text are filtered through it. The narrator—not unlike the narrator of *Crime and Punishment*—hovers over his protagonist.

As a result, Seleznev's approach often reads like fiction. The reader gets access to Dostoevsky's inner monologues, thoughts, and aspirations. Hence, we get to hear young Dostoevsky's fantasies on becoming the next Pushkin: "he [Pushkin] didn't want at all to be exiled anywhere, even though it is so pity-inducing and exalting . . . God forgive me my sinful thoughts, let this cup pass me by; don't let me anger anyone, even the school authorities or I'll end up repeating another year again—it's better to die right away" (40). This passage is a typical one. Unlike Grossman, who here and there picks up on the correspondences between Dostoevsky's life and his prose, in Seleznev's biography, Dostoevsky's prose constantly permeates his life. Thus, Dmitry Karamazov's dream about the wee one forces itself into Dostoevsky's encounter with peasants during his visit to Staraya Kikenka; in another case, as the writer laments his lack of money for tea, he anachronistically quotes the Underground Man. On becoming a member of the Panaev circle after the publication of *Poor Folk* and falling in love with Panaeva, Dostoevsky's thoughts are borrowed from *The Idiot*: "She's very pretty . . . if only she were kind" (77). Raskolnikov's prophetic dream first comes to Dostoevsky: "He fantasized at times about a vision that was at first unclear, but each time became more and more complete: that the whole world was condemned to be sacrificed to some terrifying, unheard of pestilence coming from the depths of Asia" (326). In numerous places in the biography, Dostoevsky's characters often become prototypes for their author.

If fiction penetrates life, life intrudes into prose. On numerous occasions, Seleznev not only quotes Dostoevsky's works but also rewrites them, as in an imagined scene from *The Double*: "And he ran home, to complain to himself about everything, to ask himself for some advice. He ran home, but if some strange observer suddenly saw him, he'd undoubtedly decide that Yakov Petrovich was running not to his own self but was trying to escape from himself" (69). Ultimately, the relationship Seleznev builds between Dostoevsky's life and his prose is mimetic: "Creators transfer their ordeals into their work in order to give people the possibility of reliving what they lived through over and over" (78).

In Seleznev's view, from his very first literary endeavors, Dostoevsky's major concern—like that of the contemporary radical intelligentsia—is the fate of Russia and its people. In "The Landlady" Dostoevsky already creates a sociopolitical allegory in which Russia's soul becomes the battleground for the opposing forces of the old and the new. Ordynsky, a young dreamer loses Katerina (Russia) to Murin, the old usurper, because he is lacking a concrete plan of action. At this point, the inability to act, however, is shared by the novella's author. Dostoevsky's wake-up call comes from Belinsky. The relationship between the critic and the writer plants seeds of doubt in the latter that will never be rooted out: "Never again would he be able to return to the naïve religiosity of his childhood and youth, no one would be able to make him into an Orthodox believer" (106). Unlike Grossman, however, Seleznev does not hide the role of religion in Dostoevsky's life—numerous chapters, for example, feature epigraphs taken from the Gospels. Yet, religious references obtain a rather philosophical status in the biography. They are present to frame the subject's existential struggles. Likewise, socialism does not contradict religious philosophizing; unlike religion, however, it offers its believers a course of action. The failures of *The Double* and "The Landlady" force Dostoevsky to question the power of the word to affect positive change. Belinsky offers the religious idealist Dostoevsky a concrete course of action. Under the critic's influence, "the word and the deed coalesced into a unity of his idea and passion, which took complete possession of him for a while. Perhaps forever? Who knows?" (108).

The jolt Dostoevsky receives from Belinsky leads the writer to Siberia. Just like Grossman, Seleznev treats the years of Dostoevsky's imprisonment as transformative, a threshold or a crossing through which Dostoevsky enters a period of maturity. Unlike Grossman, however, who tends to interpret Dostoevsky's transformation in Siberia as an irrevocable turn away from the progressive ideals of his youth, for Seleznev it becomes a fertile existential terrain loaded with potentiality, a place of revelation where Dostoevsky discovers his true calling. Life among other prisoners engenders Dostoevsky's most persistent ideas on the nature of good and evil. It also provides him with numerous plans, designs, and character prototypes, but most importantly, it reveals to Dostoevsky the transcendent beauty of the Russian people, who from that point on serve as the writer's indelible moral compass. Describing Dostoevsky's Siberian epiphany, Seleznev readily retells *The House of the Dead*. As seen previously, Dostoevsky's prose begets Seleznev's prose about the writer's life:

> Dostoevsky even jumped up on the bunk bed, came to and suddenly realized that he was still smiling with the same childish smile of calm as after a panic attack, as if the gentle, almost maternal smile of the serf Marei was still lingering inside of him . . . And then he, still not understanding why, crawled down from the bunk—something happened to him, as if a white dove flew through the darkness of his spiritual temple, and he suddenly went through the barracks between the bunk beds peering into the faces of the chained convicts, and for some reason no one insulted him, no one cursed him, and he felt that he could look at them completely differently than before, with a different eye, without hatred or disgust (151–52).

From this point of view, Dostoevsky's life can be seen as a prolonged meditation on the ideas present in his prose: "The idea of egotheism was completely revealed to him during hard labor as a tyrannical idea now became more odious than anything to him: the prison 'god' Krivtsov, the European idol Napoleon—aren't they the same? God doesn't reside in power, but in truth—this is the conviction of the people: it will perhaps bow to power . . . but it will only submit to truth. And if you want to be needed by your people, you have to submit to their truth—such were his thoughts now" (166). For Seleznev's Dostoevsky, Russian people and Russia are symbolic of each other. Russia *is* the people's truth and the true Russia is the ideal to which he, by following the people, will consciously direct his aspirations. Ironically, the catalyst that prods Dostoevsky to realize his affinity with the Russian people is Alexander Mirecki, one of the imprisoned Poles, who expresses his hatred for the Russians in French.

Dostoevsky's recognition of the internal beauty of the Russian people's soul and the metonymic relationship between the people and Russia gives birth to *pochvennichestvo*, which Seleznev defines as "that spiritual-moral layer of sociopolitical life on the basis of which the encounter and the organic unity between the intelligentsia and the people, between education and the people's morality, between culture and nationality become possible" (237). For Seleznev, Dostoevsky's newly discovered ideals are not much different from those espoused by the radical critics. The factors that put Dostoevsky into ideological proximity with the socialists consist of their common goal—the welfare of the downtrodden, and their common enemy—capitalism, which, undoubtedly inspired by *The Idiot*, appears in the biography as a spider, an image which seems to haunt Dostoevsky throughout his life.

Gradually and thoroughly, Seleznev debunks Soviet criticism of Dostoevsky's ideological warfare against Chernyshevsky and *The Contemporary* in his prose and journalism. While this continues the ongoing process of rehabilitating Dostoevsky within the Soviet context, it also considerably distorts and dilutes Dostoevsky's ideological polemics. In this sense, Grossman's biography, which acknowledges Dostoevsky's ideological inadequacy as it attempts to quarantine it, paradoxically provides a more accurate portrayal of Dostoevsky's views. Hence, Seleznev suggests that the sting of Dostoevsky's writing was directed against the same contingent of "cynics, egoists, and bourgeois moneymakers" as Chernyshevsky's social theory (219). What Dostoevsky railed against was not Chernyshevsky's ideals—those he shared—but their unconscionable corruption by those like Valkovsky from *The Humiliated and Insulted* or Luzhin from *Crime and Punishment*. The short story "Crocodile" is not Dostoevsky's parody on Chernyshevsky, but a mockery of those like Antonovich and Zaitsev who vulgarized Chernyshevsky's theories.

Consequently, along with the radical critics, Dostoevsky perceives the reforms of 1861 as a manifestation of Russia's deep social crisis and submits them to a sweeping critique: "Dostoevsky almost physically, as if on his own skin, perceived the germs of the start of a 'chemical disintegration' of society" (249). Seleznev's comprehensive description of Dostoevsky's polemics in the 1860s paints a continuous struggle against Russian capitalism in which Chernyshevsky remains—despite all their differences—a steadfast ally: "With Western theories people will not understand us and will not follow us—he was completely convinced of this; the only thing that surprised him was that he suddenly noticed how in his thoughts he continued to say 'we' 'us' 'to us,' in essence seeing himself as part of Chernyshevsky's and Herzen's camp, even as he clearly understood all the contradictions that separated them, all the differences in how they defined their path to reach social justice" (261–62). In the final analysis, Seleznev proposes that Dostoevsky's argument with Chernyshevsky and Dobrolyubov was not about the theory itself, but about the degree of their disagreement with the status quo and their willingness to rush history:

> Revolution? . . . No, he would not be scared by the revolution: when it was a question of freeing the people, he was ready to come out to the square and ended up in hard labor; during that time, Chernyshevsky had barely finished the seminary and Dobrolyubov was probably still a child. But now, when the main question has been resolved peacefully, without a revolt like Pugachev's (*pugachevshchina*), should we call the people to revolt? Where are you rushing

to? Society is not ready, the people are estranged from the intelligentsia; we haven't worked out a language with which to speak to the people, and you want to explain your theories to them in ten minutes. You're rushing not after history, but after theory (262).

The differences are significant, yet, for Seleznev they are not crucial; what is much more important is the commonality of their goals, which reveals itself once *The Contemporary* is temporarily shut down in 1862 and Chernyshevsky and Pisarev are arrested. Dostoevsky publishes in his journal *Time* what Seleznev calls an impassioned defense of his ideological opponents. This clearly positions Dostoevsky on the "right" side of history: "This once again was not a simple act of civic courage by *Time* and Dostoevsky personally, but also a desperate outcry and an act of defiance" (273). Over the course of the biography Selelznev continuously insists that what connects Dostoevsky and the radical critics is a relationship of productive tension where each side helps the other hone its arguments by attacking its weak spots. The leaders of Russian liberalism evoke unfailing respect in Dostoevsky:

> At the end of May he found out that Chernyshevsky was sent to Siberian hard labor, into the Nerchin mines. He clearly saw how the proud, independent character of Nikolai Gavrilovich would fare there, especially with his weak health . . . Well, it's no sin to say they weren't like-minded people; they argued and cursed each other, but both Chernyshevsky and Dobrolyubov were real fighters, loyal to an idea that might have been false, according to Dostoevsky, in the means of achieving it, but nevertheless kindred in its goals. To fight with them meant to move their common thinking towards the truth, and he still did not give up the hope of being understood. The new ones, who came to replace them only knew how to vulgarize the ideas they did not produce (310).

In a similar vein, in *Demons* Dostoevsky condemns not socialism per se, but its Bakunin-Nechaev variant.[25] Unlike Grossman, Seleznev interprets Dostoevsky's most polemical novel not as an unsuccessful caricature of Russian revolutionary movements, but as a reflection of the deviation from Chernyshevsky's true socialism. *Demons* is Dostoevsky's warning about the potential corruption of the liberal agenda even as he continues to retain a close affinity with its brand as espoused by Chernyshevsky.

In fact, Seleznev spends quite a lot of time arguing for the affinity between Dostoevsky's particular kind of Christianity and socialism and suggests that ultimately Dostoevsky would be quite happy with "socialism with a Christian face." Dostoevsky's problem with socialism comes down to his apprehensions about reason as the only basis for the formation of the socialist superstructure. As if foreseeing the Soviet twentieth century, Dostoevsky warns his contemporaries that building the future with nothing but reason, "without morality, free from the oversight of conscience," will result in a nightmare (507). Revolution without a moral center will be "immediately exploited by the global bourgeois" (499). In the final analysis, however, Dostoevsky turns out to be not so much an opponent of socialism, but a partisan of spirituality, accepting that the archetypal struggle between the forces of reason and spirituality is necessary for Russia's rebirth. Socialism and Christianity are two products born out of a single desire. Undoubtedly looking back at his country's recent past, Seleznev creates a Dostoevsky who urges socialism and Christianity to stand against their common enemy, the ominous third, the Grand Inquisitor, who personifies the power of the few over the many and seeks to exploit both for his own gains: "Here is his work of erecting the power of its mysterious temple on those who were defeated in these struggles against each other and the Christian and socialist hopes and expectations, the mocked, buried, maligned eternal values, on the ruins of man's faith in himself, in his high spiritual nature, on the crucified faith into an open—not secret—universal brotherhood for everyone and not only for select few" (508–9).[26]

In an attempt to reconcile Dostoevsky with socialist ideology, Seleznev develops a formula, the final product of which is Dostoevsky's version of a particular "Russian socialism," a synthesis between the antithetical forces of socialism and Christianity. Seleznev provides a fictionalization of Dostoevsky's meditation on the subject: "I know—he read his recently written notes, which were about to reach their readers—they might laugh at me, but my last word in the main argument, the argument between Christianity and socialism will be this: they must unite in the name of the idea of Russian socialism" (535). Ultimately, Seleznev endows Dostoevsky with a voice that is much needed for the period of late Stagnation, during which the Soviet ideological edifice had come to its most ossified point and required an injection of moral idealism in order to persevere. Only then, replete with "spiritual freedom and equality" (536), could Russia deliver to other nations its "special, final word—the word of a loving, brotherly unity of all peoples, of which, having forcefully split themselves into sects, they have not properly heard" (488).

THE WRITER

One of the difficulties of writing Dostoevsky's post-Soviet biography is that the biographers, in distancing themselves from ideological readings of Dostoevsky's works, are still preoccupied with the man and his beliefs and cannot find refuge in purely aesthetic analysis. Lyudmila Saraskina's solution is to make the figure of the artist into a cornerstone of her monumental study of Dostoevsky's life. In the most recent Dostoevsky biography in the *ZhZL* series (2011), she also foregrounds both Dostoevsky's lifelong deep religiosity and his growing political conservatism after his return from Siberia. Yet, precisely because the roles both play in Dostoevsky's life are no longer questioned, their presence in the biography serves to emphasize the book's main focus—the life of a *writer*. Hence, the simplest answer to the difference between Dostoevsky—who said that finding proof of God's existence was the main goal of his life—and his God-seeking characters is that unlike them, Dostoevsky was able to successfully overcome his demons through the consistent and heroic practice of writing.

In a single gesture in her introduction Saraskina rejects most of Soviet-era Dostoevsky criticism, but also advises against the present-day tendency to declare Dostoevsky to be a teacher and a spiritual leader. Instead of treating Dostoevsky as a means to serve present-day political and spiritual needs, Saraskina uses the biography to present Dostoevsky as an end in himself, which she argues, "would reveal his essence to those who think, read, and write about him."[27] In the footsteps of Father Sergius Bulgakov, Saraskina declares the attempt to grasp "the nature of Dostoevsky's soul" as an "intimate spiritual experience" (18).

How does this translate into an approach? To begin with, motivated by Dostoevsky's own philosophical attitude to his historical context, Saraskina separates Dostoevsky from his literal ancestry. Educated Russians, in the ideological tumult of the second half of the nineteenth century, appeared to be torn away from their family roots. As Saraskina notes, "in the space of chaos one can hardly find a place for connection between two coterminous generations" (32). Not unlike Bakhtin, Saraskina argues that while the sociopolitical context forms Dostoevsky's characters, it does not circumscribe them, instead providing them with the proper conditions for an existential crisis.[28] She collapses the difference between historical and textual realities—the lost generations she's describing are not just *raznochintsy* but Dostoevsky's *raznochintsy*. Saraskina steps over the epistemological divide and, as a result, the implied author merges with the biographical one: "the idea of decay" posited by Arkady in *The Adolescent* becomes central for Dostoevsky's vision of his own life. And vice versa: the lack of Dostoevsky's interest in his own genealogy gains confirmation by the social entropy found in his novels. In Saraskina's somber count the mortality in Dostoevsky's novels rises from twenty-one deaths in *Crime and Punishment* to forty-three deaths in *The Brothers Karamazov*: "In a world where inherited values have fallen and gotten destroyed, the roots no longer feed the crowns . . . ancestry, even if someone still remembers it, no longer helps either a person's self-identity or his greatness" (34). As Saraskina states, Dostoevsky was the only Russian writer cut off from his ancestors.

At the same time, having established Dostoevsky's existential independence and isolation from his ancestors, Saraskina insists on the importance for Dostoevsky of his *family*. In direct argument with Grossman, the first major polemical thrust of Saraskina's biography consists of a thorough rehabilitation of Dostoevsky's father, who is characterized as one of "the best people," and his parents together as a major force in providing the future writer with a happy childhood and the necessary conditions for his creative development. As Saraskina states, "The writer Dostoevsky is a rare, perhaps the single representative of Russian classical literature who was not physically punished during his childhood" (68). Moreover, Saraskina spends considerable time exposing the lack of foundation for the hypothesis about the murder of Dostoevsky's father. Challenging the conventional understanding of Dostoevsky's father's character and the manner of his death, she reexamines Dostoevsky's childhood and youth, insisting that they were not traumatic, but provided him with a well-rounded education and unconditional love, without which Dostoevsky's artistic gifts might not have blossomed.

His father's death marks the boundary between Dostoevsky's youth and mature life and determines his choice of activity. The choice, importantly, is the choice of freedom, and Dostoevsky's discovery of his literary gift is akin to "the discovery of the laws of nature" (111). Characteristically, while his first literary experiments occur alongside periods of intense reading of Western literature, his characters spring to life spontaneously, as if against this tradition: "he could hardly explain back then why against the background of romantic heroes and poetic heroines from those vivid books which excited his imagination, he fantasized about a pair of deserted misfits in *Poor Folk*—an older functionary-clerk and his dowerless orphan neighbor" (125–26). At the same time, Dostoevsky's internal artistic freedom is opposed to the external pressure from his critics. The reaction of Belinsky and the Panaev circle to "The Landlady" is predominantly ideological. Saraskina's language in describing this ideology is quite telling: "In translation from party language to one commonly understood this meant that the author of the novella betrayed the trend, deviated from the line of social condemnation and wandered into the thicket of fanciful fantasies inspired by Hoffmann and Marlinsky" (151). Thus, Saraskina describes the first occurrence of the dynamic that in Dostoevsky's life would become a constant and continue posthumously: the internally unconstrained artist struggling to brush off those who try to fit his authentic genius into the Procrustean bed of their ideology. This insight also determines the biography's polemical drive: if Dostoevsky strives to "emancipate himself from literary authorities" (151), Saraskina attempts to emancipate her protagonist from the previous tendentious interpretations of his life and works.

Dostoevsky's refusal to fit into the framework forced upon him by others becomes evident in his participation in the Petrashevsky conspiracy. The dividing line between Dostoevsky and the Petrashevsky circle's members is the same one that separates the spirit of socialism from its letter: the embrace of "the social *spirit*" by the writer is opposed by the preference for "social mechanics" (183). In this sense, Dostoevsky seems to resemble his hero George Sand, whose petit bourgeois background was sufficient for Belinsky to write her off as a social reformer and in whose works Dostoevsky "saw more socialism than in socialist circles" (ibid.). In general, Saraskina is extremely wary of the vice of ideology. As she puts it, "searching for the answer to the question of Russia's paths of development, public opinion suffered from ideological terror that came not only from the authorities, but also from opposite directions and groups.... The despotism of 'progressive ideas' and 'cutting-edge directions' was at times scarier than the despotism of the regime and, in any case, was more merciless and uncompromising" (206). Her Dostoevsky fights hard not to give in to ideological pressure from either side—conservative or liberal—and at times comes off not as a practitioner of a Bakhtinian dialogic mode of thinking but as someone who tries to resist any kind of ideological defilement at all costs. Appropriately, Saraskina depicts Dostoevsky's relationship with Speshnev as a psychological, not a political seduction. Dostoevsky's growing enthusiasm for Speshnev is presented as a psychological and philosophical problem—even the most correct ideology cannot protect one from giving up one's will to another, of turning into a follower of Nechaev. The dynamics of power transcend political affiliations.

In this biography two interrelated factors become integral for Dostoevsky's survival and his spiritual development—his faith and writing. Beginning with his imprisonment and until the end of his life, Dostoevsky is first and foremost a writer. Keeping a notebook in Siberia helps him not only to "run away from reality" but also to "transform reality" (263). In the same spirit Saraskina argues that Dostoevsky's servile poem "On the European Events in 1854," written right after his liberation, should be seen outside of its political context, called to life by the necessity to write: "Here was something else: the soldier Dostoevsky, who was just freed from hard labor, could not forget that he was a writer" (277). If writing is Dostoevsky's primary instrument of salvation, Christianity fills it with spirit. Both allow Dostoevsky to persevere. Dostoevsky's Siberian ordeal is thus framed with moments of his professions of faith. During the mock execution the difference between Dostoevsky and Speshnev is revealed in their farewell as Dostoevsky tells Speshnev "Nous serons avec le Christ" only to receive an atheistic bon mot in response: "un peu de poussière" (241). Bracketing the years of ordeal from the other end is Dostoevsky's famous letter to the Decembrist wife, Natalia Fonvizina, in which he announces Christ to be his only symbol of faith, and which Saraskina—the only Dostoevsky biographer in the series to do so—quotes in full.

If for Saraskina the ultimate goal of the biography is Dostoevsky's inner life, then the ultimate goal for Dostoevsky is writing. For years deprived of social and literary life, Dostoevsky throws himself into literary and journalistic activity after his return to Petersburg with true abandon. Yet, the tension between external constraints and internal desires remains a necessary constant: to flourish, creative freedom must push against conditions of perpetual financial dependence. Saraskina suggests that Dostoevsky's torturous relationship with his publishers secures his own literary production: "A paradoxical situation took shape: more than anything the author was afraid to work on contract, under a deadline, and for pay, within 'a system of constant debt'; yet, outside of this system, without contracts and journal creditors, he could not do anything. Dreaming of freedom, he himself, with his own will, cut off all paths to freedom and forced himself into bondage, which turned out to be a firm creative bridle" (323). Dedicated to writing, Dostoevsky's life is marked by self-sacrifice and ceaseless labor. The constant shortage of money began as early as his studies at the Engineering Institute and continued well into his midlife period, marked by obsessive gambling interspersed with periods of "ultimate poverty," and condemned Dostoevsky to work as a literary proletarian. Yet, for Saraskina, it is these very conditions that paradoxically allowed Dostoevsky's continuous absorption with writing. To stoke up the fire of creativity, Dostoevsky had to be caught in the "snare of hopelessness" (533). Continuous inspiration became a product of Dostoevsky's economic circumstances, and his publishers, especially Katkov, knew how to exploit this process.

Most of Saraskina's analysis of Dostoevsky's prose focuses on how it reflects his identity as a writer. Even in his early works, Dostoevsky appears to be a modernist avant la lettre, self-reflexively investigating the nature of creativity in his texts. What interests Saraskina in *Poor Folk* and "The Village of Stepanchikovo" is how both develop the theme of writing: "The boundless force of epistolary composition governs *Poor Folk*. Each letter takes hours of literary labor. For the two wretches, their private correspondence manifests not just a necessity to love, but also a literary debut, the habit of expressing love stylistically" (132). The figure of the writer similarly comes to the foreground in Saraskina's readings of Dostoevsky's prose after his return from exile. Thus, Saraskina reads *The Humiliated and Insulted* as a meta-novel: "Dostoevsky created a phenomenal plot: the protagonists of *The Humiliated and Insulted* read and discussed the novel *Poor Folk*, as if written by Ivan Petrovich" (348). Dostoevsky's self-reflection is partially explained by the feuilleton nature of his literary activity: when submerged into the journalistic milieu of the early sixties, Dostoevsky creates characters, "whose life, like the life of their author, is inseparably connected with the fate of the text they created. The characters/writers are the first to take on the strokes of misfortune" (ibid.).

With the mechanism of literary production in place, Dostoevsky is able to give himself fully to writing. Writing is freed from everything extraneous to it—be it money or fame—and becomes a goal in itself. Life crosses into literature, and literature, in turn, influences life. Dostoevsky's early characters take on the features of their author, "adopting and assimilating the truly fanatical commitment of the author to writing" (354). In Saraskina's rather cursory reading of *Notes from the House of the Dead*, Goryanchikov saves himself from despair by literary activity.

In contrast, beginning with *Notes from the Underground*, Saraskina's analysis of Dostoevsky's later prose strongly delineates the difference between the characters and their author. Importantly, Saraskina insists that Dostoevsky shares characteristics with his creations; indeed, some of Dostoevsky's most ethically compromised protagonists are born out of his ability for introspection. Yet, the transformation of his inner demons onto paper exorcises them and becomes Dostoevsky's saving grace. Although selfishness and coldness might have colored the last period of Dostoevsky's first marriage, unlike his Underground Man, Dostoevsky never thinks to justify such qualities. Writing allows him to work through problems as Dostoevsky continuously seeks to improve himself as a person.

Saraskina's first extensive analysis of Dostoevsky's prose is her reading of *Crime and Punishment*. She argues against the logic of crime and punishment as a path to salvation. In her interpretation, Raskolnikov is first and foremost a murderer, and it is not accidental that Dostoevsky forever leaves his promised resurrection outside the novel. Writing from the other side of the twentieth century, Saraskina sees the end of the novel as purposefully ambiguous: "the process of renewal could give an unexpected lurch. The path of Raskolnikovs in the twentieth century—this foresight contains the whole power of Dostoevsky's creative astuteness—will turn not towards personal resurrection, but towards mass terror" (450–51). What matters most here, however, is that with all the similarities between Dostoevsky and Raskolnikov ("like some of his heroes . . . Dostoevsky because of his passionate nature 'everywhere and in everything' would reach the final boundaries and 'all of his life would cross the line'" [452]), the author is radically different from the character: "to know himself and to know God, Dostoevsky did not have to commit a murder. Based on his own example he demonstrated that lack of faith and doubt are not the necessary characteristics of personal villainy. He went through Siberian hard labor, like Raskolnikov, yet it was for reading a letter from Belinsky to Gogol, not murder" (ibid.).

Similarly, in *Demons*, whose analysis is longer than that of any other Dostoevsky novel,[29] Saraskina detects a search not just for the roots of Russia's political instability but, more importantly, she sees the novel as the author's journey into the depths of his own psyche. In her reading, the existential exists on par with the political as Dostoevsky attempts to understand the inner dynamics of his attraction to Speshnev and political activity in general: "Who was Dostoevsky in that story that happened such a long time ago—considering that later on he understood it as a patient's record? Where did he see his fault and where was the fault of others?" (530). Here the connection between Dostoevsky's life and his work is visible more than in any other novel. The search for and the discovery of Stavrogin's character marks a major step in Dostoevsky's quest for self-knowledge. As was the case with the Underground Man and Raskolnikov, Stavrogin's difference from Dostoevsky is conditioned on their similarities: "human destiny and the novelistic life of the hero must be merged with the destiny and the history of the author—this was the deep meaning of depicting a demon . . . To free oneself from the demon. . . one must possess him creatively" (545). Dostoevsky endows his hero with everything he does not have himself—beauty, self-possession, aristocracy, health. In *Demons* the theme of Christ reaches its culmination—having passed through the crucible of religious doubt, Dostoevsky forces his heroes to attain self-determination through Christ. The major accomplishment of the novel is undoubtedly the thorough portrayal of the "predatorial type." As expected, this also allows Dostoevsky to forever abandon his own underground by now being fully in control of it: "to grasp the mysteries of the underground means to grasp and overcome its demons" (576–77). The biggest gamble of Dostoevsky's life pays off and the result is "not a double, but an antipode" (551). His creative endeavors have the power to realign life. As a side effect, the existential gamble of *Demons* puts a stop to Dostoevsky's obsession with roulette, and—almost mystically—finally turns Dostoevsky's desperate financial affairs around.

Unlike his characters, who are doomed to act out their inner struggles, Dostoevsky saves himself by writing. Through writing he is able to sublimate his passions and destructive obsessions (such as gambling) and also provide himself with means of sustenance. In Saraskina's biography, Dostoevsky's life appears as a tireless struggle against an incredible conglomeration of bad circumstances (the terribly unjust punishment for reading the Belinsky letter or the death of his first wife and brother during the same fateful year of 1864) on the one hand and his own passionate nature on the other. The main instrument of resistance for Dostoevsky is his work. As Saraskina writes about Dostoevsky's initial impulse for writing *The Idiot*: "The soul was unwell, but the call of work was relentless—only work was able to get him out of the trap and cure his soul" (495).

Consequently, if one of the crucial differences between Dostoevsky and Stavrogin is the latter's absence of creative talent, the writing impulse is what brings Dostoevsky close to his other protagonist, Arkady Dolgoruky of *The Adolescent*. Hence, Arkady's "spiritual growth takes place not during those four months when he . . . rushed about Petersburg from one house to another, but during that 'post-plot' time when in his notes he tried to make sense of what had happened" (627). Arkady's maturity occurs inasmuch as he grows as a writer; identifying himself as such protects his confession from corruption.

The theme of Dostoevsky as a writer is undoubtedly the main one of this biography. Beginning with his early experiments, Dostoevsky is portrayed as an inspired writer in possession of an inexhaustible imagination, a literary proletarian for whom writing is not just a chosen profession, but also a necessary means for salvation—not just from endless financial difficulties but, more importantly, from the excesses of his character. Writing is an instrument for Dostoevsky's successful battling with his own nature, but it is also a goal: notwithstanding his and his family's financial dependence on writing, it is always higher than life's troubles, it alone can take Dostoevsky to the heights of pure inspiration, it is the only endeavor that makes his life meaningful. The numerous peripeteias of Dostoevsky's life might slow down his path as a writer but are never able to interrupt its continuity. In Saraskina's summation, the salutary effect writing has on Dostoevsky's life takes on an existential dimension:

> Dostoevsky's most interesting heroes live to "work out a thought," but they do nothing else and perish either from a bullet or a noose, "eaten up by an idea." Like his heroes, Dostoevsky was similarly obsessed with ideas, tortured by God's existence, perplexed over the search for and affirmation of truth. However, in contrast to some of his heroes, murderers and suicides, he saved himself through creative work, without sinking into idleness and destructive despondency. The world of "fixed" ideas, his obsessive thinking about God plus his salvific and resurrectional writing activity—this is what Dostoevsky was, the main protagonist of all of his novels." (637)

Yet, while the biography prioritizes the philosophical and metaphysical over the social and political, Saraskina's contemporary preferences nevertheless come through in her description of Dostoevsky's polemics with his critics. In Saraskina's undeniably biased evaluation of critical responses to Dostoevsky's work, he is comparable to an old lion surrounded by a pack of young hyenas. The negative critical perception of Dostoevsky's prose was a constant during his life and largely continued into the Soviet era. In contrast to dismissive critics, Dostoevsky finds true love and appreciation from his readers. In Saraskina's account, unlike in the politically engaged criticism of Dostoevsky's time, the readers' reaction is pure: "Dostoevsky didn't think twice: it was always nicer and more important to hear a reader's encouraging words" (649). Even within Dostoevsky's lifetime, time and history are on the writer's side: "Already in the years immediately following *Demons*, Russian society was able to become convinced that the *nechaevshchina* (political devilry)—is a universal mechanism, plunging the 'pure hearted' fighter into terror as if into the abyss" (601).

Saraskina's reading of Dostoevsky's last novel most strongly reflects her own historical context. Rejecting a common interpretation of *The Brothers Karamazov*'s epilogue as an optimistic one, she insists that the novel ends with Dostoevsky's somber diagnosis for contemporary Russia. Alyosha's speech to the boys at Ilyusha's grave does not begin to wash away all the terrible, murderous devastation that occurs in the novel. The Karamazov family's destruction is symptomatic of an ineradicable social sickness. Social disintegration is carried over into the novel from life. In his delivery of the Pushkin speech, Saraskina compares Dostoevsky to Zosima and Russia to the world of the novel in which everything ends badly.

A comparative study of the three Dostoevsky biographies published in *ZhZL* clearly demonstrates that the formation of what can and cannot constitute a model worthy of emulation became a thoroughly ideological endeavor in the Soviet Union. And since *ZhZL* has always been meant for mass consumption, the series strongly reflects the changes in the Soviet ideological climate. In this sense, written in the early sixties, Grossman's biography of Dostoevsky presents its subject from within the well-established Soviet paradigm of Dostoevsky studies, put into circulation by Gorky and preserved with slight variations and several important exceptions until the late eighties. From within this paradigm Dostoevsky appeared as an artist of genius but a terrible ideologue. Seleznev's biography from twenty years later attempts to reconcile the artist-ideologue split and introduces philosophical and existential elements into its study. Likewise, while Saraskina's post-Soviet biography might push against the pedagogical ethos of Soviet biography, it still inevitably reflects its author's ideological situation. By debunking Soviet ideological censorship, Saraskina consciously strives to overcome its ideological limitations. Pledging to present its subject's inner life, the biography successfully depicts the complex life of the *writer*, yet often overlooks the *ideologue*. A thoroughly philosophical biography of such an ideologically engaged author as Dostoevsky pushes the reader to accept her own contemporary situation as post-ideological. This, however, as we know well, is wishful thinking.

NOTES

1. Vladimir Lenin, "Lev Tolstoi kak zerkalo russkoi revolutsii," in *Polnoe sobranie sochinenii* (Moscow: Izdatel'stvo politicheskoi literatury, 1968), 206–13.
2. Fedor Dostoevskii, "Pis'mo studentam moskovskogo universiteta," in *Polnoe sobranie sochinenii v tridtsati tomakh* (Leningrad: Nauka, 1972–90), vol. 30:1, 23. All translations from Russian are mine unless noted otherwise.
3. Mikhail Bakhtin, of course, finds a different way of negotiating this problem by arguing that there is no one ideological center in Dostoevsky's major fiction. See Mikhail Bakhtin, *Problems of Dostoevsky's Poetics*, ed. and trans. Caryl Emerson (Minneapolis: University of Minnesota Press, 1984).
4. Evgeny Dobrenko and Galin Tihanov, ed., *A History of Russian Literary Theory and Criticism: The Soviet Age and Beyond* (Pittsburgh: University of Pittsburgh Press, 2011), xi. Emphasis in the original.
5. Valerii Kirpotin, "Fedor Mikhailovich Dostoyevskii," *Zvezda*, no. 11 (1946): 185–86, cited in Vladimir Seduro, *Dostoevski in Russian Literary Criticism: 1846–1956* (New York: Octagon Books, 1969), 268. All further references to Seduro will be included in the text.
6. As Seduro states, the article "speaks sympathetically of the young Dostoevsky as an admirer of Belinsky, a progressive, a champion of the downtrodden, and who continues the traditions of Russian realism deriving from Pushkin's 'Stationmaster' and Gogol's 'Overcoat.' Like Tolstoy, Dostoevsky gave no quarter to false people or false ideas. Despite the change that occurred during his years in prison, Dostoevsky's writing continued to engender rebellion against social injustice in Russian youth. His rebellious characters were more forceful and clearer than his God-fearing heroes" (255).
7. David Zaslavskii, "Protiv idealizatsii reaktsionnykh vzglyadov Dostoevskogo," *Kultura i zhizn'* (Moscow, December 20, 1947). See a more detailed outline of Zaslavskii's article in Seduro, 276–82.
8. See David Zaslavskii, *F. M. Dostoyevskii: Kritikobiograficheskii ocherk* (Moscow: Goslitizdat, 1956).
9. See his *Dostoyevski in Russian Literary Criticism: 1846–1956* and *Dostoyevski's Image in Russia Today* (Belmont: Nordland Publishing Company, 1975).
10. Dostoevsky's first *ZhZL* biography was published in 1891 and written by professional biographer Evgenii Solov'ev. Since the focus of this essay is on the permutations of Dostoevsky's image in the Soviet and the post-Soviet eras, Solov'ev's biography of Dostoevsky will not be discussed here. It has been analyzed by Robert Belknap and Carol Apollonio as part of the forum on the *ZhZL* biography series (see "Dostoevsky in *The Lives of Remarkable People*," in *Slavic and East European Journal* 60, no. 2 (2016): 241–51), as has Solov'ev's work as a biographer by Caryl Emerson in "Remarkable Tolstoy, from the Age of Empire to the Putin Era (1894–2006)," *Slavic and East European Journal* 60, no. 2 (2016): 252–71.
11. At the time, Gorky was the chief of Academia's editorial board.

12. Maksim Gor'kii, "O 'Karamazovshchine'," in *Sobranie sochinenii v tridtsati tomakh*, vol. 24 (Moscow: Gosudarstvennoe izdatel'stvo russkoi literatury, 1953), 146.

13. Gor'kii, "Eshche o 'Karamazovshchine'," in *Sobranie sochinenii*, vol. 24, 154.

14. Gor'kii, "O 'Karamazovshchine'," 146.

15. Ibid., 149.

16. V. Nemirovich-Danchenko, "Protest Gorkogo. V. Nemirovich-Danchenko o proteste," *Teatral'naia gazeta*, October 6, 1913.

17. *Literaturnaia gazeta*, December 26, 1934, n.p.

18. Zaslavskii, "Literaturnaia gnil'," *Pravda*, January 20, 1935, 4.

19. Gor'kii, "Literaturnye zabavy," *Pravda*, January 24, 1935, 6.

20. Zaslavskii, "Zametki chitatelia," *Pravda*, January 25, 1935, 6. Emphasis is mine.

21. This contrast is noted in Caryl Emerson's essay in this volume.

22. Leonid Grossman, *Dostoevskii*, (Moscow: Molodaia gvardiia, 1962), 9. All further page references will be included in the text.

23. There is a noticeable difference between Grossman's take on Dostoevsky and such studies as Pereverzev's (*Dostoevsky's Writing* and *F.M. Dostoevsky*) or Lunacharsky's ("Dostoevsky as a Thinker and a Writer" or "Dostoevsky's Worldview and Writing"). They provide a Marxist reading of the writer and find the source of Dostoevsky's "contradictoriness" in his petit bourgeois background.

24. Iurii Seleznev, *Dostoevskii* (Moscow: Molodaia gvardiia, 1981). It was subsequently reprinted two times. All further page references will be included in the text.

25. The first edition of Seleznev's biography also contains a footnote in which Seleznev mentions the unconditional condemnation of Ivanov's murder by Nechaev by Marx and Engels. All of the obligatory footnotes mentioning Marx or Lenin are omitted from the later editions.

26. For Seleznev, Dostoevsky's closeness to Konstantin Pobedonostsev, the Procurator of the Holy Synod, is tangential: while he is sympathetic to some of his ideas, Dostoevsky cannot stand "Pobedonostev's dogmatic, prescriptive Christianity" (407). In the biography, the Chief Procurator of the Synod emerges not so much as the addressee of "the Poem of the Grand Inquisitor," but as his prototype.

27. Liudmila Saraskina, *Dostoevskii* (Moscow: Molodaia gvardiia, 2011), 19. All further page references will be included in the text.

28. See Bakhtin's *Problems of Dostoevsky's Poetics*: "The exceptionally acute contradictions of early Russian capitalism and the duality of Dostoevsky as a social personality, his personal inability to take a definite ideological stand, are, if taken by themselves, something negative and historically transitory, but they proved to be the optimal conditions for creating the polyphonic novel, 'that unheard-of freedom of voices in Dostoevsky's polyphony,' and this was without question a step forward in the development of the Russian and European novel" (35).

29. Having written several monographs on *Demons*, Saraskina is one of the world's renowned authorities on the novel.

Chapter 6

In Search of the "True" Chekhov
Approaches and Appropriations

Radislav Lapushin

"Chekhov's face would change every year," Ivan Bunin observed of his older contemporary.[1] Chekhov's "face," however, kept on changing even after his death in 1904 at the age of forty-four. As Irina Gitovich, a foremost expert on Chekhov's biography, has recently noted, "Though major facts of Chekhov's life . . . have remained the same, the very *image* of the writer revealed immediately after his death differs from the way he was perceived beginning in the middle of the twentieth century, and both of these images differ from how this great writer emerges in his biographies at the beginning of the twenty-first century."[2] Building on Gitovich's observation, the following essay aims to trace the dynamism of Chekhov's image as reflected through his *ZhZL* biographies of different periods, from the Stalinist to the post-Soviet. The question is what lies at the root of this dynamism: was it Chekhov's inherent ability to "change" his face or was it a response to external pressure from the shifting political environment with its ideological demands and expectations?

AN ALLY IN THE FIGHT AGAINST PETTY BOURGEOIS VALUES (1934)

In July of 1929, on the twenty-fifth anniversary of Chekhov's death, the popular magazine *Ogonek* placed on its cover a scene from Yakov Protazanov's movie of the same year, *Ranks and People (Chiny i liudi)*, adapted from Chekhov's short stories. Based on "Anna on the Neck," the emotional scene on the cover depicted the children asking their drunken father to stop drinking.[3] The caption beneath the picture read: "There is still no reason to think that this scene has lost its relevance since Chekhov's times." This cover yields two major points. The first one is the significance of the very fact that Chekhov was featured on the cover of *Ogonek* (there were also several articles devoted to him within this issue, one of them by Anatoly Lunacharsky, the other by Chekhov scholar and future biographer, Yuri Sobolev). No less telling is the emphasis put on the practical, one might say, utilitarian relevance of Chekhov's legacy rather than its artistic merits.

The *Ogonek* cover reflects well on the state of Chekhov affairs at that time. First, the Revolution, the Civil War, and the construction of the new social order appeared to put an end to the whole Chekhovian world, rendering his works completely irrelevant. However, as a prominent Chekhov scholar of the period, Abram Derman, noted in 1929, "One can assert with certainty that the decline of interest in Chekhov was only temporary and short-lived: soon studies dedicated to him began to appear again. His plays find their way back to the stage."[4] Chekhov's eventual return posed familiar questions in a new light: on which terms was he to be accepted into the new Soviet reality and what role was he to play there? Published the same anniversary year, the first (and shortest) Chekhov biography in a forerunner of the *ZhZL* series by the Marxist literary critic P. S. Kogan was an attempt to address these questions.[5]

Symptomatically, Kogan focuses on "the major tendencies of Chekhov's epoch, against which his civic image emerges."[6] This focus explains the book's structure and content. While dealing with his "epoch," the first chapters ignore Chekhov's biography proper and his literary work. Only beginning with chapter 6 and only for the next twenty-five pages at that (27–53), the author moves to Chekhov's life. He treats it in a sketchy manner and with an emphasis on socially resonant events, such as the journey to Sakhalin, Chekhov's work during the famine of 1892, the Dreyfus affair, and the "academic incident" of 1902 related to Gorky. On the subject of Chekhov's personal life, the book is virtually silent.

Regarding Chekhov's "civic image" as such, the author does not shy away from politically slanted criticism: "The idea of class struggle, of organizing workers for the struggle did not even come to his mind although the idea was being passionately debated in Marxist circles" (64). Chekhov did not understand "the essence of the class struggle between the proletariat and the capitalists" (65); subsequently, he "got confused and grew pessimistic" (66). Chekhov for Kogan is the "poet of episodes and trifles of life" who does not have an "all-embracing system of a positive worldview" (93). Why then should one read Chekhov now, in the Soviet Union? First of all, according to the biographer, Chekhov's "ideological deficiency" is not as much his "fault as his problem" (94). Furthermore, for Kogan, Chekhov is still "the voice of the positive aspirations of his time"; his negative attitude toward religion also speaks in his favor (24). There is also something that "can be learned from Chekhov" as a master of literary form. Most important, what makes Chekhov valuable to the new Socialist order is his "organic revulsion toward any petty bourgeois values (*meshchanstvo*), vulgarity (*poshlost'*), and stagnation" (109).

Unlike Kogan, Yuri Sobolev, whose *ZhZL* biography came out five years later (for another anniversary—thirty years from 1904), was a devoted Chekhov scholar who dedicated many years of his life to collecting and publishing all kinds of Chekhov materials: letters, memoirs, and documents. In the preface to his earlier scholarly book on Chekhov, he had offered a nostalgic recollection of himself as a prerevolutionary *gimnaziia* student standing, with a "sinking heart," in the hall of a newspaper's editorial offices where he had brought his very first article, which was on Chekhov.[7] Grounded in archival research, Sobolev's book is a real biography following Chekhov's life in chronological order and considerable detail, from his childhood in Taganrog to his death in Badenweiler.

In terms of political messaging, however, Sobolev does not deviate substantially from Kogan. Using as his epigraph the passage from Chekhov's famous letter to Alexei Suvorin about a "young man"—presumably himself—who "squeezes the slave out of himself, drop by drop," Sobolev makes this passage the leitmotif of Chekhov's life and endows it with an all-explanatory power. Indeed, if the quality of some of Chekhov's work for humorous journals was poor, claims Sobolev, this is because he did not take this process of "squeezing the slave out of himself" far enough.[8] Chekhov's friendship with the conservative publisher of *New Time* (*Novoe vremia*) was a blemish on his reputation for all Soviet biographers, and the fact that he was not immune to Suvorin's ideological "poison" "slowed down his struggle against his inner slave" (152). On the contrary, the Dreyfus affair "tremendously accelerated Chekhov's last struggle with his 'internal slave'" (218). References to this letter to Suvorin are ubiquitous in Sobolev's book.[9] Their very excess is suggestive of the biographer's own struggle to create an ideologically driven framework for Chekhov's life.

Still, as a whole, this biography overcomes its ideological concept. Sobolev is at his best when he forgets about the political aspects of Chekhov's life and speaks, instead, about his "vacations and entertainments" as a boy or about the vicissitudes of his relationship with Lika Mizinova. It is at these moments that Sobolev succeeds in presenting a living, breathing Chekhov. The image he presents also benefits from the fact that the writer had not yet been canonized as an official "classic" of Russian literature, which made it possible for Sobolev to quote the following passage from a letter Chekhov wrote on his way home from Sakhalin: "[I] enjoyed my share of palm groves and bronze-skinned women" (162).

Ultimately, Sobolev's Chekhov is a "courageous" person, who indeed managed to squeeze the slave out of himself in a broader sense (304). His life story, therefore, is that of a man "who straightened himself morally" (305). On the downside, his battle with the "inner slave" was a purely ethical one. Politically speaking, Chekhov did not make a decisive step in the right direction. "Which ideology did he express?" asks Sobolev in the voice of a prosecutor (305). The answer he provides is not reassuring for Chekhov's reputation: he was the "voice of the radical bourgeois ideology" (308). True, along with the bourgeoisie, he was in favor of culture, literacy, and schools and against absolutism and lack of political freedom. In concert with it, however, he was a supporter of the evolutionary (rather than revolutionary) transformation of life (305). Still, by waging his personal struggle against his inner slave, Chekhov also fought the petty bourgeois values and vulgarity that the new Soviet world inherited from the old one. The struggle against these remnants of the past is an ongoing one (recall the cover of *Ogonek*). "Chekhov infects us with a hatred toward vulgarity," declares Sobolev. "In this struggle and this hatred," he concludes his book, "Chekhov is our ally" (312).

"OUR CHEKHOV": AN EPIC HERO OF RUSSIAN LITERATURE (1946)

Vladimir Ermilov's biography signified a radically new approach toward Chekhov that determined his official image for the foreseeable future. Eleven years later, in his instructional compendium on studying Chekhov in the institutions of higher learning, Boris Aleksandrov described this biography as "the first case of a developed and wholesome depiction of Chekhov as a great national writer, completely devoid of all the remnants of the old and false perceptions of him."[10] Indeed, with this book, Chekhov, "the poet of episodes and trifles of life" and "the voice of the radical bourgeois ideology" was put on the shelf. Instead, there emerged a new and "true" Chekhov, "the author and democrat walking straight toward the fermenting Revolution" during his mature period.[11] Correspondingly, simple Russian people rather than whining representatives of the intelligentsia appeared now as Chekhov's major protagonists and the focus of his artistic attention and sympathy. Everything in Ermilov's biography is subordinated to the goal of replacing Chekhov "our ally" with "our Chekhov" (the title of Ermilov's last chapter), whose name deserves to be uttered in one breath with that of the Revolution's "stormy petrel" Maxim Gorky: "as no one else in world literature before Gorky, Chekhov was an inspired poet of labor"[12]; "along with the great 'stormy petrel' Gorky, Chekhov heard the breath of the coming storm" (390). Under Ermilov's pen, the relationship between these two writers reaches an almost intimate level: "Chekhov and Gorky found the most secret and sacred paths to each other" (388).

Yes, there are some reservations on Ermilov's part expressed in language familiar from Kogan and Sobolev. Chekhov, for example, did not "always" comprehend the true importance and meaning of his own works and only gradually learned to draw "political conclusions" (197–98). Most importantly, claims Ermilov, he had "no understanding of either the historical role of the working class, or the perspective of the Socialist revolution. He also was not connected to the great and upcoming revolutionary movement of his time" (281). In spite of all this, however, Chekhov, "with his sensitivity," expressed "the influence of the new, mighty, and decisive force—the Russian working class" (400). Thus, it comes as no surprise that Chekhov "called on all who were close to him to fight to achieve victory over everything slavish, to the struggle against all the dark forces" (136). Speaking of "Ward No 6," Ermilov writes, "It's difficult to overemphasize the social importance of this work's contribution toward the psychological preparation for the Revolution, the mobilization of all forces of protest, and the hatred of monarchy" (242). One should give credit to Ermilov for a certain level of nuance here: after all, his Chekhov only "psychologically," not politically, helped prepare the Revolution.

Ermilov coined a number of ideologically rigid formulations that were subsequently plugged into all sorts of literature by other writers: "the creator of the new, great democratic literature" (68), "an artistic representative of 'little people,' their friend and advocate" (84), "the new epic hero (*bogatyr'*) of Russian literature" (90), "a great laborer and a modest Russian" (162). The very titles of several chapters are politically loaded and communicate a clear ideological message: "We Live on the Eve of a Great Triumph," "It Is Impossible to Go on like This!," "Happiness Lies in the Future!," "Everything Must Be Beautiful about the Human Being!," "Hello, New Life!" In fairness, all these exclamations are extracted from Chekhov's texts. Divorced from their context, however, they sound like political slogans.

Most importantly, Ermilov put an end to the "firmly engraved" image of the "strikingly delicate, gentle, sensitive, and modest Dr. Chekhov" (55), replacing it with the Chekhov who waged a struggle for his talent while "mercilessly burning out everything that was slavish in his own soul and the souls of those close to him" (52); hence, the centrality of the concept of the "enemy" for Chekhov's life and work. He was an enemy of petty bourgeois values (24), despotism and lies (26), sentimentality (34), "Prishibeevs" and "Pobedonostsevs" (68). The danger posed by Chekhov's friendship with Suvorin is captured in the oxymoronic nickname Ermilov gives to the reactionary publisher of *New Time*: "The Gentle Enemy." Tellingly, the centerpiece of the book is Ermilov's close reading of the short story titled

"Enemies." According to Ermilov, Chekhov's position in "Enemies" is that "only working class people have the right to sympathy" (124). "'An enemy is an enemy'—such is the clear, sharp, and merciless mood of this story," he concludes in the context of another Chekhov work (131).

As to Chekhov's personal life, apart from his ideological battles with others and himself, it is hardly of interest to Ermilov. His Chekhov "renounces his happiness," as in his relationship with Lika Mizinova (338). "A great love entered Anton Pavlovich's life," the critic says about Chekhov's encounter with Olga Knipper, but then, there is hardly a page on the development of this love and Chekhov's marriage. Ermilov deliberately avoids anything that makes Chekhov less of an "epic hero" (*bogatyr'*) and more of a human being. At no point in his biography does the human Chekhov eclipse "our" Chekhov.

A veteran of numerous ideological campaigns against perceived literary enemies, Ermilov stops at nothing in pushing his argument. Vladimir Kataev, a major Chekhov scholar of the next generation, aptly called Ermilov's critical method a literary "swindle" the main parts of which were his manipulation of quotations and refusal to distinguish between the author and his characters.[13] Nowhere else is this "swindle" as obvious as in the book's last chapter:

> The purifying storm broke out and our native country began to turn into a beautiful garden, the laws of its life became the laws of truth and beauty.
>
> "The people should be carefully and attentively nurtured, as the gardener nurtures his precious fruit tree." These wise words of the Leader have inspired workers, peasants, and intelligentsia who merged into one single nation. Lenin and Stalin have educated these people and helped millions of the "ordinary," "common" people to learn to stand tall.
>
> "What a pleasure to respect people!" wrote Chekhov in his notebook.
>
> We have gotten to know this pleasure now. Everything that we have built and are building is inspired by a great respect for people (429).

This passage offers a practical exercise in how to turn Chekhov into "our Chekhov." While talking about the new Soviet reality, it describes it as the fulfillment of Chekhov's dreams. To emphasize this connection between Chekhov and Soviet life, the very first sentence refers to the three major Chekhov works at once: *The Three Sisters* ("the purifying storm"), *The Cherry Orchard* ("the beautiful garden") and the short story "The Student" ("truth and beauty"). The next step is to bring into the picture Lenin and Stalin, whose leadership led the Soviet people to their new gorgeous life. The book's rousing coda makes the marriage of Chekhov and this life irrevocable and eternal: "And in our every new victory, there will be seen through his work, his truth, and his dreams, the bright genius of a simple Russian man, Anton Pavlovich Chekhov" (435).

Highly influential, Ermilov's biography played a major role in solidifying Chekhov's place in the Soviet canon of Russian classical literature. Indeed, who would dare question this place after the following statement from the last chapter: "Chekhov's enemies are also enemies of all Soviet people"? Fittingly, this chilling warning is followed by another quotation from Stalin, which refers to one of Chekhov's satirical sketches: "People in our country do not like Prishibeevs" (434). In 1951, together with his book on Chekhov's drama, Ermilov's biography was awarded the Stalin Prize of the Second Degree.

THE HERO WITH A HUMAN FACE (1974)

The next Chekhov biography in the *ZhZL* series by Georgy Berdnikov represents a different type of "Sovietness" associated with the post-Thaw period of the so-called "stagnation" (*zastoi*): still restrictive in its ideological demands yet allowing for a more flexible approach. Clichés and markers of Soviet ideological discourse are ubiquitous in Berdnikov's biography. They pertain to both the book's style and its conceptual framework of Chekhov's life. As a whole, Chekhov's life emerges here as that of a true hero, who is both akin to and strikingly different from Ermilov's *bogatyr'*.

First of all, as expected from a true hero, beginning with his early years, Chekhov undergoes a series of ordeals: "the youth [Chekhov and his brothers] passed the first and most difficult ordeal"[14]; "Chekhov endured and passed successfully through these 'penal battalions' of the Taganrog *gimnaziia*" (20); "the last years of his life in Taganrog were the most serious test of his endurance and courage" (33); Chekhov "heroically labored and carried his cross" (47). Even in his personal life, this Chekhov never looks for easy paths. Describing his relationship with his wife, an actress of the Moscow Art Theater, Olga Knipper, Berdnikov comes with the quasi-oxymoronic concept of "difficult happiness": "the happiness he chose was a difficult one" (461); "he did not turn his back on his difficult happiness" (463). Realizing that he was to die soon, Chekhov "went courageously to his inevitable finale" (501).

Hence, in accord with previous Soviet biographies, the Chekhov of this book is found in a state of permanent struggle and fight (*bor'ba*), which takes place on several fronts simultaneously. It can be a "decisive, uncompromising, and consistent struggle against petty bourgeois values and philosophy" in his own family, which simultaneously was a "struggle for his personal freedom and independence" (39) or "a struggle for the formation of his own worldview" (197). The following language is typical of Berdnikov's presentation of Chekhov: "the spirit of protest began to overtake Chekhov more and more strongly" (224); "he could not reconcile himself with the lack of progressive ideas in his time" (231). Whatever Chekhov does in his personal or literary life, he always "fights." Indeed, any "active human existence" is postulated here as an act of *bor'ba*. The book's final paragraph endows this *bor'ba* with a truly universal meaning: "The more people recognize the incurable vices of the bourgeois system the more broadly the world struggle for the transformation of the society will develop on new grounds and Chekhov's works will become all the more close, clear, and precious to the people of all continents" (505). Thus, Chekhov's personal *bor'ba* is recognized as part of the "world struggle." In its tone and spirit, this bombastic conclusion parrots Ermilov. If one removes Chekhov's name from this passage, for present-day readers it would be almost impossible to assume that Chekhov is the one the author is describing.

Furthermore, similarly to his predecessor, Berdnikov presents Chekhov's life and literary evolution as an unstoppable advance, that is, "the path of tireless creative pursuits and labor, the path of great achievements and bitter disappointments, the path toward unprecedented heights of Russian and world culture" (42). In spite of all obstacles, Chekhov steadily proceeded "ever forward" (187) and "toward new creative achievements and discoveries" (316). Thus, even some temporary deviations from this path as well as Chekhov's ideological inconsistencies and hesitations are treated with the same patronizing and forgiving attitude that we encountered in Ermilov. At the end of the day, they are more than outweighed by the writer's intuitive joining the path of progress, that is, the path toward Revolution. For example, undertaking his trip to Sakhalin, "unbeknownst to himself, Chekhov was one of the first people to walk toward the new epoch" (227).

Not surprisingly, we also encounter here the same sociological approach as in Berdnikov's predecessors. The literary life of Chekhov's time, the trajectory of his literary evolution and the peculiarities of his worldview are presented as determined by political factors, such as the fact that "the ideology of the revolutionary proletariat was only forming in Russia" (312–13). Commenting on Chekhov's famous criticism of the intelligentsia in his 1899 letter to Dr. Orlov, Berdnikov does not fail to note that "at the time when Chekhov wrote these lines, Russia had already entered the third proletarian period of the liberation movement" (411). Predictably, he does not strive for objectivity or nuance while talking about Suvorin. At one point, Berdnikov characterizes Suvorin's explanations about his role in *New Time* as "sugary and nauseating lies, lies from the beginning to the end" (154).

Berdnikov also carries on a tradition of presenting Chekhov as an unwavering optimist: "no, dark impressions and bitter thoughts did not make Chekhov a pessimist" (248). His Chekhov is a "staunch supporter of progress and the scientific method" (174) as well as a "materialist and atheist believing unwaveringly in reason and science" (195). Making a passing comparison between Chekhov and Kafka (a provocative and unorthodox choice at the time!), Berdnikov claims that unlike the German writer, Chekhov "steadfastly believes in the unstoppable force—the force of the progressive development of human society" (314).

On the positive side, this voluminous book is a biography in the traditional meaning of the word. In this regard, Berdnikov is closer to Sobolev than to Ermilov. Compared to the latter, Berdnikov describes Chekhov's life in much more detail and pays more attention to the social and cultural environment against which this life emerged. There are also many more participants in this life, including the pair of mongooses Chekhov brought with him from Sakhalin: almost a page is granted to a lovely and vivid description that brings them to life (252).

As in Sobolev's biography, there is an individual and more extended chapter dedicated to Lika Mizinova and her relationship with Chekhov. The chapter includes observations and questions that would be out of place in Ermilov's book: "What do we know about Chekhov's personal life at this time? Chekhov did not like to pour his heart out and talk about his 'conquests' . . . Meanwhile, women liked him" (275). "He was very handsome," Berdnikov cites one of Chekhov's female acquaintances, and concludes, "From all appearances, there were many women who loved Chekhov" (276). Such a Chekhov, of course, substantially differs from the ascetic and incorporeal image established by Ermilov. Furthermore, in this chapter on Lika, Berdnikov is not afraid of leaving questions about the intricacies of her relationship with Chekhov without answers while describing her personality as "fluid and elusive" (282).

A similar complexity and sense of real drama are vivid in the description of the relationship between, on the one hand, Chekhov and Knipper, and, on the other, Knipper and Chekhov's sister, Masha. In the considerably detailed chapter (more than thirty pages vs. Ermilov's half a page on Knipper), Berdnikov lets the voices of Chekhov and his wife come to life through a generous citation of their correspondence. As a result, Chekhov appears as more human and more vulnerable in his humanity: "For the first time, Chekhov was looking for the right words to express not someone else's but his own love" (440). Unlike his predecessors, Berdnikov also mentions "the great misfortune" in Chekhov and his wife's life: Knipper's miscarriage (474).

The Chekhov of this biography is even allowed some minor "weaknesses," such as his short-lived infatuation with roulette during his time in Nice (388). In general, at some points, especially during his late period, Chekhov emerges as the hero with a human face who cannot and does not have to be always strong. Berdnikov quotes the memoirist who observed Chekhov without his proverbial pince-nez and not able to stop coughing, "with the big and child-like helpless eyes . . . hazy with the moisture of tears" (476). This living and breathing Chekhov is not easy to reconcile with the one who constantly wages struggles, both in his life and works, on the pages of the same book. Igor Losievsky, a contemporary scholar of the biographical genre, is justified in calling Berdnikov's image of Chekhov "mosaic-like and devoid of psychological wholeness."[15] As to the interpretations of Chekhov's works in this book, compared to Ermilov's, they are more balanced. However, Berdnikov's analysis is prone to similar acts of critical "swindle," whenever the author needs to prove Chekhov's revolutionary inclinations. The most common way to achieve this, as we recall, is to erase the difference between the author and his characters: "Pavel Ivanych whom Chekhov clearly trusts with his thoughts" (248); "Chekhov trusts Petya with his innermost thoughts" (499); "the author's voice is certainly heard in Petya's 'Hello, new life,' with which Chekhov stretches his hand out to the future generation of happy and emancipated people" (500). Like his predecessor, Berdnikov tends to break Chekhov's characters into the progressive and reactionary ones: "Never before has Chekhov divided his characters so clearly and uncompromisingly into two antagonistic camps," he comments on the novella *My Life* (375). For many sophisticated readers of the seventies, who strived to distance themselves intellectually from official discourse, such an approach to Chekhov seemed incurably dated. Luckily, these readers already had access to alternative interpretations of their beloved author.[16]

THE ELUSIVE GIANT (1993)

By the time the next Chekhov biography by Mikhail Gromov came out in the same series, there was already a different country with a different name and different political climate. Most importantly, there was neither censorship nor restrictive ideological guidelines as to how a "classic" author is supposed to look. Even if the date of this book's publication were absent from its front page, the ongoing changes would immediately become obvious for any attentive reader. In the very first sentence, for example, the characterization of Russia after the abolishment of serfdom, belongs to . . . Dostoevsky (in Soviet-era works, it would be expected to come from the works of Lenin). Several pages later, the author cites "our contemporary A. I. Solzhenitsyn."[17]

The new times did not simply bring new names; they also established new points of reference and a new conceptual framework. Thus, it is not surprising that in his evaluation of Chekhov's times, Gromov sounds very different from the Soviet-era biographers. For him, there was no "suspension of time" (*bezvremen'e*) in the 1880s, but rather, the 1880s were, according to the quote from Solzhenitsyn, "the best years of Russian thought." Consequently, the Chekhov of this book does not live his life in the context of the growing proletarian movement and eagerly anticipated revolutionary "storm." The book's preface introduces him as a contemporary not as much of Lenin as of the great Russian scientists and thinkers of his time, such as N. I. Lobachevsky, D. I. Mendeleev, and K. E. Tsiolkovsky, whose discoveries challenged and transformed the accepted perception of the world (Tsiolkovsky is quoted as saying: "I want to be Chekhov in science" [14]). Hence, there are numerous reevaluations: Gorky steps aside while Bunin comes to the spotlight. Even the villain of the previous biographies, Chekhov's "gentle enemy" Suvorin receives a fairer treatment, becoming a "rather smart and perceptive man" (148).

As expected, there are also substantial revisions to the image of Chekhov himself. "What a temptingly simplistic and wrong solution: to treat Chekhov as an atheist!" exclaims Gromov, challenging a firmly established notion of this writer's attitude toward religion (13). This does not mean that Gromov sees Chekhov as a staunch believer. His pathos reveals itself in the quotation from the artist Valentin Serov that he employs as the title for the first chapter: "Chekhov is elusive" (16). To capture this elusiveness, Gromov focuses on Chekhov's artistic legacy. For him, "Chekhov was born to become a writer" (41). Thus, the story of his life is that of his creative endeavors.

Chekhov the artist emerges from this biography as a product of centuries of Russian civilization and culture, from *The Tale of Igor's Campaign* to Dostoevsky and Tolstoy. Gromov even stretches beyond the Russian context, claiming, in particular, that Chekhov's ideal of man is "akin to the canons of the High Renaissance" (253). Such are, according to Gromov, Chekhov's artistic genealogy and the proper context for evaluating his artistic output and worldview.

It is logical, therefore, that Gromov underplays the influence "the second-and third-rate writers" associated with the "small press" could have on the future genius. Though there is a special chapter dedicated to Chekhov and the "small press," he is described here as "Gulliver among Lilliputians" (131), who "literally immersed himself in great literature" (134). As a result, "he constantly reminded his readers about Goethe, Shakespeare, Pushkin, Dostoevsky, Turgenev, about old tragedies and novels, about all the great literature, which was his natural element" (134). Hence, there is what Gromov calls Chekhov's "tragic divergence" from the style and environment of the "small press" (135). In Chekhov's early works, Gromov insists, "everything was different: plots and literary devices he used to create his images, his style and language" (142). In this context, Gromov's close attention to Chekhov's juvenile play, *Fatherlessness*, serves a similar purpose: to demonstrate that

Chekhov started his literary career not as a "careless" humorist but as a conscious descendant of a great literary tradition.

Though the book strives to follow Chekhov's life in chronological order, it is rather an intellectual biography. Some chapters—"A Natural Scientist and a Poet," "Inner Freedom," "On Love and Prototypes," "New Forms," and "Man and Nature"—read as independent essays, in which the author effortlessly moves between different periods of Chekhov's life and his numerous works.[18] Gromov writes of Chekhov's artistic manner: "Relying on his readers, Chekhov had to leave for them a certain space, creating an unusual and fragmented text with lacunae between individual chapters or parts ('why this but not that? Why that but not this?')" (337). Similar questions are warranted in relation to this biography. There is a fifty-page chapter dedicated to Chekhov's *The Steppe*, but why is there so little on "A Boring Story" or "Ward No 6"? There are individual chapters on Chekhov's first and last plays respectively, but why is *The Seagull* only briefly mentioned in a short chapter on the Moscow Art Theater, and why is no due attention given to *The Three Sisters*? On the other hand, Gromov's critical readings are invariably engaging and original while his fluency in Chekhov's oeuvre as a whole is obvious to the reader. When he states that there are almost eight thousand characters inhabiting Chekhov's prose (319), the reader can be sure that the author familiarized himself with every single one of them.

Gaps are also evident in Chekhov's personal biography. Many pathbreaking events of his life are mentioned only in passing, including, for example, Chekhov's devastating hemorrhage in 1897, his father's death, and his subsequent move to Yalta: all these developments are compressed in one short paragraph (302). Similarly, in the chapter on Sakhalin, there are only a few pages on the circumstances of the journey itself. The chapter on Chekhov's European journeys is also sketchy. The author is deliberately discreet with respect to Chekhov's intimate life: mostly, he touches upon it in the context of his literary work ("On Love and Prototypes"). The chapter on Chekhov and Knipper ("The Last Page of My Life") contains a number of insightful observations but ends too soon.

Gromov was a seasoned scholar of Chekhov, and his biography has a deeply personal tone. The book is written with a sense of proximity to its subject and, simultaneously, as it were, from a devout distance. In sum, Chekhov here is a giant of Russian literature in an everlasting dialogue with his great predecessors, so that this dialogue becomes more important than some minute details of Chekhov's life. Published at a time of great social cataclysm and uncertainty, this biography pledged continuity in the development of Russian culture and claimed this culture as an unshakable foundation of national life.[19] At the end, however, Gromov left his image of Chekhov unfinalized:

"Chekhov has no afterwards or prefaces, or predilection for preaching and moral teaching. He was probably the most unobtrusive and silent among the writers of our world" (327). In short, he was elusive!

AN INDEPENDENT AND SOLITARY INDIVIDUAL (2010)

The most recent of Chekhov's *ZhZL* biographies by Alevtina Kuzicheva, *Chekhov: The Life of a Solitary Individual*, can be described as "the most" on a number of grounds: more than eight hundred pages long, it is the most voluminous among them as well as the most detailed and documented, the most informative and informed. A product of a decades-long engagement with Chekhov, this book comes on top of Kuzicheva's previous work on the writer and his family, similarly rooted in archival research.[20] "When he would get very upset, his handwriting would slant and the lines of his letters become stretched out"[21] (740)—this apparently plain yet precise observation betrays the author as someone who has intimately familiarized herself with Chekhov's manuscripts.

At first sight, Kuzicheva's biography approaches the genre of a chronicle that indiscriminately follows Chekhov's life year by year. This chronicle offers a multifaceted picture of Chekhov in his many disparate roles: a medical student (then, a doctor) and a patient, a son and a brother, a lover and a husband, a traveler and a gardener, a public figure and a private person. The book carefully catalogs his encounters, departures for various destinations, and arrivals back home. Compared to the previous *ZhZL* biographies, it is an almost exhaustive (and in places, exhausting) account. This biography requires a patient reader, but such a reader can be certain that no important event or acquaintance from Chekhov's life will be omitted. Neither will any of Chekhov's major works nor the circumstances under which these works were created. The book offers the fullest account of Chekhov's relationship with the members of his family and Suvorin, his trip to Sakhalin, and life in Melikhovo. In its level of detail, including the intricacies of Chekhov's budget or his menu in Nice and Yalta, Kuzicheva's biography easily surpasses its predecessors.

The main competition for Kuzicheva's volume on the Russian market, however, was not the previous *ZhZL* biographies but the Russian translation of Donald Rayfield's *Chekhov: A Life* (2005; 1997 in English), in which, among other things, the British author exposed a number of Chekhov's alleged affairs. The Russian translation of this book was widely reviewed and published in multiple editions.[22] Compared to Rayfield, Kuzicheva is more understated in her account of Chekhov's intimate life. However, she does not avoid the topic, which is itself an unmistakable marker of the new times. For example, she states in a matter-of-fact manner: "Apparently, they [Chekhov and his friend, the writer Ignaty Potapenko–RL] shared a male bond based on their visits to the brothels and the knowledge of each other's secret affairs" (439).

Passages like this, which include speculation on the part of the author ("apparently"), are also an indication that she does not limit herself to the role of a silent chronicler who lets the documents and facts speak for themselves. Indeed, in addition to the features of a chronicle, Kuzicheva's biography employs some novelistic tools, which perhaps corresponds to the contemporary readers' tastes. Such novelization may be seen in the following descriptive passages: "The winter turned out to be sad" (303); "The weather happened to be warm, cloudy, and difficult for visits. In the house, everybody dispersed to their rooms early. Someone drove up to the windows quite late. Chekhov went to the porch along with his sister" (386).

Most of all, however, the novelization reveals itself in the author's attempts to introduce the inner workings of her hero's psychology. One of the devices Kuzicheva rather excessively employs throughout the book is questions asked, as it were, on behalf of Chekhov: "And he himself? Already not a journalist, but then who? A practicing doctor writing short stories for some additional income?" (91); "Does he have enough passion, boldness, and freedom? And what about the rest of his life? How is it connected with his gift of imagination for stories?" (188–89); "It was clear that he needed to write in a different way and about different subjects. But how? And about whom? New characters? New topics? New forms, as the protagonist of his *The Seagull* said"? (761). True, all these quasi-monologues are not simply the fruits of the author's imagination. As she frequently reminds her reader, they have a documentary basis, mostly in Chekhov's letters. However, taken out of their integral context, rephrased and used without quotation marks, these "monologues" lose their authenticity and create an effect of novelization.

Furthermore, this device is not limited to the title character. In the same manner, Kuzicheva channels the collective voices of literary critics ("Who is he, Mr. Chekhov? An artist of ideas, truth, beauty?" [451]) and Chekhov's contemporaries ("What is behind [his behavior]? Hidden pride? Unusual modesty? An ironic gaze, as if from aside?" [571]). The inner quasi-monologues packed with a sequence of questions are also consistently employed for Chekhov's wife: "and what—should she waste her years in Yalta, a place she did not like? In this boring and dull town, far away from her family and next to the estranged Evgeniya Yakovlevna? To observe the successes of Lilina, Andreeva, Savitskaya from a distance? To give birth to a 'half-German,' as her husband wrote to her recently?" (711); "But to be preoccupied with a daily household routine all by herself? To accept the responsibilities of a housewife? To look after an incurably sick man?" (735). In addition, there are occasional passages in the tone and spirit of other participants in Chekhov's life: the editor of *Oskolki*, Nikolai Leikin (89), Chekhov's father (256), and his sister and mother (342).

Another literary device that is ubiquitous in this biography is the employment of the construction "as if": "as if some deep melancholy and groundless dissatisfaction interfered with [Lika Mizinova's] life" (542); "as if [Chekhov] was obeying his 'prophetic feeling'" (569); "as if something was chasing him from home, contrary to common sense" (649). Many such examples refer to the dynamics of relationship between Chekhov and Knipper: "as if he was secretly warning her about the person whom she was so determined to marry" (657); "as if she had doubts about their mutual future" (658); "as if he was concerned that their correspondence was about to end" (660); "as if he was running away from everything and everyone" (662.); "as if Chekhov was challenging her idea of this feeling [love–RL]" (780). Kuzicheva's "as ifs" are ambiguous. On the one hand, they convey uncertainty about Chekhov and his contemporaries' possible motivations, but on the other, provide an illusion of the author's insight into these motivations.

Yet another major feature that differentiates this biography from an objective chronicle is the unapologetic presence of authorial judgment. Kuzicheva is not afraid of expressing strong opinions and of challenging established reputations. Consider Chekhov's sister Masha (the devoted guardian of Chekhov's legacy after his death): "Ambitious and mistrustful, she did not tolerate even a joke addressed to her, and even more, irony or criticism" (378); "the inner life of her brother was completely closed to her" (379). Consistently condescending and ironic is the author's attitude to Chekhov's younger brother Misha (209, 249, 308, 354, 406). Here is Lika Mizinova: "the subtext and subtle intonation were above her skills" [as a letter-writer–RL] (303); she was "preoccupied exclusively with herself and her perception of being insulted" (351).

The strongest criticism, however, is saved for Chekhov's wife: "her perplexity betrayed her misunderstanding of Chekhov's anguish and loneliness" (718); "Chekhov wrote to her about his love for her while she wrote about love for herself" (741); "she became attached to Chekhov as much as she could and as much as she was capable of" (744). Moreover, not only is Knipper incapable of "selflessness, dedication, and even more so, self-sacrifice," she is denied "significant talent as an actress" (708). Further on, the author is even more merciless: "nature endowed her with only a small talent" (734). None of these participants in Chekhov's life is or should be beyond reproach. However, the author would be more convincing if, in a Chekhovian manner, she let her readers make their own judgment. Such an approach would also better align with the mode of the chronicle.

What about the overall image of Chekhov that emerges from this biography? The book has the subtitle: *Zhizn' otdel'nogo cheloveka*, which could be best translated as *The Life of a Solitary Individual*, since in Russian, the adjective *otdel'nyi* means independent, solitary, separate. Kuzicheva takes this formulation from Chekhov's 1899 letter to Dr. Orlov mentioned above: "I have faith in individual people; I see salvation in individuals—intellectuals or peasants scattered here and there throughout Russia; though there are not many of them, they have strength."[23] This letter is as central to Kuzicheva's vision of Chekhov as the letter about "squeezing the slave" out of himself was to Sobolev's. Indeed, in this biography, Chekhov's "separateness" is a defining feature of his personality. It reveals itself in his childhood and is carried through his life until its very end. Kuzicheva's Chekhov is *otdel'nyi* (independent and solitary) among his classmates in the Taganrog gimnaziia and at Moscow University. So is he among his colleagues, numerous acquaintances and lovers. He is such even in the midst of his own family: "With every year, it became clearer and clearer that Chekhov is *next* to his family but not *with them*" (379, italics are Kuzicheva's). Finally, in his last years he is "separate," both geographically and spiritually, from his wife. No one in this book—from literary critics to those closest to him—has a true understanding of Chekhov. No one is up to his level as a writer and human being. Describing the internal crisis Chekhov experienced in 1887, Kuzicheva says: "The defining features of Chekhov's life are ceaseless effort and overcoming. And nothing is easy and always by himself" (106). This phrase—"and nothing is easy and always by himself"—can be seen as a guiding principle of Chekhov's life in this biography. Furthermore, unlike his Soviet-era counterparts, this Chekhov's literary evolution and worldview are not predetermined by the sociopolitical factors of his time. Neither are they evaluated within a rigid ideological framework, be it Marxist or nationalist. Chekhov is "by himself" (separate and independent) in this sense, too.

Closer to the end, Kuzicheva formulates what appears to be her overarching concept of Chekhov's life: "For years and decades, he lived in a state of resistance. During his solitary three years in Taganrog, it was resistance to the circumstances of life. During his ten years in Moscow, it was the resistance toward the endless tension within his family circle. During the Melikhovo years, it was the resistance to the hardships of rural life. During the Yalta winters, it was his resistance to his physical condition, which he described as an endless cycle of 'now I'm sick now I'm getting well'" (783). Curiously, this "resistance" is reminiscent of the "struggles" the Soviet-era Chekhov waged against petty bourgeois values and the like.

On the other hand, the Chekhov of this "life of a solitary individual" is also just a man: his corporeality, physical ailments, and suffering, especially in the last period of his life, receive considerable attention. This is the Chekhov who requested his wife to send him toilet paper to Yalta, which she neglected to do in a timely manner (813). He is anything but the demigod of the Soviet-era biographies, beginning with Ermilov's.

What is also strikingly different from that era is Kuzicheva's attempt to present Chekhov as some sort of a mystic who "more than once talked about his 'prophetic feeling,' which, as he claimed, never betrayed him either in life or in his medical practice" (145; see also 398, 569). This Chekhov is a tragic protagonist of his life, sensitive to all kinds of premonitions from his early years. He is a "fatalist" who "reconciled himself with the inevitable and with what did not depend on him" (155). Moreover, according to Kuzicheva, Chekhov's fatalism "grew stronger with the passage of time" (784). Thus, it is not accidental that she is the first of the *ZhZL* biographers to explore the "nocturnal" side of Chekhov's personality, for example, implicit references to his illness and early death scattered in his letters. She also pays attention to Chekhov's dreams, notably the one he described in the letter to Dmitry Grigorovich (8, 211, 815). Chekhov the man of dreams is a new image which would undoubtedly surprise his previous biographers.

CONCLUSION

In his famous lines, Boris Pasternak calls the artist "a hostage of eternity in the captivity of time."[24] This formulation should also apply to the artist's posthumous life. Each of the five Chekhovs sketched in this essay—an ally in the struggle against petty bourgeois values, an epic hero of Russian literature, a hero with a human face, an elusive giant, and, finally, an independent and solitary individual—is not only a "hostage" of eternity but also a "captive" of the times that brought him to life. Paradoxically, the very "elusiveness" that makes Chekhov's image as an artist and human being vulnerable to ideological manipulations precludes this image from ever becoming definitive. This lies at the root of Chekhov's ability to change his "face" and of the never-ending quest for the "true" Chekhov. There is no question that there will be new Chekhov biographies in the future. One wonders, to quote the finale of his *The Steppe*, "What kind of life is it going to be?"[25]

NOTES

1. Ivan Bunin, *Sobranie sochinenii*: 6 vols. (Moscow: Khudozhestvennaia literatura, 1988), vol. 6, 215. Unless otherwise noted, translations are mine.

2. Irina Gitovich, *Itog kak novye problemy. Stat'i i retsenzii raznykh let ob A. P. Chekhove, ego vremeni, okruzhenii i chekhovedenii* (Moscow: Izdatel'stvo "Literaturnyi muzei," 2018), 69 (italics are Gitovich's).

3. See *Ogonek*, No 27 (324), July 14, 1929.

4. A. Derman, *Tvorcheskii portret Chekhova* (Moscow: Mir, 1929), 9.

5. Published in 1929 by Moskovskii rabochii, this book is listed as "Zhizn' zamechatel'nykh liudei" on its cover and in the later bibliographical sources on Chekhov. Gorky attempted to work with several publishing houses in this interim period to establish the series, but as a series, *Lives of Remarkable People* has long been associated with Molodaia gvardiia publishing house.

6. P. S. Kogan, *A. P. Chekhov. Biograficheskii ocherk* (Moscow: Moskovskii rabochii, 1929), 64. All further references will be included in the text.

7. Iurii Sobolev, Chekhov. *Stat'i. Materialy. Bibliografiia* (Moscow: Federatsiia, 1930), 25.

8. Iurii Sobolev, *Chekhov* (Moscow: Zhurnal'no-gazetnoe ob"edinenie, 1934), 53. Further references to this book are given in the text throughout this section.

9. See pages 53, 54, 74, 77, 98, 103, 109, 120, 128, 152, 157–58, 176, 218, 222–23, 265, 268.

10. Boris Aleksandrov, *Seminarii po Chekhovu. Posobie dlia vuzov* (Moscow: Gosudarstvennoe uchebno-pedagogicheskoe izdatel'stvo Ministerstva prosveshcheniia RSFSR, 1957), 86.

11. Ibid., 87.

12. Vladimir Ermilov, *Chekhov* (Moscow: Molodaia gvardiia, 1946), 349. Further references to this book are given in the text throughout this section.

13. Vladimir Kataev, *Slozhnost' prostoty: Rasskazy i p'esy Chekhova. V pomoshch' prepodavateliam, starsheklassnikam i abiturientam* (Moscow: MGU, 1998), 69.

14. Georgii Berdnikov, *Chekhov* (Moscow: Molodaia gvardiia, 1974), 17. Further references to this book are given in the text throughout this section.

15. Igor' Losievskii, *Nauchnaia biografiia pisatelia: problemy interpretatsii i tipologii* (Kharkov: Krok, 1998), 122.

16. For new developments in the field of Chekhov studies in the 70s, see Igor' Sukhikh, "Chekhov (1960–2010): Novye opyty chteniia," in *A. P. Chekhov: Pro et Contra. Lichnost' i tvorchestvo A. P. Chekhova v russkoi mysli XX–XXI vekov (1960–2010). Antologiia*, vol. 3 (Saint Petersburg: Izdatel'stvo russkoi khristianskoi gumanitarnoi akademii, 2016), 13–20.

17. Mikhail Gromov, *Chekhov* (Moscow: Molodaia gvardiia, 1993), 8. Further references to this book are given in the text throughout this section.

18. See his collection *Kniga o Chekhove* (Moscow: Sovremennik, 1989) which overlaps with this biography.

19. It was also a time of great cataclysm and uncertainty in the publishing world, and Gromov's book was one of the first biographies to come out as the press was rebuilding itself. In 1992 only two books came out and in 1993 it was one of three new titles published. See *Katalog 'ZhZL': Zhizn' zamechatel'nykh liudei 1890–2010* (Moscow: Molodaia gvardiia, 2010), 192.

20. See for example *Vash A. Chekhov (Melikhovskaia khronika 1895–1898)* (Moscow: Iskona, 1994); *Chekhovy: Biografiia sem'i* (Moscow: Artist. Rezhisser. Teatr, 2004). Kuzicheva was also editor in chief and complier of volume 4 in two books of *The Chronicle of Chekhov's Life and Works* (Moscow: IMLI RAN, 2016).

21. Alevtina Kuzicheva, *Chekhov. Zhizn' "otdel'nogo cheloveka"* (Moscow: Molodaia gvardiia, 2010), 740. Further references to this book are given in the text throughout this section.

22. For the response this biography received among Chekhov scholars in Russia, see for instance Vladmir Kataev's review of the original book (*Chekhovskii vestnik*, 2 [1997]: 6–12) and Irina Gitovich's review of its Russian translation, "Made in, ili snova o biografii. Zametki chitatelia" (*Chekhovskii vestnik*, 17 [2005]: 2–36) reprinted in her *Itog kak novye problemy*, 224–236. The book also had an impact outside of academia. See for instance an interview with Donald Rayfield on Russian television: "Doktor Chekhov. Retsept Bessmertiia," series "About Everything" (January 24, 2017 https://www.youtube.com/watch?v=hBQd1oKF70A).

23. A. P. Chekhov, *Polnoe sobranie sochinenii i pisem:* 30 vols. *Pis'ma*, vol. 8 (Moscow: Nauka, 1980), 101.

24. Boris Pasternak, "Noch'" (1956), in his *Polnoe sobranie stikhotvorenii i poem* (Saint Petersburg: Gumanitarnoe agentstvo "Akademicheskii proekt," 2003), 420.

25. Chekhov, *Polnoe sobranie sochinenii i pisem. Sochineniia*, vol. 7 (Moscow: Nauka, 1977), 104.

Chapter 7

From Idol to Villain and (Almost) Back

Gorky as Editor and Subject of Lives of Remarkable People

Irene Masing-Delic

Tovah Yedlin, an early Western biographer of Gorky, grappled with the complexity of Gorky's personality and concluded: "Maxim Gorky was and remains a hard man to know, a perception that still holds true."[1] This essay explores two themes: Maxim Gorky's (real name Alexei Maximovich Peshkov) editorship of the series *The Lives of Remarkable People* (*Zhizn' zamechatel'nykh liudei*, *ZhZL*) and the presentations of his life (1868–1936) in the three biographies of him in that same series. What goals did the writer pursue as editor of *ZhZL* (1933–1936), and how did the biographies (1958, 2005, 2016) present him? Given the large time gap between the writer's first notion of the purpose of biography and his editorial practice when in charge of *ZhZL*, as well as the large chronological divides between the first two biographies of him in the series and the very different approaches to the subject in all three of them, the foci of discussion will be the variations within the two parameters indicated.

GORKY'S PHILOSOPHY OF BIOGRAPHY

Longtime *ZhZL* editorial collaborator G. E. Pomerantseva in her informative *Biography in the Flow of Time* offers a detailed discussion of Gorky's editorial ambitions for the series when he resurrected it in 1933 (after its interruption during World War I, the October Revolution, and its aftermath).[2] Like his prerevolutionary predecessor F. Pavlenkov, Gorky wanted a "pedagogical" series for the still largely undereducated majority of the peasant and worker population of his country, but his vision transcended the goal of telling the mass reader about the "great people of the world" and what they had created, discovered and invented. His series was to serve "knowledge of humankind" (*chelovekovedenie*), its past and current ontological status as well as "knowledge" of its future potential development (see Trigos and Ueland in this volume). Before discussing Gorky's concept of this goal in greater detail, it is important to go back to the incident that "triggered" his philosophy of biography. It is described in the autobiographical sketch "The Cemetery" ("Kladbishche"), part of the collection of sketches *Through Russia* (*Po Rusi*, 1913), and it took place during Gorky's years of wandering "all over Russia." Pomerantseva too sees this text as important for understanding Gorky's editorial policies.

"The Cemetery"

In this sketch, young Peshkov (he became "Gorky" after the publication of the story "Chelkash" in 1895) had fallen asleep in the hollow between two graves in a provincial cemetery which he frequented to find relief from, to his mind, the disgustingly animalistic and annoyingly vulgar inhabitants of the steppe city he lived in at the time. He was suddenly woken up by an elderly man who claimed that he saw a snake crawling up to him. The snake proved to be harmless, but the narrator, in spite of being irritated about his interrupted sleep and with the man who had so rudely woken him, struck up a conversation about human mortality and the prospects of human progress.[3] In my view, the irascible (but kind) old man offers a fictionalized version of the "immortality philosopher" Nikolai Fyodorov (1829–1903) whose *Philosophy of the Common Task* ("Filosofiia obshchego dela," 1906–1913) deeply impacted Gorky.[4] Certainly the narrator's interlocutor delivers very much the same message as Fedorov in his magnum opus—minus his Orthodox faith. Thus, he angrily denigrates the current state of Russian burial grounds, especially their stereotypical gravestone inscriptions "Here rests God's servant XYZ" [in Orthodox religious terminology, the term used for servant is "slave"—*rab*]. Instead, he sees it as imperative to give descriptions of the *contributions* the dead had made to their communities on the stones or crosses, replacing non-informative data with "chapters" of an endless *Book of Life* (*Kniga zhivota*), in which, similarly to the *Book of Life* of Revelation, all people who had done something good for the common weal would have their deeds recorded.[5] Given the limited space of a gravestone or cross, there were to be archives located near the cemetery keeping records of all these good deeds, however minor, written up in captivating narratives (akin to biographies). Khorvat, as the cemetery philosopher is called, urges all people, educated or not, to explore the "treasures" the cemetery is harboring (*klad*-bishche—*treasure*-site),[6] both the evidence for the science of the biological processes taking place inside the graves and the recorded data in the archives.[7] In the course of conversation, the narrator comes to understand the ultimate message the elderly man drives at—the necessity to eliminate death itself at the very site of death, the cemetery. He has a sudden vision of warm red blood flowing over the gravestones infusing the remains of the buried dead with vital energies. His vision of this "blood transfusion" is inspired by the red glow of the setting sun.[8] It arguably was *the* moment when young Peshkov accepted a mission to be pursued for the rest of his life, or a "project" (a Fedorovian term used in Gorky's sketch) that would give a special direction to his subsequent numerous publishing ventures and editorships, not least to the biographical series *Lives of Remarkable People*. This project was to abolish death by keeping the traces of the activities of the dead recorded and archived (Gorky's version of "eternal memory") and by celebrating immortalizing science.

GORKY AS EDITOR

Returning to Pomerantseva who also sees "The Cemetery" as a key to Gorky's approach to biography,[9] she characterizes Gorky's expansion of the educational goals *ZhZL* had established under Pavlenkov as the comprehensive study of the human mind in its past manifestations and future potential. Nor was the human body forgotten—for that matter, in Gorky's view, the mind was part of the body, physically located in the brain, and manifested as mental energy. At the same time as Gorky was shaping *ZhZL*'s policies, he was deeply engaged in establishing the All-Union Institute of Experimental Medicine (*Vsesoiuznyi Institut Eksperimental'noi Meditsiny*, or *VIEM*) in Moscow. *VIEM* was to research the human species not only as biological beings in their current condition, but also to investigate how it might evolve and improve, i.e., engage in eugenics research. Brain research was of special interest, especially the question how the human brain processed information received from its physical and social surroundings and what occurred when the brain's responses to these "signals" from reality were translated into the activity of the human mind. Armed with that knowledge, scientists could proceed to experiments on how to improve brain capacity.[10] This two-pronged "study of the human being" was complementary. Neurophysiological research of brain functions and their reflex reactions to outer stimuli belonged to the sphere of the Institute, while examining the already formed minds of remarkable people of the past manifested in their activities was *ZhZL* territory. The task of the series was to convey the cultural "heritage" (Pomerantseva, 80), i.e., the accumulated "accomplishments" of outstanding people who had improved their sociopolitical environment through their artistry, or heroism, or perspicacious political acumen, or incisive intellect. Vital questions to be researched were of the type: how could one explain the non-profitable (to them themselves) self-sacrifices most of the "remarkable" people gladly accepted as part of their professional activities emotionally and physiologically? What work habits did the geniuses of the past develop to promote their work capacities? How did geniuses explain their own genius and why they possessed it while the majority of people did not? What brain structures produced genius and which ones hampered it?[11] In brief, the ultimate goal of Gorky's cultural-scientific endeavors of the 1930s was the "formation of newborn people" (Pomerantseva, 81), based both on medical research and historical studies of outstanding people who were to be "examined from all angles," just as Gorky already had recommended in his "manifesto cum credo," the prose poem *Man* (*Chelovek*, 1904). For this purpose of creating a superior humanity, Gorky required scientists who were able to think "futuristically" in *VIEM*, as well as biographers who were "scientifically and scholarly thinking artists" (Pomerantseva, 81). In the second case, the biographers were to create a vivid portrait of the subject, via the prism of his/her accomplishments, presented within the contexts of the contemporary state of art of the subject's sphere of creativity and of current sociopolitical conditions.

A proper balance between factual information and artistic presentation in the biographies produced by *ZhZL* was deemed crucial by Gorky. Well aware of the limits of what was possible in the political and artistic climate of the 1930s, he usually favored facts (if politically acceptable) over artistry. Mikhail Bulgakov's biography of Molière was rejected as too "playful" by his coeditor A. N. Tikhonov (Serebrov), and Gorky fully endorsed his decision.[12] They both acknowledged that it was good art, but rejected it for lacking a "dense historical fabric," i.e., for not being sufficiently "scientific and scholarly" (Pomerantseva, 139). Theoretically in favor of balance between "magical" artistry conjuring up the life of a person no longer among the living and factual information about a genius's achievements in his/her time and environment, Gorky increasingly favored the latter and "the human being was drowned in analysis of the epoch" (Pomerantseva, 143). The biographies of the series were not to commemorate the complex psyche of an exceptionally endowed unique personality, but rather to serve as a "brick" in the grand structure of the Gorkian—Fyodorovian "common cause" that, relying on information offered by past accomplishments, would help "newborn" humanity to evolve to ever higher levels, surpassing the current peak of "Man" (as shown in *Chelovek*).

It could be argued that Gorky betrayed the "epiphany" which his fictionalized self experienced in "The Cemetery" when he envisioned his *Book of Life* as a complete record and archive of the "small deeds" of average people in his collectively compiled future "endless book" of humanity's accomplishments. As its title already reveals, *ZhZL* was a series focused solely on "remarkable" people. As Gorky, however, had implied already in his credo-poem *Man*, the purpose of studying people of genius was to learn how to make ordinary people (*liudi*) into *Cheloveki*, i.e., a superior, continuously active and progressive Humankind under the motto "forward and higher").[13] The biographies of *ZhZL* were to keep "eternal memory" alive—not so much of people per se though, as of their *accomplishments*—small or large—that would eventually fuse into a "common task" culminating in the conquest of nature's main weapon of terror against humankind—death. In view of Gorky's iconic status, his editorial guidelines were practiced by *ZhZL* long after his death, even if their Fedorovian subtexts were not openly acknowledged, or even registered by its biographers.[14]

Let us now turn to the three Gorky biographies that were published in the *ZhZL* series.

GRUZDEV'S *ZhZL* BIOGRAPHY

In his review article of Ilya Gruzdev's works on Gorky's life, including his *ZhZL* biography (from 1958/1960),[15] Barry Scherr points out that "to write a good biography of Gorky in Soviet times" was "difficult" (682).[16] Gruzdev's works on Gorky's life did not overcome these difficulties and were, as a result, not "entirely successful" (690), Scherr opines, and his evaluation includes the *ZhZL* biography. It is indeed a "factographic" work, which ignores its subject's inner conflicts and divisions (the "duality" most Gorky scholars see as a crucial part of his psyche), the specifics of character and demeanor, his relations with women and ideological quandaries (or if mentioned always with the comment that Gorky came to see his mistakes). Political considerations undoubtedly were an important reason for Gruzdev's cautious approach including the "canonization" of the writer (Scherr, 681) that was part of Gorky's status after his return to the Soviet Union (1928–1936) and that precluded any probing analysis. Nor did the poetics of Socialist Realism permit it. Much space was instead given to historical and social contexts, contemporary events and Bolshevik Party policies, Lenin's ideological "guidance" of sometimes "errant" Gorky, and other such parameters. Any blunder in dealing with the iconic writer's life was indeed fraught with dangers that did not cease after Gorky's death. In 1938, for example, it was "discovered" that deposed and later executed NKVD (and former OGPU) commissar Genrikh Yagoda, a personal friend (and "observer") of the writer and his household, had had the writer (and his son) "murdered" on the behest of Leon Trotsky and his right-wing bloc sympathizers within the Soviet Communist Party (including M. Bukharin and A. Rykov). Undoubtedly, therefore, Gruzdev's laconic treatment of Gorky's personal life and his virtual non-mention of his death was a wise move. In regard to the latter, even though the year of the first publication of his *ZhZL* biography was 1958, i.e., during the thaw era, Gruzdev merely states that the writer told him that he feared his "heart would stop before he would have completed the fourth volume of his chronicle-novel *Klim Samgin*," adding that "this did indeed happen—the novel was not finished" and that "on June 18, 1936, Gorky was no more" (341). The result of this and many other taboos leaving numerous lacunae in their wake, was a biography that tells what an icon like Gorky, "founding father" of numerous sacrosanct Soviet institutions, "should" be like, especially after his return to the Soviet Union, namely: a man who had no private life, lived for the triumph of socialism, and knew that Soviet Russia was "the land whose mission it was to pour creative energy over the whole world shaped by man" and already was doing so (257). Usually Gruzdev finds his evidence for Gorky's convictions in the writer's own declarations of "faith," leaving it to him to express his passionate and unshakable belief that all productive knowledge was the source of "endless possibilities—when backed by the *magic* of labor and eulogized by *enthusiastic* socialist-realist art.[17] This quote from the writer's description of a paper mill's "astonishing" accomplishments gives a good example of one of Gorky's pillars of faith—the omnipotence of labor and of the technology created by the scientific mind serving progress:

> "The timber brought from the Volga shore *moves by itself* from the water to the saw, and then, sawed up into logs—*without any human interference*—the logs crawl on into the drum where they are washed and stripped of their bark. They then move upward a pipeline to a height of hundreds of feet, from where they fall down, forming pyramids; in this pyramidal shape they move into a machine which grinds them into porridge-like pulp which flows onto cloth-covered receptacles in another machine. From there it lowers *itself* in the shape of huge rolls of paper straight onto a freight train. All this is so strikingly simple and clever that—I say it again—*poems* ought to be written about such factories hailing them as the triumph of human reason" (267; emphasis all mine).

This quote demonstrates both Gorky's faith in the omnipotence of labor and in literature's sacred task to support it in a both "realistic and romantic" manner (262).

In view of Gorky's editorial policies discussed above, caution was perhaps not the only reason for the numerous lacunae in Gruzdev's biography, but also Gorky's own demand for a contextual approach that valued "great historical events," "the stupendous achievements of the Soviet people," "unstoppable progress" and the like, presented according to the norms of Soviet political correctness, much more than individual experience, even that of inspiring personalities, including Gorky.[18] As Basinsky, Gorky's main *ZhZL* biographer to date, states, it is "interesting to note that Gruzdev who had frequent both epistolary and personal contacts with the writer, never published any memoirs of him" (89);[19] presumably they could have lowered the image of the "great Russian Artist and great Russian Man," by showing him as all too human, or even just human. The Stalinist demand that leaders be icons and presented in terms of hagiography was certainly applied to Gorky up to the 1990s.

The Soviet cult of the invariably great, patriotic, and morally impeccable icon "Gorky," logically, found its iconoclasts in the 1990s when the Soviet empire was being dismantled. Criticism of Gorky's apparently enthusiastic endorsement of forced labor as an efficient means for "reforging" criminals, not least political "criminals," already prepared for by Alexander Solzhenitsyn's impactful GULAG narratives (which included ironical and highly critical references to Gorky), as well as Gorky's apparently sincere hate campaigns against "wreckers" and "traitors," his increasingly narrowing vision of literature's role and his apparent mental comfort within Stalinism, offered ample sources for drastic revaluations.[20] Post-Soviet intelligentsia "denunciations" of the writer soon evoked sharp protests by traditional Gorky scholars and critics, however, who saw him as a great writer of the pre-Soviet school of Realism and who admired him as a writer who had garnered international recognition, nay, worldwide fame and worldwide ideological influence. After the Soviet Union had abandoned its internationalism in the 1930s for the motto "Socialism in one country," many Soviet patriots valued his not joining the emigration, in spite of many years abroad, remaining loyal to Socialist ideals in spite of pre-return periods of critique of Soviet policies. As perestroika failed to bring about all the positive changes its adherents had envisioned, eventually an "exposé-fatigue" (George Gibian's term) set in, not only in regard to Gorky but, more generally concerning the entire Soviet period when the country had been a world power and Gorkian visions of its grandiose future in which the world would be transformed according to Soviet models, had been inspiring the nation. Gorky scholars of the twenty-first century advocated a more balanced view of the "great writer, thinker and humanist" who, according to some of them, had himself been victimized during the last years of his life, spent in virtual house arrest and perchance murdered on Stalin's orders.[21] The two *ZhZL* biographies that are analyzed in the rest of this article belong to the rehabilitating type, but they do not deny that some aspects of Gorky's activities were problematic, or at least misguided, even if well-intentioned. The dominant current trend of critical reception is to see Gorky as a "tragic" figure of "titanic" stature.[22] The well-known Gorky scholar V. S. Barakhov, for example, describes the writer as "astonishing, grandiose, and beyond reach" (*udivitelen, grandiozen i trudnopostizhim*, 6).[23] The influential Gorky scholar Pavel Basinsky also represents this trend of putting Gorky "beyond good and evil" in the sense of seeing him as a personality that cannot be judged by conventional moral criteria.

BASINSKY'S GORKY

Basinsky's biography (2005) clearly aims at restoring Gorky's reputation as both a writer of indisputable merit (in spite of some artistic failures when yielding to overt didacticism) and as a public figure whose ideals were impacting people worldwide. Basinsky, like Barakhov, hyperbolizes Gorky's personality and mind, declaring that they transcend all boundaries, pointing to Gorky's almost superhuman breadth of erudition, acquired virtually without any schooling, exclusively through constant reading and contacts with cultural elites, including international ones. The scholar even sees Gorky as "not entirely a human being" (*ne sovsem chelovek*), but as an "emissary" from "another world, more "developed" than ours" (440), tasked with raising earthly humanity to a higher level.[24] As already stated, the biographer does not present a flawless Gorky, but rather a personality *tragically great* in his very flaws, one who should not be measured by "ordinary yardsticks," certainly not the narrow criteria of a conventional bourgeois world.[25] Both Tolstoy and Chekhov, according to Basinsky, distinctly felt that "some unknown quantity" had entered the world with the appearance of Gorky. Even if one were to concede that Gorky's "visit" to earthly reality was "a mistake made by God or nature, it was a mistake of colossal proportions" (103), and as such, again, beyond conventional judgments. Basinsky rejects the émigré writer I. D. Surguchev's opinion of Gorky as a "mediocrity" who had made a pact with the Devil, since how else could one explain that, in spite of modest literary talent, he enjoyed huge success, as well as fame, wealth and "women's deceptive love?" (101). Marking his independence from conventional opinion, Basinsky states that Gorky's encounters with Russian devils were much more interesting than Faust's pact and meetings with Mephistopheles, and, apparently, extending this favorable comparison to many other writers generally deemed greater than Gorky. Although Basinsky sees Gorky's rejection of religion as a mistake, he still deems Gorky's stance of fearless "god-fighter" (*bogoborets*) as worthy of respect, probably implying that God himself likes a sincere opponent.

GORKY'S "RELIGIOSITY"

Gorky certainly rejected Russian Orthodoxy. Agreeing with Ludwig Feuerbach that "man had created God in his own image" (to have a model to emulate), as well as with Friedrich Nietzsche's notion that the Church's almighty "God had died" and Mankind now should step into his shoes, Gorky fought with the images of God that various religions had "invented," especially Christianity in the form he knew best—Russian Orthodoxy. He did however appreciate the spiritual excitement that religion could offer and, therefore, attempted to imbue a monotonous political Socialism with dimensions that could diversify it and add to its appeal, founding his own (pseudo-) religion of god-building (cocreated with Anatoly Lunacharsky and Alexander Bogdanov). Following in the footsteps of other Silver Age founders of "revised" religions, such as Dmitry Merezhkovsky, Vassily Rozanov, and Leo Tolstoy (in his later works), he too launched a radical religion (or "religiosity") that dispensed with the traditional creator-deity. Whether one sees his god-building as a religion or a pseudo-religion (103),[26] Gorky clearly was a determined opponent not only of the Christian deity, but also of this religion's ethical values, such as humility, patience, all-forgiveness, and others connected with traditional piety. Relying on the axioms of monistic materialism and Nietzsche's cult of the Overman (Übermensch),[27] he proclaimed that humankind was its own evolving god, one whose endless potential was being realized in the "forward and higher" trajectory of eternal Progress (the leitmotif of his credo poem "Man.")[28]

In his sophisticated, thoroughly researched[29] and critical but, at the same time, idolizing biography of Gorky, Basinsky opts for seeing a religious tragedy as the key to the "numerous conflicting aspects of Gorky's multifaceted (*pestryi*) personality" (263). To him, Gorky is a Russian Job, but unlike the biblical Job, he is one who does not ultimately make his peace with God, but instead engages in a lifelong struggle with him and his unjust world order. This is an arguably paradoxical position, since Gorky did not believe in the biblical God, but although he viewed the deity as a chimera, it is a fairly lively one.[30] The irreconcilable Russian Job, Gorky, makes it his goal to become, at a minimum, the equal of the *demiurgical* deity called God.[31] He wants to stand right next to him (*vstat' riadom*) in order to show him that it would not take much to "shove [him] aside" (38).[32] In other words, Gorky wishes to see the concept of God "killed" a second time (after Nietzsche), now by him personally and on his own conditions—those of his religion of socialist god-building.[33]

THE PHASES OF GORKY'S "TRAGEDY"

Basinsky posits that Gorky's religious tragedy, his misguided, yet valiant, struggle with God, began in his childhood, when his father died because his three-year-old son infected him with cholera. God absurdly made him—a child—"guilty without having any guilt" (to quote the title of N. Ostrovsky's play *Bez viny vinovaty*). It continued with his mother's rejection of her little son—equally absurdly she was blaming him for her husband's death. The boy was taken care of by his grandparents, especially by his strangely fascinating babushka, who exuded endless kindness toward all living (and phantasmagorical) creatures (including "little devils").[34] She was an inexhaustible source of fascinating folklore and had intimate daily conversations with her pagan-Christian God, praying to him, and even more often, to his Mother, telling them both all about her everyday concerns in remarkably poetic and ever-varied language. As soon as grandfather (*ded*) would leave for some professional engagement, she had "vodka-happy" drinking feasts (*russkoe 'dionisiiskoe' deistvo*, Basinsky, 31) with simple people whom some "good citizens" would call "dregs of society." From a "proper" point of view, she was an alcoholic, who enjoyed many happy moments of inebriation, who held nobody to account for virtually anything and who had no appreciation whatsoever of dogmatic purity, instead "flowing out in all directions" as even testified to by her ample figure. Her family was loath to take their "wayward tippler" (*shaloputnaia p'ianchushka*, 30) along when visiting "decent company." The little boy Alexei adored his babushka, but the youth Peshkov increasingly realized that her life lessons were not for him. She was easily exploited, and, generally, not respected, since her all-forgiving and indiscriminate kindness made her vulnerable. Facing the harsh realities of the life he was beginning to get to know, he understood that her path could not be his. She had to be "torn" out of his heart, and she was, when the youth went "out into the world." The future "Prometheus" (as Bertram Wolfe sees Gorky[35]) and babushka were incompatible. His merciless and detested grandfather had more useful lessons to teach about life, including his severe beatings of the boy, which were "tests of mettle" of sorts, judging by Gorky's autobiography *Childhood* (*Detstvo*, 1913). In an early act of "self-violation" (to be followed by many more), young Peshkov *forced* himself to reject on principle a world that made "no sense" to him (babushka's), for a world that could be "molded" into having meaning and purpose created by "proud" men, such as his rebellious "barefoot" characters from the lower social layers (*bosiaki*) and Satin in the play *The Lower Depths* (*Na dne*, 1902), who felt that the word *Man* (*Chelovek*) had a "proud ring" to it. Escapism in all forms, whether into drink or dreams, not followed by subsequent efforts to make them become reality, also evoked the youth's growing contempt. Eventually, "concrete-clad, iron humanism" (263) increasingly prevailed over unprincipled self-indulgence and uncritical acceptance of "unworthy" people. Gorky's famous duality, i.e., his basic conflict between "petty" individual empathy and grand transformations of all mankind, between earthly homelands and their future cosmic habitats, was rooted in this childhood choice between pitying "small" people and heroic collective self-transcendence, "meaningless" good deeds done for individuals (unless they were remarkable and as such had value for Progress) versus the total transformation of all humanity. There was also the choice between enjoying beautiful nature as she was and forcing her to "realize" and "redeem" her flaws scientifically by learning to "obey her master," omnipotent humankind, in which material "energies" had evolved into human intelligence capable of restructuring her. The "universal" principle usually won out (as it had done in the choice between unprincipled babushka and severely disciplinarian *ded*), but Gorky at times, even later in his life, did engage in acts of "just kindness" even with people who had no "value" for the Cause. He famously often teared up on many occasions, and his "weepiness" may well have been a "physiological" reaction to the strain of constant self-control. This is my personal interpretation of Gorky's famous penchant for tears noticed by Vladimir Mayakovsky, Kornei Chukovsky, Nina Berberova and many others.[36]

Since the writer's inner duality is such a staple of Gorky scholarship, I would here like to digress to a well-known essay by Kornei Chukovsky which already in 1918 discussed the notion of Gorky as "schizophrenic." In his "The Two Souls of Maxim Gorky" ("Dve dushi Maksima Gor'kogo," 1918),[37] the famous literary critic made the writer's dichotomies his main theme. The title of his article alludes to Gorky's own polemical article "Two Souls" ("Dve dushi," 1915) which was met with much indignation by the reading public. In this article the writer postulated that there was an "Asiatic" and a "European" Russia and that the "Asiatic" one should be "overcome" (to use a Nietzschean term). Disagreeing with this perception, Chukovsky claims that Gorky would have been a better writer had he written less about "European" Russia (mainly the westernized intelligentsia) which he *forced* himself to endorse, but did not feel "at home" with; he "should" have focused on the "Asiatic" Russia of the folk which he *made* himself hate, but understood and described well, and, most likely, loved against his conscious intent to abhor it. Undoubtedly babushka was an "Asiatic."[38]

Basinsky agrees with Chukovsky's and many other critics' diagnosis of a split in the writer's psyche that led to inner tensions and created a false sense of duty to false values, especially those he apparently endorsed during the last years of his life. Seeing Gorky as a "multiple" personality, he also sees his spiritual "breadth" deepen into a radically "split personality" in which

"Peshkov" (his real name) and "Gorky" (his pseudonym) came to lead separate lives (159), with the assumed personality becoming a mask covering his [true, or no longer true?—IMD] face. Since duality is an important component in Basinsky's overall religious interpretation of Gorky, I would here like to disrupt his chronological narrative by bringing up his very detailed discussion of the friend-enemy relationship between Gorky and Leonid Andreev (in the early twentieth century and up to World War I). It offers a partial replay of the writer's childhood choice between a "feminine" lack of principle and a "masculine" stance of steadfastness and unbending determination. The replay of the fundamental choice between babushka and *ded* made in his early youth apparently created a pattern that also determined Gorky's subsequent life.

Basinsky endows the two writers Gorky and Andreev with symbolic gender roles where Gorky is the "stern" man of principle and Andreev, who is "always begging for something and demanding something" (264), plays the female role. Andreev constantly declared his "love" for Gorky and sought solace in his strength in times of crisis, even though the latter tried to "rein him in" by pointing out that there were more important issues in this world than individual emotional crises, however terrible, and the clinging need for support and thirst for shared enthusiasms which Andreev was constantly demanding. Unwittingly reenacting the dynamics of the relationship between Gorky and his all-forgiving childhood babushka, "feminine" Andreev did not judge his friend when Gorky left his wife (Ekaterina Volzhina) and their children for the married MKhAT actress Maria Andreeva (her stage name; she was not related to Andreev), but sympathized with his friend, as well as Andreeva, who found themselves in difficult circumstances at the time. As babushka would *not*, so Andreev did *not* fan the flames of scandal or take the opportunity to read moral lectures about the virtues of fidelity and steadfastness to his friend.[39] It cannot be said that Gorky returned Andreev's solicitous concern. Gorky never abandoned his stance of "manly contempt" for Andreev's frequent moments of "feminine" (and alcohol-induced) weakness, not even when Andreev was devastated by the death of his beloved first wife. At that time, Gorky was busy working out the specifics of his new religion of god-building and had no time to take a deeper interest in his friend's grief.[40] However, he himself was emotionally quite dependent on Andreev, as Basinsky perspicaciously notes in analyzing Gorky's "play-acting." Hiding his own emotional need of Andreev, carefully maintaining his outward "no-nonsense" stance, he secretly allowed himself some inner space for empathizing with his friend's inner chaos, because it made him see his own suppressed anxieties more clearly without confessing to them (265). He had his cake and ate it too, as it were. Over time Gorky apparently overdid his superior bearing in which there was no room for what he claimed to be self-indulgence on his friend's part. Their friendship gradually cooled into indifference and, eventually, violent dislike on Andreev's part. Ideological issues separated the former friends forever. Andreev's final remarks about Gorky denounced his "crimes" against the Russian people and his guilt in the "destruction of Russia," i.e., his support of the Leninist principles that Andreev had come to believe led to Russia's ultimate defeat in World War I, opening the floodgates to subsequent revolutions (306). Upon hearing of Andreev's death in Finland in 1919, Gorky burst into tears and told his colleagues at the World Literature (*Vsemirnaia literatur*a) publishing house that he had lost his "only true friend" (252–53).

In addition to Gorky's passion for "self-violation," i.e., for forcing himself to suppress personal inclinations in favor of the pursuit of "higher" things, there was, in his youth, his "mania for suicide" (*suitsidomaniia*, 59). Basinsky delves into this topic in some detail, because one could not discuss this psychopathology of Gorky's in Soviet times (63). The root cause of Gorky's suicidal despair the biographer sees in a sense of "spiritual insult" (*obida*) that the young man keenly experienced at the time. Basinsky interestingly argues that in the novel *Three of Them* (*Troe*, 1901), the protagonist Lunin kills the disgusting old merchant Poluektov, not to "prove" something (like Raskolnikov), but because he is "offended" by the man's sheer disgustingness, which he perceives as an "insult" to him personally (see the section "Punishment without Crime," 168–74). Lunin seems to share (express) Gorky's own loathing for a fallen and ugly world and its "vulgar and smug" inhabitants, one which in the writer's case, was combined with the alienation of a misunderstood prophet. Gorky already early in life saw himself as the bearer of a salvific message of self-transcendence that he was keen to spread to his fellow men (81). Not many "saviors" have an immediate broad appeal and, in Gorky' case, few in his immediate surroundings in the years before he transitioned from vagabond to *intelligent* were able to understand his message. This made the young man and many of his autobiographical protagonists "strangers to all" (*chuzhoi vsem*, 80), an "alien," to continue Basinsky's *inoplanetianin* image of Gorky. As already stated, Basinsky sees the root cause of Gorky's tragedy in the anti-religious choices he made: his hostility toward a God he did not believe existed and his realization that the notion of God as a creator had distorted humankind's development, as well as his subsequent relentless pursuit of Progress. These were the remedies that he passionately believed would set everything right.

In this context of deep alienation from the inhabitants of this planet, the autobiographical story "The Boss" ("Khoziain," 1912) offers Basinsky important clues to his subject's inner life and his suicidal tendencies. "The Boss" shows Gorky as a "religiously anti-religious" personality, even a "deformed Christ" (81). In the critic's intriguing close reading, this story's main character, the baker Semyonov for whom young Peshkov worked, emerges as a slovenly, exploitative and generally disgusting petty bourgeois (*meshchanin*) who, however, is not devoid of some perspicacity. In fact, he even plays the unlikely roles of Pontius Pilate, as well as the Devil himself in the story. Just as Pilate was "stumped" by Jesus's "strangeness," so Semyonov was baffled by, but also curious about, Peshkov's bizarre character and morality, wherefore he tried "tempting" him into abandoning his unusual ideas for more conventional ones. The bakery itself, located in a dark cellar with a huge flaming oven, was the localized "hell" ruled by its devilish master. Demonic Semyonov was also the owner of numerous coddled and beloved pigs which his apprentices had to feed and look after; they, initially, seem to be cast in the role of the biblical Gadarene swine. In a twist of the story,[41] it is not the pigs that prove to be the demon-ridden swine, however, but the human bakery workers who poisoned them. They did so partly because they misinterpreted Peshkov's inflammatory speeches about the need for a better world, thinking their killing the pigs of their boss would contribute to that goal by avenging their wrongs, thus aiding the cause of justice. They afterward celebrated their "heroic act" in a drunken orgy crowned by a disgusting "dog-fight" (83). In another twist of the story, Semyonov prefers his animalistic men to aloof "Gnostic" personalities disdainful of the primitive creatures called "humans" and makes his peace with the workers who had killed his swine, but not with "Grokhalo," as Peshkov was known in the bakery, because of his loud-voiced criticism of both his boss's and his workers' crude and senseless lives. Another reason for the boss to be annoyed with Grokhalo was that he had thwarted all his sly attempts to figure him out. Semenov, like the Devil who tempted Christ in the desert, was unsuccessful and perhaps he too was "annoyed" about that.

Leaving Semyonov's bakery in Kazan soon after the "swine incident," Peshkov made his most famous suicide attempt in that city in 1887, which he recorded in his story "An Incident from the Life of Makar" ("Sluchai iz zhizni Makara," 1912). He subsequently overcame this "mania" of trying to depart from our world to another planet for good. After surviving the Kazan suicide attempt, he made his irrevocable choice for a "better" religion than the one offered by the Orthodox Church. He refused the light "educational punishment" of a penance (*epitim'ia*) that he was given by the city's Spiritual Consistory to atone for his sin of attempted suicide, and having threatened to commit another if forced to obey the Church's order, he was excommunicated (*otluchen*) from the Church for some years. Having become "Gorky" and having chosen the "loneliness and tragedy" (111) of a prophet of a "truer" faith, one that authorized humanity to initiate its own quest for redemption, the writer made this divorce from the Church permanent. Basinsky states that "Gorky did not know how to repent" (346). The biographer sees this formal and final separation as a fateful decision in Gorky's life, one that sealed his choice of an ambiguous spiritual path at a "crossroads" of life for which Kazan provided the locale.

Basinsky interprets the subsequent periods of Gorky's life and later phases of ideological developments in the light of the writer's unwavering commitment to promoting Humankind as the Deity of the future, and collective labor as the "rational magic" that this deity had at its disposal to create a new world. He sees his "proud" ("Luciferian") decision to break with metaphysical spheres whose existence he emphatically denied, while still acting as if they mattered, as the prime mover of his actions in the subsequent stages of his life. There was his god-building religion (which he retained even after Lenin's criticism of it) that made him protect the intelligentsia for its brainpower and erudition when he feared that revolution and civil war violence might destroy the educators of future divine Over-humanity. In keeping with his dualism, there was, simultaneously, his criticism of Lenin's cultural policies and his admiration for his personality which he saw as one not prone to his own duality, as being that of a "whole (*tsel'nyi*), undivided, purposeful" leader who never deviated even an inch from a set goal (162). While disliking Dostoevsky's cult of Slavic virtues, including piety, he himself was a Soviet Slavophile, extending Nietzsche's cult of the proud man to his multiethnic nation which he saw as capable of becoming the proud and all-victorious savior of the world. Gorky was convinced that humanity's "rights" had been "violated" by the "God-created" world order, and his own innermost sense of being irreconcilably *offended* by an unacceptable reality remained a cornerstone in his sense of having a mission and destiny to rectify the insults of the past world order. These were the factors that made him don his final mask of "Soviet prophet." Edith Clowes identifies 1928 as the year when Gorky saw his "chance to act out his God-building fantasy and return to Russia as the greater-than-human "father of Soviet culture." His "myth had come true in the birth of a new and 'just' society in which the masses had become the creators of a new world and he himself *their* mentor."[42] Basinsky shares this assessment, at least insofar as also seeing Gorky's return as motivated by his sense of self-imposed duty (see below).

Gorky's return to the Soviet Union has raised endless speculation about the most likely reasons behind this decision. Basinsky considers all the current explanations for Gorky's homecoming from life abroad to a new life in Soviet Russia before offering his own explanation. Was it financial security with guaranteed mass sales of his literary works and "a bit more" (an urban art nouveau–style villa, a palatial dacha near Moscow, a Crimean dacha) that enticed him to, and kept him in, Russia?[43] Was it the need to salvage the ("Dostoevskian") image of himself as the true "spiritual leader of his universal nation" which was called upon to save the world in a spirit of not orthodox, but god-building, brotherhood? Was it his sense of obligation to maintain "the creed of god-building Socialism" (the Gospels of which were his novels *Mother* and *Confession*), which he had "dogmatized" while undergoing his usual "self-violations" during the years of exiles and homecomings? Was it family pressure and his own longing for his native land and language (he mastered none other)? Was it not receiving the Nobel Prize that instead went to the émigré Ivan Bunin (who frequently declared and wrote about his enmity for the "Soviet" Gorky, a sentiment largely shared by the émigré community), thus once more confirming Gorky's belief that his mission had to begin in Soviet Russia, where there was faith in unending progress.

Giving most plausible motivations their due—most of them undoubtedly contributed something to his last major life decision—Basinsky sees the dominant parameter in Gorky's personal and spiritual paradigm in his "faith" in collectivized Soviet Russia's potential to redeem nature and change world history—no less—as the decisive factor. He believes that Gorky went to Stalin's Russia in order to "sacrifice himself" (*soboi zhertvoval*, 245) to correct the mistakes and misconceptions that Mother Nature had made and not corrected in the course of her evolutionary development (*nedorazumenie*, 254; *oshibku*, 408). In a letter to Stalin he had hailed "collectivization," in terms that suggest that he saw it as a first step toward the "common cause" of eliminating death by united labor (409), backed by advanced science.[44] It was this desire to redeem a flawed nature by harnessing her to technology that made him return to Soviet Russia where he would meet the paradoxical fate awaiting him in Soviet Russia—the fate of both "leader and prisoner" (*vozhd' i uznik*, 251). In Stalin's Russia, Gorky would become the King in Stalin's political chess games (long ago having superseded the "pawn" status of his name "Peshkov") and, like this chess figure, he was the crucially important figure, but also essentially—and increasingly—powerless, since highly restricted in his movements (cf. 388).

To sum up Basinsky's approach to his subject: the critic sees in Gorky the *heretic* who, having broken his ties with the official church and created his ideology of god-building, ventured upon outsmarting the politicians Lenin and Stalin. He had some successes in this game (many "valuable" intelligentsia lives were saved under Lenin, some—temporarily—under Stalin), but it was he who, in the end, proved to be their "dupe," certainly Stalin's. He made himself see positive results emerging from Stalinist politics that furthered the projects of his god-building faith, but his ruthless "humanism" (311), paradoxically combined with a "boundless faith in Man" (*isstuplennaia vera v Cheloveka*, 312), led to Gorky being determined to see as successes even those developments that perhaps did not coincide with his expectations. In line with his view of Gorky as a *Great* Sinner, Basinsky, however, wants his readers to see Gorky's actions in the 1930s as based on an essentially noble vision of Humankind living in complete harmony with itself and dwelling in a vastly ameliorated Nature which no longer harbored inescapable mortality. At the end of his biography, Basinsky describes how Gorky, living in Sorrento in the winter of 1930 (until 1933 Gorky divided his time between Sorrento and Moscow), found himself close to a major earthquake in nearby Villanova that killed 3,700 people. He was profoundly shaken by this event (as he had been during the even more destructive 1908 earthquake of Messina, which he saw as a call for cooperation in regulating nature; 438–39).[45] The biographer comments: "This tragic event occurred one year before Gorky's final departure for the USSR" (439). He seems to imply that this event confirmed in Gorky the belief that he and his country had a "mission" to save the world by developing a socialist society that would bring out the full potential of humankind. He decided that, returning to the Soviet Union, he would be serving that mission. He committed to its collectivist ideology because he was convinced it would realize the "common task" to realize goals that had haunted mortals since the inception of time. His "newborn" country would take charge of nature, not allowing "her" to wreak havoc with human beings and societies anywhere in the world. "Knowing" that the USSR was the land of the future in which a collective and comradely, science-guided and art-inspired, humanity had begun the common cause of worldwide salvation, his return became a "task," "cause," and "mission" from which he could not withdraw.

BYKOV'S GORKY

Dmitry Bykov is the author of the voluminous and thought-provoking *Pasternak* (2005), the much-lauded and repeatedly prize-awarded *ZhZL* biography of the innovative poet and author of *Doctor Zhivago*. A milestone in the series, it offers an outstanding example of the "new biography" that *ZhZL* began to publish at the turn of our century. In his *Gorky* (in the small-format *Small Series* [*Malaia seriia*], 2016),[46] Bykov, like Basinsky, is rehabilitating the Russian and Soviet writer, but also allowing himself ironical double entendres, ambivalent judgments, and outspoken criticism. A Pasternak biographer's choice of Gorky as a subsequent subject for the *ZhZL* series may surprise those who are unaware of Bykov's enormous productivity and "omnivorous," approach to literature, as well as his penchant for reevaluating standard views of writers, sometimes audaciously and innovatively, sometimes somewhat overly mindful of surprise effects. He disputes that Gorky had anything in common with Socialist Realism (5), even though the writer in the past was seen as its "progenitor." He sees the writer as being "one of the most powerful prose writers of the Russian Silver Age" (7)—although later on he declares most of his novels to be dull—reserving his praise for the writer's shorter prose, including memoirs, satire, and polemical journalism. The biographer is glad that "no one is forced to love Gorky anymore," but he also thinks that to "remember him is necessary," for one because few writers could teach us better than he "how to resist the standard opinions of the majority and to respect the truth of the lonely individual" (*odinochek*, 9). This statement seems somewhat startling in view of Gorky's alliance with Stalinist values during his last years, but Bykov may have in mind Gorky's early rebellions against tsarist autocracy and his constant attacks on the "petty bourgeoisie" (*meshanchstvo*) as the social layer that represented the moral and aesthetic values known as *poshlost*.'[47] He may also have in mind Gorky's anti-Bolshevik journalism after the October Revolution and during the Civil War, above all, *Untimely Thoughts* ("Nesvoevremennye mysli," 1917–1918), which Bykov admires (they have "guaranteed his immortality," 182). In this work Gorky did take an independent stance which contributed to his being sent into his second Italian quasi-exile (1921–1928/1933). Or he may be ironically pointing to Gorky's turning from defiant rebel to yes-man to pursue "higher goals" than those of the current moment.[48] Like Basinsky, Bykov sees Gorky in "titanic" terms—for example, as a "titan of the Russian Enlightenment, on a par with Nekrasov, Chernyshevshy, and Lunacharsky" (9). Far from all readers would call these three writers and critics "titans" of enlightenment thought. But perhaps Bykov seeks to create "shock effects" by his reevaluation of, for example, Chernyshevsky's simplistic materialist philosophy and his usually ridiculed pamphlet-novel *What Is to Be Done?* (*Chto delat'?*, 1863), which illustrates its doctrines. After all, even sophisticated Vladimir Nabokov paid tribute to Chernyshevsky's moral integrity (even when writing satirically about him in *The Gift* [*Dar,* 1938]), and Bykov often deplores the lack of this particular quality in contemporary society. In any case, he is not afraid of challenging "conventional" readers' claims to "good taste," as when he states that Gorky's "Song of the Stormy Petrel" (1901) "inspires the reader with angry enthusiasm" (*groznyi vostorg,* 122). Now usually seen as a fairly gauche piece, however popular it was in its time, when it aroused ecstatic responses from hundreds of thousands, if not millions, of socialist believers worldwide, it pleases the critic by its energetic rhythms and message. His message states that there "is no point in putting any hopes in legal means of struggling [with the government, IMD] and the "stupid penguins" of all times (read the *poshliaki* who love the status quo and embrace expedient politics, 47). They will always hide their "fat bodies" in some large crevice or other, rather than join the revolutionary cause of a worthy "petrel" of our times. He admits that the "song" is "primitive" but "its energy makes up for everything" (122). Clearly, this positive evaluation is Bykov's subjective response to Gorky's theme of rebellion as it relates to the Russia of today immobilized by political and moral entropy.

Bykov values Gorky as an important writer for the less-sophisticated reader. He repeatedly praises Gorky's talent as "entertaining" (65), "colorful" (*iarkii*), focused on "action" and "events" (66). His first two volumes of short stories are "entertaining reading even now" (65), particularly when seen against the lack of intriguing plots in the literature of the beginning of the twentieth century. True, Gorky never worried about good taste when piling one melodramatic action upon another, but he usually managed to create genuine art out of any crude "chunk" (*bolvanka*) of reality, even if the effect was not particularly subtle (66). Still in a laudatory vein, Bykov praises him as a master of the "unexpected move," which aligns him with modernism even though the writer did not approve of this movement. Gorky was also a good satirist, according to Bykov—his *Russian Fairytales* (*Russkie skazki*) are a brilliant satire on the Russian intelligentsia (171).[49] He has high praise for the stories of 1922–1924 and the *Diary Notes* (*Zametki iz dnevnika*) belong to his best achievements (214). Bykov, however, also criticizes much of Gorky's literary output: "Let us note that Gorky is prone to indulge in artificial pathos, verbosity and that his novels often are but a chain of chaotically combined episodes." In the writer's late publicistic articles it is "very difficult" to find "amidst the tin rattle" a "single statement emanating from a human being" (171).

If Bykov's evaluation of Gorky the writer is at times ambiguous—some of his effusive statements suggest backhanded compliments—his evaluation of Gorky's political stance is less so. Thus he declares that it is time to part with "the legend of Gorky's anti-Stalinism" (248), however much Russian consciousness may have a problem with the fact that a "great, truly great and universally famous writer lived in a time of terror and warmly welcomed it" (250).[50] Here Bykov departs from those who see Gorky as duped and victimized, or as a hero who, to the extent possible, was trying to rein in Stalinist excesses, or even as a "two-faced hypocrite" (248). He supports his view of Gorky as a sincere Stalinist by arguing that the writer "in general, very rarely stood up for anybody," for example, doing nothing to save Isaac Babel (who was executed), or help Iurii Olesha, who "fell silent," or Boris Pasternak who had problems with the republication of his *Safe Conduct* (*Okhrannaia gramota,*1931) (255). He did nothing for them, because he did not want to do anything for them. On the contrary, he actively provided the Stalinist regime with the logic and vocabulary (251–52) for its actions toward cultural outsiders. One reason was his conviction that "Stalinism was the only alternative to Fascism" (252); another may have been that he began to view the Communists as the "future builders of a red empire" (249). His contemporaries could not polemicize with Gorky since he enjoyed iconic status and only the team of Ilf and Petrov, in the foreword to their novel *The Golden Calf* (*Zolotoi telenok*, 1931) satirized "a severe citizen" of the Russian land who sternly told them that any satire, even satire that accepted the regime, or any form whatsoever of "giggling" or "smirking" (*smeshki*) at any aspect of Soviet life in the "period of reconstruction" was harmful (261). This "severe citizen" (Gorky) could only think of one appropriate reaction to contemporary events—"to trumpet forth hymns and psalms" (262), glorifying the powers in charge. Gorky never budged from the position he took in the 1920s, namely that only the Bolsheviks could save Russia. However, once again, Bykov surprises the reader with an unexpected conclusion, stating that Gorky deserves not only criticism, but "also respect" for "never budging" from his principled stance (261). However misguided such loyalty may have been, accepting a corrupt status quo in which "consuming as much as possible" combined with "thinking as little as possible" (284–85) prevails, is reprehensible as well. In fact, the current cult of "stability" at any cost is "not much better than Stalinism—let's not be sly" (*nemnogo luchshe stalinisma–ne budem zhe lukavit'*, 261). Presumably, this is not a rehabilitation of Gorky's pro-Stalinism, but rather, another attack on the current cultural climate in Russia. Bykov's final evaluation of Gorky is a "mixed bag." Recommending that his works be "read and reread," his ultimate verdict is that the "strange, uneven and powerful writer Maxim Gorky" is an undeniably "real" part of Russian culture, one which cannot be excised, whatever one's opinion of him may be.[51]

CONCLUDING REMARKS

The three biographies discussed above present three basic approaches to the personality and works of the writer over the course of the second half of the twentieth century to the twenty-first—of a man who is still "hard to know" (see the opening to this essay). The first is to present a Soviet "icon" which almost does not qualify as biography, if one believes that this genre's focus should be the interpretation of a unique personality, the keys to which have to be sought in her/his psyche as reflected in his/her actions and works. It seems safe to say that this type of depersonalized biography-hagiography is not just passé, but beyond resurrection. The second is still partly hagiographic, but creates a cultural mythology of considerable complexity, in which Gorky finds a niche in the country's cultural history as a Russian archetype—the rebel and petrel who like Lermontov's persona in "The Sail" (*Parus*) thinks that "peace can only be found in storms." The third biography seeks "relevance" in juxtapositions between past and contemporary realities. The last two biographical approaches resulted in sophisticated and subjective works which illuminate not only Gorky but also some major trends of the current cultural climate in Russia. Will their intriguing works keep interest in Gorky alive? Is their passion for the subject shared by their contemporaries? Will there be many more biographies in *ZhZL* or by other publishing houses of a still-elusive writer whose larger-than-life image is still maintained by not a few scholars?

The days when Gorky "captivated the popular imagination in a way few writers in any society have ever done" (163) are undoubtedly gone.⁵² His works can no longer be the petrels of social revolution, nor claim unique insights into the current life of the Russian folk, nor will a majority of readers accept them as superior to Chekhov's and Bunin's, nor be shocked by their scenes of violence and cruelty. Bykov in his *Soviet Literature* (*Sovetskaia literatura,* 2012) points to one aspect of Gorky's literary legacy that might be of continued interest in the future, however—it is his vision of the only revolution envisioned by him that still has the power to attract attention: the "anthropological revolution."⁵³ The Nietzschean-utopian theme of creating the superior *Chelovek* of the future, the science fiction theme of the future metamorphoses of matter (would it "disappear" in its "material" form, dissolve into pure energy? [*Soviet Literature*, 14]) combined with the Fyodorovian quest for immortality—in these spheres Gorky might still interest readers who like him do not consider the evolution of mankind and material nature a completed process. As for future Gorky biographers, they still have the challenge to break away from mythologizing the writer and to create a portrait of a complex personality impacted by childhood memories, pursued by ambitious dreams, undermined by inferiority complexes, driven by the need to prove himself and pretending to be what he was not, or whatever future psychological features biographers may find to have been decisive factors in his life. As to his belonging to the history of Russian culture, he was clearly a significant part of it and the "reality" (to evoke *The Life of Klim Samgin* once more) of his being in it for good is beyond dispute.

NOTES

1. Tovah Yedlin, *Maxim Gorky: A Political Biography* (Westport, CT, and London: Praeger, 1999), xi.

2. G. E. Pomerantsev, *Biografiia v potoke vremeni, ZhZL. Zamysli i dostizheniia serii* (Moscow: Kniga, 1987). All translations from Russian are mine.

3. Every detail of this scene is highly symbolic—the snake crawling up to the sleeper's mouth, apparently trying to crawl into it, is a (Nietzschean) symbol of *taedium vitae*. The hollow between the graves where the narrator falls asleep, referred to as a "cradle," intimates that humankind still is but an infant resting on Mother Nature's bosom instead of being her master, and the elderly sage is a savior figure. He is an "awakener" who shows the way out of the darkness of unawareness (sleep)

to the light of consciousness and knowledge and he gives the sleeper the mission to bring about this transition for himself and others.

4. For the resemblance to the "resurrection philosopher" Nikolai Fedorov, see Irene Masing-Delic. "Fedorovian Resurrecting in Maksim Gorky's 'The Cemetery'" in *Christianity and the Eastern Slavs*, III (Berkeley, Los Angeles, London: University of California Press, 1995), 181–98. The timing of Gorky's knowledge of Fedorov is discussed there as well.

5. The biblical book—as a document for Judgment Day—recorded all deeds, both good and bad, however.

6. Fedorov was fond of puns and "etymologies" of this type—*tselomudrie*, for example, is the "full wisdom of chastity."

7. The notion that the cemetery is the given space of resurrection evokes associations to the Orthodox paschal troparion that states that Christ "trampled down death by death" ("smertiiu smert' poprav") and that this victory "bestows life to those in their tombs."

8. One is reminded of Alexander Bogdanov's fascination with blood transfusions as a means of universal bonding, as well as life span–extending, strategy, already presented in his science fiction novel *Red Star* (1907) and later in his scientific work *The Struggle for Increased Vitality* (*Bor'ba za zhiznesposobnost'*, 1927).

9. See Pomerantseva's discussion of the sketch in *Biografiia*, 59–63.

10. Pomerantseva stresses that Gorky was "deeply interested in human physiology, especially the capacity (*emkost'*) of the brain and how it could be increased" (137).

11. After Lenin's death it became common to extract the brains from the skulls of deceased "remarkable" people and subject them to a "slicing procedure" (created by German neurologist Oskar Vogt, who was in charge of Lenin's brain for some years) that was to reveal the secrets of the structure of the outstanding brain. The brains eventually ended up in the Moscow Institute of the Brain accompanied by a biographical account of the brains' former owners. Gorky's brain was removed immediately after his death for research purposes. For details on the Institute and Oscar Vogt's role, see Monika Spivak, *Posmertnaia diagnostika genial'nosti* (Moscow: AGRAF, 2001).

12. In a letter to Tikhonov (Serebrov) about Bulgakov's biography, Gorky wrote: "In its present shape this is not serious research and you rightly point out that it will be sharply criticized . . . , therefore it is necessary . . . to change its "playful style" [11: 506], or reject it. For details, see Svetlana M. Demkina's "M. Gor'kii i seriia *Zhizn' zamechatel'nykh liude*i," *Voprosy kul'torologii* 4 (2014): 65–72. Nor did Gorky wish to support the publication of Platonov's *Chevengur*, since he strongly suspected it would be futile in the given cultural and political climate. Examples of similar cautious nonsupport could be multiplied.

13. The wanderer Luka in Gorky's play *The Lower Depths* (*Na dne*, 1901) makes the famous distinction between *liudi* and *cheloveki*. "Those are—just *liudi*, but those are—*cheloveki*," indicating the difference between ordinary and extraordinary people. Vladislav Khodasevich points out that Luka in this instance speaks for Gorky himself and that the *cheloveki* cry out to be spelled with an uppercase letter. Gorky-Luka sees in them "heroes, creative people, movers of the progress Gorky idolized." Cf. http://

hodasevich.lit-info.ru/hodasevich/vospominaniya/nekropol/gorkij.htm. Last accessed June 12, 2020.

For Gorky's transformation of Nietzsche's Overman (*Chelovek*) into Over-Humanity (*Cheloveki*), see Hans Günther's *Der sozialistische Übermensch, Gor'kij und der Sowjetische Heldenmythos*. (Stuttgart: J. B. Metzler, 1993).

14. Gorky never abandoned his Fedorovian convictions even long after having apparently acquiesced to Lenin's demand to give up god-building. Among many other indicators, this is evidenced by his cautious epistolary contacts with the Fedorov disciples A. K. Gorskii and N. A. Setnitskii, active in Harbin and, later, in Soviet Russia. His noncommittal letters were prudent, since the Soviet authorities were suspicious of both his correspondents. Setnitsky was executed in 1937 and Gorsky died in prison in 1943. See I. A. Bocharova, A. G. Gacheva, "M. Gor'kii i mir filosofskikh idei. N.F. Fedorova (perepiska s A.K. Gorskim I N. A. Setnitskim)," *Gor'kii i ego korrespondenty*. Ed. L. Spiridonova i drugie (Moscow: IMLI RAN, 2005), 501–45.

15. I. A. Gruzdev, *Gor'kii* (Moscow: Molodaia gvardiia, 1958). A second edition was published in 1960. All references in this article are to the 1960 edition and included in the text.

16. See his "Il'ia Gruzdev—Biograf Gor'kogo" ("Ilya Gruzdev, Gorky's Biographer"), *Revue des Études Slaves* 71, no. 3 (1999): 681–91.

17. Gruzdev's own term was "many-layered realism" (290) and one "layer" of this realism was undoubtedly the notion that the topic of utopias coming true under Stalinist-Soviet rule with magical speed was a legitimate component in it.

18. Gorky clearly did not share André Maurois's view of biography—"not to discard or keep hidden anything at all" relevant about the subject (Pomerantseva, 15).

19. Pavel Basinskii, *Gor'kii* (Moscow: Molodaia gvardiia, 2005). All further references will be included in the text.

20. A succinct survey of Gorky's reception history up to the perestroika period, complemented by a useful bibliography can be found in Yedlin's book, 241–47.

21. The issue of "murder" versus "death due to natural causes" is still debated. Several murder scenarios have been eliminated, however (such as poisoned chocolates, not to mention Trotskyite intrigues). For an overview of the issue and an account of the writer's last days, see Geir Kjetsaa, *Maksim Gor'kii. Sud'ba pisatelia* (Moscow: Nasledie, 1997), 287–93.

22. The image of the titan already occurs in Igor Gouzenko's fictionalized account of Gorky's last years in his bestselling novel *Fall of a Titan* (1954).

23. V. S. Barakhov, *Drama Maksima Gor'kogo. Istoki, kollizii, metamorfozy.* (Moscow: IMLI-RAN), 2004.

24. In the later essay "Strannyi Gor'kii" in *Skripach ne nuzhen* (Moskva: ACT, 2014), 52–77, Basinsky uses the term *inoplanetianin* to the writer's "ontological" status (77). His vision of the writer as a man from "another planet" makes the scholar envision Gorky's "relief" after his "liberation" from earthly fetters when "diving into the cosmic abyss on his way home" (77).

25. This Tiutchevian/Dostoevskian perception of Gorky as an emanation of the quintessential Russian character, "unfathomable in his spiritual largesse," harmonizes with Basinskii's (and scholar Vadim Kozhinov's) view of the Russian Revolution(s)

as phenomena of cultural "overflow" (*izbytochnost'*, Basinsky, 68). "Russian overflow" is a key concept of the biography; it tallies with Dostoevsky's notion that the Russian character is "too broad" and should be narrowed—but not too much—largesse, breadth and "overflow" being essentially positive features.

26. George Kline saw it as a "pseudo-religion." *The 'God-builders' Gorky and Lunacharsky," Religious and Anti-religious Thought in Russia* (Chicago and London: The University of Chicago Press), 1968, i.

27. This term became known in Russian as *sverkhchelovek*.

28. Gorky's cult of Progress alienated some of his colleagues. See Irene Masing-Delic, "Incompatible Collaborators: Gor'kii, Khodasevich and 'Belfast,'" in the forum *Maksim Gor'kii and Vladislav Khodasevich. Slavic and East European Journal*, 62:4 (2018), 643–62.

29. Following the traditions of the series addressing cultured but not necessarily academic readers, authors do not offer footnotes and page references, but (at least lately) offer a list of sources and recommended readings. Basinskii's knowledge of his subject is indisputable, although he too does not offer direct references or identify quotations beyond the name of the source.

30. According to the nurse (and family friend) Olimpiada Chertkova who lovingly looked after Gorky during his last illness, she overheard how Gorky "quarreled with God in his sleep" (Basinskii, 397).

31. Gorky's god-fighting religiosity and personality displays Gnostic features, such as his cult of the intellect and contempt for *existing* humankind, especially *hylic* consumerists and other petty bourgeois people (*meshchane*). For Gnostic features in Silver Age culture and in Gorky's world view, see my *Abolishing Death. A Salvation Myth of Russian Twentieth-Century Russian Literature*. Stanford, CA: Stanford University Press, 1992.

32. The wish to push God aside, ironically (and, probably, involuntarily), parodies the Underground Man's "duel" with the officer who pushed him aside at a gambling table, leading to the former's decision to avenge himself by bumping into him in the street in order to make him feel that he—the lowly nonentity—was just as good as the officer. He succeeded in creating a slight collision, but it is doubtful that the officer took note of it. Did Gorky ever consider the notion that God too might not pay much attention to his pushing him aside?

33. God-building is the ideology he would embrace for the rest of his life. Dmitrii Bykov in his *ZhZl* biography of Gorky [see footnote 42 for publication data] sees *bogostroitel'stvo* as "the idea that he never ever fully abandoned," 145).

34. Basinskii points out that "devilry" was a major motif in Silver Age Poetry. Alexander Blok's poem "The Old Woman and the little Devils" (1905) certainly comes to mind when reading about babushka in Gorky's *Childhood*.

35. Bertram Wolfe, *The Bridge and the Abyss. The Troubled Friendship of Maxim Gorky and V. I. Lenin* (New York: Frederick A. Praeger, 1967).

36. For this aspect of Gorky's personality, see Daniel A. Brooks, "Bitter Tears: Emotions in Texts by and about Maksim Gor'kii" (in the Forum *Maksim Gor'kii and Vladislav Khodasevich*). *Slavic and East European Journal* 62, no. 4 (2018): 706–26).

37. K. I. Chukovskii, "Dve dushi M. Gor'kogo," *Sobranie sochinenii*: v 15 tomakh, t. 8: *Literaturnaia kritika*, 1918–1921 (Moscow: TERRA-Knizhnyi klub, 2004), 183–238.

38. Somewhat illogically Gorky loved folklore, presumably an "Asiatic" folk heritage. He transformed it into a political message, however, in his speech at the 1934 *First Congress of Soviet Literature*, adding the notion that this art of the folk had served the purpose of expressing people's dreams of a future better life that industry someday would realize and give to humankind: the flying carpet, for example, was the folk's dream of the future airplane.

39. The scandalous aspect of this double divorce and subsequent civil marriage was intensified by the suicide (or, possibly, murder) of the multimillionaire Savva Morozov, patron of the MKhAT theater, who, as all knew, was infatuated with Andreeva. Did he die because of unrequited love, i.e., by suicide, or was he murdered because he had told Andreeva that he had left her 100,000 rubles in his will that the Bolshevik party deemed it had good use for? In any case, being a dedicated Bolshevik and friend of Lenin, Andreeva handed over the money to the Party.

40. Gorky's "overman stoicism" could be quite frightening, as demonstrated in the conversation he had with Dr. Aleksei Speranskii when, in 1934, he was waiting for his son Maxim's death agony to end in a room above the one where he was discussing medical research with the famous *VIEM* physician. There can be no doubt that the loss of Maxim was a terrible one to Gorky (although he hardly fulfilled any dreams Gorky may have harbored about his becoming a "proud Man"), but he again proved that he could *force* himself to see a personal issue as irrelevant to the universal and cosmic "tasks" he felt he had to fulfill, in this case to move experimental research forward to its eventual goal—mankind's total control of nature and the human body. He presumably hoped that once medicine had "abolished" death, no fathers would ever again have to go through his own sufferings.

41. Unexpected plot twists are an important feature of Gorky's poetics. See Bykov's discussion of Gorky's poetics below.

42. See Edith Clowes's article "Gorky, Nietzsche, and God-building," *Fifty Years on: Gorky and His Time*. Ed. Nicholas Luker (Nottingham, UK: Astra Press, 1987), 127–44, citation from 143.

43. For example, Fazil Iskander saw guaranteed publication and income as a major factor. In his *Rabbits and Boa Constrictors*, he ridicules a Poet who "writes poems only about storms" [such as "The Stormy Petrel"] in exchange for "guaranteed lifelong fame" and income. See E. Klius (Edith Clowes), "Parodiinye alliuzii na M. Gor'kogo v neofitsial'noi belletristike poststalinskoi epokhi," in *Neizvestnyi Gor'kii. M. Gor'kii i ego epokha. Materialy i issledovaniia*, vyp. 4 (Moscow, 1995), 111–16.

44. The devoted Fyodorov followers A. Gorskii and N. Setnitskii returned from émigré life in Harbin to the collectivizing Soviet Union, seeing the conditions there for a possible foundation of the "common task." Fyodorov-influenced god-builder Gorky may well have returned, harboring similar hopes (cf. note 14).

45. For an interesting discussion of Gorky's reaction to the Messina earthquake, see Jennifer Presto, "The Revolutionary Ecology of Gor'kii's Italy," *Slavic and East European Journal* 61, no. 3 (2017): 423–44.

46. Dmitrii Bykov. *Gor'kii*. Malaia seriia, vyp. 105. (Moscow: Molodaia gvardiia, 2016). All further page references to this book are given in parentheses in the text.

47. For a well-known description of *poshlost'*, see Vladimir Nabokov's "Philistines and Philistinism," in *Lectures on Russian Literature* (London: Pan Books, Picador edition, 1983), 329–314.

48. In that regard, he also suggests that Gorky feared his lack of inner barriers and total readiness to commit any act of defiance whatsoever, regardless of consequences, and that therefore he was prone to "throwing himself into limiting constraints with the same glee as others seek freedom" (47).

49. Although Gorky's character Smertiashkin (from one of these fairytales) is usually seen as a satirical portrait of the writer Fyodor Sologub, Bykov somewhat surprisingly sees him as a self-portrait (172).

50. He refers to Pushkin's classical notion (in *Mozart and Salieri*) that genius and evil acts (*zlodeistvo*) are incompatible.

51. Speaking of Gorky's "indisputable reality," Bykov alludes to a scene in his last novel *The Life of Klim Samgin*, in which two children, a girl and a boy, drown. Since the boy's body is never found, one character searching for it asks the eponymous main character, "if that boy had ever really existed" (Da byl li mal'chik-to)?"

52. Andrew Barratt, "Games Tramps Play. Monster and Man in Gorky's 'Chelkash'." *Fifty Years on: Gorky and His Time*. Ed. Nicholas Luker (Nottingham UK: Astra Press, 1987), 163–91.

53. Dmitrii Bykov, *Sovetskaia literatura. Kratkii kurs* (Moscow: PROZAiK, 2012), 11. All further references will be included in the text.

Chapter 8

Alexander Blok as the Model Modernist

Jonathan Stone

Despite having died in 1921 at the age of forty, the poet Alexander Blok cast a long shadow over the whole of twentieth-century Russian literature and culture. Writers born decades after his death found themselves immersed in his legacy. Significantly, this influence extended well beyond his writing—the very memory of Blok seemed to linger and resonate generations after he was gone. In 1968 Wladimir Weidle elevated twenty-eight year-old Joseph Brodsky to the pantheon of Russian poets by wistfully noting how he "remembers the Petersburg of 1921 . . . the Petersburg in which we buried Blok but could not bury Gumilyov."[1] What the young Brodsky purportedly remembers a half century after Blok's death are not just the poems and articles he wrote, but the entire ethos of an era. For many Soviet writers, readers, and scholars, Blok served as a capacious stand-in for the complex aesthetic, cultural, and political life of the early twentieth century. His central position in the Russian literary landscape, his engagement with revolutionary politics, and his formal contributions to the development of Russian modernist poetry all served as potential common ground between a variety of audiences and interlocutors. With Blok at their side, Soviet readers can inhabit the same intellectual sphere as cautious Soviet scholars. By reminiscing about Blok, those who remained in Russia after the 1917 Revolution can share memories with those who left. Blok's biography occupies a crossroads between Imperial and Soviet Russian culture and can be twisted and turned to speak to a range of readers. After a seventy-year history of Blok's life and work being manipulated and repositioned, his post-Soviet biographers faced the task of unraveling Blok from rather monolithic narratives and placing him back into the now more fully articulated and accessible story of Russian modernism.

As a model modernist for generations of Russians, Blok has been the focal point for understanding twentieth-century literature and art since the earliest responses to his poetry. Blok's ability to shape and define modernity becomes most evident when his writing is inscribed onto his biography.

Blok was the subject of two separate volumes in the *ZhZL* series. The first, by Andrei Turkov, published in 1969 (with a second edition in 1981), was superseded by Vladimir Novikov's volume from 2010 (quickly followed by a second edition in 2012).[2] Neither of these biographies existed in isolation as Blok had been a familiar presence in Russian culture without a break since the first years of the twentieth century. He was an ideal figure for Soviet readers. Despite Blok's intellectual and bourgeoise background, his perceived acceptance of the revolution and embrace of proletariat culture inoculated him from the critiques leveled at many of his modernist peers. The simplified and straightforward version of Blok's life, as presented in his *ZhZL* biographies, developed alongside scholars' attempts to preserve the complexity of his aesthetics through a *Collected Works* and a series of volumes of articles dedicated to him. The numerous strands of Blok's legacy represented in these various projects created divergent appreciations of his identity and incompatible conceptual understandings of modernism which persisted into the post-Soviet period. This chapter will discuss the development of Blok's popular persona through the *ZhZL* volumes as a significant indicator of the Soviet and post-Soviet views of culture and literature in the decades preceding the 1917 revolution. The *ZhZL* versions of Blok's biography complement the other ways that his life story was told and incorporated into Russian literary culture. They were never the only forms in which readers encountered Blok's life and work and, while they can function as stand-alone biographies, they are most informative when seen as a part of a complex web of approaches to early twentieth-century culture. Blok resides at the hub of both popular and scholarly understandings of modernism. His biography can be used to present divergent views of modernism and, in the century since his death, has been pressed into service of various aesthetic, cultural, and political agendas.

Indisputably among twentieth-century Russia's greatest poets, Blok both helped to usher Russian literature into the age of modernism while also representing the final moments of its classical traditions. He was arguably the most significant and successful poet of Russian symbolism. His works exemplify the movement's debts to Romanticism, particularly through the highly lyrical nature of his verse, while also demonstrating its modernist traits of linguistic, formal, and general aesthetic innovativeness. Blok's infusion of mystical and Gnostic topoi into his early poetry, particularly that concerned with the *Prekrasnaia Dama* (Most Beautiful Lady), directly shaped the direction and characteristics of the poetry of Russian symbolism's younger generation. His subsequent disenchantment with that stage of his poetry (which he would later designate as thesis followed by antithesis) would mark a fissure in the movement that would lead to its eventual moment of crisis and fall from dominance. Blok's poetic output follows a distinct trajectory that has been described (building upon Blok's own terminology) as a path. A consequence of this reading of his career is a remarkable degree of cohesion within his work and interconnections between his poetry and his biography. Blok's first book of poetry, *Verses on the Most Beautiful Lady* (*Stikhi o Prekrasnoi Dame*, 1905), was fueled by the impulse to imbue his life story with the idealism and mystically charged transformative capacities of symbolist poetry. His early period primarily focuses on the disjunction between the earthly and the celestial as evidenced in poems about love and passion. The hauntingly mystical language of these works, their spirituality and intimacy, expressed a discernable optimism about poetry's capacity to transcend the mundane world and achieve the ideal. Once Blok began to question the heavenly nature of his heroine (the embodiment of Vladimir Solov'yov's Divine Feminine), his verse took on a more ambiguous and darker tone. This marked the start of his next literary phase, that of "antithesis."

The shift in Blok's poetic tone is accompanied by the transformation of his Most Beautiful Lady to the Unknown Woman ("Neznakomka," the titular hero of a programmatic poem and play from 1906). This deeply ambiguous figure, both a heavenly creature and a prostitute, reflected Blok's struggles with the extent to which symbolist aesthetics penetrated the poet's daily life. His play *The Puppet Show* (*Balaganchik*, 1906) openly ridicules the mysticism that had been a hallmark of Blok's earlier poetry and resituates his art's focus onto the illusory and artificial aspects of literature. Blok's poetic trajectory followed a rather organic course that led him from the otherworldly ideals of his early verse to the mundane banality of this next period. Its imagery is marked with earthliness (a section of poetry from this period is titled "Bubbles of the Earth" ["Puzyri zemli"]) and an engagement with the city as a key literary topos. While always closely tied to Blok's biography, his poetry takes on a particular intimacy in this stage as reflected in one of his most lyrical books, *The Snow Mask* (*Snezhnaia maska,* 1907)—a declaration of love to both a flesh-and-blood woman and the city of Petersburg. Blok's connection to his native city and country would find expression in the more overtly historicized, and at times politicized, poetry of his latter period coinciding with the decline in symbolism's prominence around 1910.

Blok's cycle of "Italian Verses" (*Italianskie stikhi*, 1910) embodies some of the significant shifts his poetry undertook in the final decade of his life. It shows a concern with culture and history more readily aligned with the burgeoning school of Acmeism than symbolism. He also investigated his own history and lineage in the unfinished long poem *Retribution* (*Vozmezdie*, begun in 1910), a distinctly decadent depiction of his (vampiric) father and the Russia of his childhood. Blok was by no means immune from the social upheaval of early twentieth-century Russia (he witnessed the 1905 Revolution firsthand and served in the Russian army during World War I), but the presence of distinct political themes in his poetry is a later phenomenon marking the final phase of his career. The best examples of these are in his 1915 collection *On Russia* (*O Rossii*) and, most famously, his 1918 long poem *The Twelve* (*Dvenadtsat'*). The latter follows a group of Red (Bolshevik) soldiers as they carouse and murder while on patrol in Petrograd. It employs an astounding variety of lexical registers (ranging from the vulgar to the liturgical) and meters (including the modernist tonic *dol'nik*). The poem is fraught with ambiguity, particularly surrounding the final image of Christ at the head of the group, and earned Blok acclaim and disparagement from numerous circles. The poem was officially received as pro-Bolshevik and thus cemented Blok's posthumous acceptance into the Soviet canon. It was also the cause of the deepest rift between Blok's Soviet and émigré image. The poem left a bitter and bewildering taste in the mouth of Blok's friends and admirers who left Russia after 1917 and the lasting memory of Blok in the Russian communities of Berlin and Paris was of a tragic figure out of step with the time. Following on Blok's own forays into inscribing his life onto his poetry, a surge of publications in the years after his death began to establish the contours of how he was remembered and the relationship between his biography and his art.

The intertwined processes of memorializing, republishing, and studying Blok (with one ultimate goal being to write his biography) are centered around the emerging and shifting definitions of aesthetic and cultural modernism. As Katerina Clark notes, Petrograd of the 1920s was a "crucible of cultural revolution" and the epicenter of the theatricality and ritualism that marked early Soviet intellectual society.[3] Blok had been at the forefront of introducing Russians to a performativity and interactiveness of art that was essential to both the avant-garde and the revolution. His plays in particular mobilized both camps, potentially uniting them at least briefly since, "[f]or many intellectuals, theater provided the charter myth of revolution, not theater up on a stage than an audience watched passively, but theater as a construct for a totalizing experience."[4] By the time of his death, Blok had opened the door for multiple ways of linking modernist aesthetics and revolutionary politics. As he was eulogized and as the print legacy of his life was fixed, a tension emerged between Blok's association with art of the nineteenth century and art of the twentieth century. On the first anniversary of Blok's death, Osip Mandelshtam famously recalled,

> Blok was a nineteenth-century person and knew that the days of his century were numbered. He greedily expanded and deepened his inner world in time, much like how the badger digs in the earth to make its home, digging out two

exits. A century is a badger hole and a person of the century lives and moves in a meager portion of space, feverishly trying to expand his territory and, more than anything, appreciating the ways out of this hole. Moved by this badger-like instinct, Blok delved deeply into his knowledge of nineteenth-century poetry.[5]

Whether he is the last nineteenth-century poet or the poster child of modernism, Blok was perpetually presented as a person out of time. His first work was received as "a book that was born precisely outside of temporality" while, with his following publications, critics noted that his works "are moving away from the motley and chaotic tendencies of the new art. It sometimes seems that there is something old in it, something half cut off, the riddles of distant, distant ancestors' dreams."[6] Even in strictly aesthetic terms, Blok cuts a protean figure. His poetry exudes Romantic influences, his artistic gaze is drawn to the lines and forms of Italian architecture, his diction is taken from the streets and taverns of early twentieth-century Petersburg, his poetic form echoes the fragmented perspectives of modernist painting. His biographers had to contend with these multiple artistic identities while reinforcing the unity of his life and work.

While other works were more apt for delving into the complexities of Blok's poetic persona and the contradictory elements of his aesthetics, the *ZhZL* volumes on Blok strive to smooth out the differences between his many literary phases and poetic modes. Inherent to this approach are significant divergences in the prevailing understanding of modernism. Differing as well was the degree of familiarity with Silver Age culture that could be assumed in the reader of the 1960s versus the reader of the 2010s. Both volumes present an aesthetically cohesive Blok, but the different means by which they do so reflect a shifting sense of priorities. The two representations of the years 1906–1907 are telling. Turkov's 1969 edition embraces the trope of masks in Blok's work from this period. He focuses on the play *The Puppet Show* from 1906 and the poetry collection *The Snow Mask* from 1907. Representative of the second, post–*Most Beautiful Lady*, phase of Blok's writing (Blok's notion of "antithesis"), these works are unquestionable milestones in his career. For Turkov, these years are marked by decline and pessimism, by death and tragedy. Blok's interest in masks and the theater are part of his disillusionment with the world around him, a stance justified by both Blok's own retrospective presentation of his poetry and Soviet scholarship on symbolism and modernism. The trends of discussing Blok's writing established in the previous decades shaped Turkov's emphasis on Blok's personality as the anchor of his aesthetics and as a window into the themes and forms that defined modernism. A formative text in this process was from the grimmest year of Stalin's repressions. In 1937, the prestigious *Literary Heritage* (*Literaturnoe nasledstvo*) series issued a double volume dedicated to three politically palatable modernists: Valery Bryusov, Andrei Bely, and Blok. This nearly seven-hundred-page collection of articles and publications set the tone for discussions of their lives and works. Considerations of symbolist language and poetics were predicated on a complete picture of the writers' identities and had to be supplemented with an abundance of documentary evidence—correspondence and contextual commentary on their lives. Turkov employs a poet-centered approach to Blok's aesthetics that was cemented in the *Literary Heritage* volume's advancement of a canonical narrative about Russian modernism.

The *Literary Heritage* treatment of these authors sought to articulate their "literary heritage" quite literally. The lion's share of the volume focuses on their epistolary and bibliographical legacies with an eye to filling in scholarly gaps. Couched within that context are more general discussions of Russian symbolism's language, theory, and worldview, articles that go beyond the blinkered personality–focused representation of the era. Yet those are quantitatively overwhelmed by the more empirical facets of the volume, and its true purpose seems to reside in furthering a biographical understanding of the movement centered on these acceptable figures. Implied in this approach is the certainty that, regardless of their upbringings, these poets would ultimately turn out to be Soviet true believers. In part, this reflects a Stalin-era conservatism about literary experimentation and purely aesthetic analyses of literature. But these ideological mandates are not the only forces driving this approach. In his lifetime, Blok's collected poetry was reorganized and reprinted three times (in 1911, 1916, and 1918), with two additional editions coming out soon after his death (1922 and 1923). The guiding principle of these collections was to bring the publication of Blok's poetry into alignment with his biography. Blok was at the forefront of retrospectively rearranging and recontextualizing his work such that it mapped the contours of his life. This is the crux of biographical symbolism, a trend that marked the shift in symbolism's engagement with the reader following the movement's 1910 crisis.[7] Symbolism's insularity and ephemerality (exemplified by Blok's favorite word from his early period—"unsayable" [*neskazannoe*][8]) were replaced by a semblance of order and structure that significantly increased the poetry's audience. By moving away from the limited sphere of readers that were part of symbolism's early identity, the entirety of Blok's work became accessible to a mass public. This trajectory suited Soviet treatments of modernism well and the 1937 *Literary Heritage* volume reflected a trend that had been set in motion by Blok himself.

Blok never vanished from public view in the half century following his death. The regular publication of biographical materials, scholarship, and literary works kept him squarely in the reader's mind. Turkov's *ZhZL* biography draws from and builds on this visibility while also reflecting a shift in the representations of modernism that began to take root in the 1960s.

Leonid Livak explains the "toponymical labyrinth" of Soviet modernist studies by noting the tensions that emerged in the post-Stalin cultural landscape since, "[i]n the USSR, the issue of critical metalanguage resurfaced with the political Thaw of the late 1950s. The terms elaborated in the 1930s were now marred by unwanted Stalinist resonance. The attendant revision of critical lexicon breathed new life into underused cognomens, "modernism" in particular."[9] While émigré communities gravitated to the more value-laden term "Silver Age" to describe the period from the 1890s through 1917, Soviet scholars were left to wrestle with the legacy of the negative connotations of "modernism." A renewed opportunity to convey the capaciousness of this aesthetic and the depth and breadth of its literary output was stymied by an uncertainty in how best to navigate its terminology. Blok, whose life came into contact with most of the figures and works represented in the movement, could be called into service as an alternate umbrella under which they could be grouped and discussed.

> After Blok had become an indisputable [Soviet] classic, his name became ideological cover for the legalization of other Silver Age poets as his "contemporaries." Scholarship on the history of early twentieth-century Russian poetry was often conducted under the mask of "Blok studies." With his patent "revolutionariness," Blok opened the gates for his less revolutionary compatriots.[10]

This impulse to fit many of modernism's aesthetic tenets into analyses connected to Blok's work resulted in the establishment of the *Blok Volumes* (*Blokovskii sbornik*) series out of Tartu (Estonia) in 1964. The inaugural issue abounds with topics that expose the reader to the broader tendencies of modernism including its engagement with mysticism and reliance on artifice and theatricality. Blok's early poetry and dramatic works offer an entry point to a relatively unfiltered view of early twentieth-century aesthetics. Readers' access to these texts had been enhanced by the eight-volume *Collected Works* of Blok, published between 1960 and 1965 in an edition of 200,000 copies. Turkov used a wealth of sources, as noted in the back matter of his biography, including numerous archival materials and family documents (most notably the unpublished memoirs of Blok's wife, Lyubov Mendeleeva).[11] Turkov could assume several levels of familiarity with Blok by the time his *ZhZL* biography was published in 1969 and comfortably aim for his contribution to complement both the growing amount of material about the poet's life as well as the new directions in defining his era.

Turkov's section on the second phase of Blok's career amplifies his overarching argument about Blok's ability to move fluidly between various aesthetic modes and forms. He re-creates the artistic milieu in which Blok wrote his first mature works in 1906–1907 with the expected tools of the biographer—Blok's own letters and recollections, firsthand accounts from the memoirs and diaries of writers, actors, and musicians in his circle, reproductions of photographs from the period and illustrations of the books, and excerpts from the texts themselves. While Turkov's poet-centered approach puts all of these materials in the context of Blok's experiences, he nevertheless creates a dynamic picture of the polemics and responses from the movement's practitioners that helps establish the cultural context for Russian modernism. This is a significant step toward the more capacious and nuanced understanding of the movement toward which the *Blok Volumes* series and the new *Collected Works* publications were also striving.

By focusing on *The Puppet Show* and *The Snow Mask*, Turkov highlights the rifts between modernist writers and draws out the messy process of establishing this new art in Russia, "[t]he Verses on the Snow Maiden were received by his former friends as the poet's even further downfall. Interestingly, in their detractions they speak in nearly the same terms as Blok's later critics who employed a vulgar sociological approach."[12] Turkov shows the dialogue that was modernism. Blok resides at its center, but Turkov goes to great lengths to fill in its peripheries and educate the Soviet reader on the debates that shaped it. He implicitly weaves the various strands that had been scattered by Soviet scholarship in the preceding decades together into a reasonably complete picture of the movement. The touchstones of artifice and theatricality, among Russian modernism's most salient aesthetic traits,[13] become ways for the mass readership of the *ZhZL* series to engage with Blok's life, his work, and the artistic culture of prerevolutionary Russia. The large Soviet audience of Turkov's work (it was published in a print run of 150,000 copies) got an account of modernism that went beyond the fragmented and blinkered version of it widely available through the limited number of authors of the period published in Russia since the 1920s.

For Turkov, Blok is a means to introduce forgotten people and buried concepts to a broad readership. Much of his account of the aesthetics of modernism is part of an act of remembering and re-creating an epoch. When Vladimir Novikov undertook the task of writing the second version of Blok's *ZhZL* biography in the early 2000s, Blok no longer had to serve as a cover for otherwise impermissible discussions of modernism. In the decades following the end of the Soviet Union, the process of remembering the Silver Age and republishing an avalanche of works of Russian modernism had returned many of Blok's contemporaries to the reading public. When Novikov writes about Blok's poetry, he is promoting an approach to modernism that differs from Turkov's. The representative work from Blok's second phase for Novikov is not *The Puppet Show*, but the poem "The Unknown Woman." This 1906 poem is used to promote the perception of Blok's singular poetic genius and provide insight into the inspiration for his writing. He dismisses

The Puppet Show as a parody and caricature meant to deflect from Blok's troubled marriage. In general, Novikov is quite open and blunt about Blok's sexual proclivities, affairs, and venereal disease. But his depiction of the creation of "The Unknown Woman" is shrouded in mystique that adds an otherworldliness to Blok's habit, at this time, of immersing himself in the taverns of Petersburg:

> For Blok, "to drink" wasn't an illness or addiction (depending on the type of drink, he, evidently, didn't get drunk), but rather a means of escape, a means of entering a parallel world. It was its own sort of action, the reification of the concept of the "Dionysian." He looks rather eccentric when intoxicated.[14]

Novikov is invested in combining a close reading of the poem with a fully mythologized depiction of the symbolist poet (which occasionally slips into the present tense, as if Novikov and the reader are witnessing the scene firsthand). He is operating with an understanding of modernism that evolved significantly since the 1960s and he is writing for a readership with a potentially more varied and nuanced conceptual picture of early twentieth-century literature and culture.

When Novikov discusses Blok's aesthetics, he no longer has to treat him as the model modernist in the Soviet sense. Readers knew the nuance, hints, and musicality that populated Konstantin Balmont's lyrics; the cosmic interconnectedness and mystically charged power of Zinaida Gippius's language; the cult of art and beauty that marked Mikhail Kuzmin's writing. Blok's work no longer encompassed the monologic approach to modernism that was the essence of Turkov's representation of his life and works. He is now part of a cacophonous and multifaceted aesthetic crowd that better reflects the diversity and messiness of Russian modernism.[15] In Novikov's work such a polyphonic understanding restores the complexities and nuances of modernism without lessening Blok's centrality to the movement. He is still the modernist most amenable for the mass reader of the *ZhZL* series, and his aesthetics are still representative of the broad qualities of modernism for a post-Soviet audience. Novikov emphasizes the longevity and continuity of Blok's relationship with modernity. He draws out the poet's affinity with the upheavals of the twentieth century and aligns Blok with modernism's disruptive and destructive forces as well as its penchant for the ideal and otherworldly. He begins his biography with the scene of Blok's death. The implications of disease and degeneration that marked the turn of the century and distinguished its cultural milieu from the preceding age are foregrounded by this moment. Blok dies repeatedly in the opening pages as Novikov compiles numerous responses to the news of his demise. Beginning the biography with this series of testimonials asserts Blok's fundamental position for all of Russian literature. Novikov then establishes Blok's notably decadent heritage by focusing on his father's family. The malignant and even vampiric figure of Blok's father, absent for much of his life, imbues Blok with a pointedly modern persona—he is the product of a spent era who embraces the aesthetic and social revolutions of the first decades of the new century.

Even though he is far from the only example of the Russian modernist poet available to the general reader of the 2000s, Blok still carries an oversized burden to convey the tenets of modernism. The avant-garde associations of his late poem of the revolution, *The Twelve*, are anticipated in the cover of Novikov's edition. The cubist features of Aristarkh Lentulov's painting of the Kremlin's Ivan the Great Bell Tower and one of Yuri Annenkov's illustrations for *The Twelve* (both in color) are joined by a tightly cropped sepia photograph of a young Blok defiantly staring out at the reader. The concept of "life creation" (*zhiznetvorchestvo*) is an inescapable element of this volume. The crafting of an artist's biography to align with their aesthetics was a particularly prominent facet of Russian symbolism. The intentional and fluid movement between life and art produced poetry deeply rooted in a transformed and idealized vision of the world. As Vladislav Khodasevich retrospectively summarized the practice, the symbolists

> attempted to transform art into real life and real life into art. The events of life were never experienced as merely and solely life's events; instead, because of the lack of clarity and the instability of the boundary lines that outlined reality for these people, the events of life immediately became part of the internal world, a piece of creation. Conversely, something written by any member of the circle became real, an event of life for all.[16]

Blok was among the most accomplished practitioners of life creation and, when his life is first seen through the tragic lens of his father's fate, his art acquires a meaning that exceeds its solely aesthetic function. Novikov establishes this as an entry point into Blok's writing. His analyses of the poetry, particularly from the second phase of Blok's career, indulge in the myth-making and legends to which Blok lends himself. The section of Novikov's biography which discusses "The Unknown Woman" is titled "The Drama Continues" and it focuses on the turbulent episode in the Blok's life when Andrei Bely actively courted his wife, Lyubov. Turkov details this period in his earlier *ZhZL* volume, but his account of it is more matter-of-fact and indicative of the interpersonal relationships between these figures. For Novikov, it plays into his use of life creation as the dominant trope for Blok's life and the overarching theme informing his presentation of modernism.

By making life creation the centerpiece of his biography of Blok and his approach to modernist aesthetics, Novikov is rendering both the poet and the movement accessible to a wide readership. By arguing for the seamless fusion of Blok's life and work, he instills a structure and orderliness onto both. Turkov's Soviet-informed approach prioritized the person over the work, the biography over the symbolism. This allowed him to define modernism by detailing the actions of its practitioners and the value of his biography is in the tangential stories of those other modernists as much as in the telling of Blok's own life. This was the by-product of biographical symbolism and also achieves a degree of comprehensibility and clarity that makes modernism accessible. However, it is a reflection of a poet-centered version of modernism that creates the movement from the aggregate of figures involved in it, with Blok as the central hub of this network. This is how Turkov fosters the cultural contexts of modernism and fills his biography in with the supporting cast that were essential to Blok's career. The notion of modernism as a network of writers and intellectuals who bridged the gap between the nineteenth and twentieth centuries runs throughout his biography. Instead of opening with the creation of a myth of Blok through representations of his death and paternal lineage (Novikov's tactic), Turkov paints a thorough picture of the idyllic and comfortable intellectual life of the rarified sphere into which Blok was born. It is a world filled with art, literature, and ideas, and in describing it Turkov can return a Soviet reader to the people and places that established early twentieth-century Russian culture. He re-creates the intricate webs of interactions that occupied Blok for his entire creative life and defined the content and form of his writing. The shifting alliances and extended polemics of Russian modernism fuel this presentation of Blok and make Turkov's biography far more than a retelling of his life. Even the book's supplementary material has an aura of discovery—the label "published for the first time" is appended to twenty-one of the images included in the volume, primarily photographs of Blok's family and friends. As part of the sea change in the Russian discussion of prerevolutionary culture, Turkov's *ZhZL* contribution brings the scholarly approach of rediscovering forgotten or suppressed authors and integrating them into the narrative of Russian literature to a very wide audience. It takes the notion of modernism mainstream.

Novikov also brings more sophisticated academic concepts to a general readership in the guise of establishing the cultural context of Blok's life and work. His treatment of *The Snow Mask* veers notably from Turkov's by reading it as a "cold book" whose emotional register is more appealing to a future reader than it was to Blok's contemporaries.[17] Here Novikov introduces the concept of the modernist book as a holistic entity that encompasses the author's life, the process of its composition, its physical attributes, and its reception. The book is placed into a specific historical and biographical setting while also analyzed through the lens of material culture. One element of a sociological turn in Russian modernist studies,[18] this approach elevates the structure of the book to one of the primary facets of Blok's biography. As Novikov claims, Blok "creates each new book like a new life."[19] His biography consequently is both the book of Blok's life and the life of his books. This was aided by a project that coincided with the publication of Novikov's new *ZhZL* entry. As Blok's popular biography was being updated, so was the standard scholarly edition of his work. The eight-volume *Collected Works* that had shortly preceded Turkov's book was replaced by a projected twenty-volume *Complete Collected Works and Letters* initiated in 1997. When Novikov's 2010 work was published, seven volumes of the *Complete Collected Works* had come out containing all of Blok's poetry and the majority of his prose. Unlike the 1960–1965 *Collected Works*, this compilation of Blok's writing has an extensive apparatus that focuses on contextualizing the works and supplementing them with numerous biographical details and excerpts from related memoirs, diaries, and letters. Novikov's volume is, to an extent, a rearrangement and distillation of such notes. Nevertheless, in the *Complete Collected Works*, the poems are primary, and the context is a secondary (and even optional) component of the reader's experience of them. For Novikov, the two are inextricably bound together. Such a combination of life and works is, naturally, standard for a biography. But in the case of Blok, it fosters a symbiotic relationship between the two that makes life creation the only feasible way to read his biography. The poet cannot be understood without being refracted through the myth of his life. His idealism, his tragedy, his theatricality, his patriotism are all in service of the concept of the writer as one who confronts modernity head-on and copes with its unknowability by aestheticizing their world. In this way, Blok is still the model modernist whose personality succeeds in capturing his era.

Blok's license to represent the Silver Age for generations of Soviet and post-Soviet readers is derived in part from the capacious and paradigmatic qualities of his aesthetics. But his patriotic and political stances, his relationship to the people and the revolution, cemented his durability as an ideologically acceptable figure. The delicate balancing act that Soviet scholars of modernism had to perform is well documented in the 1974 correspondence between Leonid Dolgopolov, a specialist in Blok and Bely, and the editors of the third edition of the *Great Soviet Encyclopedia*. Dolgopolov's article on Russian literature of the turn of the century came under heavy scrutiny and was ultimately rejected for, among other infelicities, not discussing Socialist Realism and taking an overly narrow view of the era by minimizing the "social-historical character of the period," namely the revolution of 1905, the appearance of the Communist Party, and Lenin.[20] Turkov had to thread the same needle and ultimately land on a version of Blok that prioritizes his interest in the folk and shows his response to the 1905 revolution as a turn toward Russian history and themes. Even old Dmitry Mendeleev (the renowned chemist and Blok's father-in-law), who had not left his home in years, is recounted to have ordered his carriage and rushed to his friend the minister Sergei Witte on the nineth of January.[21] Mendeleev's disgust at Witte's unwillingness to stop the bloodshed serves as a modicum of redemption for all of Blok's intellectual circles, a precursor to the poet's patriotic tendencies and revolutionary sympathies. When Blok's perceived (or imposed) political views are incorporated into his identity as a modernist, the biographer must dwell on class relations and use Blok to draw out the "social-historical character of the period." Turkov's volume signals his interest in doing so from the beginning. The image of Blok on the cover is not from his youth, but from among the last of the poet—the photographer Moisei Nappelbaum's 1921 portrait of a worn and weathered Blok. The illustrations are also from Annenkov's suite for *The Twelve*, but their washed-out green-gray tones and evocation of the black night, white snow, and relentless wind of the poem's opening emphasize revolution and social upheaval over artistic modernism. Turkov's focus on *The Twelve* informs much of the final third of his biography. In Turkov's estimation, the culmination of Blok's third poetic phase, around 1910, saw the crystallization of his revolutionary outlook:

The world had changed and it had to be built anew!

His contemporaries were shocked by the poem *The Twelve*, as if it has been written by a "new poet" with a "new voice."

But in literature nothing happens "suddenly." In order to be able to "capture" the stormy, frothing current of the revolution and imprint it on the readers' hearts for good, one needs an experienced eye, a keen sense of history, the hand of a master capable of crafting a monumental quilt; one needs a studio for working with the epic of the times. In Blok's life, his work on the poem *Retribution* turned out to be such a studio.[22]

Novikov had opened his biography with Blok's father, the hero of *Retribution*, to establish the myth of the poet's modernist life story. For Turkov, this episode is the precursor to *The Twelve*. He makes it integral to Blok's position as the fusion of twentieth-century aesthetics and Soviet ideology. His biography is no less sweeping an account of the Silver Age as its post-Soviet counterpart, but the conditions under which Turkov could convey the flavor of that era required the ultimate triumph of Blok the citizen.[23]

Novikov accepts the political elements of Blok's biography as part of his intellectual and civic life, but also as a precondition for keeping Blok in public discourse and on Soviet syllabi for several generations:

Blok did not make it into the ranks of official classics, into courses of study, immediately and without some hesitation and difficulty. In order to include the poet into the Soviet literary iconostasis, he had to be diligently contrasted with the "Decadents," ripped from the context of Russian Symbolism. The poem *The Twelve* was a focal point, although in a stringently singular interpretation: the author was pro revolution with no hint of contra. All of his previous work began to be analyzed as part of the path towards the revolution.[24]

Released from the fetters of a "stringently singular interpretation" of Blok, Novikov can present his political writings as part and parcel of the poet's aestheticization of life and the surrounding world, "*The Twelve* is not simply the "music of the revolution," but a symphony of life in all its fullness."[25] The doctrine of life creation holds to the very end. Even after the revolution, which incontrovertibly ended his native era and exterminated his social milieu, Blok uses poetry to weave the images, people, and voices of this historical moment into the artistic fabric of twentieth-century Russia. The final pages of Novikov's biography loop back to its opening, the scene of Blok's death. He doubles down on the unity of the poet's life and the paradigmatic nature of his work. While acknowledging that modernity was a complex and multifaceted phenomenon and admitting that the Soviet-era capaciousness of Blok's career was a legal fiction to allow for discussions of other modernists, Novikov does ultimately make Blok the keystone of the era. He is "ground zero" for some of the most talented and significant poets of the twentieth century.[26]

Russian modernism shared many traits with Western modernism, and indeed the Russian poets in Blok's circle were aware of and in contact with their European counterparts. Yet the tenor and general shape of Russian modernism differed significantly from the relatively austere modernism that dominated the West. While the Russian movement's individual aesthetic components might align with the theoretical and scholarly descriptions of European modernism, Russian modernism was marked by a pervasive preference for the ideal over the real. Russian modernism was concerned with the transformative capacity of the word and, for a brief moment in Russia, it appeared that art's power to change and even save the world would triumph. This short-lived utopianism would leave an indelible mark on all of twentieth-century Russian literature and culture. Blok's life served as a vessel for that literature and culture and helped to preserve it throughout the Soviet period and beyond. Modernism entailed a particular relationship to time, one that privileges change and renewal:

> The historicist feeling that we live in totally novel times, that contemporary history is the source of our significance, that we are derivates not of the past but of

the surrounding and enfolding environment or scenario, that modernity is a new consciousness, a fresh condition of the human mind—a condition which modern art has explored, felt through, sometime reacted against.[27]

For Turkov and Novikov, Blok's biography allowed them to re-create Russia's engagement with modernity and partake of its affirmation of the significance of contemporary history. It was a means for them, and their readers, to come to terms with the twentieth century and articulate the interconnections between aesthetics, culture and ideology. They varied in how they did so, and the versions of Blok they produced reflect the sea changes in both politics and scholarship that Russia endured in the course of the century following Blok's death. Yet Turkov and Novikov both recognized the power of Blok's work and the allure of his life to tap into deeper currents that reveal a new consciousness and fresh condition of the human mind. They made him into the model modernist and, with that, an eternally present and eternally central figure for generations of Russian readers.

NOTES

1. Wladimir Weidle, "Petersburg Poetics," in Nikolai Gumilev *Sobranie sochinenii* (Washington, D.C.: Victor Kamkin, 1968), xxxv–xxxvi.

2. Biographical sketches of Blok had been included in several other *ZhZL* editions of the era: Kornei Chukovskyii's *Sovremenniki* (1962), Maksim Gorkyii's *Literaturnye portrety* (1963), Konstantin Paustovskyii's *Blizkie i dalekie* (1967). These were, however, framed as reminiscences by literary figures who knew Blok and inhabit a liminal space between biography and memoir.

3. Katerina Clark, *Petersburg: Crucible of Cultural Revolution* (Cambridge: Harvard University Press, 1995).

4. Ibid., 75.

5. Osip Mandel'shtam, "A. Blok [1922]," in *Aleksandr Blok: Pro et contra*, ed. N.Iu. Griakalova (St. Petersburg: RKhGI, 2004), 413.

6. Zinaida Gippius, "Review of 'Stikhi o Prekrasnoi Dame' [1904]," in *Aleksandr Blok: Pro et contra*, ed. N.Iu. Griakalova (St. Petersburg: RKhGI, 2004), 27; Boris Griftsov, "Ob Aleksandre Bloke, iskresnnosti i dekadentstve [1907]," in *Aleksandr Blok: Pro et contra*, ed. N.Iu. Griakalova (St. Petersburg: RKhGI, 2004), 70.

7. See Jonathan Stone, *The Institutions of Russian Modernism: Conceptualizing, Publishing, and Reading Symbolism* (Evanston, Ill.: Northwestern University Press, 2017), 203–40.

8. Zinaida Gippius, "Moi lunnyi drug. O Bloke [1925]," in *Zhivye litsa* (Moscow: Russkaia kniga, 2002), 9.

9. Leonid Livak, *In Search of Russian Modernism* (Baltimore, Md.: John Hopkins University Press, 2018), 70.

10. Vladimir Novikov, *Aleksandr Blok* (Moscow: Molodaia gvardiia, 2010), 96.

11. Additionally, he would have been aware of much of the Western scholarship on Blok thanks to the extensive fifteen-page bibliography published by Avril Pyman in the 1964 *Blok Volume* (557–73).

12. A. M. Turkov, *Aleksandr Blok* (Moscow: Molodaia gvardiia, 1969), 123.

13. See Colleen McQuillen, *The Modernist Masquerade: Stylizing Life, Literature, and Costumes in Russia* (Madison: The University of Wisconsin Press, 2013).

14. Novikov, *Aleksandr Blok*, 129.

15. In the post-Soviet era, *ZhZL*'s program had expanded in step with the greater awareness and wider availability of nearly every significant modernist author. Among formerly taboo writers receiving their first *ZhZL* biography in the years leading up to Novikov's new Blok edition were: Vladimir Solov'ev (2000), Marina Tsvetaeva (2002), Osip Mandel'shtam (2004), Maximilian Voloshin (2005), Valerii Briusov (2006), Nikolai Gumilev (2006), Andrei Bely (2007), Dmitrii Merezhkovskii (2008), and Anna Akhmatova (2009). These constituted a mixture of new works and republishing other, older, biographies under the *ZhZL* imprint.

16. From "The End of Renata" (1928), quoted in Irina Paperno, "Introduction," in *Creating Life: The Aesthetic Utopia of Russian Modernism*, ed. Irina Paperno and Joan Delaney Grossman (Stanford: Stanford University Press, 1994), 2–3.

17. Novikov, *Aleksandr Blok*, 148–49.

18. See A. I. Reitblat, "Russkaia literatura kak sotsial'nyi institut," in *Pisat' poperek* (Moscow: Novoe literaturnoe obozrenie, 2014) and A. I. Reitblat, "Simvolisty, ikh izdateli i chitateli," in *Ot Bovy k Bal'montu* (Moscow: Novoe Literaturnoe Obozrenie, 2009).

19. Novikov, *Aleksandr Blok*, 150.

20. L. K. Dolgopolov, *Progulki s Blokom* (Saint Petersburg: Nestor-Istoriia, 2019), 225.

21. A. M. Turkov, *Aleksandr Blok*, 75–76.

22. Ibid., 203.

23. Irene Masing-Delic explores this facet of Turkov's biography in Irene Masing-Delic, "Two Bloks and One Pasternak: When, How and Why Does One Get into *The Life of Remarkable People*?," paper presented at AATSEEL Conference (Chicago 2014).

24. Novikov, *Aleksandr Blok*, 95.

25. Ibid., 313.

26. Ibid., 333.

27. Malcolm Bradbury and James McFarlane, eds., *Modernism: A Guide to European Literature, 1890–1930* (New York: Penguin, 1991), 22.

Chapter 9

Narrating Eccentricity
The ZhZL Biographies of Anna Akhmatova and Marina Tsvetaeva

Alexandra Smith

As cultural products, Russian biographies of writers play an important role in the construction of cultural capital in post-Soviet Russia. Pierre Bourdieu links cultural capital to a social order that "is progressively inscribed in people's minds"[1] through its educational system, language, values and everyday activities. According to Vasily Gatov, Russia's attempt in the 2000s to "re-establish the country's importance and exceptionality" is inseparable from the recycling of traditional beliefs. They are deeply "rooted in Russian culture, literature and philosophy."[2] Gatov, commenting on political storytelling in Putin's Russia, concedes that Russian mass media's communication revolves around this myth: "Mother Russia is the absolute good. Positive, educated and well-behaved, it fosters the good for all the neighbors and even non-neighbors. Though sometime before Russia was humiliated and surpassed by some obscure forces, it persistently revives itself and wants to spread the good it represents."[3] In this context, exemplary accounts of lives of remarkable writers who endured suffering and who preserved their belief in Russia's greatness and spiritual resilience appear more important than ever in a country where a new ideology comprises a hybrid mix of facts, myths, legends, and conspiratorial interpretations of reality.

In this chapter I will examine the biographies of Anna Akhmatova and Marina Tsvetaeva published in the *Lives of Remarkable People* series (*ZhZL*) in the 2000s in the light of Pierre Bourdieu's ideas about the reception and evaluation of works of art. "The relationship between a creative artist and his work, and therefore his work itself," writes Bourdieu, "is affected by the system of social relations within which creation as an act of communication takes place, or to be more precise, by the position of the creative artist in the structure of the intellectual field." Bourdieu compares the intellectual space to a magnetic field that features "a system of power lines."[4] In the last three hundred years Russian literary culture was more conservative than Western culture, so it comes as little surprise that women poets came to be taken seriously only at the beginning of the nineteenth century. Yet prominent Russian women poets such as Anna Bunina and Karolina Pavlova became widely appreciated in Russia only in the beginning of the twentieth century. According to Maria Nesterenko, Anna Bunina was the first woman poet in Russia whose themes and tropes were developed by Russian female poets of subsequent generations.[5] Likewise, Alessandra Tosi views Bunina as "the first woman poet of note in Russia."[6] Yet many contemporaries of Bunina ostracized her for being totally devoted to literary craftsmanship and self-education. Tosi explains:

> Writing as a full-time activity was deemed inappropriate and immoral for a lady, whose literary accomplishment was confined to the spontaneous and artless expression of her innocent feelings. Bunina (a rare case among women writers of the time) rejected such a view: she regarded literature as a work of craft requiring dedication and serious study, quite independently from any consideration of gender (322).

Tosi praises Bunina as an archetypal image of the Russian female poet who defended her choice to become a professional author: "As in her life, also in her work Bunina did not conform to the standard image of women, providing an important archetype for the full acceptance of female authorship in Russia" (Ibid.). While Akhmatova used Bunina as her role model, Tsvetaeva paid homage to Pavlova by defining her own art as a sacred craft. This definition appears in Pavlova's poem "You have survived in the poor heart." ("Ty utselevshii v serdtse nishchem"). Tsvetaeva uses a particular line from Pavlova's poem—that equates poetry and sacred craft—as an epigraph for her collection *Craft* (*Remeslo*).

While Pavlova and Bunina were important to Russian modernist poetry's exploration of the subjectivity and fluidity of individual identity, there have been no biographies dedicated to Pavlova or Bunina in the *ZhZL* series in Russia. The existence of the 1916 biography of Pavlova written by the Russian poet and critic Boris Rapgof[7] escaped the attention of Soviet and post-Soviet editors of the series. It is therefore unusual to see biographies of twentieth-century female poets published while their nineteenth-century predecessors go without serious acknowledgment. In the absence of knowledge of Pavlova's and Bunina's lives, a post-Soviet reader lacks information to place in any perspective the exceptional qualities of the lives and works of Akhmatova and Tsvetaeva.

Similarly, the Soviet literary canon was selective in the promotion of female poets. With the small exception of female war poets and children's poets, Soviet authorities were not eager to canonize modernist authors whose complexity and poetic personae were too difficult to capture in the round. Leonid Heller points out that Soviet culture was characterized by its philosophical and ideological rejection of traditional aesthetic values and metaphysics. He claims that "they were re-examined and revised from the perspective of the class history of mankind." As Heller puts it, "the famous triad 'of ideological commitment,' 'Party-mindedness,' and 'national popular spirit' constituted the core of socialist realist aesthetics."[8] In contrast, Akhmatova and Tsvetaeva worked on the margins of Soviet society: they experienced displacement as émigré and internal émigré authors. Most of their controversial and politically independent works became known to the Russian mass reader from the late 1980s or early 1990s.

The marginal position of such important Russian women poets as Tsvetaeva and Akhmatova within the Soviet canon can be largely explained by their independent political views and their use of religious and classical allusions in poetry. Their works foreground the notion of female consciousness and transgress the boundaries of established social norms pertaining to sexuality and gender. In the post-Soviet context, the emergence of three *ZhZL* biographies of Akhmatova and Tsvetaeva might be partly explained by their eccentric lifestyles and the unorthodox views on Russian history and culture they expressed in their poetry in an innovative manner. In addition, the cult of writers as heroes and martyrs in Russia appears an important factor in the post-Soviet canonization of Akhmatova and Tsvetaeva as victims of Soviet totalitarian policies. As Andrew Wachtel aptly notes, Russia literature does not just reflect reality, but it often constructs "new identities and new social and political realities."[9]

Wachtel thinks that the inclusion of biographies of many writers into the *ZhZL* series is unsurprising. In his view, a strong interest in writers' lives can be explained by the special place assigned to writers in Russian society as creators and social critics. It appears that the post-Soviet cult of writers is firmly rooted in that tradition. Today, complementing the traditional view of these writers from the past as martyrs, many are seen as celebrities who having mastered their lives treated them as another artifact. Yet Wachtel suggests that the Russian readership in the post-Soviet period is still influenced by the Romantic view of writers as heroes, as evident in Pavlenkov's and Gorky's series *Lives of Remarkable People*. He also thinks that in Russia there is a somewhat old-fashioned distance between the reader of remarkable people's lives and the objects of biographical study. Wachtel finds this disturbing by

Western standards: "Russians venerate their writers, believe that they were and are far more than mere creators of insightful fictions, and they want to connect the writers and their texts to their lives in ways that contemporary Western criticism finds problematic."[10]

In the space that follows I would like to examine how the reception of the lives of Akhmatova and Tsvetaeva in the 2000s follows existing patterns of the cult of the author and how the absence of the critical apparatus developed in the West has prevented the authors of their biographies to do full justice to the representation of their experimental poetry and their complex personalities. It will be demonstrated that both Akhmatova and Tsvetaeva are often assessed in biographies and critical studies as eccentric women and mythmakers in the style of their famous male nineteenth-century predecessors, especially Alexander Pushkin and Mikhail Lermontov.

CANON-FORMATION AND THE EMERGENCE OF THE CULT OF THE AUTHOR

The celebration of Russian writers' lives, including those of lyric poets, emerged in the second half of the nineteenth century in parallel with the construction of the Russian literary canon in the high school curriculum that was oriented toward classical education. "The study of classics," maintains Alexey Vdovin, "was meant to teach students the 'proper' way of interpreting their own national culture."[11] As Vdovin puts it, "Russian literature became 'classic' because it became part of classicist curriculum."[12] Similarly, Russian biographies of prominent literary figures were meant to educate Russian readers in how to comprehend valuable works of literature in relation to the specific history of Russian canon formation. Vladimir Stoiunin's book *On Teaching Russian Literature* (1864), famous for its eight editions in the second half of the nineteenth century, promoted students' competence in moral values more than in aesthetics. Vdovin explains: "Stoiunin's method was based on the discussion of behavioral and moral ideas communicated by a text rather than its aesthetic merits. Students were invited to put themselves in the shoes of literary characters and model their own life choices under the given circumstances (this was called a 'conversation about life')."[13] Such an approach is evident in the canonization of Pushkin, the first and foremost Russian national poet. Yuri Lotman explains that the desire of Russian readers to see Pushkin's life and art as a part of one single narrative is rooted in the Romantic tradition: "The poet's art came to be seen as one big autobiographical novel, in which short and long poems formed chapters, while the biography served as the main plot. . . . This romantic view of life . . . was pivotal for Pushkin. Based on it, he went further and created not just a wholly unique verbal art, but also a wholly unique art of living."[14] The original founder of the *ZhZL* series, Florenty Pavlenkov, saw life's activities as the heart of the biographies in his series and wanted to use these biographies for educational purposes. Similarly to Dmitry Tolstoy's attempt to bring together the works of antiquity and contemporary Russian works in the school curriculum, Pavlenkov used the book *Plutarch for Youngsters* as the model for his biographical series.[15]

Maxim Gorky's version of *ZhZL*, founded in 1933, revised Pavlenkov's ideas significantly in order to produce Soviet biography. Although Gorky's vision of biographical writing is rooted in the Russian tradition of utilitarian approaches to biography, his series was more diverse: for example, he attempted to commission several foreign authors to write biographies of Western writers. Gorky's attempt at illustrating important events of world history by narrating the lives of heroes, scientists, writers, and artists whose careers had a significant impact on various historical events was in line with a revived interest in Thomas Carlyle's vision of history as the biography of great men.[16] According to Angela Brintlinger, the main goal of Gorky's series was to promote the idea of life as a feat. "And as the 1930s progressed," writes Brintlinger, "it became clear that the series of biographies was the perfect institutional home for the Soviet enterprise of monumental hero-worship."[17]

However, Gorky's vision did not go unchallenged. The idea of the biographer who could stimulate the imagination of readers better than any poet or novelist was widely debated in the Soviet Union. In the early 1980s, it culminated following the publication of volumes in the series that deviated from the ideals of Pavlenkov and Gorky. In September 1980 the prestigious literary journal *Literary Issues (Voprosy literatury)* had published articles by prominent critics, writers, and scholars on the biographical methods used by the series in the 1970s and 1980s.[18] Picking up on the criticism of many volumes in propaganda magazines and newspapers, the discussion focused on the quality of the latest biographies of Suvorov, Gogol, and Goncharov. A prominent participant in the discussion, the Soviet scholar Nikolai Skatov, welcomes the displacing of the didactic approach to literature offered by canonical nineteenth-century critics such as Nikolai Dobrolyubov, Nikolai Chernyshevsky, and Vissarion Belinsky. Skatov sees these critics as being inseparable from the Soviet educational canon but he questions the uncritical attitude to them prevailing in 1930–1970s Soviet literary criticism.

Commenting on Igor Zolotussky's book *Gogol*, Skatov admires the biographer's approach to Gogol's controversial and ambiguous behaviour. Not only does Skatov welcome Zolotussky's interest in Gogol's spiritual development and search for a higher truth, he suggests that all *ZhZL* biographies should follow this trend and present remarkable people as exemplary truth seekers. Skatov's enthusiastic comments about Zolotussky's book clearly deviated from the established bond between Pavlenkov's project and the educational goals of the series that were also closely adhered to by Gorky and his followers. Skatov suggests that the series should contribute to the character-building and personal development of Soviet readers more than to political education. Skatov finds the appeal of Zolotussky's biography in its shift away from the tendentiousness of the conception of the series by Gorky and subsequent editors: "The idea of seeking the truth through personal development stands out at the most important part of the representation of Gogol found in I. Zolotussky's book; the author himself appears to be a truth-seeker. Such an approach should become exemplary for all volumes published by *ZhZL*."[19] It is difficult to say whether the authors of post-Soviet biographies of Akhmatova and Tsvetaeva consciously followed Skatov's advice, but the image of the two major twentieth-century female poets constructed in their books invokes Skatov's implicit idea that the fluidity of creative identity deserves to be studied in its own right and that lives of remarkable people should be seen as models for emulation in personal growth.

Certainly, Skatov's views contributed to the dismantling of the metanarrative oriented toward monumental art and the construction of a collective self. With the collapse of the Soviet Union in 1991, there was a rapid demise of monumental hero-worship. Brintlinger's aforementioned observation about the vision of Soviet biography as an embodiment of heroic life cannot be fully applied to the new wave of auto/biographical writing started in Putin's Russia. It is clear that in the 2000s the cult of the hero was gradually replaced with the cult of celebrity. The cult of celebrity has been largely shaped by a culture of consumption that sees glamour as the new utopia.[20]

Several commentators have noted that the popularity of biographies in post-Soviet Russia indicates how outmoded Florenty Pavlenkov's vision of a series of books on exemplary lives in service of enlightenment has become. Many contemporary bestselling authors have written biographies of writers and celebrities more for commercial than educational reasons. Many books have been also written with the aim of subverting the images of famous writers and public figures created by the Soviet canon in order to titillate the reader's imagination or to create a scandal. Commenting on books produced after 1991, Brintlinger points out that many biographies written in today's Russia are meant for ordinary people, not for the scholar. Her explanation of the popularity of *ZhZL* biographies of Russian poets includes the common belief among Russian readers that "poets lead interesting lives." She also stresses the commercial success of the series and the attractiveness of the opportunity for the successful author to write a sellable book. "Keeping in mind both the subject and the reader," Brintlinger elucidates, "allows a writer to bridge the past and the present," especially because a *ZhZL* biographer has an intimate knowledge of an audience. As Brintlinger puts it: "these books continue to sell on brand reputation alone."[21] Pavlenkov's original idea to produce a series of biographies aimed at general audience resonates well with the post-Soviet market that is eager to consume the lives of celebrities alongside those of remarkable people.

In the last two decades, discussion of what the new post-Soviet *ZhZL* biography should emphasize has emerged. Recently critic Inna Bulkina has found an exemplar for the post-Soviet *ZhZL* series in narrating the lives of Russian writers. She welcomes Lev Loseff's *ZhZL* volume about Brodsky that presents his life as of remarkable interest for his poetic personality and creative response to life inside and outside Russia. Philological biographies by such critics and scholars as Dmitry Bykov and Oleg Lekmanov have become a very popular genre. Bulkina thinks that post-Soviet *ZhZL* writers "shifted somewhat the traditional poles of the biography genre." Bulkina states: "The *Molodaia Gvardiia* series grew out of Plutarch's *Moralia,* out of admonitions to 'a young man pondering how best to live,' but it has of late reverted to the pre-Plutarchian 'museum of oddities' which, as we recall, itself proceeded not from 'the evaluative idea of what makes "a great man"' (Averintsev) but from mere notions of 'celebrity.'"[22] In Bulkina's opinion, despite the commercial pressures on publishers to produce sellable books, the writers' series stands out as a lofty genre in contrast with the biographies of tyrants, military heroes, and other public figures.

AKHMATOVA'S BIOGRAPHY AS A MUSEUM OF ODDITIES

Svetlana Kovalenko's 2009 biography of Akhmatova published in the *ZhZL* series[23] is representative of the new trend in Russian literary culture which can be described as less controlled and more anarchic in comparison with the Soviet period. Soviet educational and censorship hierarchies were replaced by private publishers who secure their powerful position though advertising and promotional strategies conducted by public relations professionals. The values of homogeneity and unity promoted by Soviet literary culture were replaced by the notions of plurality and diversity. With today's rise of visual mass culture, Russian television tries to compete with written biographies by creating documentary films about Russian twentieth-century writers in a conscious attempt to create a unified view of Russian history through the prism of narratives of literary lives that mix fiction and reality.

Kovalenko's posthumously published book about Akhmatova appears to represent the market-oriented trend of Russian contemporary culture. It is an unfinished biography of Akhmatova that was prepared for publication by Kovalenko's husband, Aleksandr Nikolyukin, and the editor, Lyubov

Kalyuzhnaya. The book's structure is chaotic; fragmented in many places, it lacks a coherent narrative. Kovalenko often mixes together early and late periods of Akhmatova's life. The fascination with Akhmatova's early life might be partly explained by a widespread nostalgia for the late imperial period that is evident in films and documentaries featuring Russian aristocracy and prominent public figures. Russian television constantly revives and reassesses Russian life before the Bolshevik revolution in order to create a bridge between that forgotten past and the revolution. The discussion of Stalin's legacy is problematic in today's Russia, and Kovalenko's desire not to extensively probe into Akhmatova's life between the early 1920s and 1946 parallels the approach of official textbooks on Russian modern history adopted under Putin by Russian secondary schools.

It is not clear if Kovalenko lacked the theoretical apparatus to evaluate Akhmatova's life during the period of heavy censorship, or whether she chose to avoid the controversial issues related to Stalin's terror. There are occasional references to some people who knew Akhmatova well in the 1920s to early 1940s, yet the reader is not given any detailed description of Akhmatova's encounters and friendships with such important twentieth-century authors as Boris Pasternak, Osip Mandelshtam, Lydia Chukovskaya, Nikolai Khardzhiev, and Marina Tsvetaeva. In her editor's preface, Kalyuzhnaya describes the first half of the book as a historical and biographical interpretation structured around the use of Akhmatova's five male lovers as muses in her poetry. She does not explain why many important events in Akhmatova's life—such as her period in Tashkent, her war poetry, and her translations of other poets—have been completely omitted from this book. In Kalyuzhnaya's view, the three chapters comprising part 2: "Narrative Poems and the Theater," "Literary Contexts," and "Anna Akhmatova's Autobiographical Prose," focus on Kovalenko's evaluation of Akhmatova's craftsmanship rather than on political contexts of Soviet life. Such a fragmentary perspective on Akhmatova's life creates the impression of Akhmatova as a lyric poet preoccupied with her inner life rather than with Russia's tumultuous history. Akhmatova's stoic character and spiritual values praised by Cold War–era critics in the West become less prominent in Kovalenko's narrative than in the studies by Amanda Haight or Elaine Feinstein.

In contrast to preceding biographers, Kovalenko's portrayal of Akhmatova's personality and her idiosyncratic growth as a poet comes across as highly subjective and imbalanced. In her review of Kovalenko's book, Sonia Ketchian even writes: "The reader discerns latent resentment for the person Akhmatova."[24] The image of Akhmatova is blurred partially because Kovalenko prefers the accounts of Akhmatova's male friends and lovers, Boris Anrep, Nikolai Nedobrovo, and Sir Isaiah Berlin and seems to disdain Nikolai Gumilev. Ketchian also finds Kovalenko's insufficient treatment of

Akhmatova's common-law husband Nikolai Punin and son Lev Gumilev as patchy and misleading. Ketchian criticizes Kovalenko for not mentioning Punin and his family's mistreatment of Akhmatova and her son and for whitewashing aspects of Soviet history in her depiction of Lev Gumilev's imprisonment and forced labor.

Ketchian also finds fault with the second part of Kovalenko's book, which allegedly focuses on Akhmatova's craftsmanship in the postwar period, but gravitates more toward the sensational and the subjective. She notes that in places Kovalenko seems to write her own narrative that provides lengthy descriptions of her conversations with Berlin, her professional links with the editor and scholar Vladimir Orlov and her interviews with Irina Punina. She goes on to say: "Kovalenko . . . appears happiest writing about the men in Akhmatova's life (other than Gumilev and Punin). Anatoly Naiman is forgotten. Even as Kovalenko seeks to depict Akhmatova in and from her legacy, surroundings, and circle, somehow the real person and the genuine creative poet remain remote and hidden, as it were, behind the four men around her who are depicted in greater relief" (Ibid, 369). In sum, Ketchian finds Kovalenko's biographical method of writing questionable and inappropriate, though she suggests that the book's introduction of some new materials could be a basis for future studies beyond this first biography of Akhmatova in Russian.

It can be added to Ketchian's observations that Brodsky has not been mentioned in Kovalenko's book either. Given the importance of Akhmatova's legacy for the generation of poets who emerged during the Thaw, it is strange to see the absence of any references to Brodsky or other prominent contemporary poets such as Dmitry Bobyshev, who dedicated several poems to Akhmatova and saw her as a mentor, and Nataliya Gorbanevskaya, who acknowledged her indebtedness to Akhmatova and who was prominent in circulating Akhmatova's "Requiem" through samizdat in the 1960–1970s. Kovalenko also overlooks philosophical aspects of Akhmatova's late poetry, focusing instead on the autobiographical overtones of her long poem "Poem Without a Hero" (*Poema bez geroia*) as well as on the use of fragment in her late works.

Unlike many Akhmatova scholars, such as Roman Timenchik and Alexandra Harrington, Kovalenko insufficiently questions Akhmatova's methods of shaping her own public image and mythmaking. As many biographical accounts of Akhmatova's life demonstrate, her biographical legend revolves around the myth of the poet as a tragic hero. Commenting on Akhmatova's obsession with her biography and skillful mythmaking, Harrington writes:

Akhmatova projects the image of herself in her late poetry ... as someone who perished and was subsequently reborn, and highlights the split from her former self evinced by her encounter with a historical fate. This chthonic narrative of life, death and revival is frequently encountered in Russian post-revolutionary poetry. The mythology which has arisen around Akhmatova thereby conforms broadly to a traditional pattern, stressing her fortitude in the face of undeniable suffering in the tragic terms of the Russian poet's Golgotha.[25]

In contrast, Kovalenko suggests briefly that Akhmatova consciously made an attempt to inscribe herself into the classical and romantic traditions of European poetry. She notes in passing that the notion of "the Akhmatova myth" is associated with the classical roots of Akhmatova's poetry.

Kovalenko maintains that the "Akhmatova myth" is carefully constructed by Akhmatova herself with the use of the fragment in her works. The omission of important details and the use of allusive language, Kovalenko implies, create a sense of mystery. Her overall perspective on Akhmatova's life suggests that Akhmatova's autobiographical works constructed a plot that prominently features those events of her life that fit the image of a neo-classical poet's life. According to Kovalenko, in many written and rewritten accounts of her life, Akhmatova emphasized that her childhood identity was largely shaped by encounters with antiquity, especially during her visits to Chersonesus, the ancient Greek colony founded 2,500 years ago in south-western Crimea. Kovalenko also thinks that Akhmatova ascribed symbolic meaning to some events of her life, including her discovery of a marble stone featuring a part of the larger ancient Greek text that Akhmatova donated to the museum in Chersonesus.[26] It would have been useful to develop this conceptual framework further, especially because Kovalenko notes the abundance of references to characters found in Greek mythology and canonical ancient Greek texts in Akhmatova's poetry. Similarly, Kovalenko finds borrowings from German Romantic texts and from Shakespeare but does not highlight any specifics of Akhmatova's appropriation of images from the past. The allusive language of Akhmatova's poetry analyzed extensively in the works of scholars interested in intertextuality (notably Timenchik and Susan Amert) altogether escapes Kovalenko's attention. It is unclear from her book why Akhmatova's life was remarkable. In his review of Kovalenko's biography of Akhmatova, the prominent Akhmatova scholar Vadim Chernykh rightly asks: "How is it possible to publish a biography of any author if thirty years of this author's life are not included in the biography?"[27]

On the other hand, one important achievement of Kovalenko's book is her attempt to bring Akhmatova's prose, autobiographical writing, and notebooks together. In her concluding paragraphs, Kovalenko highlights the interrelationship between Akhmatova's autobiographical writing and poetry as a manifestation of Akhmatova's self-reflexivity. She suggests that Akhmatova's fascination with James Joyce's novel *Ulysses* had an impact on her own style. It enabled Akhmatova to address different aspects of her personality in her notebooks as well as in her poetry in a thoughtful, introspective way. Kovalenko thinks that in the future an attentive reader will be able to reconstruct Akhmatova's creative psychology through an analysis of her notebooks. She writes: "Her notebooks . . . contain a complex labyrinth of her creative thought. . . . In these notebooks each word, each poetic line and each stanza as well as each reference to a letter, or a place where the poet lived at some point of her life, or a particular addressee of her poem contain an unsolvable mystery; this mystery represents Akhmatova's *Ulysses*."[28] Kovalenko's observation is in line with British studies of modernism that suggest that a focus on personality constitutes a paradigm shift in recent scholarship emphasizing the centrality of auto/biographical writing for modernist literature.

Sadly, Kovalenko's biography overlooks many of Akhmatova's important works, including her cycle "Wreath for the Dead" ("Venok mertvym") which Akhmatova worked on for twenty-two years. The cycle's preoccupation with commemoration reveals Akhmatova's religious feeling. Akhmatova's process of recollecting turns the material of the past into an event occurring in the present due to her strong sense of responsibility to herself and to her silenced contemporaries. As Mikhail Meilakh and Vladimir Toporov point out, by interweaving her present life with memories of the past, Akhmatova "imports her own life into history."[29] In contrast to Meilakh's and Toporov's study, Kovalenko's book understates Akhmatova's religious outlook. Akhmatova's preoccupation with memory is also given insufficient attention. Kovalenko's main interest lies not in Akhmatova as a thinker but in Akhmatova as a person who uses her lyric poetry as a diary to chronicle her everyday life.

Kovalenko's suggestion that future scholars and biographers should embrace the contradictory elements of Akhmatova's personality rather than attempting to construct a finished portrait reinforces the idea popular among Russian and European modernists that a person might have multiple selves. In the opinion of modernists, a person's different selves manifest themselves variously in different moments of his/her life. Kovalenko's unusual stance, as a biographer interested only in certain aspects of Akhmatova's life, recalls Gorky's rebellious position as a biographer of Tolstoy as evident in Gorky's *Reminiscences of Leo Nikolayevitch Tolstoy* (Hogarth Press, 1920 and 1921) published in London with the help of Virginia Woolf and Samuel Koteliansky. The book features Gorky's reflections on Tolstoy composed in the style of fragmentary notes casually jotted onto scraps of paper, presenting Gorky's changeable attitude to Tolstoy and questioning the stability of biographical character. Woolf praised Gorky's biographical style and saw it as an embodiment of the new biography capable of embracing gaps, fragments, and unexplained aspects of the biographical character. As Claire Battershill points out, Woolf used Gorky's idea of recording biographical notes on scraps of paper as "a metaphor for the compositional and formal structure of a desirably candid biography."[30]

It is difficult to know whether Kovalenko was consciously attempting to employ modernist biographical methods in her portrayal of Akhmatova or not, but most passages of the book focus on Akhmatova's personality rather than the contextual settings of her works and historical events. In modernist-like manner, Kovalenko's biography succeeds in portraying Akhmatova as a biographical character difficult to capture in the whole. It resists the monumentalization of Akhmatova by focusing on private moments of her life. It also overcomes the image of the martyr created during the Cold War through the depiction of Akhmatova's complexity and the use of a candid biographical method. Sarah Krieve's assessment of Akhmatova's canonization shows the shortcomings of such a clichéd image of Akhmatova the martyr that had been created by critics and readers from the 1980s to the 2000s:

> During perestroika, Akhmatova came to be identified with Russia's urgent need to articulate Russia's resistance to the atrocities of Stalinism. This is, as I see it, the primary reason for her contested value during that period. Pigeonholed by Western and émigré scholars as an 'internal émigré', Akhmatova's name came to serve as shorthand for suffering and near martyrdom at the hands of Soviet authorities.[31]

It is difficult to say whether Kovalenko's intention to create a fragmentary narrative of Akhmatova's life was modeled on Gorky's method of writing about Tolstoy or whether Kovalenko did not want to create a monumental image of Akhmatova for the consumption of the post-Soviet reader in order to articulate a gap between Akhmatova's private life and her public persona. In an era of multihistoricism characterized by a lack of consensus on the legacy of Stalinism and a lack of political continuity the possibility of objective historical representation remains problematic. As the Russian cultural historian Alexander Etkind maintains, "Stalinism is not dead, and the pervasive multihistoricism contributes to a dearth of proper memorials."[32]

In fact, Kovalenko's book is not the first portrait of Akhmatova in the *ZhZL* series. It is a pity that Kovalenko did not incorporate into her book Kornei Chukovsky's memoir about Akhmatova in the *ZhZL* volume *Contemporaries* (*Sovremmeniki*) published in 2008. Chukovsky's essay on Akhmatova written in 1964–1968 can be seen as an early attempt to inscribe Akhmatova into the twentieth-century canon of Russian and European poetry. It describes Akhmatova's trajectory from a highly analytical poet of loneliness engaged in making new forms of subjectivity to a poet of considerable historical imagination molded by the tensions between place and space. In Chukovsky's hands, while Akhmatova reflected on the sense of place and historical space in Russian poetry, she also belonged to the European tradition. Chukovsky not only comments on the wide range of Akhmatova's interests comprising various poetic traditions and cultural spaces, including those of Pushkin, Dante, ancient Egypt, and ancient Greece, he also thinks that she created her own version of historical lyric poetry. On a personal level, he portrays Akhmatova as a complex person who had a gift for producing epigrams and witty comments: "Akhmatova's character comprised a wide variety of qualities that would be impossible to fit into a simplistic model. Her rich and complex personality combined many features that would rarely be found in one person."[33] Given that Chukovsky's essay contains references to his daughter and Akhmatova's close friend Lydia Chukovskaya's as-yet-unpublished diaries, which were available to him in the 1960s, it raises the question of the possible collective authorship of this memoir. The fact of inclusion of his essay about Akhmatova in this post-Soviet *ZhZL* volume exemplifies the growing interest in developing Skatov's aforementioned approach to biography. Given that Skatov's model of biographical writing foregrounds spiritual development and complex personality, it can be seen as a perfect template for producing an inspiring narrative of life for any Russian author of significance. Such a model would reinforce in the eyes of post-Soviet readers the uniqueness of the Russian literary tradition rooted in nineteenth-century concerns of such writers as Tolstoy and Dostoevsky about truth-seeking and spirituality.

TSVETAEVA'S *ZhZL* BIOGRAPHIES AS POST-SOVIET HAGIOGRAPHIES

Viktoria Shveitser's 2003 *ZhZL* biography of Marina Tsvetaeva is a shorter version of her biography *Everyday Life and Being of Marina Tsvetaeva (Byt i bytie Mariny Tsvetaevoi)* published in Paris in 1988 by the émigré publishing house Syntaxis.[34] Rosette Lamont, who reviewed the English translation of the Paris biography praises Shveitser's study for its insights and intellectual rigor: "For Schweitzer, a scholar educated in the Soviet Union, the writing of this book must have been cathartic. It enabled her to reappraise her own skewed education, the received ideas and ideological propaganda her generation had to spout back as their own thinking. Again and again she states that she now sees things differently, that she has read Tsvetaeva anew." As Lamont notes, Shveitser was particularly suited to be Tsvetaeva's biographer because she was expelled from the Moscow Writers Union for her involvement in the Sinyavsky-Daniel affair and an émigré. Her unique perspective has allowed her to reevaluate Tsvetaeva's works and life from both artistic and political standpoints. Lamont stresses that the book mirrors the experiences of both women: "it is a fresh decoding of the poet's phenomenal political intuition and an autobiographical sketch as well. . . . This biography is more than an intellectual study; it chronicles a meeting between two heroic women. Tsvetaeva, who worked at the outer edge of the aesthetic of the limit, needed to be understood in this fashion."[35] Akin to Lotman's aforementioned description of Pushkin's biographers who tend to see the poet's art "as one big autobiographical novel," Shveitser's book displays the tendency to show Tsvetaeva's life as being closely entwined with her art. The structure of the book implies that Tsvetaeva's life can be read as a novel that revolves around important events and people: "Seryozha," "Alya," "Revolution," "Irina's Death," "After Russia," "Pasternak," "My Pushkin," and "Nostalgia for Motherland." Shveitser also inserts a chapter about her visit to Elabuga, where she hoped to see Tsvetaeva's grave and talk there with people who knew Tsvetaeva. Shveitser, one of the first biographers of Tsvetaeva (as well as Irma Kudrova), should be recognized as an important compiler of information on Tsvetaeva over several decades. Her findings have laid the foundation for other books about Tsvetaeva.

As a supporter of Andrei Sinyavsky who was persecuted by Soviet authorities in the 1970s, Shveitser is especially fascinated by Tsvetaeva's independence and her political views. She pays special attention to those works and events of Tsvetaeva's life that were impossible to discuss openly before the late Soviet period. The complex art-life nexus is treated well in her biography, but she does not differentiate clearly between Tsvetaeva the author of poetic and fictional works and Tsvetaeva the person. She is often influenced heavily by Tsvetaeva the perceived autobiographer who created a mythologized account of her own life. Shveitser tends to treat Tsvetaeva's autobiographical writing uncritically. The implied reader of her biography is expected to be a "voyeur" who would enjoy many private details of Tsvetaeva's day-to-day life.

To a large extent, Shveitser romanticizes Tsvetaeva and portrays her as a neo-Romantic author. This is how she explains the absence of a physical portrait of Tsvetaeva's mother in her autobiographical stories: "Tsvetaeva sees her mother as a romantic heroine. . . . When she was 21, she wrote to Rozanov: 'Her tormented soul continues to live in us; with the difference that we reveal to others those aspects of our personalities that she used to suppress. Her rebellious nature, her madness, her thirst for sublimity became embodied in us in the most extreme manner.'"[36] In her review of Shveitser's biography, Revekka Frumkina states that it is difficult to render adequately Tsvetaeva's romantic personality that longs to attain spiritual heights and defines Tsvetaeva as an unusual and eccentric person who always behaved outside established societal norms.

In Frumkina's view, Tsvetaeva's life was full of paradoxes that are difficult to comprehend. Frumkina notes that Shveitser successfully renders Tsvetaeva's inconsistencies and paradoxes because she empathizes with Tsvetaeva's inner struggle between being a woman and being a poet: "Shveitser's book succeeds most of all in finding the right tone of narration that does not downplay tragic overtones of Tsvetaeva's life. Shveitser does not justify Tsvetaeva the person; she does not patronize. Despite her occasional pejorative comments about Tsvetaeva's behaviour, she shows empathy."[37] Frumkina points to the commercial success of the book shown by its multiple print runs. It appeals to the mass reader who finds Tsvetaeva's life to be out of the ordinary and fascinating.

Interestingly, Shveitser repeatedly discusses irrational aspects of Tsvetaeva's behavior, including her problems with motherhood. In Shveitser's view, it is impossible to comprehend why in the early 1920s Tsvetaeva showered with love her daughter Alya yet was totally indifferent to her younger daughter Irina, who had learning difficulties. Furthermore, she claims Tsvetaeva failed as a mother. In Shveitser's view, Tsvetaeva wanted to be a good mother to her three children but struggled due to her excessive emotionality and creative ambitions: "Tsvetaeva was a difficult mother. This is true not only regarding Irina. It is evident in her treatment of all three children. Perhaps, her poetic gift and inner obsession with creativity prevented her from being calm and balanced? The ability to be patient is important in communicating with children in everyday life. Tsvetaeva interfered with the personal growth of her children: she wanted Alya to be molded in her own image; she was indifferent to Irina; and she loved her son Mur excessively."[38]

While discussing many oddities of Tsvetaeva's behaviour, Shveitser fails to align her eccentricity with the emergence of the New Woman in Russia and in Europe. This definition was usually applied to women who smoked, rode bicycles, abandoned corsets, and wore comfortable clothes. In Tsvetaeva's story about Maximilian Voloshin, "The Living about Living," Voloshin's mother epitomizes all the qualities of the New Woman who does not look like a proper Victorian lady. New Woman novels were popular among Tsvetaeva's contemporaries: they inspired young women in the 1900–1910s to embark on the inner journey toward the self and embrace the outward task of changing the world. Shveitser lacks any interest in gender studies and does not question the challenges of modernity to traditional gender roles when she discusses Tsvetaeva's eccentric behavior and views.

Shveitser overlooks the fact that Tsvetaeva's poetic persona was largely influenced by such cultural icons as Marie Bashkirtseff—to whom Tsvetaeva dedicated her 1910 collection of poetry *Evening Album* (*Vechernii al'bom*)—and the French actress Sarah Bernhardt who was famous for playing male roles, including Shakespeare's Hamlet. Judy Simons emphasizes the nature of Bashkirtseff's appeal to modern artists: "Bashkirtseff's diary with its startling, candid tone and its unabashed personal confidences, had caused a literary sensation, and had started something of a vogue for intimate confessional reminiscences among young well-bred young women with imaginative aspirations."[39] The influence of Bernhardt on Russian women authors and artists was even more subversive. As Catherine Schuler points out, while Bernhardt "drew large crowds in Russia," her reputation in Russia was scandalous: many conservative critics saw her as a living embodiment of "the antithesis of traditional sex/gender ideology."[40] In contrast to Shveitser, who does not link Tsvetaeva to modernist trends pertaining to gender transgression and androgyny, Olga Hasty sees Tsvetaeva's preoccupation with advocating women's superiority to men as an extension of the cultural debates of the 1900–1920s. Hasty asserts that in her autobiographical fiction, Tsvetaeva "directs women away from fulfilling men's expectations." Hasty summarizes Tsvetaeva's outlook as follows: "Rather than perpetuate conditions that are inhospitable to their creative self-realization, women can come together in the poetic domain that is rightfully theirs."[41]

Shveitser also misreads the representation of the transgressive aspects of identity construction and ambivalence of love manifested in Tsvetaeva's letters, stories, and poems. In the chapter devoted to Tsvetaeva's relationship with Sophia Parnok, a Russian modernist lesbian poet, Shveitser suggests that the reader can only be puzzled by Tsvetaeva's passionate attraction to Parnok. In Shveitser's view, such an attraction is difficult to explain by a lack of happiness since Tsvetaeva's needs as a woman and as a mother were satisfied by her husband Sergei and her daughter Ariadna. Shveitser thinks that Tsvetaeva's affair with Parnok derives from her risk-seeking behavior and her status as a genius. Shveitser's comment implies that geniuses tend to be mad and are driven by their irrational desire to explore new territories: "Perhaps, the explanation lies in Tsvetaeva's thirst for novel experiences that constitutes an important feature of a genius's mindset? Her obsessive desire to explore new things might have driven her to this unexplored, mysterious and dangerous path?"[42] In her review of the English version of Shveitser's biography, Hasty notes: "The portrait of Tsvetaeva that emerges from Schweitzer's outstanding biography shows slight but unmistakable signs of the prevailing tendency to apply to Tsvetaeva the stereotypical, romantically infused image of 'The Poet' as an irrational being driven by excessive emotions. The chaos and unruliness of Tsvetaeva's day-to-day life does not in fact invade her poetry which, for all its variety and intensity, is ruled by a remarkable consistency."[43] Hasty's observation is fully applicable to Shveitser's shortened

ZhZL biography in Russian, which focuses on the interrelationship between genius and madness.

In his 2017 *ZhZL* biography, Ilya Falikov treats Tsvetaeva more evenhandedly than Shveitser does. While it continues to rely heavily on quotes from Tsvetaeva's letters, diaries, and stories, the metatextual aspect of Falikov's biography makes the narrative of Tsvetaeva's life less controversial and more orderly. As Hasty's aforementioned observation suggests, the chaos of Tsvetaeva's everyday life does not enter her poetry, which displays exceptional clarity of expression and craftsmanship.

It appears that Falikov's biographical method derives from Lotman's view of literary biography. David Bethea sums up Lotman's views as follows:

> It is my hypothesis that Lotman, who has learned from Bakhtin but has also learned where he departs from his antipode, is trying to use his method to get as close as possible to the headwaters of poetic creativity itself—how poets use the material of life, beginning with its implicit codes, not only to write but to live creatively. The connection between life and art, text and code, can be, Lotman comes more and more to see, generative of meaning-the ultimate semiotic gesture.[44]

In Bethea's view, Lotman perceives "signifying turning-points in a biography" as belonging more "to the authoring personality than to the modelling codes." Literary roles chosen by Pushkin, Bethea thinks, allowed him freedom in the privacy of his own thoughts "to develop personalities that had little to do with those masks and indeed could be seen in retrospect to actually oppose them."[45]

Falikov, in Lotman-like manner, is keen to identify semiotically important utterances and metaphors in Tsvetaeva's poetry that can be defined as modeling codes. Thus, in his comments on her unfinished long poem about Esenin, Falikov suggests that some stanzas sound prophetic: "She, a citizen of the central part of Moscow, was destined for the rest of her life to live in a suburb, regardless of the country she lived in. In her poem, "The Lute" ["Liutnia," 1923], she already discusses this. This poem is a metaphor of the things to come."[46] In this passage, Falikov refers to Tsvetaeva's formulaic assertion that life is a suburb without showing any awareness that the theme of displacement constitutes one of the most significant tropes of modernist poetry.

Nevertheless, Falikov's interest in identifying Tsvetaeva's codes of behavior makes his biography unique. Its emphasis on the "authoring personality" that creates his/her own life rather than on Tsvetaeva the woman stands in sharp contrast to Shveitser's biography. Such a vision of poetic behavior, as Bethea explains, derives from theoretical studies produced by Bakhtin and Lotman. Bethea writes: "Thus, the code, rather than being synonymous, in

Bakhtin's phrasing, with 'an intentionally fixed, killed context,' is that formal unit which, while not determining the outcome, enables poetic behavior in life. It gives an element of choice, not the free choice of result but the opportunity to provoke change, back to the authoring *lichnost'*."[47] Bethea's description of Pushkin's life is fully applicable to Tsvetaeva: "Pushkin, then, was using the code, not the finished plot, in order to be the author of his life up to the end. As terrifying as it sounds, it really did not matter what happened: in any case, it would be on Pushkin's terms. There were things that mattered to Pushkin more than merely staying alive (his honor, his family's privacy, his reputation in the eyes of 'History.'"[48] Likewise, Falikov suggests that Tsvetaeva's suicide was an extension of her poetic behavior that led to her death. In contrast to leading Tsvetaeva's biographers such as Kudrova and Shveitser, he concludes with a reference to Tsvetaeva's last note to her son Mur. It defines Tsvetaeva's suicide as a manifestation of her psychological dead-end state of mind. The last words of the biography laconically state: "There is nobody to blame."[49] This conclusion implies that Tsvetaeva's death was on her terms because it fit the poetic persona of the Romantic poet promoted in her poetry.

Unlike Shveitser, Falikov is an established poet and biographer. His acclaimed biographies of Evgeny Evtushenko and Boris Ryzhy were written in a similar vein: his main interest lies in the construction of his subject's poetic persona. In her review of Falikov's biography, Elena Elagina praises his attentiveness to Tsvetaeva the poet. She thinks that Falikov succeeded in portraying Tsvetaeva as a great poet. Yet she does not think that being a complex and difficult person would make Tsvetaeva's life interesting to ordinary Russian readers. As she puts it, "geniuses are always difficult in day-to-day life."[50] She welcomes Falikov's decision to treat Tsvetaeva as a poet rather than as a woman or simply as an interesting person because she firmly believes that Tsvetaeva's poetry overshadows her personality.

Falikov's narrative strategy that privileges Tsvetaeva the poet and the autobiographer enables him to avoid lengthy discussions of Tsvetaeva's life that reveal her anarchistic behavior, controversial political views, and anxieties about gender identity. It also overcomes the Cold War image of Tsvetaeva as a martyr and victim of Stalinism which strongly pervades other biographies of Tsvetaeva. Like Kovalenko's biography of Akhmatova, it avoids analyzing in detail the tragic circumstances of Tsvetaeva's life in Stalin's Russia. Both books reflect multihistoricist approaches to biographical writing in post-Soviet Russia. It appears that Falikov avoids difficult questions because he is well aware of the lack of consensus on the legacy of Stalinism in contemporary Russia. Although Falikov refers extensively to Mur's diaries of the late 1930s, he downplays Mur's critical portrayal of the political atmosphere in Russia under Stalin.

Falikov explains his main goal in writing this biography: "The goal of my book is to show what was happening in Tsvetaeva's consciousness or what might have affected her thinking."[51] Since Falikov's biographical method is informed by his own Lotman-like preoccupation with central codes and metaphors, his book gives the impression that Tsvetaeva followed in the footsteps of Pushkin by controlling her own image as a Russian poet up to the last moment. In Falikov's hands, the authoring personality of Tsvetaeva is more important that any of the reminiscences about her everyday life produced by her contemporaries. Such a version of Tsvetaeva's life appears to be a good fit for the *ZhZL* series, which glorifies remarkable lives of those people whose immense contribution to Russian cultural life benefits both national unity and transnational monumentalization of Russian heroes.

CONCLUSION

As the present chapter has demonstrated, in post-Soviet Russia the names of Akhmatova and Tsvetaeva have ceased to serve as shorthand for suffering and martyrdom at the hands of Soviet authorities. In the absence of an uncontested view on the legacy of Stalinism, it does not seem possible to commemorate fully the lives of these major twentieth-century female poets. Lotman's model of treating Pushkin as the author of his own life has been applied to these poets due to the lack of a critical apparatus that takes into account the peculiarities of modernist aesthetics and gender politics. The goal of the *ZhZL* biographies discussed here is to show how poets use the material of their lives for their poetic and autobiographical works and how they practice the art of living in a Pushkinian manner. The conservative nature of the *ZhZL* biographies of Tsvetaeva and Akhmatova does not undermine their success among post-Soviet readers. Not only does the centrality of reading to the construction of Russian national identity remain as strong as ever in Russia in the 2000s, the prestige of the *ZhZL* series enables the publishers to breach the gap between popular and high cultures as well.

NOTES

1. Pierre Bourdieu, *Distinction: A Social Critique of the Judgement of Taste*, translated by Richard Nice (Cambridge, Massachusetts, 1984), 471.
2. Vasily V. Gatov, "Contagious Tales of Russian Origin and Putin's Evolution," *Society* 53 (2016): 619–24, cited on 619.
3. Gatov, "Contagious Tales, 621.

4. Pierre Bourdieu, "Intellectual Field and Creative Project," *Information (International Social Science Council)*, 1969, 8 (2): 89–119, quote from 89.

5. M. Nesterenko, "Uroki 'neopytnoi muzy'," in Anna Bunina, *Neopytnaia muza. Sobranie stikhotvorenii* (Moscow: B.S.G.-Press, 2016), 11–25, quote from 19.

6. Alessandra Tosi, "Anna Bunina (1774–1829) and the Origins of Women's Poetry in Russia," *Journal of European Studies* 28, no. 3 (1998): 322.

7. B. E. Rapgof, *Karolina Pavlova. Materialy dlia izucheniia zhizni i tvorchestva* (Petrograd: Trirema, 1916).

8. Leonid Heller, "A World of Prettiness: Socialist Realism and Its Aesthetic Categories," in Thomas Lahusen and Evgeny Dobrenko, eds. *Socialist Realism Without Shores* (Durham, NC: Duke University Press, 1997), 51–75, quote from 52.

9. Andrew B. Wachtel, "The Cult of the Author," *Slavic and East European Journal* 60, no. 2 (2016): 280–83, quoted on 280.

10. Wachtel, "The Cult of the Author," 283.

11. Alexey Vdovin, "Dmitry Tolstoy's 'Classicism' and the Formation of The Russian Literary Canon in The High School Curriculum," *Ab Imperio* (4/2017): 108–37, 109.

12. Vdovin, 110.

13. Vdovin, 119.

14. Yurii Lotman, *Aleksandr Sergeevich Pushkin: Biografiia pisatelia. Stat'i i zametki* (Sankt-Peterburg: Iskusstvo-SPB, 2003), 57. Translation from Russian here and elsewhere is mine unless specified otherwise.—A.S.

15. Ludmilla A. Trigos and Carol R. Ueland, "Literary Biographies in the *Lives of Remarkable People Series (Zhizn' zamechatel'nykh liudei)*," *Slavic and East European Journal* 60, no. 2 (2016): 207–20, 211.

16. Thomas Carlyle's book *On Heroes, Hero-Worship and the Heroic in History* was translated into Russian in 1891 by Valentin Yakovenko. In the early 1930s, Tsvetaeva's sister, Anastasiia, a close friend of Gorky, prepared a new translation of this book. See: Anastasiia Tsvetaeva, "Tomas Karleil' v moei zhizni," in *Neischerpaemoe* (Moscow: Otechestvo, 1992), 208–13.

17. Angela Brintlinger, "The *Remarkable* Pushkin," *Slavic and East European Journal* 60, no. 2 (2016): 221–40, cited on 232.

18. "Knigi o russkikh pisateliakh v ZhZL," *Voprosy literatury*, no. 9 (1980): 179–251.

19. N. Skatov, "Dvizhenie vpered," *Voprosy literatury*, no. 9 (1980): 199–203, 200.

20. Helena Goscilo and Vlad Strukov, eds. "Introduction," *Celebrity and Glamour in Contemporary Russia: Shocking Chic* (London: Routledge, 2011), 1–26, 4.

21. Brintlinger, "The *Remarkable* Pushkin," 237.

22. Inna Bulkina. "The Lives of Remarkable People," *Russian Studies in Literature* 49, no. 2 (2014): 87–95, 95.

23. Svetlana Kovalenko, *Anna Akhmatova* (Seriia biografii: Zhizn' zamechatel'nykh liudei, Moscow: Molodaia gvardiia), 2009.

24. Sonia. I. Ketchian, "Svetlana Kovalenko. Anna Akhmatova. Ed. Aleksandra N. Nikoliukina. Seriia biografii: *Zhizn' zamechatel'nykh liudei*. Moscow: Molodaia gvardiia, 2009," *Slavic and East European Journal* 54, no. 2 (Summer 2010): 368–69, 368.

25. Alexandra Harrington, "Anna Akhmatova's Biographical Myth-Making: Tragedy and Melodrama," *Slavonic and East European Review* 89, no. 3 (July 2011): 455–93, 459.

26. Kovalenko, 262.

27. V. A. Chernykh, "Svetlana Kovalenko. *Anna Akhmatova*," *Znamia*, no. 8 (2009), http://znamlit.ru/publication.php?id=4015 Last accessed: 10/23/.2019.

28. Kovalenko, 263.

29. M. B. Mejlax and V. N. Toporov, "Akhmatova i Dante," *International Journal of Slavic Linguistics and Poetics* 15 (1972): 29–75, 51.

30. Claire Battershill, "Life Before 'The New Biography': Modernist Biographical Methods in the Hogarth Press's 'Books on Tolstoi,' 1920–24," *a/b: Auto/Biography Studies* 31, no. 1 (2016): 109–32, 116.

31. Sarah A. Krieve, "A Transcultural Monument: Anna Akhmatova in Postsocialist Russia," *South Atlantic Review* 74, vol. 2 (2009): 62–81, 78.

32. Alexander Etkind, "Hard and Soft in Cultural Memory: Political Mourning in Russia and in Germany," *Grey Room* 16 (Summer 2004): 36–59, 55.

33. Kornei Chukovskii, *Sovremenniki. Portrety i etiudy* (Moscow: Molodaia gvardiia, 2008), 305–39, 337.

34. The 1988 book was translated into English and published in New York in 1993. Viktoria Schweitzer, *Tsvetaeva*. trans. Robert Chandler, H. T. Willets, Peter Norman, ed. Angela Livingstone (New York: Farrar, Straus & Giroux, 1993).

35. Rosette C. Lamont, "Tsvetaeva by Viktoria Schweitzer," *World Literature Today* 68, no. 4 (Autumn 1994): 843.

36. Viktoriia Shveitser. *Marina Tsvetaeva* (Moscow: Molodaia gvardiia, 2003), https://www.e-reading.life/chapter.php/95744/3/Shveiicer_-_Marina_Cvetaeva.html [date of access: 1/11/2019] All further references are to this edition. To date, the book went through three additional reprintings in the series with slight variations of the title. The comprehensive catalog of *ZhZL* publications through 2012 does not indicate that there were any changes in these editions.

37. Revekka Frumkina, "Zhizn' Tsvetaevoi, rasskazannaia Viktoriei Shveitser," *Troitskii. Nauka. Variant* (1.02.2011), https://trv-science.ru/2011/02/01/zhizn-cvetae-voj-rasskazannaya-viktoriej-shvejcer/ [date of access: 11/1/2019]

38. Shveitser, *Marina Tsvetaeva*, https://www.e-reading.life/chapter.php/95744/24/Shveiicer_-_Marina_Cvetaeva.html [date of access: 11/2/2019].

39. Judy Simons, "Secret Exhibitionists: Women and their Diaries," in *Diaries and Journals of Literary Women from Fanny Burney to Virginia Woolf* (London: Palgrave Macmillan, 1990), 1–18, 1.

40. Catherine A. Schuler, *Women in Russian Theatre: The Actress in the Silver Age* (London and New York: Routledge, 1996), 13.

41. Olga Peters Hasty, *How Women Must Write: Inventing the Russian Woman Poet* (Evanston, Illinois: Northwestern University Press, 2020), 142.

42. Shveitser, *Marina Tsvetaeva*, https://www.e-reading.life/chapter.php/95744/14/Shveiicer_-_Marina_Cvetaeva.html [date of access: 11/2/2019]

43. Olga Peters Hasty, "Tsvetaeva by Viktoria Shweitser, trans. Robert Chandler and H. T. Willetts," *Slavic Review* 54, no. 1 (Spring 1995): 229.

44. David M. Bethea, "Bakhtinian Prosaics versus Lotmanian 'Poetic Thinking': The Code and Its Relation to Literary Biography," *The Slavic and East European Journal* 41, no. 1 (Spring 1997): 1–15, 2.

45. Bethea, "Bakhtinian Prosaics," 8–9.

46. Il'ia Falikov, *Marina Tsvetaeva. Tvoia nelaskovaia lastochka* (Moscow: Molodaia gvardiia, 2017), 412.

47. Bethea, "Bakhtinian Prosaics," 11.

48. Ibid.

49. Falikov, *Marina Tsvetaeva*, 839.

50. Elena Elagina, "Ne ko vremeni i ne ko dvoru," *Druzhba narodov*, no. 6 (2017), http://www.intelros.ru/readroom/druzhba-narodov/d6-2017/33229-ne-ko-vremeni-i-ne-ko-dvoru.html [date of access: 11/2/2019].

51. Falikov, *Marina Tsvetaeva*, 794.

Chapter 10

Mikhail Bulgakov
Refractions of a Writer's Life

J. A. E. Curtis

Alexei Varlamov opts to preface his *ZhZL* biography of Mikhail Bulgakov with an epigraph taken from Alexander Blok's unfinished narrative poem *Retribution* (*Vozmezdie*, 1910–1921): "Life is without a beginning or an end. / Chance lies in wait for us all. / Above us there is inescapable darkness, / Or else the brightness of God's face."[1] Blok's poem is a meditation on family, set in a period of Russia's history extending from the 1870s until the time of writing, and reflecting on the ways in which retribution has been passed down to the blasé generation of the fin de siècle, until finally some new child may appear who will "grasp the wheel that drives human history." It is a poem of guilt and of foreboding. These opening lines by Blok emphasize the vagaries of fate in human destiny, suggesting that chance may lead us either toward the temptations of the dark side or toward spiritual redemption. These are also the terms in which Varlamov asks us to consider the life of his subject, Mikhail Bulgakov, as a "duel" fought over his soul between the forces of good and evil, a battle in which, broadly speaking, he seems to believe that Bulgakov's spiritual integrity was compromised.

This moral struggle is also evoked in the brief summary of Varlamov's book (on the page that provides publication details), where Bulgakov's entire existence (*bytie*) is presented as a ceaseless, conscious duel fought with fate, leading to his defeat in life but brilliant successes in literature. Varlamov frames his account of Bulgakov's life, however, not in terms of the Erinyes, the three ancient Greek deities of vengeance and retribution, but instead divides his account of Bulgakov's life somewhat more prosaically into three parts named for his three wives, Tatyana, Lyubov, and Elena. For this he has been praised by the literary scholar Alexei Kholikov: "I think that Varlamov needs the three leading ladies as witnesses without whose testimony the book would never have happened. In that—and in that alone—lies their central role. He understands that the 'personal, family, secret relationships between a man and the women in his life are not so very important to the creative biography of our hero.' In this time of moral color-blindness, a position like that deserves the highest accolades."[2] Avoiding the prurient preoccupations that sometimes appear to dominate Western biographical writing, Varlamov uses the three wives' intimate knowledge of their husband, and their letters, diaries and memoirs, to chronicle the travails of Bulgakov's public life, rather than his domestic inclinations.

As it happens, Blok's opening lines are immediately followed in this "Prologue" to *Retribution* with an affirmation of the artist's unique gift and capacity to "believe / in ends and in beginnings," to know "where heaven and hell" await us, to "wipe away" chance events, and to see that the world is, in fact, beautiful, even if the singer ultimately perishes for his song. However, Varlamov clearly does not feel that Blok's more hopeful vision of the artist in the rest of his poem can be applied to Bulgakov and to the way in which he faced the challenges with which he was confronted in his lifetime, which extended across such turbulent years in Russia's history, from his childhood in Kyiv, where he was born in 1891, up until his early death in Moscow in 1940.

Varlamov's biography of Bulgakov for the *ZhZL* series first appeared in 2008, with a print run of five thousand copies, soon followed by a reprint that same year of seven thousand further copies. A third edition came out in 2012 and is now out of print. It was translated into German in 2010 but has not appeared in English. The volume is 840 pages long, apparently making it one of the lengthier *ZhZL* books: one critic described it as "the plumpest" (*naipukhleyshii*) in the series.[3] Varlamov suggests that he had no choice in writing such a lengthy study: "I don't even like how bulky this biography is, but the book came out the way it did. The reason for it lies not in the scale of the person but in the number of sources and in the literary status enjoyed by Bulgakov, who always stood at the center of the cultural life of his time."[4] It consists of the three named sections reflecting his three marriages, followed by thirty pages of footnotes (providing little more than page references to sources), a ten-page chronology of the principal dates of Bulgakov's life and works, plus three and a half pages of bibliography. As is typical of the *ZhZL* series, there is no index. Each of the three sections contains seven to ten chapters, mostly with rather cryptic titles, such as: I, 5: 'Duck-like noses' (*Utinye nosy*); I, 11: "Valya, you're a bum" ("*Valya, vy zhopa*"). These somewhat coy attempts to intrigue the reader (possibly an echo of Bulgakov's practice in some of his own fiction) make it even more difficult to work out from the table of contents where any specific topic can be found in the narrative. All this suggests that Varlamov assumes that his readers will already be broadly familiar with the outlines of his subject's life, that they will orient themselves fairly easily in the book without any finding aids—and it also assumes, presumably, that he expects every reader to read all the way through the volume from beginning to end, rather than dipping into the book to find particular episodes of interest. Mikhail Bulgakov is an immensely popular author: it has been estimated that in his centenary year of 1991 as many as one book in ten published in the USSR during the final year of the Soviet state's existence was written by him. The likely readers of this *ZhZL* volume, first published seventeen years later, are therefore likely to belong to a generation born and educated in the Soviet era, for whom Bulgakov became a cult author when they were young adults. By 2008 these would be middle-aged readers, many of them belonging to the new, post-Soviet middle class.

The choice of Alexei Varlamov to author this volume would have been made in order to guarantee that loyal *ZhZL* readers would be tempted to buy the book: Varlamov is not known particularly as a Bulgakov scholar, which in itself might have been an advantage, since he was less likely to belong to one of the fiercely competitive critical schools that have grown up around Bulgakov's legacy, whose members have disputed everything from the textology of his works to his moral and political stance and his views on Russian, Jewish, and Ukrainian identities. As Varlamov put it himself: "I had no problem with whether or not I should write a biography of Mikhail Bulgakov. It was all purely 'technical': the publishing house made an offer and I accepted it. In this case the publishing house was prompted by the fact that there was as yet no Bulgakov biography in the *ZhZL* series."[5] He never met any of Bulgakov's wives or close relatives, nor did he undertake new archival research in writing this book, relying entirely instead on published sources. On the other hand, he is the very well-regarded author of several previous titles in the *ZhZL* series, including by now volumes on writers contemporary to Bulgakov such as Mikhail Prishvin (2003)—Varlamov wrote both of his doctoral dissertations on him—Alexander Grin (2005), Alexei Tolstoy (also in 2008), and Andrei Platonov (2011), as well as on Grigory Rasputin (2007) and the Thaw-era writer Vasily Shukshin (2015). In an undated interview with Zakhar Prilepin Varlamov affirmed that the genre of biography attracts him because it enables him to explore the ways in which God's will, predestination, and fate interact to shape human destinies, and that "the choice of a subject is not for that matter all that important."[6]

Born in 1963, Varlamov has reached the highest echelons of the literary establishment in the Putin era, as a university lecturer and distinguished member of literary editorial boards, and now serves as the Rector of the Gorky Literary Institute in Moscow. Since 2011 he has been a member of the Presidential Council of the Russian Federation on Culture and the Arts. He has won multiple prizes for his own fiction as well as for his nonfiction writings.

In 2006 he was awarded the Alexander Solzhenitsyn prize "for his subtle exploration in fiction of the strength and the vulnerability of the human soul, and of the soul's fate in the modern world; and for making sense of the paths of Russian literature during the twentieth century through the genre of literary biographies."[7] Perhaps it is notable that when he won the national "Big Book" (*Bolshaya kniga*) prize in 2007 it was for a "documentary novel" about Alexei Tolstoy with the title *The Red Jester* (*Krasnyi shut*): this unusual genre definition gives us a clue to the distinctly belletristic narrative tone he sometimes adopts in the writing of biography. He swiftly followed *The Red Jester* with his ZhZL volume about Alexei Tolstoy in 2008, in the same year as the one about Bulgakov; the Tolstoy volume interestingly commanded an initial print run of ten thousand copies, twice the size of the first Bulgakov printing. In other words, entrusting the task of writing what should become a canonical biography of Bulgakov to Alexei Varlamov was in no sense a controversial step—his was a safe pair of hands, and he had a high-profile reputation as an influential and likeable person and a readable author, knowledgeable about the period, who would write a well-researched, thorough book.

Many previous biographies of Bulgakov exist, of course, and Varlamov refers frequently to the major scholars of his life such as Marietta Chudakova, Anatoly Smelyansky (whose work he describes as "a classic," 488), Lydia Yanovskaya, Boris Sokolov, and Boris Miagkov, and he also mentions more specialized studies such as Devlet Gireev's 1981 study of the author's time spent in the Caucasus, *Mikhail Bulgakov on the Banks of the Terek* (*Mikhail Bulgakov na beregax Tereka*). He draws extensively on the abundant memoirs assembled by Bulgakov's relatives, and the several editions of the correspondence and diaries that document his life. Despite knowing English reasonably well (Varlamov studied at a specialist English school) he does not take into account any of the pioneering studies in English such as those by A. C. Wright, Ellendea Proffer, Lesley Milne, and others. In general, Western scholarship on Bulgakov (including studies by émigré writers) is passed over in silence. He situates his own project as follows:

> I found myself to a significant degree in dialogue with the books that I consider most important. There are, in the broader perspective, two of those: Chudakova's *A Life of Mikhail Bulgakov* (*Zhizneopisanie Mikhaila Bulgakova*) and Anatoly Smelyansky's *Mikhail Bulgakov at the Art Theater* (*Mikhail Bulgakov v Khudozhestvennom teatre*). All the rest are interesting but, in my opinion, not pivotal. I also very much like what Miron Petrovsky wrote about Bulgakov. I made some use of the works of Lydia Yanovskaya and Boris Sokolov—although Sokolov provides too many interpretations that say more about himself than about Bulgakov. Among foreign authors, I used, for example, an article by Sergio Trombetta, an Italian journalist, titled "Meridian: The Best Works of the

Author of *The Master and Margarita*." In general, I relied a lot on journalists, because they reflect the conventional opinion, the stereotypes. . . . Grappling with the multiplicity of interpretations and evaluations surrounding Bulgakov is outside my field. In that sense I did not aspire to read all the literature about Bulgakov and to follow up 500 books on him with the 501st. My book addresses not Bulgakov scholars, who will already be up-to-date with 90 percent of what is in it, but Bulgakov's readers.[8]

However, Varlamov's claim here that he is not writing a new contribution to scholarly debates about interpretation, but offering a reflection of popular views, aimed at illuminating Bulgakov's life for the general reader, sits somewhat uneasily alongside the sheer volume and density of the biographical tome under discussion.

In the opening section of the biography, entitled "Tatyana," Varlamov points out that Bulgakov was perhaps atypical for a writer in having a genuinely happy childhood alongside his six brothers and sisters, all brought up together in a lively, highly cultured middle-class household in Kyiv. He is perhaps not quite correct when he also claims that Bulgakov was unique as a twentieth-century Russian writer in having parents who both came from families of priests (9)—we have only to think of his close friend Evgeny Zamyatin, who very similarly was descended from a family with numerous members of the clergy on both sides. For Varlamov this issue is of prime significance because of the way in which his religious background offered a set of spiritual standards for Bulgakov to live up to, an endeavor in which he apparently failed. Varlamov argues that faith was a key issue in Bulgakov's outlook, and from the outset of his biography he articulates an argument to which he will return more than once, namely that Bulgakov wrote a book of genius in *The Master and Margarita* (*Master i Margarita*), "which is also a spiritually 'seductive' novel about the power of the devil and the weakness of Him Who opposes him" (9). Varlamov does disagree with the more extreme of modern-day Russian Orthodox responses to Bulgakov's life and works, such as the view expressed in a number of different forums by the priest Iov (Gumerov) that after Bulgakov's father's death in 1907 secular culture was allowed to obscure religion in his upbringing, and that "the path of his life undoubtedly constitutes a spiritual tragedy" (34). Similarly, Varlamov refers to the "many people" who believe that Bulgakov corrupted both those close to him, and also his millions of readers, by tempting them toward atheism, mysticism, and occultism (43). On the one hand, Varlamov argues that these opinions represent a superficial or distorted account of the truth, but on the other hand it is striking how often in the course of his biography he, in fact, cites such opinions. His own conclusion in this section appears to be that:

There is no need to idealize or simplify the spiritual path of this book's hero, nor to ignore the awkward twists in his biography, but neither do you need to demonize or vulgarize it. Having rebuffed the Church, Bulgakov did not move towards primitive nihilism or atheism. . . . here we have an embodiment of the eternal story of how man's soul becomes a battleground between God and the devil. (45)

In a striking (but ultimately puzzling) comment, Varlamov adds: "Bulgakov was doomed to lose his faith, because he was a writer 'from God'" (45).

In his opinion, Bulgakov's first novel *The White Guard* (*Belaya gvardiya*), a nostalgic, clearly autobiographical account of the travails of a middle-class family in Kyiv during the Civil War, in 1918–1919, provides confirmation of this trajectory in his life from innocent virtue toward sin. Written in the early 1920s when he had moved to Moscow and was living under the new atheistic Bolshevik regime, the novel is described by Varlamov as "the most irreproachable of all his creations" (251), a book which was explicitly Christian, and indeed "one of the most Christian books of twentieth-century literature" (78). Many readers would perhaps take issue with this view, not least because the novel *The White Guard* is explicitly framed by glimpses of a pagan universe represented by Venus and Mars, the pre-Christian Roman deities of love and war. When taken together with the scathing account of the decadent Rusakov's hysterical obsession with Holy Scripture, and with the quasi-autobiographical hero Dr. Alexei Turbin dreaming of a highly unconventional heaven to which even good Bolsheviks would be admitted—since what counts is not faith, but deeds—Bulgakov's *The White Guard* precisely seems to challenge a religious view of the world that is contained within the bounds of conventional, let alone Orthodox Christianity. In contradiction to Varlamov's interpretation, the novel seems to posit spiritual values and notions of good and evil that remain true for all times, irrespective of religious practices.

Varlamov rightly points out that Tatyana, whom Bulgakov met when they were still teenagers and married while he was still a student, is a crucial figure in his biography, despite having been somewhat eclipsed by his later wives both in her own lifetime and also during the period after Bulgakov finally emerged into celebrity from the late 1960s, when portions of *The Master and Margarita* were first published. She may not have been a confident society figure as Lyubov and Elena both were, in rather different styles, but she was married to him longer than they were (from 1913 to 1925), and shared with him truly formative experiences, though these are not recorded in the form of extensive diaries or memoirs. Varlamov also seems to find significance in the fact that she was the only one of his wives to whom he was married in church (*stala ego edinstvennoi venchannoi zhenoi,* 49). Once Bulgakov had qualified as a doctor in 1916 she joined him as a nurse and shared with him distressing experiences on the front line during World War I, including several operations involving amputations. She then traveled with him to a small Russian village where he spent about eighteen months as a country doctor. Being the only medical practitioner for miles around and tending to largely uneducated patients not only confronted him with a wide range of medical challenges, but also eventually led to his own addiction to morphine. Tatyana was the one who had to endure his impossible behavior and demands, and it was she who, together with his doctor stepfather, managed eventually to wean Bulgakov off the drug after they returned to Kyiv early in 1918. Varlamov expresses his "deep conviction" that this became a sacral moment in his life, when in exchange for being cured Bulgakov "signed a contract" with the higher powers, in other words with fate, that he would abandon medicine to become a writer (86–87).

Tatyana also joined Bulgakov in 1919 when he left Kyiv, probably as a medical volunteer with the White army, and traveled to the town of Vladikavkaz in the north Caucasus, where he first started to write and publish some articles, short stories and plays. There he succumbed to typhus, and by the time he was recovering the town had passed into Bolshevik control. Bulgakov apparently blamed Tatyana for having failed to get him out of Vladikavkaz while he was ill, to escape the Reds. Their marriage had in any case reached a fairly rocky point, and in 1921 Bulgakov made an attempt to emigrate across the Black Sea, telling Tatyana that she should move to Moscow without him. At this, Tatyana apparently "'started to cry' . . . as she confided in M. O. Chudakova with feminine trustingness," according to Varlamov (173). There is no doubt that Bulgakov treated her badly after they both ended up in Moscow, and he felt guilty about this right up to the end of his life. And indeed, Varlamov cites a number of other episodes in which Bulgakov may not have behaved in an admirable way as a young man: an experiment with cocaine as well as the addiction to morphine (61–62); the two abortions undergone by Tatyana in the early years of their relationship, plus a later abortion undergone by his second wife Lyubov; he and Tatyana ceasing to wear their holy crosses; the egoism and "satanic" arrogance described by one of his sisters (46–47); and his not entirely ethical exploitation of the lives of people from his immediate circle to provide material, sometimes mercilessly caricatured, for his fiction (96–102). But one online reviewer of this biography has argued that in sharing Bulgakov's multiple weaknesses and human faults with the reader, Varlamov simply succeeds in making the reader love him all the more.[9]

After Bulgakov moved to Moscow in 1921, he and Tatyana had to endure some years of hardship as he struggled to establish himself, but within two or three years he had largely succeeded in that goal. Varlamov suggests that it was precisely another of his own *ZhZL* subjects, Alexei Tolstoy, who rescued Bulgakov from obscurity and poverty by giving him opportunities to be published, even though Bulgakov despised Tolstoy for his opportunistic political outlook (199, 216). In another of Varlamov's startling swerves into pious subjectivity, he also suggests that the death of Bulgakov's mother in February 1922 coincided with this upturn in his fortunes, and that it would not take a huge stretch of the imagination to suggest that this was because of his mother's prayers for her son from beyond the grave (197). The first section of Varlamov's book concludes with one of his 'intimate' authorial interventions, echoing a narrative device of Bulgakov's in *The Master and Margarita*, when he addresses the reader and explains that he will be discussing Bulgakov's drama "a little later on. But in the meantime, let us introduce a new and very important heroine" (280).

These occasionally tiresome authorial mannerisms should not, however, be allowed to distract from the fact that overall Varlamov does provide us with a very thorough account of Bulgakov's life. He draws, as most of Bulgakov's biographers have done, on the very extensive documentary records of his life and career that have survived in the archives in the form of letters and diaries, and which have by now been published in scholarly editions. Most of the best-known studies of Bulgakov have taken advantage of these unusually rich resources, which have been preserved partly because of Bulgakov's own determination to create a personal archive for posterity, especially after 1929, even while his contemporaries were rejecting all his writings. Nevertheless, Varlamov insists that memoirs, letters, and diaries are never to be trusted, unless you can find at least two to four independent sources to confirm what they tell you (556). In particular, Varlamov is well informed about the more recent published archival discoveries, many of which have offered a fuller picture of how the Soviet authorities regularly gathered information on Bulgakov, his writings and his political opinions, and about how these matters were regularly debated at the highest levels of government, including even by the Politburo, chaired by Stalin himself. Studies by scholars such as Benedikt Sarnov in Russia, or Katerina Clark and Evgeny Dobrenko in the West, have done a great deal over recent decades to demonstrate just how attentively and actively Stalin-era government figures engaged in every twist and turn of the lives of leading cultural figures, including writers, composers, theater directors, and many others.

The second section of the biography opens with an account of one of Bulgakov's more craven acts of betrayal, when he decided to remove the dedication to Tatyana he had written for his novel *The White Guard*, in which so many experiences she had shared with him feature in fictional disguise. Instead, to her dismay, those portions of the novel which were published in early-mid 1920s Moscow appeared with a dedication to the new love in his life, Lyubov Evgenevna Belozerskaya. Lyubov was a sophisticated woman, previously married, who had spent time in emigration. Together, the new couple started to move in elite literary and theatrical circles, and as Bulgakov's reputation soared after the controversial 1926 staging of a dramatic adaptation of *The White Guard* under the title *The Days of the Turbins* (*Dni Turbinykh*) at the Moscow Art Theater, he found himself one of the most sought-after writers of the NEP period. And at the same time, he came under the close scrutiny of the OGPU, even being subjected to an interrogation shortly before the premiere of *The Days of the Turbins*. Bulgakov conducted himself with dignity on this occasion, spoke frankly and forthrightly about his political convictions, and seems to have earned some sort of immunity from the more threatening aspects of secret police scrutiny in subsequent years. This was undoubtedly helped by the fact that Stalin himself was known to be exceptionally fond of the "Turbin play," which he attended over a dozen times. Varlamov also suggests that Bulgakov earned his relatively advantageous position by simply speaking the truth to his interrogators (like Ieshua in his later novel, when speaking to Pontius Pilate), claiming somewhat improbably that these Soviet authorities "neither then nor later on meted out punitive measures to those who had concealed nothing from them" (337). Varlamov concludes that while Bulgakov deserves to be criticized for his personal beliefs, as well as for his high-handed treatment of some of those around him, "this could never be said of his stance as a writer and creative artist, nor of his civic position" (393). It is certainly striking that Bulgakov never allowed the endless reverses in his professional life to deter him from further creative endeavors, and he never stooped to speaking untruths or to attacking his enemies in public.

The brief period of theatrical successes in Bulgakov's life in the mid-1920s came to an end with his play *Flight* (*Beg*), in which he portrays middle-class intellectuals and other members of the White movement a year or so after the events depicted in *The White Guard*, as they are chased by the Bolsheviks out of Russia through the Crimean peninsula and into emigration in Constantinople and, for some, eventually in Paris. Varlamov is not alone in considering *Flight* to be Bulgakov's best play (430), although here as elsewhere he does not explore the work in much detail for its actual content or aesthetic innovations. In this respect he follows in the long-standing Russian biographical tradition of "separating literary history from literary criticism. ... The literary works were discussed as facts in the lives of writers, but were not the basis for the kind of creative psychological profile that one began to find in Western biography with the onset of the Freudian approach in the early twentieth century."[10] Instead, he is fascinated by the tortuous path *Flight* took toward being staged, and the high-level debates that eventually led to it being banned from the stage before its premiere, after a Politburo discussion early in 1929. His tracing of this story takes up the best part of thirty pages of the book and includes the unabridged quotation (over six pages) of an account of the play's political weaknesses prepared for the Politburo by the critic R. Pikel (408–14). Here there is a slight sense that the shape of some of Varlamov's narrative has been driven by the availability of documents, especially relatively new ones such as this, which are not so familiar even to Bulgakov scholars. This is also true of his investigation of the question as to why *The Days of the Turbins* was taken off the stage at the same time, notwithstanding Stalin's fondness for the work. A recently uncovered document providing an account of a meeting Stalin held with Ukrainian writers on February 12, 1929, suggests that the ban was imposed not so much because of the play's blatant class-based sympathies for the enemies of Bolshevism, but because it was perceived by the Ukrainians as offending their national pride (441).

The catastrophes of 1929, which in the end involved the banning of four of Bulgakov's plays in various stages of production, was to prompt the first of a series of letters which he addressed to government leaders, to the father figure of Soviet literature Maxim Gorky, and even to Stalin himself over the ensuing ten years. Extraordinary though this practice was in framing the last decade of Bulgakov's life, this is familiar material from all the well-known biographies, and the story has often been told. Well-known too is the story of his first meeting with Elena Sergeevna Shilovskaya, a very beautiful married woman with two sons, in February 1929: after a couple of difficult years, she would become his third wife in 1932, as well as figuring without any doubt as the prototype for Margarita in his greatest masterpiece. His new-found love did much to assuage the acute distress of 1929. That culminated in the notorious personal telephone call Bulgakov received from Stalin in April 1930, in which he declined the opportunity to emigrate, and instead accepted the opportunity of regular work as an assistant director at the Moscow Art Theater. He was left with a half-promise of further conversations with Stalin, which to his intense disappointment never, in fact, materialized. Overall, Varlamov shrewdly describes this episode as a tactical victory but a strategic defeat for Bulgakov (481).

One nuance that Varlamov addresses in detail, however, is a suggestion initially floated in the second, expanded 1988 edition of Marietta Chudakova's seminal *Life of Mikhail Bulgakov* (*Zhizneopisanie Mikhail Bulgakova*), in which she seized the opportunities rapidly opening up as glasnost' established itself to be more outspoken about certain controversial topics than had been possible even earlier in that same year. The issue was the rumor that Elena, Bulgakov's third wife, might have had connections with the OGPU, and indeed that she might even have been "planted" by them to report back on Bulgakov and his activities. Varlamov also quotes Chudakova's "elegant subtlety" (466) in suggesting in a later article of 1998 that it was not inconceivable that both Bulgakov's third wife Elena, and indeed her sister Olga Sergeevna Bokshanskaya, who worked in the administration of the Moscow Art Theater, might possibly have been Stalin's mistresses during the 1920s. There is, incidentally, no hint of such a story in respected post-Soviet biographies of Stalin such as those by Edvard Radzinsky (1996), Simon Sebag Montefiore (2003), or Robert Service (2004). Be that as it may, the suggestion about her OGPU connection, which has gained a little more credence, arises from comments made by one of Elena's daughters-in-law, who apparently raised questions about how Elena always somehow managed to live a privileged and apparently untouchable life, with access to luxurious food and services, in the midst of the 1930s Terror, and even after Bulgakov's death in 1940 and the later deprivations of World War II. This is, admittedly, a question which has never been entirely explained. Varlamov describes Elena as a tough and complex figure, patronizingly adding: "She was a woman with all those characteristics that come naturally to the descendants of Eve, as well as the fact that a fiery blend of two bloods—Jewish and Russian—made itself felt" (540). This kind of egregious—and evidently subconscious—sexism on his part (combined with crude assumptions about national characteristics) also colors his discussion of how trustworthy the evidence for Elena's secret 'mission' may be, and why Chudakova took up the theory so readily, when he queries "the logic and the motives of these two women" (546). Ultimately, Varlamov concludes that despite Chudakova's "feminine intuition" (597) with regard to this question, the full documentary evidence for her theory so far has proved lacking. Even if it is conceivable that Elena was initially asked to report on Bulgakov to the OGPU, he argues, their relationship soon became one of deep and genuine love, and this was how this particular stroke of "fate" played out (434). Instead, he suggests that Bulgakov and Elena were simply very well aware of the close attention the security services were paying to their every word. Furthermore, the personal sympathy of Stalin himself, which was widely known, may have served to insulate them from the worst horrors of the arrests, imprisonment, torture, or execution suffered by others in their immediate circle during the Terror (603).

One episode in which Varlamov takes a particular interest, for understandable reasons, is the story of how Bulgakov came to write a biography of Molière for the very same *ZhZL* series in which his own book has appeared. This project came at a moment when the *ZhZL* series was being relaunched in 1933 under the aegis of Maxim Gorky, after a hiatus since 1915. As Trigos and Ueland have observed, the Soviet permutation of the series was designed to reshape the behavior of the masses by offering a glimpse of exemplary lives, using "a detailed Marxist analysis of that social milieu in which great people had to live and work" in order to highlight the instructive differences between the epochs of capitalism and socialism.[11] Bulgakov undertook the task with enthusiasm, reading widely in the available sources in Russian (and a few in French). But having done his research, he then allowed himself considerable creative license, particularly in casting his narrator as a writer contemporary to Molière, who welcomes the newborn infant into the world with a lengthy chat with the midwife. He also focused more on the difficulties of his professional, public, and family life than he did either on Molière's plays, or on the process of their composition. This idiosyncratic approach did not find favor with the editor, Alexander Tikhonov, who wrote a lengthy criticism of the way that Bulgakov had approached the biographical undertaking. As Bulgakov described it to one of his friends: "My narrator, who is in charge of the biography, is described as a casual young man who believes in sorcery and demons; he possesses occult skills, has a fondness for salacious stories, makes use of dubious sources and, worst of all, is inclined to royalism."[12] Bulgakov scarcely even bothered to protest, and the project was shelved. Varlamov comments that our sympathies are naturally inclined to be with the inventive writer and his challenges to convention but asks us to consider whether Tikhonov did not in fact have good grounds for some of his objections (he notes that Gorky also agreed with Tikhonov). Bulgakov had written a passionate, subjective piece with certainly autobiographical—and almost certainly political—resonances, and this was not supposed, as Varlamov understands it, to be a typical biographer's approach: "The ZhZL books . . . assumed . . . a distinct separation between the author and his hero and the observing of a reverential and respectful distance; it was assumed that you were writing a book which would be a monument" (535). Incidentally, Varlamov makes a curious slip in discussing Molière, referring to one of his plays (*Les Précieuses ridicules* / lit. *The Absurd Pretentious Ladies*) in a quite inaccurate Russian translation, which would translate back into English as *The Comical Valuables* (536). As Trigos and Ueland observe, the effect of the rejection of Bulgakov's conceptually original approach was to "set limits on the use of creative license in the series for years to come."[13] Gorky and Tikhonov instead commissioned Stefan Mokulsky, a well-known expert on French theater, to write on Molière for ZhZL in Bulgakov's place. The Mokulsky version was published in a print run of 50,000 copies in 1935. Only in 1962 did the beginnings of the rehabilitation of Bulgakov's name during the Thaw lead to the first publication of his own account of Molière in the series. That publication, incidentally, also saw the first-ever mention in print of the existence of the novel *The Master and Margarita*, which was described in several lines of the introduction written by Veniamin Kaverin.

Varlamov comments ruefully on the several attempts Bulgakov made to travel abroad during the 1930s, all of which were frustrated. He points out that, however bitter his disappointment, this particular stroke of fate did at least ensure that Bulgakov stayed in Moscow to carry on writing, and in particular to continue work on *The Master and Margarita*. He gives an extensive account of the traumatic banning of his play about Molière in 1936, alongside the struggle to get his biographical play about Pushkin put on. Both of these ventures were, predictably, just as unconventional in the biographical sense, the Molière play in resolutely refusing (despite Stanislavsky's determined efforts) to depict the "genius" Molière composing his immortal works on stage, while the Pushkin play went even further and described the poet's final days without ever bringing Pushkin himself physically into the view of the audience.

As the Terror unfolded around him, Bulgakov left the Moscow Art Theater for the Bolshoi, to work there on librettos, composing his unfinished satire on Stanislavsky's theater under the title *A Theatrical Novel* (*Teatral'nyi roman*) for his own private amusement in the evenings. And all the time individuals would turn up in his life who were blatantly reporting on him to the NKVD (formerly OGPU). There were occasional lighter moments during these bleak years, including the improbable episode of his being befriended by American diplomats in the mid-1930s, who offered him glimpses of a luxurious and free life which must have seemed utterly extraordinary in Stalin's Moscow. He also returned to his drafts of *The Master and Margarita*, a novel which Varlamov affirms to be essentially about the year 1937, the most frightening year of the Terror, "when a mysterious mystical and evil force bursts into people's lives, against which there is no protection" (726). This somewhat problematic reading of Bulgakov's masterpiece assumes that Woland unequivocally represents the powers of evil, even though the novel's epigraph from Goethe's *Faust* ("I am a part of that power which wishes forever evil but does forever good") precisely warns us against such an unambiguous interpretation. However, Varlamov disputes that this is how Woland should be viewed, insisting instead that "All-powerful Woland is repellent and abominable" (747). He concludes that even though Woland departs from Moscow before the resurrection promised by Easter, there is no triumph of good in the novel: "For all the lightness, phantasmagoric aspects and entertaining qualities of Bulgakov's novel, there is scarcely in Russian literature a more tragic and hopeless work of literature" (728). It does seem difficult to reconcile this reading of his with the ultimate destiny painted by Bulgakov for his autobiographical hero and heroine in the text, a Romantic idyll in which art, music, and friendship will fill their days, and anxiety and worry will pass into oblivion.

Ultimately, though, Varlamov is somewhat tentative in his overall conclusions about the work, suggesting that it contains heretical features, but also moments of truth and beauty. His account is also somewhat fragmentary, focusing above all on what he calls the "confessional" aspects of *The Master and Margarita* (733), an approach which he justifies by pointing out that in a sense Bulgakov's novel did little to shape the author's own life, since it remained unknown until so long after his death. But several readers of Varlamov's biography have found this disappointing, pointing out that he devotes more pages to the subject of Bulgakov and Molière than are set aside to discuss *The Master and Margarita*. Varlamov has responded as follows: "I am sometimes scolded for having given so much space in the book to the plot of *Molière* and so little to *The Master and Margarita*. But this is an issue of principle, since *The Master and Margarita* influenced Bulgakov's fate in no way, whereas *Molière* hurt him in numerous respects."[14] This disjunction between what Bulgakov achieved in his own lifetime and his modern-day reputation becomes a broader issue too, in that if F. F. Pavlenkov's "overarching concept" for the ZhZL series he founded in 1890 "was that individuals, rather than abstract ideas, served as the prime movers in history,"[15] then Bulgakov's life signally fails to meet this criterion. Almost entirely frustrated for the last decade and more of his life in his attempts to get published or staged, his name was destined after his death to slip into obscurity for over twenty years, until the more liberal atmosphere of the Thaw after Stalin's death allowed for his name to reemerge and for his works at last to start to be published. To speak of his impact is therefore a question of a sensational but very belated, posthumous reputation, not an influence—or not at least one that could be acknowledged—upon those around him.

The major event of Bulgakov's final years was the writing of his biographical play about Stalin's early revolutionary activities, *Batum*. The story of the Moscow Art Theater's pleas to him to provide them with a work for Stalin's Jubilee celebrations at the end of 1939, his drafting of the play, and the deep shock he suffered when the production was cancelled, is a very well-known episode. Varlamov is reluctant to say much about the play itself since he "doesn't like it" (764), which is perhaps a pity since it certainly deserves to be examined on its own terms for what it is. But Varlamov concludes that above all the writing of this work constituted "a betrayal of self" for Bulgakov, as well as triggering an acute crisis in his health which shortened his life and prevented him from completing *A Theatrical Novel* or polishing *The Master and Margarita* (760).

Bulgakov's death after a few months of a very painful and distressing illness fell on March 10, 1940, which Varlamov observes was the Sunday before Lent, known in the Orthodox calendar as "Forgiveness Sunday." On this day the faithful ask each other for forgiveness, in order to cleanse themselves before they start to approach the rites accompanying the Easter celebrations. Varlamov concludes that "This, if you like, provides the decisive argument in the debate about who received the soul after death of this son of a theology professor and a schoolteacher from a small provincial town" (793–94). This somewhat winsome judgment, which presumably assumes that the sinful author was granted forgiveness in the hereafter, rounds off Varlamov's biography of Mikhail Bulgakov with a little wishful thinking. It also continues to assume that all his *ZhZL* readers share his own religious outlook and will judge Bulgakov and his writings above all in terms of his spiritual journey within the Russian Orthodox Church.

Varlamov's biography of Bulgakov has provoked mixed responses. One reader at least, has concluded that "for all the mass of details and information which are adduced about him and his 'unsuccessful life' in this book, he still doesn't come to life."[16] In a volume assembled for the 112th anniversary of Bulgakov's birth in 2011, the editor John Givens summarizes the opinions of one contributor, the Russian literary scholar Alexei Kholikov, as follows:

> At 839 pages, it is too detailed and bogged down with documentary sources (often quoted at length) for the tastes of average readers. But despite all of its documentary qualities, it has little new to offer the critic already familiar with the writer's life and works. As if to compensate for its more scholarly passages, the biography attempts to make something of a novel out of Bulgakov's life, dividing the book (rather arbitrarily, according to Kholikov) into sections named after each of the writer's three wives and trying to keep the reader's attention by means of "innuendos and other gimmicks," such as saucy chapter titles. As if that is not bad enough, Varlamov devotes more space in his work to an analysis of Bulgakov's *The Life of Monsieur de Molière* than to the work for which he is most famous—*The Master and Margarita*. The end result, in Kholikov's assessment, is highly unsatisfactory: a biography "made to order," but one that does not deliver on its promises.[17]

What can we infer from Varlamov's approach about his implied and intended reader? In conversation with Kholikov Varlamov claimed: "I don't think that the number of readers should influence the extent of the biographer's responsibility and conscientiousness at all. Nor does the number of readers define the difficulty presented by a given 'leading man.' In writing books, I do think of the reader, but only in the sense of hiding nothing from him, of telling everything I know." This is surely disingenuous; or does it in fact mask a failure to consider carefully enough exactly who he was writing for? Kholikov concludes that "the biography is too gossipy for a scholarly work but too reliant on documents for a popular one. . . . The paradox is that the non-specialist reader may be hampered by Varlamov's membership of the 'castes' of both scholars and writers." Kholikov notes that Varlamov seems to do everything possible to turn Bulgakov's life into a kind of novel, recounting it in the style of an ancient tragedy, as a duel between the hero and his fate. Kholikov also feels that he allows the documentary to prevail over the narrative in a way which damages the overall project: "He holds strictly to his documentary sources, which are enough to drown the reader, no matter how hard he or she tries to stay afloat. Or more accurately, to bog the helpless creature down in the agendas, minutes, applications, and certificates that Varlamov quotes copiously and almost always unabridged. But alas, the meticulous historian has won out over the writer, whose job would have been to give the non-specialist's 'ear' a break by conveying the meaning of a given set of minutes in a more accessible form." Varlamov's response to this criticism has been to argue the importance of the document in the post-Soviet cultural sphere:

> All the documents I quote had been previously published. But they weren't in Chudakova's book, since that was published in 1988. In my opinion, the paraphrase of documents weakens the biographer's position. My readers are skeptically inclined, distrustful, and picky. Everywhere they want to see a certificate, a paper, a document. I read books that way, too. I want everything to be brought together between a single set of covers, and I try to saturate my life stories with all the information I have. These books are not fine writing. They are not designed to be read at one sitting.[18]

In a roundtable discussion on the art of biography in 2008, the year his Bulgakov volume was published, Varlamov claimed that the main criterion for a good biography was simply to make it interesting: "My task as an author is to show as little of myself as possible." He also argued that it is crucial to understand an individual, rather than judge him.[19] To what extent has he met these two criteria in his biography? Perhaps the most striking feature of this work, in which his own voice, beliefs and opinions are actually far from being hidden, is the preoccupation with Bulgakov's spiritual journey. Correspondingly, the traumas of Stalinist oppression and censorship recede somewhat into the background, seemingly taken for granted rather than constituting the greatest tragedy of Mikhail Bulgakov's career. Does Varlamov's biography reflect the cultural priorities of the Putin era—and perhaps even the Putin administration? The close personal links between Vladimir Putin and the Russian Orthodox hierarchy have recently seen religious convictions reinstated as a primary measure of patriotic behavior and cultural practices in the modern state. At the same time, a new, careful "management" of the narratives of history has seen the traumas and horrors of Stalinist oppression blurred and obscured, in favor of a triumphalist vision of Russian national identity. While not evidently written to serve these priorities of the second decade of the twenty-first century, Alexei Varlamov's 2008 biography chimes in well with the current Zeitgeist.

NOTES

1. Alexei Varlamov, *Bulgakov* (Moscow: Molodaia gvardiia, 2008). Page references to Varlamov's biography will be given in parentheses after relevant citations.
2. Aleksei Kholikov, "Mikhail Bulgakov 'Made to Order,'" *Russian Studies in Literature* 47, no. 2 (Spring 2011): 64.
3. Vladimir Tsybul'sky in a review of 14 January 2009 in Gazeta.ru, at http://litena.ru/news/item/f00/s01/n0000130/index.shtml (accessed 9 December 2019). It is striking that, by contrast, the early biographies in the *ZhZL* series were typically just 70–90 pages long (Ludmilla A. Trigos and Carol R. Ueland, 'Literary Biographies in the *Lives of Remarkable People* series (*Zhizn' zamechatel'nykh liudei*)', *Slavic and East European Journal* 60, no. 2 (2016):208).
4. Kholikov, 63.
5. Kholikov, 70.
6. Interview of Varlamov by Prilepin at http://zaharprilepin.ru/ru/litprocess/intervju-o-literature/aleksej-varlamov-.html (accessed 9 December 2019).
7. Quoted from Varlamov's homepage at the Gorky Literary Institute: http://www.litinstitut.ru/content/varlamov-aleksey-nikolaevich (accessed 24 November 2019).
8. Kholikov, 68–69.
9. "Trompitayana" at https://www.livelib.ru/book/1000312008-mihail-bulgakov-aleksej-varlamov (accessed 9 December 2019).
10. Trigos and Ueland, 209.
11. Trigos and Ueland, 212–13.
12. Quoted from my detailed account of Bulgakov's writing of his biography of Molière in *Bulgakov's Last Decade: The Writer as Hero* (Cambridge: Cambridge University Press, 1987), 50–64 (citation from 51).
13. Trigos and Ueland, 214–15.
14. Kholikov, 67.
15. Trigos and Ueland, 207.
16. Vladimir Tsybul'sky in a review of January 14, 2009 in Gazeta.ru, at http://litena.ru/news/item/f00/s01/n0000130/index.shtml (accessed 9 December 2019).
17. John Givens, "Bulgakov's Anniversary," *Russian Studies in Literature* 47, no. 2 (Spring 2011): 4–5.
18. Kholikov, 69.
19. "Biografiia glazami biografa,"*Voprosy literatury* 6 (2008), cited in *Russian Studies in Literature*, vol. 46, no. 1 (2009–2010):14.

Chapter 11

Between Biography and Mythology

The Russian and American Lives of Joseph Brodsky

Carol Ueland

One of the major tasks for *ZhZL* in the late Soviet, and even more so in the post-Soviet series, was to expand the range of subjects for literary biographies to include figures who were ideologically impossible to write about in the Soviet period. Among them were a large number of authors who had left Russia either by voluntarily emigrating or who were forced to become exiles, many of whom then went on to achieve outstanding literary success abroad. Some of these figures left after the Revolution, such as Vladimir Nabokov and Ivan Bunin, and others at various later stages of Soviet history.[1] But the achievements of such figures, along with more recent exiles and émigrés like Joseph Brodsky, Alexander Solzhenitsyn, Sergei Dovlatov, Vasily Aksyonov, and others were too great to ignore for the post-Soviet *ZhZL* series and demanded inclusion into the canon of biographies of Russia's foremost writers.[2] The biographies of exiles were always problematic for the series. F. F. Pavlenkov had hoped to include a biography of Russia's most famous exiled writer of the nineteenth century, Alexander Herzen, early in his series, but due to censorship issues his biography only appeared in 1898.[3]

In both Tsarist and Soviet culture, Russian émigrés and exiles were traditionally seen as outcasts, traitors to the state. As historian Richard Freeborn explains: "Russian literary attitudes are frequently surrounded by fierce public debate and far from disinterested official concern.... They are often tragically enmeshed with government policy. In certain notorious cases they have become the pretext for persecution, exile, or death."[4] Although Maxim Gorky himself maintained relations with many émigré Russian writers, after his death a hostile attitude toward exiled or émigré writers hardened even further in the Soviet period and was reflected as well in their omission as biographical subjects in the Soviet *ZhZL*. During the Third Wave emigration of the 1970s and 1980s, more prominent writers, many of Russian-Jewish origin, left the Soviet Union than even after the Bolshevik Revolution. By the late Soviet period their literary works began to be published in their homeland, often unofficially at first, but with the arrival of Gorbachev's glasnost' also in official publications, thus rejoining the contemporary Russian literary canon. G. S. Smith remarked on the significance of the publication of Brodsky's poems in *Novyi mir* in December 1987 that this was "the first time since the early 1920s that poetry by a living Russian émigré was published in Russia without being sheathed in some sort of prophylactic denigration."[5] More recently as poets and writers of the 1960s passed away, renewed interest in all writers of this period has led to new *ZhZL* biographies, starting in 2002 with one on the immensely popular Vladimir Vysotsky and more recently those of Andrei Voznesensky, Yevgeny Yevtushenko, and Bulat Okudzhava as well as a collective biography on the sixties by Dmitry Bykov.[6] In some cases the émigré designation was now problematized by the fact that some writers of this period, such as Yevtushenko, lived both in Russia and elsewhere or sometimes returned to their homeland permanently as in the cases of Solzhenitsyn or Aksyonov. Biographers now have the task of depicting multiple settings for the complex series of events that formed their subjects' lives and works.

In terms of biographical appeal, the dramatic events of Joseph Brodsky's life stood out: his trial for "parasitism" in 1965 and subsequent first period of exile in the Russian Far North aroused worldwide outrage against the Soviet government's treatment of a little-published poet who a few years later was more or less forced to become an émigré in a second and permanent exile abroad. He subsequently rose to the heights of literary fame in Western intellectual circles, culminating in his winning the Nobel Prize for Literature in 1987 and then became the first Russian-born Poet Laureate of the United States, his adopted country. The events of Brodsky's early life in the Soviet Union fit perfectly into the biographical myth of the poet as martyr, first applied in the nineteenth century to Alexander Pushkin and then embodied in the early twentieth century by Alexander Blok and later by Anna Akhmatova, Marina Tsvetaeva, Osip Mandelstam, Boris Pasternak, and others.[7] This chapter explores the choices made in the portrayals of Brodsky in the two radically different *ZhZL* biographies of the poet by Lev Loseff in 2006 and Vladimir Bondarenko in 2015.

The key moments in Brodsky's life are not only open to interpretive possibilities but also rife with deliberate ambiguity. Early on in Brodsky's career,

Anna Akhmatova famously remarked "What a biography they have created for our redhead. As if he had hired someone on purpose."[8] While the first part of Akhmatova's comment seems presciently to both sum up and predict the tumultuous course of the poet's life, the less noted second half already suggests a degree of self-fashioning. William Wadsworth, longtime executive director of the Academy of American Poets (and earlier Brodsky's student in a poetry seminar at Columbia) describes his appeal in American intellectual circles: "Joseph was a heroic figure, the paradigm of the dissident writer, a tremendously romantic figure who had stood up to the Soviet 'establishment,' paid the consequences, and prevailed nonetheless."[9] Wadsworth concludes that this life story gave Brodsky a moral authority that no contemporary American poet could claim. However, Wadsworth also recalls the remark of American poet Charles Simic, who after summing up Brodsky's life at a reading, remarked: "No poet could ever wish for more."[10]

Even before his death in January 1996, a torrent of books and articles on Brodsky's life and works appeared in Europe and the United States, and soon in Russia as well, augmented by posthumous recollections of the poet, both by scholars and friends. In a 2004 conversation with another seminal Brodsky scholar, Valentina Polukhina, Loseff joked "'Brodsky studies,' something which you and I initiated some twenty years ago, is now galloping along at an industrial pace."[11] The pace has not diminished since then. In the months after the poet's death, the Brodsky estate, under the direction of his longtime editor Ann Kjellberg and the poet's widow Maria Brodsky, honored the poet's wishes in supporting his ongoing projects such as the establishment of a foundation to support fellowships for Russian artists at the American Academy in Rome. It also was deeply involved in the collection and translations of the Brodsky's poetry in both English and Russian. But the estate also set guidelines that limited any access to the poet's personal papers, a restriction that would seem to make a comprehensive biographical account of his life next to impossible. A close friend of the poet, Yakov Gordin, cites several places that confirm Brodsky's consistent views on the matter. In making a will in 1994 Brodsky added a letter in which he wrote, "A request to my friends and family not to collaborate with the publishers of unauthorized biographies, biographical research, diaries and letters." Gordin goes on to explain that "he feared that the world of poetry would be exchanged for the political world.... He was deathly afraid that the high drama of his existence (*bytie*) would be lowered to the level of vulgar everyday life (*poshlyi byt*)."[12] This decision was not uncontroversial. As the scholar James Rice wrote in a letter of response to the estate's announcement: "one might object to 'reading poetry through the lens of biography' but it is quite wrong (also pointless) to object to the lens of biography itself. Good biography should be written so that it further *enhances* the reading of poetry for what it is—the richest human communication," and adds "Your suggestion that the poet's wishes could be honored by *destroying* material that sheds light on his life makes my archival soul cringe!"[13] Rice's objections were supported in a separate letter by Loseff, "After the death of a great writer destroying any scrap of paper with his handwriting amounts to a cultural crime, much worse than unauthorized publications." He goes on to note that there is much greater interest in Brodsky in Russia than the United States and asks that the estate make Brodsky's own words on the subject of his legacy available, "even though I have no intentions of writing Joseph's biography."[14] In subsequent years archives containing approved scholarly materials were set up both in Russia and the United States, but access to Brodsky's personal materials were to be closed for a fifty-year period.

The division between a poet's activities in daily life and a poet's life as reflected in his works is central to the foundational cultural model presented by Pushkin. His disdain for the exposure of petty or sordid details of an artist's life to the common reader is perennially cited in discussions of Russian writers' biographies, "The mob devours confessions, memoirs, etc. because in its baseness it relishes the humiliation of the supreme, the weakness of the powerful. Upon discovering any unsavory detail, it is delighted: *He is despicable, just like us; revolting, just like us!* That's a damn lie, bastards: even when despicable and revolting, he is not like you—he is different."[15] As opposed to debasing details, moments of inspiration which are manifested in great art are then the only legitimate concerns of poets' biographies. Several of Pushkin's most famous lyrics, such as "The Poet" (*Poet*, 1827), "The Prophet" (*Prorok*, 1826), "The Poet" (*Poet*, 1827), "To the Poet" (*Poetu*, 1830) have been read as illustrations of this biographical dichotomy. This traditional view prevailed to the twentieth century as in the notion of the "biographical legend" of the formalist Boris Tomashevsky, and to the views of Brodsky's mentor, Anna Akhmatova, who discussing the greatness of poets said, "About this/verses tell about them best."[16]

THE RELUCTANT BUT TALKATIVE SUBJECT

Joseph Brodsky's own statements on the relationship between life and biography emerge from this tradition. For Brodsky, as for many Russian poets, from the beginning of his career, Pushkin was the role model whose literary status and life fashioning he most tried to emulate.[17] Brodsky's contemporary, the semiotics scholar Yuri Lotman, rejected the idea of Pushkin as a victim of the state in his 1981 biography of Pushkin. Instead, he introduced the poet's potential for self-fashioning, an idea Brodsky also employed. However, once he landed in the West in 1972, in the words of another major Brodsky scholar, Cynthia Haven, "Brodsky became the poster boy for Soviet persecution: a 'victim,' in other words, and therefore a cliché."[18] Brodsky fought this characterization, and Haven notes that Akhmatova taught him something else—how to craft his own image: "She had taught him how to position himself; she was an expert in such self-fashioning. . . . Brodsky told one friend that he would make exile his personal myth and so he did."[19] Another close friend and fellow poet Tomas Venclova confirmed the statement, adding "He succeeded in the highest degree."[20] Ellendea Proffer, who with her husband Carl at Ardis Press became the main publisher of Brodsky's Russian verse as well as setting him up as poet in residence at the University of Michigan after his departure from the Soviet Union, later commented that, "Joseph imagined that it would be possible to control what was written about him."[21] So while Brodsky professed that a poet's real biography lies only in his verses, during his lifetime he also gave numerous interviews and wrote autobiographical essays, largely in English, which were instrumental in attracting an audience beyond that for his poetry itself. Others have noted that he regularly used poets' biographies in teaching about their poems. Yet he repeatedly asserted his views on poets' biographies:

> A poet is not a man of action. His existence, his qualities are not defined by his actions, but by what he makes. He is a maker. The crucial thing for the maker is the material. You may lead whatever life you like . . . whatever it is. It doesn't really matter. You can do something totally unrelated to this other activity. And for that reason, we have these biographies of poets, which is a totally ridiculous thing . . . The poet's métier is words, making words, language. So if you are of a mind to write a biography of a poet, you have to write a biography of his verses.[22]

Biographical materials about Brodsky were accumulated throughout his lifetime, including interviews, transcripts of readings and speeches, visual records, featuring numerous photographs, videos, films, and even an interview on national television in 1981 with Morley Safer on *60 Minutes*. A first book of collected Brodsky interviews with Solomon Volkov was published in 1998.[23] In 2002 Haven published a wide range of collected interviews and recordings from the poet's readings. The first of these interviews are notes from a conversation with an American student in Leningrad in 1970 that were later found after Brodsky's death by her Russian history professor at Mount Holyoke, Peter Viereck, who was also a poet admired by Brodsky. The book ends with a question-and-answer session for students at Southwest Texas State University in November 1995, about ten weeks before the poet's death. What is particularly helpful to scholars about Haven's format is that she publishes the introductory comments for these appearances as well, thus documenting the context of the interview, alongside Brodsky's own comments, which sometimes are quite at odds with the introduction. For example, Viereck says in his introduction to the first piece, that Brodsky's heart condition "was caused by his gulag labors," a statement which Haven corrects saying, "Joseph Brodsky was never in a labor camp, or gulag, although he served twenty months of a five-year sentence for hard labor in the Archangelsk region."[24] While Brodsky spoke repeatedly of the positive side of his experience of exile in Archangelsk, the image created for the public more resembled that of a figure from Solzhenitsyn's *One Day in the Life of Ivan Denisovich*. In the *60 Minutes* program, entitled "Exiled," Morley Safer calls the "theme" of Brodsky's poetry "the Soviet poet as Soviet victim."[25] Brodsky's refutation of such a characterization appears more than once in commencement addresses: "Above all, try to avoid telling stories about the unjust treatment you received at their hands; avoid it no matter how receptive your audience may be. Tales of this sort extend the existence of your antagonists."[26] In an interview from 1975, Brodsky talks about going back to Russia if it changes ("I think I will be back to those streets and people") which is repeated in an interview of 1978. In 1991 he answers the question of his possible return to Russia by an aphorism derived from Heraclitus, "You can't step twice into the same little river."[27] Later in a 1995 interview when asked if his line "Home! Where you won't be back ever" is his own view, he says that more or less, it is.[28] Yet Polukhina states, "In the summer of 1995, Brodsky wrote a letter to A. Sobchak [then mayor of St. Petersburg] expressing his regrets at not being able to go to St. Petersburg, despite the fact that he had already accepted the invitation."[29] The result is that Brodsky's biographers have to sort through an abundance of such inconsistent or contradictory material from the subject himself.

THE RELUCTANT BUT OBSESSIVE BIOGRAPHER

Despite his statement soon after Brodsky's death on not intending to become Brodsky's biographer, Loseff in many ways seemed the ideal choice of author for the *ZhZL* biography.[30] Émigré Russians had periodically appeared as authors in the series history, often because of their personal relationship with the subject.[31] In her history of *ZhZL*, former editor Galina Pomerantseva summarized the reasons for selecting this type of biographer, noting that the classics of biography, such as Boswell's *Life of Samuel Johnson*, are written by people who knew their authors personally. The idea persists that the best biographer is a contemporary and that personal acquaintance with the subject is an indispensable condition for the creation of a masterpiece. She notes that in Russian biography this idea was supported by Annenkov's biography of

Pushkin and Aksakov's biography of Tiutchev. She also takes from Harold Nicolson his notion that biographers who have personal knowledge of the subject do not have to search for a conception, their views are already fixed, and they can portray the hero's time as well as physical details. Successful biographies by contemporaries convey both the atmosphere of the time and the character of the hero.[32] But Loseff was much more than a fellow Russian émigré. A native of Leningrad, he traveled in many of the same circles as Brodsky and states that while he was working at the Leningrad children's journal *Campfire (Koster)*, he was responsible for Brodsky's first publication in the Soviet Union.[33] Like Brodsky, as a Russian Jew he was allowed to emigrate in 1976. He went to Ann Arbor, Michigan, where he also worked with Carl and Ellendea Proffer at Ardis Press. He, his wife and children actually lived with Brodsky during their first weeks in Michigan. After completing a PhD at the University of Michigan he went on to a successful career as both a writer and academic; at the time of his death in 2009 he was the chairman of the Russian Department at Dartmouth College. During his life in the United States, in addition to books and articles on Russian themes, Loseff wrote twelve collections of poetry, some of which have been translated by the British scholar Gerald Stanton Smith, and others. He has been increasingly recognized as a major poet in his homeland.[34] The longtime director of Molodaya gvardya, Valentin Yurkin. in discussing Loseff's book for the *ZhZL* series, calls him one of the most interesting poets of the emigration.[35] The incredible parallels of the biographer's and subject's lives beautifully facilitated Russian readers' interest in the biography since much less was known about Brodsky's life in the United States. Loseff was one of the few people who could explain the choices Brodsky made in emigration based on living through many of the same experiences and the larger task of having to remake his identity based on a very different set of cultural norms.

But Loseff's most striking qualification as Brodsky's biographer came from his singular knowledge of Brodsky's poetry itself. While in the Soviet Union, Brodsky did little to organize his early work into collections. The earliest major attempt to do so was the compilation of a typed five-volume samizdat collection from 1971 to 1974 by Vladimir Maramzin, with the participation of Efim Etkind and Mikhail Heifitz. Maramzin was arrested in 1974 and sentenced to five years in prison but was allowed to emigrate in 1975. Before his own emigration, Loseff also worked on the Maramzin collection.[36] He brought this knowledge to his work at Ardis where he, along with Alexander Sumarkin, edited Ardis' books of Brodsky's Russian verse.[37] The Maramzin collection, revised by Maramzin and Loseff in emigration with Brodsky's participation, became the basic source for all subsequent Brodsky collections. Another major collected edition, *Works (Sochineniia)*, was started in Russia after the fall of the Soviet Union with Brodsky's approval. Its first volume was published in 1992, under the editorship of G. Komarov. By the time the third and fourth volumes of this edition came out, it was clear that there were notable mistakes or omissions, and Yakov Gordin took over the editorship, reworking and continuing this edition with the assistance of Komarov. Earlier Gordin had been selected by Brodsky's father to be the caretaker of the poet's remaining personal effects in Leningrad, and he eventually took on the role of de facto Brodsky executor in Russia, including the completion of the *Works* edition. As it had been started on a subscription basis, the edition needed to be completed, and eventually produced seven volumes. The many letters between Loseff and Gordin (joined also by Polukhina) in the years immediately after the poet's death attest to their constant collaboration and meticulous attention to preserving Brodsky's written legacy. During Brodsky's lifetime there had been several other collected editions of his works, some incomplete or unauthorized.[38] Shortly after Brodsky's death in 1996, the poet Alexander Kushner, in his capacity as editor in chief of the *New Library of the Poet* series, considered the most prestigious editions of Russian poetry, turned to Loseff to edit a two-volume Brodsky edition. It included a biographical introduction entitled "The Shield of Perseus. A Literary Biography of Joseph Brodsky" (*Schit Perseia. Literaturnaia biographiia Iosifa Brodskogo*) and an extensive commentary to the poems.[39] Loseff later explained that he took on the *ZhZL* biography as a result of the close readings of Brodsky's work that he undertook for this project. The *New Library of the Poet* edition finally appeared only in 2012 after several years' delay due to negotiations with the Brodsky estate over changes that Loseff had not managed to complete before his death in 2009.[40]

But these were not Loseff's only writings about Brodsky. In 1998 he published *Epilogue* (*Posleslovie*), the first section of which contained poems connected with his memory of Brodsky.[41] Barry Scherr, in an introduction to a bilingual selection of Loseff's work, says of his poems about Brodsky: "for many years he consciously avoided allowing any Brodskyan elements into his own writing. Then the floodgates opened after Brodsky's death in 1996, when he wrote an entire cycle of poems lined to the memory of his close friend."[42] In accepting the offer to write for *ZhZL*, Loseff did so adhering to the guidelines laid down by Brodsky, the Brodsky estate, and the traditionally conservative Russian norms for writing about poets. In the Russian preface to his biography, Loseff explains his decision to write it:

> Perhaps I shouldn't have written this book. For over thirty years its hero was my close friend, and the absence of distance doesn't enable a sober approach. . . . It was interesting for me in the course of several years to write commentaries to his poems. When I was finished with the commentaries, it seemed, that to

accompany them with a connected text, outlining the background of the life in his poems, was not only interesting but also essential (12).[43]

LOSEFF'S *ZhZL* BIOGRAPHY OF BRODSKY

Loseff begins with the most conventional of biographical openings, giving the date and place of birth of his hero. He then goes on to add that in the Orthodox calendar this day celebrates Sts. Cyril and Methodius, but that being born into an assimilated Jewish family his hero would only later connect his birth with that of the birth of the Cyrillic alphabet (13/1). The notion of a "philological biography" is thus inscribed in the biographer's first sentences. His opening paragraph consists of three sentences, with three inserted poetic quotations. This alternation between factual data, a description of an event, and the relationship of the poet to language itself is a miniature preview of the narrative technique that Loseff employs on a larger scale thereafter in alternating throughout his narrative between the events and the stages in the formation of Brodsky's poetics. Loseff notes that if we knew nothing of Brodsky's poetry but only his sayings about poetry, we would have a false impression of what kind of poetry he wrote. One clarification he makes early on about Brodsky is that he is often self-contradictory especially in his use of his well-known aphoristic statements, a phenomenon that Loseff ultimately traces to Brodsky's hatred of fixed systems. He is especially emphatic about his subtitle—that this not a biography but "an experiment in literary biography" and notes "Brodsky was categorically opposed to turning his own life, or indeed any human life into narrative, along the lines of a nineteenth century novel. . . . Life is too unpredictable and absurd, to be able to turn it into narrative. . . . Therefore, Brodsky always insisted that he be judged not by his biography but his works" (11).[44]

The book's ten chapters follow chronologically in a traditional manner from birth and background, to location, family, education, early vocations, friends, influences, literary tastes, early poetic role models, and then Brodsky's own early verse. Of the ten chapters, the first five cover Brodsky's life and development in the Soviet Union, followed by a sixth explicating several of the poet's most famous and famously difficult works. The concluding section of the seventh chapter, "The World Through the Eyes of Brodsky," sums up the poet's mature philosophical views, grounded in existentialism, which Loseff concludes remained essentially the same for the rest of his life (172–73/163). The book's last three chapters are devoted to Brodsky's life in the United States, but cover few events as such, the exceptions being his Nobel Prize in Literature award in 1987 and a detailed account of the recurring heart problems that led to his early death. The paucity of dates in the chapters can be explained by the inclusion in the appendix of a typical feature of most *ZhZL* biographies: a chronology of Brodsky's life and works, compiled by Valentina Polukhina with Loseff's participation. It is unusual in its length—101 pages—and for the inclusion of writing and publication dates (sometimes generalized) for each of Brodsky's works. The result is that the narrative flows quite smoothly, organized by themes. Loseff's discussion of Brodsky's private life is confined to published sources or his personal witnessing and he avoids writing about the poet's many relationships except where they were already common knowledge. He does note the change in Brodsky's attitude from his earlier insistence that his poems were self-sufficient and not in need of critics' explanations to his acknowledgment at the end of his life that commentaries were necessary "for young readers." The need to accurately record the historical background of the events of Brodsky's life is a prime mover for Loseff's work, as he notes, "Poems are created in history, and many historical realia, existing openly or hidden in the text with time inescapably begin to need explanations" (11). Loseff's main narrative technique is to support his interpretation of the events of the poet's life with lines from Brodsky's verses. He is incredibly self-effacing given how long and continual their friendship was. There are only a handful of times when he allows himself to become a character in the text, although he was such a major figure in Brodsky's life, serving as his editor from Leningrad days to his last years as well as one of the leading scholars of his work.[45] In the following passage, Loseff's narration seamlessly flows from direct quotations by his hero, into a mimicking of the poet's own ironic tone:

> Over the stove stood a black plaster bust of Lenin, which in later, less dangerous times gave way to a marble bust "of some woman in a flouncy bonnet, the kind [of bust] they used to sell in antique stores," and over his bed hung a portrait of Stalin, apparently meant as a hint to the casual visitor that the boy had been named for that particular Iosif (19/8).

In the few instances where Loseff seeks to distance his own views from Brodsky's (such as their differing views on formalism as a literary theory or their views on Ukrainian independence from Russia), Loseff generally only expands on his own views in the footnotes.

What are the large biographical issues Loseff tackles? First, Brodsky's Jewishness and question of whether he was a believer. He cites Brodsky's self-identification: "I am a Jew, a Russian poet and an American citizen" (21). He contextualizes the problem by providing background on the period of heightened anti-Semitism in the Soviet Union of Brodsky's formative years and the impact it had on his family. While he is careful to say that no one can really know another's innermost beliefs at a given moment in their life, he describes Brodsky as an existentialist agnostic who valued Christian notions of love and forgiveness without accepting any belief system. While praising Loseff's biography as one of the best in the recent series, "excellent, exact and many-sided," Valentin Yurkin also somewhat surprisingly remarks, "the author is a researcher, and it is impossible not to notice his objectivity, even a certain coldness, with which he looks at the life and works of his hero."[46] Yurkin here refers to Loseff's inclusion of an early and little-known episode in Brodsky's life in which he agreed to participate with two friends, Oleg Shakhmatov and Alexander Umansky, in the hijacking of a plane in Samarkand in order to fly out of the Soviet Union. He gives two versions of the episode: one where they had agreed to toss the pilot off the plane and simply failed because the flight was changed, and another, told by Brodsky, that they had abandoned their plan because he had qualms about harming an innocent pilot (57–59/45–48).

The most detailed account of events in the biography is a revisiting of Brodsky's trial and subsequent exile, first to Norenskaia in the Arkhangelsk region, and his eventual exile to the West in 1972. The story of the trial has been told in many other accounts starting with the smuggled courtroom transcripts taken by Frida Vigdorova. By the time of Loseff's biography, it had already become a canonical story (even included in a major second-year Russian-language textbook for English-speaking students),[47] a twentieth-century version of Socrates' trial, with the presiding judge, Savelyeva, long having taken on the role of stereotypical Soviet bureaucrat and archvillain. Loseff refines the clichés and shifts the focus onto the person who actually was responsible for Brodsky's arrest and persecution, one Yakov Lerner, and Lerner's background and subsequent biography. Loseff's is the first account to integrate the personal emotional shock of what was happening in Brodsky's life—the affair that his common-law wife, Marina Basmanova, was having with one of Brodsky's closest friends, Dmitry Bobyshev at the same time as his arrest—with the larger context of the ideological demands and political mechanisms that led to his arrest. He includes such details as the origin of the "druzhina" (a kind of people's auxiliary police), one of which Lerner headed, and ultimately locates the source of the event in the careerism that motivated officials' decisions, from local police to party officials to writers' union bureaucrats, at every phase of the process—a trajectory of the banality of evil. In describing the illegitimate trial practices and in this extraordinary case, the eventual review of the trial and lessening of Brodsky's sentence as a result of a unified protest against it, Loseff gives a detailed description of how trials in the "bureaucratic Leviathan state" which was the Soviet Union could be successfully exposed. He writes, "The decisive conduct of the three witnesses for the defense (the poets V. G. Admoni and Natalya Grudinina and the scholar Efim Etkind), the city's intelligentsia's passionately aroused concern for the proceedings, and the solidarity with the accused were unexpected for those who arranged the mock trial" (91–95/82–86). Loseff comments even more forcefully in a footnote: "In the history of the dissident movement of the 1960–1970s the Brodsky case was the first big battle to be fought and won" (299/277).

Loseff sees Brodsky's subsequent experience of exile in Norenskaia as the most significant event in his formation as a poet because it was Brodsky's first opportunity to seriously study the English poets to whom he was attracted. Loseff credits his "epiphanic" experience in reading Auden's poem "On the death of T. S. Eliot" as the most important moment in Brodsky's intellectual formation. In concluding remarks about the Soviet period of Brodsky's life, Loseff asserts that his worldview never essentially changed after his internal exile: he simply became a more complete and nuanced poet until his death. On his exile to the West in 1972, Loseff repeats verbatim Brodsky's account of the implied threats of the authorities if he did not accept their invitation and calls it part of a plan to purge the country of dissidents (147–48/137). Newer accounts, such as Ellendea Proffer's memoirs, put that explanation in a different light, saying that the proposal came at a time when Brodsky really wanted to leave, if necessary by marriage (fictitious or real) to a foreigner.[48]

In turning to Brodsky's life in the United States and Europe, Loseff's historical and social contextualization of its course serves to explain to the Russian reader why Brodsky lived as he did and is clearly drawn on Loseff's analysis of his own experience:

> All new Americans experience "culture shock" as they try to adapt to a society built on principles entirely different from those on which they themselves were reared. The basic concepts of American civilization were dizzyingly different from the Russian concepts. Success and failure, wealth and poverty, people and government and even such concrete notions as a house, a town, a car, a dinner, visiting friends meant something different (183/173).

Loseff notes that Brodsky's traumatic Russian experiences and his love of American movies actually prepared him better than most, and what attracted him to American culture were its notions of individual responsibility and personal initiative which resulted in a dual love of American poetry and law. This section is marked by the arrival of "the author of these lines" in the text. He concludes this section with Brodsky's observation, "So some of us, coming here, had the sense that we were coming home: we seemed more American than the Americans" (185/174). The book's last three chapters are devoted to Brodsky's life in the United States, mainly in very generalized descriptions of his teaching, lectures and publishing. They are filled with remarkable insights into discussions of whether a writer can truly be bilingual, the basic differences between the Russian and English languages and the problems thereby created for translators, and very detailed information on the lack of prosodic equivalents in things like the association of certain meters with subject matter and tone in the two poetic traditions. The depictions of Brodsky's friends in the émigré community and his new American environment lack the precision of earlier descriptions of his relationships with friends in Russia. There are short accounts of squabbles within the émigré community. The one extended discussion of this milieu is on the relations between Brodsky and Solzhenitsyn and their changing opinions of each other. Loseff concludes, "Their differences had nothing to do with their international status or with émigré squabbles; it had everything to do with Russian culture, with the old quarrel between Slavophiles and Westernizers." However, Loseff notes, "Brodsky, 'the Westernizer,' was just as eager as Solzhenitsyn, 'the Slavophile,' to leap to the defense of Russia and Russians, especially when the latter were accused of being aggressors by nature, or slaves by nature, or some sadomasochistic combination of both" (225/208). He gives a brief account of Brodsky's poem "On the Independence of Ukraine," written in 1992, but only read once at Queens College in New York in February 1994, noting its implementation of harsh language, including the use of criminal jargon to describe the Ukraine breakaway. Loseff notes that it was the only poem that Brodsky decided not to publish because of its political implications—Brodsky thought it a good poem. But he concludes, "We remember, that Brodsky felt Ukraine, and more precisely Galicia, to be his ancestral home" (265).[49]

Loseff's survey of the poetry of Brodsky's final years includes an extensive account of the mostly negative reactions to the poet's self-translations and original poems in English. He clearly agrees that, unlike prose, poetry can only be written in one's native language, and seconds Isaiah Berlin's statement, "How could anyone who had not read him in Russian understand him by his English poems?" (245/225). While he returns to questions of poetics in his final chapter, none of the poetry in English is explicated. The events of the last five years of Brodsky's life including his marriage to Maria Sozzani in 1990 and the birth of his daughter Anna in 1993 are compressed into a short paragraph, while the closing pages of the biography discuss at length Brodsky's illness and the theme of illness and death in his late works. The biography closes with a brief description of Brodsky's death at home and the decision to bury him in Venice. In a letter to Brodsky's wife of April 20, 2006, as he is preparing for the *ZhZL* biography to be published later that year, Loseff asks her for the name of the book that was open on Brodsky's desk the evening he died.[50] The simplicity of the closing pages is particularly moving.

While creating his "philological biography," Loseff was at various times writing his personal memoirs of the poet, entitled *Meandr*. They remained unfinished at the time of Loseff's death in 2009. But in 2007, his friend the poet Sergei Gandlevsky visited him and asked for a copy, which he later annotated for a book publication.[51] The memoirs consist of short passages, many of which are on the same topics as in the biography, and are at times are identical to it, but in other places Loseff records personal details of experiences with Brodsky in a more intimate and revealing fashion. He describes Brodsky's physical appearance and habits, such as his scratching like a cat on his friend's jacket and making cat sounds. In their early years in emigration, they were both fond of hunting for secondhand clothes in thrift shops. At one point, Loseff remembers wearing a jacket given to him by Brodsky, who had bought it secondhand and recalls that he always thought Brodsky was taller and broader than himself, that he was "bigger" than him. The pieces are random with few precise time markers, but full of the kind of remembrances of relationships and personal feelings that are lacking in the biography itself. They include his dreams of Brodsky: one from 1996, a few months after the poet's death, and others in 2001, 2002, and 2004, all connected with attempts to understand poems. On the whole these fragments present a vivid and intimate contrast to the tone of the biography.

CRITICAL REACTIONS TO LOSEFF'S BIOGRAPHY

Loseff's biography was widely reviewed in both the United States and in Russia, first when the *ZhZL* original was published, and again when the English translation appeared.[52] Andrei Ranchin describes the concept of a "philological biography": "The biographer/scholar trances how the texts refract the events of the poet's life, the moods he experienced and the ideas that fascinated him," seeing Loseff's detailed linguistic analyses as an integral part of his narrative.[53] But he does argue with two of Loseff's analyses of poems, adding that "There is language too complex for the 'lay' reader who is this series' target audience" (45). On the other hand, he commends the restraint of his hero's depiction, "Loseff transforms Brodsky neither into an epic hero boldly challenging a bloodthirsty Soviet minotaur nor into the target of scandalous chitchat. Loseff's text is absolutely free of any drooling over intimate details, gossip or rumors." He criticizes Loseff instead for disregarding "Brodsky's mythopoetic strategy" (41). E. Lutsenko criticizes Ranchin in turn, noting that "Loseff is here working at the intersection of two genres, the traditional life story and the literary biography" and focuses on the author's other merits: "Suddenly breaking through this logically verified and punctilious text is an intimately personal *impression* that supplies the basis for the image of the poet."⁵⁴ British critic Belinda Cooke agrees with the latter point, even though she calls the biography "an unashamedly hagiographic portrayal of Brodsky."⁵⁵ Émigré journalist Lilia Pann advances a different argument for the book's success—Loseff's focus on existentialism as the key philosophical underpinning of Brodsky's life and writings:

> Brodsky accomplishes the task of existentialism—to transform *existence into essence*—"to be that by which language lives." Loseff's "experiment in literary biography" succeeds because to Brodsky, literature was a field on which the battle for his own existence was waged. Loseff has seen for himself that "there is no fundamental distinction between Brodsky in life and Brodsky in poetry."⁵⁶

Pann notes Solomon Volkov, whom she calls "the patriarch of Russian studies," has said Loseff's book is a "biography that will remain definitive for the next twenty years or so."⁵⁷ On the other hand, some Brodsky specialists already yearned for more. As Haven writes,

> Yet *Joseph Brodsky: A Literary Life* is simultaneously enlightening, perplexing, and exasperating. The knowledgeable reader is left feeling rewarded and cheated at once, as if invited to a sumptuous banquet and offered only canapés. The protean figure remains beyond the range of these pages. The door remains at once half open and half closed to us.⁵⁸

Evidently *ZhZL* editors felt there could be a new approach even before the twenty years expired.

VLADIMIR BONDARENKO: THE BIOGRAPHER AS PILGRIM

A new biography of Brodsky in the *ZhZL* small series by Vladimir Bondarenko, *Joseph Brodsky: Russian Poet* (*Iosif Brodskii: Russkii Poet*) was timed to coincide with the date of what would have been Brodsky's seventy-fifth birthday in May 2015.⁵⁹ The author is a conservative literary critic and journalist who is a prolific writer and has served as an editor for several right-wing publications, including the newspapers *Tomorrow (Zavtra)* and *Day of Literature (Den' literatury)*. In determining the canon, he views Russian literary history through the recurring presence of imperial themes as demonstrated in his first book for Molodaya gvardiya press, *Last Poets of the Empire: Essays on Literary Fates* (*Poslednie poety imperii: ocherki literaturnykh sudeb*, 2005). Bondarenko later authored a biography of Mikhail Lermontov (2012) and after the Brodsky biography one on Igor Severyanin (2018), both also in the *ZhZL* small series.⁶⁰ Educated in Leningrad, he says he was introduced to Brodsky by Evgeny Rein in 1967. He describes himself at that time as being an avant-garde poet but when he gave Brodsky his poems, the poet tore into them so badly that he gave up writing poetry and instead turned to his true vocation as a journalist and literary critic.[61] While not having Loseff's close personal relationship with Brodsky, Bondarenko mentions in an interview with journalist Sergei Vinogradov that he had several meetings with Brodsky in his family's apartment in the Muruzi House and that Brodsky gave him a copy of his first collection of poems published in the United States (242). He continued to correspond with the poet and later met and spoke with Brodsky by phone in the United States (243). In the same interview Bondarenko states that he has been collecting and writing articles on the poet for more than thirty years.[62] The biography includes a picture of the author at Brodsky's grave site, where he tells us he recited Brodsky's *Christmas Poems* on a December visit to Venice (413).

Bondarenko adopts one of the most traditional strategies of a biographer, one that first appeared in late eighteenth- and early nineteenth-century European biographical practice, that of the pilgrim who goes to the significant places in his subject's life to reexperience the inspiration those places provided to his subject and to use them as a guide to his readings of the works. During his travels he stays in the same hotels where Brodsky stayed, even sleeping in the peasant hut of Brodsky's Norenskaia exile, and enjoys a month in Sweden, where he experiences an affinity to Brodsky's love of the north (since his own family had northern roots) and enjoys the poet's favorite Swedish vodka. These research trips become part of the narrative fabric. In contrast to Loseff's self-effacement, Bondarenko continually inserts himself and his personal reactions to these physical and intellectual quests. He seems to assume that the reader already knows the main events of Brodsky's life so he can jump forward and backwards in time. The reader follows not a chronology of Brodsky's life as much as Bondarenko's discovery of "his" Brodsky. As the interviewer notes regarding the biographer's sources, "He believes that talking to people in the street is a no less effective scientific method than working in the archive."[63] At times his tone is self-congratulatory. He interviews a childhood playmate of the poet, Mirsaid Saparov who relates his envy of Brodsky's long pants, sewn on his mother's sewing machine, to which Bondarenko adds, "Such details you can't invent" (44). At the end of his book Bondarenko lists the places he found to be the most significant in Brodsky's life: Vnukovo, Petersburg, Cherepovets, Konosha, Gotland, Venice (433); although he mentions visiting Brodsky's Morton Street apartment in New York, neither that, nor Ann Arbor, nor South Hadley, nor Washington is deemed worthy of mention in the book since he ultimately stresses Brodsky's alienation from his American life.[64] Bondarenko dismisses all of Brodsky's post-Nobel interviews as being false because of his necessity to adapt to

American "political correctness," although he does cite them occasionally, in particular Brodsky's conversations with Solomon Volkov. Since *ZhZL* biographies do not require scholarly documentation, the author's list of sources often omits any information confirming a number of tantalizing assertions in the text. He borrows long passages from others, including Loseff, and cites verbatim conversations of years past. Bondarenko often describes some aspect of Brodsky's life through ruminations and conjectures, introducing his ideas as rhetorical questions and then labeling his deductions as factual. He repeats his main conclusions at numerous places in the text. Bondarenko's overall compositional strategy seems to be to align Brodsky's religious and political views with his own.

THE IDEOLOGICAL BIOGRAPHY

As always with *ZhZL*, the subtitle *Russian Poet* is telling. Bondarenko reworks Brodsky's self-description as "A Jew, a Russian poet, and an American citizen."[65] While Bondarenko's main focus is on Brodsky's life as a poet, he also extensively discusses his Jewishness, but dismisses the importance of his life in the United States and the works he created there, especially the poems written in English, which he calls those of "a miserable poet writing dull and superfluous poems," although he acknowledges the greatness of his English-language essays.[66] His only comment regarding Brodsky's American citizenship is that he was "law-abiding."[67] While Loseff started his biography with the notion that Brodsky was a genius whose complex personality can best be apprehended though his poetry, Bondarenko's opening thesis is that Brodsky was always about creating a grand narrative. He notes that the poet's first reaction to life in the West, recorded in an interview in Vienna in 1972, was to be stunned by the centrality of "shopping." Bondarenko states: "Not for a moment, did he live a consumer's life himself. Brodsky was compelled all his life to be drawn to the 'grandeur of the conception,' to oppose himself to Western consumer civilization" (10). This famous phrase, used by Pushkin to describe Dante's oeuvre, is applied to Brodsky's. He lives "at a higher note" in his poetry (11). There he can reject the worldly and remember his predestination (80). Bondarenko concludes: "The steam engine of poetic greatness dragged Joseph Brodsky from flat jokes and versified jibes to genuine religiosity (*religiosnost'*), support of the state *(gosudarstvennost')* and love of empire (*imperkost'*)" (14). These plus the additional concepts of *narodnost'* (a love of the people), *russkost'* (innate Russianness), and even *sovetkost'* (Sovietness) are the foundations of Bondarenko's understanding of Brodsky's character.

In the biography's most controversial section, Bondarenko asserts that Brodsky was secretly a Russian Orthodox Christian, baptized during World War II in Cherepovets by his nurse Grunya. While this was a common practice during the war in an attempt to protect Jewish children from the Nazis, Bondarenko claims to be the first to track down evidence. He goes to the village seeking interviews with wartime survivors who knew the family, and purports to have found the church where the ceremony was performed, although no documents survived. He frames his discovery with what he sees as telling coincidences: on the church doorstop is a cat (Brodsky loved cats), in the church as he enters a child is being baptized: "She is the same age Brodsky was when he was brought here."[68] As further proof of the poet's faith, he mentions that Brodsky was photographed wearing a cross, but those photographs are not included (14). The nature of Brodsky's beliefs is a recurrent and controversial question that arises in almost every interview with the poet's close acquaintances. In his own biography, Loseff circumvents the question by saying it would be inappropriate for him to speculate but goes on to quote lines from various poems and prose texts that touch on the question, reaching the conclusion: "The God that Brodsky speaks of has nothing to do with organized religion" (157). Ultimately Bondarenko relies on the "genuine religiosity" of Brodsky's Nativity poems (14). Father Mikhail Ardov, an Orthodox priest and close friend of Brodsky's comments, "I think those poems are just a reflection of the holiday itself. The spirit of the festival got into his blood. It's the Christmas trees and all that—January and the pine needles. It's got nothing to do with God made flesh."[69] Among the poet's other close friends, opinion on Brodsky's religiosity is sharply divided. Alexander Kushner recalls the poet's skeptical attitude toward religion and his indignation at Anatoly Naiman, a converted Jew, when he told Brodsky he should be baptized.[70] Evgeny Rein says that Brodsky "walked that razor's edge between theism and atheism."[71] Some friends and colleagues agree with the notion that Brodsky was a Christian poet, though often with reservations. Tomas Venclova writes, "Some of his poems express the Christian view of the world with a rare profundity and perspicacity" and as such "they justify calling him a Christian poet." But he adds the Brodsky "had an allergic reaction to the 'hardline Russian Orthodox' and their ilk."[72] Bengt Jangfelt agrees with the phrase "Christian poet" since Brodsky's admiration for European culture was permeated by Christianity, but that Brodsky didn't like Orthodoxy since it was a "national religion."[73] Michael Scammel concurs: "He responded to Christianity aesthetically" but also adds "I think he responded to the aesthetics but he also responded to the ethics of Christianity."[74] Of course the nature of anyone's religious beliefs may change over time and ultimately be inaccessible. Of these many opinions, Bondarenko's stands alone in his absolute assertion of Brodsky as an Orthodox believer. He explains that Brodsky needed to keep silent about his faith in order to achieve success in the United States as "an elite New York intellectual" (86).

Like Loseff, Bondarenko sees the poet's experience of exile in Norenskaia, or as he prefers to emphasize, the nearby small settlement of Konosha, as the most formative one in Brodsky's life, one that Brodsky later called the happiest time of his life (245). Bondarenko even compares it to Pushkin's productive exile at Mikhailovskoe (though without the hard labor). While Loseff sees this time as a period when Brodsky's reading of John Donne and other English poets formed his aesthetics in a way that never substantially altered thereafter, Bondarenko has a very different reading: "I am more interested in the movement of the poet to the people (*k narodu*), to the people surrounding him, the sensation of merging with them" (90). He agrees with Alexander Solzhenitsyn that if Brodsky had only been allowed to serve out the full five years of his sentence, he would have become an even greater poet (180). While Loseff also saw Brodsky's internal exile as transformative, he characterizes it quite differently: "But the transformation took place thanks to his profound immersion in books and not thanks to the plough, the birch trees and the peasantry."[75]

The themes of this biography mimic Loseff's in many ways. Like Loseff, Bondarenko begins with a history of the city of Brody, that of the poet's Jewish forbears. Whereas he paraphrases Loseff as saying the poet considered all of Ukraine, including Brody, a common cultural space with Russia, he goes on to contradict Loseff by saying Brodsky connected this cultural space with Poland, and from his youth had no feelings for Ukraine. He attributes Brodsky's antipathy with a wild speculation: Brodsky almost became an actor in Ukraine, but the movie shots in which he appeared were ordered to be cut and his name was removed from the cast list: "Maybe from this time Brodsky hated Ukrainian officials? And maybe because of this he related his historical homeland not to Ukraine but to Poland?" (36). The reader is treated to a fifteen-page explication and defense of Brodsky's short poem "On the Independence of Ukraine" ("Na nezavisimost' Ukrainy"), which he considers one of Brodsky's best poems (378). The political implications of this praise soon become clear, rising to this rhetorical climax: "This private poet, autonomous from everyone, alienated both from Jews and Americans, and all other nations and religions suddenly takes on himself the highest responsibility in the name of all Russians to rebuke Ukrainians for their departure from a united imperial space, from a united Russia" (*iz edinoi Rossii*), the last phrase coinciding with the name of Putin's political party (379). While Loseff did note the poem's authenticity, he also emphasized that Brodsky feared that it would be misunderstood so never authorized its publication.[76] Bondarenko says the poem from year to year receives waves of new liberal attacks and rebukes the editors of Russian Brodsky editions for not including it, especially the definitive *New Library of the Poet* edition of Brodsky which Loseff edited. Bondarenko sees Brodsky's "On the Independence of Ukraine" as proof of the poet's gift of prophecy, a traditional role for Russian poets, by linking it to the Ukrainian revolution of 2014. Katharine Hodgson and Alexandra Smith have analyzed Bondarenko's views in detail and note that he "puts forward an uncritical idea of empire associated with the might of the Russian state, both under tsarist and Soviet rule, and the assertion of an identity that is distinct from and opposed to that of Western Europe."[77] For Bondarenko, Brodsky is a poet of the empire, even the Soviet one. He also describes what he characterizes as Brodsky's standing up for Russia in a dispute with Central European writers at the Wheatland Foundation Conference on Literature in Lisbon in 1988. Václav Havel and others accused the Russian writers present of not understanding their degree of complicity in the Soviet imperialist project. However, Irena Grudzinska-Gross has a different reading of this incident. She analyzes Brodsky's response as coming from the concept of history as the history of the state: "He reached back—to Latin, to Roman history—for him the Soviet Union was an *imperium*. For Brodsky, too, it was an imperium, though he lived in its prosaic, rotting present. From which he escaped."[78]

CRITICAL REACTIONS TO BONDARENKO'S BRODSKY

Needless to say, since its publication, the Bondarenko biography has provoked a storm of reaction, on both sides of the ideological divide. A review of Bondarenko's book on May 25, 2015, by Alexander Chalenko in the online journal *Russian Spring* (*Russkaia vesna*), is entitled "The Return of Brodsky to the Russians" ("Vozvrashchenie Brodskogo russkim"). The author concludes: "The critic Bondarenko simply put before himself the ambitious and noble goal of returning, at last, the last Russian Nobel laureate to the Russian people, shattering the liberal-Westernizer myth about him, as a rootless cosmopolitan, as a potential supporter of the Orange revolution and Maidan . . . and Molodaia gvardiia agreed to help the critic and patriot in this."[79] Egor Kholmogorov, writes that the book has come out in the context of the events in Ukraine which have led to a current questioning of Russian self-identity and concludes that Bondarenko's "attractive book . . . gives the possibility of looking at Brodsky outside of the usual liberal discourse." A short anonymous review in Fontanka.ru is more restrained, "Well, Bondarenko's point of view has a place to exist, although the conclusions about the poet's imperial consciousness, perhaps, are exaggerated."[80] Smith and Hodgson also discuss his biography in the context of his nationalist views but stress that he can only fit Brodsky into his canon by ignoring aspects of his life and career.[81]

BRODSKY'S PERSONAL LIFE AND FUTURE BRODSKY BIOGRAPHIES

There are limitations to Bondarenko's biographical methodology. The reader is convinced of his admiration for Brodsky, but the visits and interviews mask a lack of research and proofreading by misleading characterizations or simple factual errors. By ignoring the American years of Brodsky's biography, he incorrectly states that Brodsky could find no role in his life in exile (326). On the contrary, a complete biography will show that during this period he was in constant demand in literary circles and an active participant in literary organizations, especially his work as the American Poet Laureate and for the PEN American Center.[82] Bondarenko tries to assert Brodsky's alienation from his Jewish roots by stating that he never appeared in venues connected with Jewish organizations, but in fact he repeatedly appeared at the 92nd St. YMHA (Young Men's Hebrew Association) and arranged readings for friends at Workmen's Circle. He misstates the duration of researchers' lack of access to Brodsky's personal papers (done at the poet's request) in his archive as seventy-five years, rather than the actual fifty (9). Meanwhile, ignoring the request, he tries to discuss Brodsky's love life, naming a number of women including Zofia Kapuscinska, Veronica Shilts, Faith Wigzell, Masha Vorobieva, Annelisa Alleva, and myself.[83] Most of his attention is focused on Marina Basmanova and the poems dedicated to her, "New Stanzas to Augusta" (*Novye stansy k Avguste*), which he finds among the poet's best because she is the only true love of his life, a "senseless love" (*bezumnaia liubov'*) which he foresees as a future novel. The emotional tonality of a romance novel colors his depiction of Brodsky's wife, Maria Sozzani, when he writes of her decision to bury her husband in Venice, rather than St. Petersburg: "Maybe he truly told Maria his wish to be buried in Venice. And perhaps, this was only her will—to take care of the grave, located in her country, was more convenient. In addition to give the body to Petersburg—meant to give back Joseph forever to her rival Marina Basmanova" (429–30). In the closing pages on Brodsky's funeral in New York there are both factual errors and similar tasteless moments. The Cathedral of St. John the Divine in New York, where a memorial service was held forty days after the poet's death, is not a Russian Orthodox Church (411). Bondarenko also repeats a gruesome account of the poet's coffin splitting in two first when being transported to Venice and flooding at the grave that Loseff had earlier refuted.[84] In the final analysis, the necessity to make the details of Brodsky's life conform to the author's ideological preconceptions and his constant shifts in tonality totally undercut whatever new information a reader may glean. But Brodsky fans have already turned elsewhere: new biographical details complete with photos and fragmentary narratives emerge daily on the Joseph Brodsky Facebook pages, which numbers upward of 300,000 participants, as well as films and video interviews with Brodsky's contemporaries.[85]

NOTES

1. A. M. Zver'ev, *Nabokov* (Moscow: Molodaia gvardiia, 2001). Bunin was included in K. G. Paustovskii's book of sketches, *Blizkie u dalekie* (Moscow: Molodaia gvardiia, 1967) and a full biography was published thereafter, M. I. Roshchin, *Bunin* (Moscow: Molodaia gvardiia, 2000).

2. Lev Losev, *Iosif Brodskii. Opyt literaturnoi biografii* (Moscow: Molodaia gvardiia, 2006). It has been reissued five times to date. My citations are from the third edition of 2008. An English version was published as Lev Loseff, *Joseph Brodsky, A Literary Life*, trans. Jane Ann Miller (New Haven and London: Yale University Press, 2011). English translations will be taken from this publication except where noted. The other Brodsky biography in question is Vladimir Bondarenko, *Brodskii* (Moscow: Molodaia gvardiia, 2015). Other examples of this trend are: L. Saraskina, *Aleksandr Solzhenitsyn* (Moscow: Molodaia gvardiia, 2009), Valerii Popov, *Dovlatov* (Moscow: Molodaia gvardiia, 2010), and Dmitrii Petrov, *Aksenov* (Moscow: Molodaia gvardiia), 2012.

3. E. A. Solov'ev, *A.I. Gertsen: Ego zhizn' I literaturnaia deiatel'nost'* (St. Petersburg, Zhizn' zamechatel'nykh liudei, 1898).

4. Richard Freeborn, *Russian Literary Attitudes from Pushkin to Solzhenitsyn* (London: Palgrave, 1976), n.p.

5. G. S. Smith, "Going Back (Mainly on Brodsky)," *Canadian American Slavic Studies* 33, Nos. 2–4 (1999): 335.

6. V. Novikov, *Vysotskii* (Moscow: Molodaia gvardiia, 2002). This biography's first printing was 10,000 copies, twice the *ZhZL* norm, and was issued in its ninth edition in 2021. The other titles are: D.L. Bykov, *Bulat Okudzhava* (Moscow: Molodaia gvardiia, 2009); I. Vyrabov, *Andrei Voznesenskii* (Moscow: Molodaia gvardiia, 2015); Il'ia Falikov, *Evtushenko. Love story* (Moscow: Molodaia gvardiia, 2017); D.L. Bykov, *Shestidesiatniki* (Moscow: Molodaia gvardiia, 2019).

7. In the application of the idea of the myth of the poet in the *ZhZL* series, see the essays on Pushkin by Angela Brintlinger, on Blok by Jonathan Stone and on Akhmatova and Tsvetaeva by Alexandra Smith in this volume.

8. This second sentence is translated differently by others. My translation is closer to the original: "kak budto on kogo-to narochno nanial." See A. G. Naiman, *Rasskazy o Anne Akhmatovoi* (Moscow: Khudozhestvennaia literatura, 1989), 10.

9. William Wadsworth, "A Turbulent Affair with the English Language," in Valentina Polukhina, *Brodsky Through the Eyes of His Contemporaries*, Volumes I

and II (Boston: Academic Studies Press, 2008), 2:471. Valentina Polukhina, a prolific scholar of the poet, wrote one of the earliest scholarly monographs on Brodsky's writing, *Joseph Brodsky: A Poet for Our Time* (Cambridge: Cambridge University Press, 1989).

10. Polukhina, 2: 467.

11. Lev Loseff, "He Lived at Extraordinary Pace," in Polukhina, 2:90.

12. Iakov Gordin, *Rytsar i smert', ili Zhizn' kak zamysel. O sud'be Iosifa Brodskogo* (Moscow: Vremia, 2010), 6–7.

13. Letter of James Rice to Ann Kjellberg, April 25, 1996 in the Loseff Papers, folio 1, Bakhmeteff Archive, Rare Books and Manuscripts Library, Columbia University. I wish to thank Tatyana Chebotareva, the director of the Bakhmeteff Archive in the Rare Books and Manuscript Library at Columbia University, for providing me with access to several letters from the Loseff papers.

14. Letter of Lev Loseff to Ann Kjellberg, April 26, 1996. Loseff Papers, folio 1.

15. The original Pushkin citation is from a November 1825 letter written in Mikhailovskoe to P. A. Vyazemskii. This translation is from the English version of Loseff's preface but did not appear in the original Russian *ZhZL* biography. The English "Preface" differs considerably from the longer version in the Russian, possibly in an attempt to make it more appealing to an English language readership.

16. Losev, *Iosif Brodskii*, 7. This phrase does not appear in the English version.

17. Anatolii Naiman is credited as being the first to draw the parallels between Brodsky and Pushkin, followed by many other contemporaries, such as Bella Akhmadulina, who remarked "Perhaps Brodsky is the second coming of Pushkin." See Polukhina, 2:64, fn 8; 110.

18. Cynthia Haven, "The Unknown Brodsky," *The Nation,* Apr. 11/18, 2016, 42.

19. Ibid., 44. The friend was Andrei Sergeev, and the remark found in his memoirs "O Brodskom" in *Omnibus* (Moscow: *Novoe Literaturnoe obozrenie*, 1997), 448.

20. Tomas Venclova, "He Tended to Ascribe his Own Traits to Other Poets," in Polukhina, 2:187.

21. Ellendea Proffer Teasley, *Brodsky Among Us: A Memoir* (Boston: Academic Studies Press, 2017), 174. The book was actually published first in Russia as Ellendeia Proffer Tisli, *Brodskii sredi nas* (Moscow: Izdatel'stvo AST, 2015), where it was an enormous success.

22. Blair Ewing, "An Interview with Joseph Brodsky," in Cynthia Haven, ed., *Joseph Brodsky: Conversations* (Jackson, Mississippi: University Press of Mississippi, 2002), 167.

23. Solomon Volkov, *Conversations with Joseph Brodsky* (New York: The Free Press, 1998). A Russian edition was published, *Dialogi s Iosifom Brodskim* (Moscow: Eskimo, 2013) with a new introduction by Iakov Gordin entitled "Svoia versiia proshlogo," 5–13. The Brodsky estate did not approve of this book on the grounds that Volkov did not supply the original tapes on which it was based to confirm the authenticity of the conversations, but they were all done with the poet himself during his lifetime. Another longtime friend of Brodsky's, the writer and publisher Igor Efimov, has reservations about the way in which Brodsky's voice comes through in these interviews, suggesting that they may have been somewhat overedited. But

Iakov Gordin stresses their uniqueness because of the presence of the microphone and calls them invaluable for any biographer of Brodsky. See Iakov Gordin, "Versiia proshlogo," in *Rytsar' i smert', ili Zhizn' kak zamysel*, 143–50. See also Igor Efimov, "Navigators in the Ocean of Spirit," in Polukhina, 2: 116–17.

24. Haven, *Conversations*, 3–5. Haven corrects similar mistakes in footnotes in the volume.

25. Haven, *Conversations*, 101.

26. Joseph Brodsky, "Speech at the Stadium," in *On Grief and Reason* (New York: Farrar, Straus, Giroux, 1995), 146.

27. Haven, *Conversations*, 155. This is a variant of a well-known saying of Heraclitus.

28. Ibid., 47, 51, 175.

29. Polukhina, 2:402.

30. Lev Vladimirovich Losev was born Lev Lifshitz on June 15, 1937, and died May 6, 2009. He adopted a different last name because his father was a well-known author. He sometimes used the name Aleksei Losev, but generally used the spelling Loseff for his last name in English.

31. See our introductory chapter in this volume.

32. Pomerantseva, *Biografiia v potoke vremeni*, 202, 219.

33. Lev Loseff, "A New Conception of Poetry," in Polukhina, 1:142.

34. The leading writer and critic, Dmitrii Bykov, writes in a preface to an interview with Losev, "Lev Losev is one of the most famous Russian (*rossiiskikh*) poets. And, perhaps, the best of all living ones." Dmitrii Bykov, "Ia chuvstvuiu Brodskogo obvorovannym," *Ogonek* 44 (27 Oct-2 Nov. 2008): n.p.

35. Valentin Yurkin, "Piatyi laureat," in *Vremia i knigi*, 180.

36. Loseff in Polukhina, 1:141.

37. Personal communication of 7/25/2021 from Ronald Meyer, Publications Director at the Harriman Institute at Columbia, who also worked with the Proffers at Ardis.

38. For a complete account of the previous editions of Brodsky's works and how the *New Library of the Poet* edition was composed see *Sostav nastoiashchego izdaniia* in Iosif Brodskii, *Stikhotvoreniia i poemy* (Saint Petersburg: Izdatel'stvo Pushkinskogo Doma/Izdatel'stvo "Vita Nova," 2012), 419–24.

39. Losev explains his work on this volume in an article entitled "Primechaniia s primechaniiami," *Novoe literaturnoe obozrenie* 5 (2000). Accessed 3/29/2020. He notes that he took on this work joyfully because it resulted in a kind of a daily meeting with Joseph, although he worries that Brodsky may not have approved.

40. A detailed explanation can be found in Iosif Brodskii, *Stikhotvoreniia i poemy*, 419.

41. Lev Losev, *Posleslovie* (Saint Petersburg: Pushkinskii fond, 1998). For an overview of Losev's poetry see Gerald S. Smith, "Flight of the Angels: The Poetry of Lev Losev, *Slavic Review* 47, no. 1 (Spring 1988): 76–88. Comments on Loseff's poems on Brodsky can be found in Barry Scherr, "Introduction," in Lev Loseff, *As I Said— Kak ia skazal*, trans. G. S. Smith (Todmorten, UK: Arc Publications, 2012), 16–17.

42. Barry Scherr, "Introduction," 17.

43. My translation. The English preface (ix–xi) has been considerably reworked with the last paragraph of the Russian moved to the opening. However, the essential elements are retained, albeit in a different order. Hereafter, citations will list the page numbers of the *ZhZL* original first, followed by those of the English version where the two texts exactly coincide.

44. This passage is omitted in the English translation of the preface which is reworked.

45. Among Loseff's major scholarly works on Brodsky are *Poetika Brodskogo. Sbornik statei red.L.B. Loseva* (Tenafly, N.J.: Ermitazh, 1986), *Joseph Brodsky: The Art of a Poem*, ed. Lev Loseff and Valentina Polukhina (New York: Palgrave, 1999), *Brodsky's Poetics and Aesthetics*, ed. Lev Loseff and Polukhina (New York: Palgrave, 1990).

46. Valentin Yurkin, "*Piatyi laureat*," 180–82.

47. See Richard Robin, et al, *Golosa: A Basic Course in Russian*, Book 2, 3rd edition (Upper Saddle River, NJ: Pearson Prentice Hall, 2003), 229–30.

48. Proffer, 76–77.

49. My translation here is closer to the original.

50. Letter to Maria Brodsky of April 20, 2006, Loseff Papers, folio 1, Bakhmeteff Archive, Columbia University Rare Books and Manuscripts Library.

51. It is beyond the scope of this study to do a full comparison of these sketches with the finished episodes in the *ZhZL* biography. Lev Losev, *Meandr* (Moscow: Novoe Izdatel'stvo, 2010) at www.litres.ru/lev-losev/meandr/ Last accessed 5/23/2020.

52. The book was such a literary event that a selection of reviews by Russian critics was translated for *Russian Studies in Literature* [hereafter *RSL*] 46, no. 1 (Winter 2009–2010).

53. Andrei Ranchin, "A Philological Biography" in *RSL* 46, no. 1 (Winter 2009–2010): 40. Further references to this article will be given in the text.

54. E. Lutsenko, "A Valediction: Forbidding Mourning (The Biographer and His Critics)" in *RSL* 46, no. 1 (Winter 2009–2010): 22.

55. Belinda Cooke, "Review of *Joseph Brodsky: A Literary Life*," *The Russian Review* 73, no. 1 (January 2014): 125–26.

56. Lilia Pann, "A Biography of the Mind," in *RSL* 46, no. 1 (Winter 2009–2010): 35.

57. Ibid., 31.

58. https://bookhaven.stanford.edu/2011/12/quarterly-conversation-for-brodsky-poetry-was-a-ticket-out-of-this-world/ Last accessed 7/28/2021.

59. Although in the "Small Series," Bondarenko's biography is considerably longer than Loseff's. All further references to this book will be given in the text.

60. Vladimir Bondarenko, *Poslednie poety imperii: ocherki literaturnykh sudeb* (Moscow: Molodaia gvardiia, 2005); *Lermontov: Misticheskii genii* (Moscow: Molodaia gvardiia, 2012); *Severianin. Vash nezhnyi, vash edinstvennyi* (Moscow: Molodaia gvardiia, 2018).

61. Aleksandr Chalenko, "Vozvrashchenie Brodskogo russkim," on *Russkaia vesna*: https://rusvesna.su/recent_opinions/1432843354. Last accessed 1/5/2016.

62. Vladimir Bondarenko, "Kreshchenie Iosifa Brodskogo," interviewed by Sergei Vinogradov, *Zhurnal 'Russkii mir'* at https://m.rusmir.media/2014/08/01/kreshenie. Accessed 1/5/2016.

63. Bondarenko, interview.

64. Vnukovo is the airport from which Brodsky emigrated, Petersburg his hometown, Cherepovets is where he spent World War II with his mother during the siege of Leningrad, Konosha is a village where Brodsky lived at times during his exile in the Far North, Gotland is the northern part of Scandinavia, visited by Brodsky and Bondarenko in their mutual love of northern lands, Ann Arbor and South Hadley are the locations of the University of Michigan and Mount Holyoke College, two of the places Brodsky taught, and Washington, D.C., was the site of his residency as the Librarian of Congress.

65. Cited by Loseff, 21.

66. Bondarenko, interview.

67. For a different picture of Brodsky's relations with American law, see the memoirs of his friend Ludmila Shtern, *Osia, Iosif, Joseph* (Moscow: Izdatel'stvo Nezavisimaia Gazeta, 2001), 225.

68. Bondarenko, interview.

69. Mikhail Ardov, "Leaving this Place is Impossible. . ." in Polukhina, 2:159.

70. Personal communication from Aleksandr Kushner, 9/6/2021.

71. Evgenii Rein, "The Introduction of the Prosaic into Poetry," in Polukhina, 1:76.

72. Tomas Venclova, "Development of Semantic Poetics," in Polukhina, 1: 183–84.

73. Bengt Jangfelt, "The Terrible Fate of a Russian Poet," in Polukhina, 2:237.

74. Michael Scammell, "He Responded to Christianity Aesthetically," in Polukhina, 2:570. Polukhina also comments on this question in her "Introduction," 2: xxii–xxiii.

75. Lev Loseff, "A New Conception of Poetry," in Polukhina 2:95.

76. Loseff, *Brodsky,* 242–44.

77. Katharine Hodgson and Alexandra Smith, *Poetic Canons, Cultural Memory and Russian National Identity after 1991* (Oxford, Bern, et al.: Peter Lang, 2020), 54. In their further discussion of Bondarenko's biography they thoroughly analyze motifs of empire in Brodsky's work, with close readings of Bondarenko's favorite Brodsky poems, including "On the Death of Zhukov" and "On the Independence of Ukraine," 75–87.

78. Irena Grudzinska-Gross, *Czesław Miłosz and Joseph Brodsky: Fellowship of Poets* (New Haven and London: Yale University Press, 2009), 215.

79. This site provided a selection of positive reviews of the book at the time: http://www.rusvesna.su Last accessed 5/1/2016.

80. Ibid.

81. Hodgson and Smith, 81.

82. For a detailed example of his work there see my article, "Joseph Brodsky as Cultural Mediator between the Emigre Community and the Homeland," *Russian Emigration at the Crossroads of the XX–XXI Centuries. Proceedings of the International Conference Dedicated to the 70th Anniversary of the New Review/Novyi Zhurnal* (New York: The New Review Publishing, 2012), 66–73.

83. Most of these women have written about their relationships with Brodsky, except the late Masha Vorobieva, who was a neighbor at 44 Morton St and often described as a kind of sister to Brodsky. With regard to myself, this is absolute nonsense (see Bondarenko 168, 392). I knew Brodsky and worked with him on perhaps a dozen occasions, mainly in my role as Aleksandr Kushner's translator. In that capacity I attended Brodsky's funeral. I wrote to Andrei Petrov, the head editor of *ZhZL* on Feb 28, 2016 and received a reply several hours later from Bondarenko in which he apologized and said he was guilty for taking my name from an unnamed source. He promised to remove it in subsequent editions, but I have no evidence this was done. Curiously, Bondarenko seems not to know of Brodsky's other daughter, Anastasia, by another Petersburg lover, the ballerina Marianna Kuznetsova.

84. Loseff was so offended by this account, attributed to Ilya Kutik, that he wrote a letter to a newspaper to deny it. Loseff, "He Lived . . ." in Polukhina, 2:99.

85. The main page on Facebook is maintained by Victoria Chulkova, but I have occasionally found others. For example, see https://www.facebook.com./JosephBrodsky /posts/August 1, 2021. Since the events commemorating the poet's 80th birthday in 2020, such interviews regularly appear on YouTube: *Razgovory o Brodskom* from the Anna Akhmatova Museum and Nataliia Shariymova's series, *N'iu Iork plius Brodskii*.

Bibliography

Akimova, Alisa. "Istoriia i biografiia." *Prometei* 1 (1966): 346–53.
Aleksandrov, B. I. *Seminarii po Chekhovu. Posobie dlia vuzov.* Moscow: Gosudarstvennoe uchebno-pedagogicheskoe izdatel'stvo Ministerstva prosveshcheniia RSFSR, 1957.
Andreev, N. F. "Nechto o N. V. Gogole." *Prometei* 5 (1968): 333–68.
Arndt, Walter. *Pushkin Threefold: Narrative, Lyric, Polemic, and Ribald Verse. The Originals with Linear and Metric Translations.* New York: E.P. Dutton & Co., 1972.
Aron, Leon. "A World Fiercely Observed," *The Wall Street Journal.* January 15–16, 2011, C7.
Backscheider, Paula R. "Opportunities for Comparative Biography," *Slavic and East European Journal* 60, no. 2 (2016): 272–79.
———. *Reflections on Biography* (2013).
Bakhtin, Mikhail. *Problems of Dostoevsky's Poetics.* Edited and translated by Caryl Emerson. Minneapolis: University of Minnesota Press, 1984.
Barakhov, V. S. *Drama Maksima Gor'kogo. Istoki, kollizii, metamorfozyi.* Moscow: IMLI-RAN, 2004.
Barratt, Andrew. "Games Tramps Play: Monster and Man in Gorky's 'Chelkash'." *Fifty Years on: Gorky and His Time.* Ed. Nicholas Luker, 163–91. Nottingham (UK): Astra Press, 1987.
Basinskii, Pavel. *Gorky.* Moscow: Molodaia gvardiia, 2005.
———. *Lev Tolstoi—Svobodnyi chelovek.* Moscow: Molodaia gvardia, 2016, reissued under the ZhZL imprint and Series cover in 2017.
———. *Lev Tolstoi: Begstvo iz raia.* Moscow: Izdatel'stvo ACT, 2010 / 2017.
———. "Strannyi Gor'kii" in *Skripach ne nuzhen.* Moscow: ACT, 2014. 52–77.
———. *Sviatoi protiv L'va: Ioann Kronshtadtskii i Lev Tolstoi. Istoriia odnoi vrazhdy.* Moscow: Izdatel'stvo ACT, 2013.
Basinsky, Pavel. *Leo Tolstoy. Flight from Paradise.* Translated by Huw Davies and Scott Moss. London: Glagoslav Publications, 2015.
Battershill, Claire. "Life before 'The New Biography': Modernist Biographical Methods in the Hogarth Press's 'Books on Tolstoi,' 1920–1924." *a/b: Auto/Biography Studies* 31, no.1 (2016): 109–32.

Belknap, Robert, Carol, and Apollonio. "Dostoevsky in *The Lives of Remarkable People.*" *Slavic and East European Journal* 60, no. 2 (2016): 241–51.
Berdnikov, G. P. *Chekhov.* Moscow: Molodaia gvardiia, 1974.
Bethea, David M. "Bakhtinian Prosaics versus Lotmanian 'Poetic Thinking': The Code and Its Relation to Literary Biography," *Slavic and East European Journal* 41, no. 1 (Spring 1997): 1–15.
———. "How Black was Pushkin: Otherness and Self Creation." In *Under the Sky of My Africa: Alexander Pushkin and Blackness*, edited by Catherine Theimer Nepomnyashchy, Nicole Svobodny and Ludmilla A. Trigos, 122–49. Evanston, IL: Northwestern University Press, 2006.
———. *Realizing Metaphors: Alexander Pushkin and the Life of the Poet.* Madison: University of Wisconsin Press, 1998.
"Biography through a Biographer's Eyes, Materials from a Roundtable Discussion." *Voprosy literatury* 6 (2008), *Russian Studies in Literature* 46, no. 1 (Winter 2009–2010): 8–16.
Blium, A. *Pavlenkov v Viatke.* Kirov: Volgo-Viatskoe knizhnoe izdatel'stvo, Kirovskoe otdelenie, 1976.
Bocharova, I. A., and A. G. Gacheva. "M. Gor'kii i mir filosofskikh idei N. F. Fedorova (perepiska s A. K. Gorskim i N. A. Setnitskim)." *M. Gor'kii i ego korrespondenty.* Edited by L. Spiridonova, 501–45. Moscow: IMLI RAN, 2006.
Bojanowska, Edyta. *Nikolai Gogol: Between Ukrainian and Russian Nationalism.* Cambridge: Harvard University Press, 2007.
Boldyrev, Nikolai. "Chelovek v nepreryvno meniaiushchemsia landshafte." *Ivan Groznyi, Petr Velikii, Menshikov. Potemkin. Davidovy. Biograficheskie ocherki.* Ed. Nikolai Boldyrev, 5–12. Chelyabinsk: Ural Ltd., 1994.
Bondarenko, Vladimir. *Brodskii. Russkii poet.* Moscow: Molodaia gvardiia, 2015.
Bourdieu, Pierre. *Distinction: A Social Critique of the Judgement of Taste.* Translated by Richard Nice. Cambridge, Massachusetts: Harvard University Press, 1984.
———. "Intellectual Field and Creative Project." *Information (International Social Science Council)* 8, no. 2 (1969): 89–119.
Bojanowska, Edyta. *Nikolai Gogol: Between Ukrainian and Russian Nationalism.* Cambridge: Harvard University Press, 2007.
Bradbury, Malcolm, and James McFarlane, eds. *Modernism: A Guide to European Literature, 1890–1930.* New York: Penguin, 1991.
Brintlinger, Angela. "The *Remarkable* Pushkin," *Slavic and East European Journal* 60, no. 2 (2016): 221–40.
———. *Writing a Usable Past: Russian Literary Culture, 1917–1937.* Evanston, IL: Northwestern University Press, 2000, 2008.
Brintlinger, Angela, and Benjamin Richards. "Perechityvaia Bulgarina: Byl li Faddei Venediktovich podletsom i naskol'ko nas eto dolzhno volnovat'?" *A.S. Griboedov: epokha, lichnost', tvorchestvo, sud'ba, Khmelitskii sbornik*, no. 16. Viaz'ma. 2014.
Brodskii, Iosif. *Stikhotvoreniia i poemy.* 2 vols. St. Petersburg: Izdatel'stvo Pushkinskogo Doma/ Izdatel'stvo "Vita Nova," 2012.
Brodsky, Joseph. "Speech at the Stadium." *On Grief and Reason.* New York: Farrar, Straus, Giroux, 1995.

Brooks, Daniel, A. "Bitter Tears: Emotions in Texts By and About Maxim Gor'kii." Forum on *Maksim Gor'kii and Vladislav Khodasevich. Slavic and East European Journal* 62, no. 4 (Winter 2018): 706–26.
Brooks, Jeffrey. "The Breakdown in Production and Distribution of Printed Material, 1917–1927." In *Bolshevik Culture,* edited by Abbot Gleason, 151–74. Bloomington: Indiana University Press, 1985.

———. "Readers and Reading at the End of the Tsarist Era," in *Literature and Society in Imperial Russia, 1800–1924*, edited by William Mills Todd. Stanford, CA: Stanford University Press, 1978.

———. *When Russia Learned to Read: Literacy and Popular Literature, 1861–1917.* Princeton: Princeton University Press,1985.

Bulkina. Inna. "The Lives of Remarkable People." *Russian Studies in Literature* 49, no. 2 (Spring 2013): 87–95.

Bunin, I. A. *Sobranie sochinenii v shesti tomakh.* Moscow: Khudozhestvennaia literatura, 1988.

Bykov, Dmitry. *Gor'kii.* Malaia seriia, vyp. 105. Moscow: Molodaia gvardiia, 2016.

———. "Ia chuvstvuiu Brodskogo obvorovannym." *Ogonek* no. 44 (Okt. 27/Noia.2, 2008. n.p.

———. "O knige Vladimira Bondarenko *Brodskii. Russkii Poet.* Otzyvy i retsenzii." http://denlit.ru/index.php? Last accessed 1/5/16.

Chalenko, Aleksandr, "Vozvraschenie Brodskogo russkim." http://www.rusvesna.su. 5/28/2015. Last accessed 1/5/16.

Chekhov, A. P. *Polnoe sobranie sochinenii i pisem v 30-ti tomakh.* Moscow: Nauka, 1974–1983.

Chernykh, V. A. "Svetlana Kovalenko. *Anna Akhmatova.*" *Znamia* 8 (2009). http://znamlit.ru/publication.php?id=4015 Last accessed: 10/23/.2019.

Choldin, Marianne Tax. *A Fence Around the Empire: Russian Censorship of Western Ideas*. Durham, NC: Duke University Press, 1985.

Chukovskii, K. I. "Dve dushi M. Gor'kogo." In Chukovskii, K. I. *Sobranie sochinenii v 15 tomakh*, Tom 8: *Literaturnaia kritika*, 1918–1921, 183–238. Moscow: TERRA-Knizhnyi klub, 2004.

———. *Sovremenniki. Portrety i etiudy.* Moscow: Molodaia gvardiia, 2008.

Clark, Katerina. "Little Heroes and Big Deeds: Literature Responds to the First Five Year Plan" in *Cultural Revolution in Russia, 1928–31,* ed. Sheila Fitzpatrick. Bloomington: Indiana University Press. 1978.

———. "The History of the Factories" as a Factory of History: A Case Study on the Role of Soviet Literature in Subject Formation." in *Autobiographical Practices in Russia—Autobiographische Praktiken in Russland*, edited by Jochen Hellbeck and Klaus Heller, 251–77. Goettingen: V&R Unipress, 2004.

———. *The Soviet Novel History as Ritual.* Chicago: University of Chicago Press, 1985.

———. *Petersburg: Crucible of Cultural Revolution.* Cambridge: Harvard University Press, 1995.

Clowes, Edith. "Gorky, Nietzsche, and God-building." *Fifty Years on: Gorky and His Time*, edited by Nicholas Luker, 127–44. Nottingham (UK): Astra Press, 1987.

———. (Klius, E.) "Parodiinye alliuzii na M. Gor'kogo v neoffitsial'noi belletristike poststalinskoi epokhi," in *Neizvestnyi Gor'kii. M. Gor'kii i ego epokha. Materialy i issledovaniia.* vyp. 4 (Moscow, 1995): 111–16.

Cooke, Belinda. Review of *Joseph Brodsky. A Literary Life* by Lev Loseff and Jane Anne Miller. *The Russian Review* 73, no. 1 (January 2014): 125–26.

Curtis, Julie. *Bulgakov's Last Decade. The Writer as Hero.* Cambridge, UK: Cambridge University Press, 1987.

Demkina, S. M. "M. Gor'kii i seriia Zhizn' zamechatel'nykh liudei'." *Voprosy kul'torologii* 4 (2014): 65–72.

Derman, A. *Tvorcheskii portret Chekhova.* Moscow: Mir, 1929.

Desiaterik, Vladimir. *Pavlenkov. Zhizn' zamechatel'nykh liudei.* Moscow: Molodaia gvardiia, 2006.

Dobrenko, Evgeny, and Galin Tikhanov, eds. *A History of Russian Literary Theory and Criticism: The Soviet Age and Beyond.* Pittsburgh: University of Pittsburgh Press, 2011.

Dolgopolov, L. K. *Progulki s Blokom.* St. Petersburg: Nestor-Istoriia, 2019.

Dostoevskii, Fedor. "Pis'mo studentam moskovskogo universiteta." in *Polnoe sobranie sochinenii v tridtsati tomakh,* vol. 30:1. Leningrad: Nauka, 1972–1990.

Eidel'man, N. Ia. *Byt' mozhet, za khrebtom Kavkaza.* Moscow: Nauka, 1990.

Eikhenbaum, B. M. "Tvorchestvo Iu. Tynianova," in *Vospominaniia o Iu. Tynianove: Portrety i vstrechi,* edited by V. A. Kaverin, 210–23. Moscow: Sovetskii pisatel', 1983.

Elagina, Elena. "Ne ko vremeni i ne ko dvoru." *Druzhba narodov* 6 (2017): http://www.intelros.ru/readroom/druzhba-narodov/d6-2017/33229-ne-ko-vremeni-i-ne-ko-dvoru.html [date of access: 11/2/2019].

Emerson, Caryl. "Bakhtin, Lotman, Vygotsky, and Lydia Ginzburg on Types of Selves: A Tribute." in *Self and Story in Russian History,* edited by Laura Engelstein and Stephanie Sandler. Ithaca: Cornell University Press, 2000.

———. "Our Everything." *Slavic and East European Journal* 48, no. 1 (2004): 79–98. *JSTOR,* www.jstor.org/stable/3220151. Accessed 6 May 2020.

———. "Remarkable Tolstoy, from the Age of Empire to the Putin Era (1894–2006), *Slavic and East European Journal* 60, no. 2 (2016): 252–71.

Ermilov, V. *Chekhov.* Moscow: Molodaia gvardiia, 1946.

Etkind, Alexander. "Hard and Soft in Cultural Memory: Political Mourning in Russia and in Germany." *Grey Room* 16 (Summer 2004): 36–59.

Falikov, Il'ia. *Marina Tsvetaeva. Tvoia nelaskovaia lastochka.* Moscow: Molodaia gvardiia, 2017.

Fanger, Donald. *The Creation of Nikolai Gogol.* Cambridge: Harvard University Press, 1979.

Filippov, Aleksei. "Griboedov v teni." *Nezavisimaia gazeta,* May 15, 2003.

Fomichev, Sergei. *Aleksandr Griboedov: Biografiia.* St. Petersburg: Vita Nova, 2012.

Fomichev, Sergei (ed.). *A. S. Griboedov. Tvorchestvo. Biografiia. Traditsii.* Leningrad: Nauka, 1977.

———. *A.S. Griboedov v vospominaniiakh sovremennikov.* Moscow: Khudozhestvennaia literatura, 1980.

France, Peter, and William St. Clair, eds. *Mapping Lives: The Uses of Biography*. Oxford: Oxford University Press, 2002.
Freeborn, Richard, *Russian Literary Attitudes from Pushkin to Solzhenitsyn*. London: Palgrave, 1976.
Frumkina, Revekka. "Zhizn' Tsvetaevoi, rasskazannaia Viktoriei Shveitser." *Troitskii. Nauka. Variant* (1.02.2011), https://trv-science.ru/2011/02/01/zhizn-cvetaevoj-rasskazannaya-viktoriej-shvejcer/.
Gatov, Vasily V. "Contagious Tales of Russian Origin and Putin's Evolution." *Society* 53 (2016): 619–24.
Gippius, Zinaida. "Moi lunnyi drug. O Bloke [1925]." In *Zhivye litsa*. Moscow: Russkaia kniga, 2002.
———. "Review of 'Stikhi o Prekrasnoi Dame' [1904]." In *Aleksandr Blok: Pro et contra*, edited by N.Iu. Griakalova. St. Petersburg: RKhGI, 2004.
Gitovich, I. E. *Itog kak novye problemy. Stat'i i retsenzii raznykh let ob A. P. Chekhove, ego vremeni, okruzhenii i chekhovedenii*. Moscow: Izdatel'stvo "Literaturnyi muzei," 2018.
———. "Made in, ili snova o biografii. Zametki chitatelia." *Chekhovskii vestnik*, 17 (2005): 2–36; reprinted in *Itog kak novye problemy*, 224–36.
Givens, John. "Bulgakov Anniversary: Editor's Introduction." *Russian Studies in Literature* 47, no. 2 (Spring 2011): 3–6.
Gorbunov, Iunii. *Florenty Pavlenkov. Ego zhizn' i izdatel'skaia deiatel'nost.'* Cheliabinsk: Ural Ltd., 1999.
Gordin, Iakov, *Rytsar' i smert', ili Zhizn' kak zamysel. O sud'be Iosifa Brodskogo* Moscow: Vremia, 2010.
Gor'kii, Maksim. *Chelovek*. 1904. http://gorkiy-lit.ru/gorkiy/proza/rasskaz/chelovek.htm.
———. "Eshche o 'Karamazovshchine.'" in *Sobranie sochinenii v tridtsati tomakh*, vol. 24. Moscow: Gosudarstvennoe izdatel'stvo russkoi literatury, 1953.
———. "Khoziain." 1912 http://gorkiy-lit.ru/gorkiy/proza/hozyain/hozyain.htm.
———. "Kladbishche." 1913. http://gorkiy-lit.ru/gorkiy/proza/rasskaz/kladbische.htm.
———. "Literaturnye zabavy." *Pravda*, January 24, 1935.
———. *Na dne*. 1902. http://gorkiy-lit.ru/gorkiy/pesy/na-dne/na-dne.htm.
———. "O 'Karamazovshchine'." in *Sobranie sochinenii v tridtsati tomakh*, vol. 24. Moscow: Gosudarstvennoe izdatel'stvo russkoi literatury, 1953.
———. "Sluchai iz zhizni Makara." 1912. http://gorkiy-lit.ru/gorkiy/proza/rasskaz/sluchaj-iz-zhizni-makara.htm.
———. *Sobranie sochinenii v tridtsati tomakh*. Moscow: Gosudarstvennoe izdatel'stvo khudozhestvennoi literatury, 1955.
Goscilo, Helena, and Vlad Strukov, eds. "Introduction." *Celebrity and Glamour in Contemporary Russia: Shocking Chic*. London: Routledge. 2011, 1–26.
Griboedov, A. S. *Polnoe sobranie sochinenii v 3 tomakh*, edited by N. Piksanov. Saint Petersburg: Izdatel'stvo Imperatorskoi Akademii Nauk, 1913.
———. *Sobranie sochinenii*. edited by S. Fomichev. Moscow: Khudozhestvennaia literatura, 1988.

Griftsov, Boris. "Ob Aleksandre Bloke, iskresnnosti i dekadentstve [1907]." In *Aleksandr Blok: Pro et contra*, edited by N.Iu. Griakalova. St. Petersburg: RKhGI, 2004.
Grinchenko, N. A. "K istorii izadetl'skoi diatel'nosti F. F. Palvenkova. Pis'ma F. F. Pavlenkova k P. I. Sementkovskomu (1890–1899)." in *Knizhnoe delo v Rossii v nachale XIX–XX vv.,* no. 20 (2019): 12–62.
Gromov, M. P. *Chekhov.* Moscow: Molodaia gvardiia, 1993.
———. *Kniga o Chekhove.* Moscow: Sovremennik, 1989.
Gross, Irena Grudzinska. *Czesław Miłosz and Joseph Brodsky: Fellowship of Poets.* New Haven and London: Yale University Press, 2009.
Grossman, Leonid. *Barkhatnyi dictator.* Moscow: Moskovskoe tovarishchestvo pisatelei, 1933.
———. *Dostoevskii.* Moscow: Molodaia gvardiia, 1962.
———. *Pushkin.* Moscow: Molodaia gvardiia, 1939.
Gruzdev, Il'ia. *Gor'kii.* Moscow: Molodaia gvardiia, 1958
Gudzii, N. K. *L. Tolstoi.* Moscow: Molodaia gvardiia, 1944.
Günther, Hans. *Der sozialistische Übermensch, Gor'kij und der Sowjetische Heldenmythos.* Stuttgart: J. B. Metzler, 1993.
Hamburg, G. M. "Tolstoy's Spirituality." *Anniversary Essays on Tolstoy.* Edited by Donna Tussing Orwin, 138–58. Cambridge: Cambridge University Press, 2010.
Harrington, Alexandra. "Anna Akhmatova's Biographical Myth-Making: Tragedy and Melodrama." *Slavonic and East European Review* 89, no.3 (July 2011): 455–93.
Hasty, Olga Peters. *How Women Must Write: Inventing the Russian Woman Poet.* Evanston, Illinois: Northwestern University Press, 2020.
———. "Tsvetaeva by Viktoria Shweitser. Translated by Robert Chandler and H.T. Willetts." *Slavic Review* 54, no. 1 (Spring 1995):229.
Haven, Cynthia, ed. *Joseph Brodsky: Conversations.* Jackson: University Press of Mississippi, 2002.
———. "The Unknown Brodsky." *The Nation.* April 11, 2018, 42.
Hellbeck, Jochen. "Galaxy of Black Stars: The Power of Soviet Biography." *American Historical Review* 114, no. 3 (June 2009): 615–24.
Heller, Leonid. "A World of Prettiness: Socialist Realism and Its Aesthetic Categories." In *Socialist Realism Without Shores*, edited by Thomas Lahusen and Evgeny Dobrenko, 51–75. Durham, N.C.: Duke University Press, 1997.
Hodgson, Katharine and Smith, Alexandra. *Poetic Canons, Cultural Memory and Russian National Identity after 1991.* Oxford, Bern, et al.: Peter Lang, 2020.
Ilchuk, Yuliya. *Nikolai Gogol: Performing Hybrid Identity.* Toronto: University of Toronto Press, 2020.
Iurkin, Valentin. *Vremia i knigi: Molodaia gvardiia v epokhu peremen.* Moscow: Molodaia gvardiia, 2010.
———. *Zhizn' zamechatel'nogo izdatel'stva: Molodaia gvardiia—75 let.* Moscow: Molodaia gvardiia, 1997.
———. *ZhZL: Letopis' tsivilizatsii: 120 let serii "Zhizn' zamechatel'nykh liudei."* Moscow: Molodaia gvardiia, 2010.

Jones, Polly. *Revolution Rekindled: The Writers and Readers of Late Soviet Biography*. Oxford: Oxford University Press, 2019.

———. ed. *Writing Russian Lives: The Politics and Poetics of Biography in Modern Russian Culture*. Modern Humanities Research Association. 2018.

Jones, W. Gareth. "Biography in Eighteenth-Century Russia." *Oxford Slavonic Papers* 22 (1989): 58–81.

Kalugin, Dmitrii. *Proza zhizni: russkie biografii v XVIII i XIX vv.* St. Petersburg: European University in St. Petersburg, 2015.

———. "Soviet Theories of Biography and the Aesthetics of Personality." *Biography* 38, no. 3 (Summer 2015): 343–62.

Karlinsky, Simon. *The Sexual Labyrinth of Nikolai Gogol*. Chicago: University of Chicago Press, 1967.

Kataev, V. B. Review of *Anton Chekhov: A Life*, Donald Rayfield. *Chekhovskii vestnik* 2 (1997): 6–12.

———. *Slozhnost' prostoty: Rasskazy i p'esy Chekhova. V pomoshch' prepodavateliam, starsheklassnikam i abiturientam*. Moscow: MGU, 1998.

Katalog "ZhZL," 1890–2010. Edited by E. I. Gorelik. Moscow: Molodaia gvardiia, 2010.

Kelly, Laurence. *Diplomacy and Murder in Tehran: Alexander Griboedov and Imperial Russia's Mission to the Shah of Persia*. London: I. B. Tauris, 2002.

Ketchian, Sonia I., "Svetlana Kovalenko. Anna Akhmatova. Ed. Aleksandra N. Nikoliukina. Seriia biografii: Zhizn' zamechatel'nykh liudei. Moscow: Molodaia gvardiia, 2009." *Slavic and East European Journal* 54, no. 2 (Summer 2010): 368–69.

Khodasevich, Vladislav. "Vospominaniia." http://hodasevich.lit-info.ru/hodasevich/vospominaniya/nekropol/gorkij.htm.

Kholikov, Aleksei. "Pisatel'skaia biografiia: Zhanr bez pravil." *Voprosy literatury* (Noiab.-dek. 2008): 41–76.

———. "Mikhail Bulgakov 'Made to Order.'" *Russian Studies in Literature* 47, no. 2 (Spring 2011): 61–71.

Kjetsaa, Geir (Kh'etso, G.). *Maksim Gor'kii. Sud'ba pisatelia*. Moscow: Nasledie, 1997.

Kline, George. *Religious and Anti-religious Thought in Russia*. Chicago and London: The University of Chicago Press, 1968.

"Knigi o russkikh pisateliakh v ZhZL," *Voprosy literatury* 9 (1980): 179–251.

Kogan, P. S. *A. P. Chekhov. Biograficheskii ocherk*. Moscow: Moskovskii rabochii, 1929.

Koshelev, V. A., "Blesk i nishchita 'neprelozhnykh istin.'" *Novoe literaturnoe obozrenie*, no. 6 (2003): https://magazines.gorky.media/nlo/2003/6/blesk-i-nishheta-neprelozhnyh-istin.html.

Kovalenko, Svetlana. *Anna Akhmatova*. Seriia biografii: Zhizn' zamechatel'nykh liudei, Moscow: Molodaia gvardiia, 2009.

Krieve, Sarah A. "A Transcultural Monument: Anna Akhmatova in Post-socialist Russia." *South Atlantic Review* 74, no. 2 (2009): 62–81.

Kurbatov, Valentin. "Taina na kraiu 'Zakaza.'" In Zverev and Tunimanov, *Lev Tolstoi. Zhizn' zamechatel'nykh liudei*. Moscow: Molodaia gvardiia, 2006. 5–10.
Kuzicheva, A. *A. P. Chekhov. Zhizn' "otdel'nogo cheloveka."* Moscow: Molodaia gvardiia, 2010.
Kuziv, Ivan. "Mykola Hohol' u svitli kritiki P. Kulisha i V. Belinsk'ogo." PhD Dissertation, Ottawa, Canada, 1966.
Lamont, Rosette C. "Tsvetaeva by Viktoria Schweitzer." *World Literature Today* 68, 4 (Autumn 1994): 843.
Lee, Hermione. *Virginia Woolf's Nose: Essays on Biography*. Princeton and Oxford: Princeton University Press, 2005
Lenin, Vladimir. "Lev Tolstoi kak zerkalo russkoi revolutsii." in *Polnoe Sobranie Sochinenii*. Moscow: Izdatel'stvo politicheskoi literatury, 1968.
Levinton, G. A. "Griboedovskie podteksty v romane 'Smerti' Vazir-Mukhtara." *Tynianovskii sbornik. Chetvertye Tynianovskie chteniia* (1990): 21–34.
Levitt, Marcus. *Russian Literary Politics and the Pushkin Celebration of 1880*. Ithaca, NY: Cornell University Press, 1989.
Levitt, Markus Ch. *Literatura i politika: Pushkinskii prazdnik 1880 goda*. Translated by I. N. Vladimirov and V. D. Rak. St. Petersburg: Akademicheskii proekt, 1994.
Lipking, Lawrence. *The Life of the Poet: Beginning and Ending Poetic Careers*. Chicago: University of Chicago Press, 1981, 1984.
Livak, Leonid. *In Search of Russian Modernism*. Baltimore, Md.: John Hopkins University Press, 2018.
Loseff, Lev. *Joseph Brodsky: A Literary Life*. New Haven, CT: Yale University Press, 2011.
———. Papers. Series: Correspondence, 1945–2006. Subseries I: Correspondence with Individuals, undated, 1945–2005. Bakhmeteff Archive. Columbia University.
Losev, Lev. *Iosif Brodskii: Opyt literaturnoi biografii*. Moscow: Molodaia gvardiia, 2006.
———. *Meandr*. www.litres.ru/lev-losev/meandr/.
———. "Primechaniia s primechaniami." *Novoe Literaturnoe Obozreniie* 5, 2000.
Losievskii, I. Ia. *Nauchnaia biografiia pisatelia: problemy interpretatsii i tipologii*. Kharkov: Krok, 1998.
Lotman, Iurii. *Aleksandr Sergeevich Pushkin: Biografiia pisatelia. Stat'i i zametki*. St. Petersburg: Iskusstvo-SPB, 2003.
———. "Literaturnaia biografiia v istoriko-kul'turnom kontekste." 804–16. In *O russkoi literature. Stat'i i issledovaniia (1958–1993)*. St. Petersburg: Iskusstvo-SPb, 1997.
Lovell, Steven. *The Russian Reading Revolution: Print Culture in the Soviet and Post-Soviet Eras*. Basingstoke: Macmillan and St. Martin's Press, 2000.
Luckyj, George S. N. *Between Gogol' and Ševčenko: Polarity in the Literary Ukraine*. Munchen: Wilhelm Fink Verlag, 1971.
Lutsenko, E. "A Valediction: Forbidding Mourning (The Biographer and His Critics)." *Russian Studies in Literature* 46, no. 1 (Winter 2009–2010): 17–29. English translation by Liv Bliss of Russian text "*Proshchanie, zapreshchaiushee pechal': biograf i ego kritiki*." *Voprosy literatury*, no. 6 (2008): 63–76.

Maguire, Robert. A. *Gogol from the Twentieth Century: Eleven Essays*. Princeton: Princeton University Press, 1974.

———. *Red Virgin Soil: Soviet Literature in the 1920s*. Ithaca, NY: Cornell University Press, 1987.

Makolkin, Anna. "Probing the Origins of Literary Biography: English and Russian Versions." *Biography* 19, no. 1 (Winter 1996): 87–104.

Mandel'shtam, Osip. "A. Blok [1922]." In *Aleksandr Blok: Pro et contra*, edited by N.Iu. Griakalova. St. Petersburg: RKhGI, 2004.

Masing-Delic, Irene. *Abolishing Death: A Salvation Myth of Russian Twentieth-Century Literature*. Stanford (CA): Stanford University Press, 1992.

———. "Fedorovian Resurrecting in Maksim Gorky's 'The Cemetery'." *Christianity and the Eastern Slavs*, III. Berkeley, Los Angeles, London: University of California Press, 1995. 181–98.

———. "Incompatible Collaborators: Gor'kii, Khodasevich and 'Belfast.'" *Maksim Gor'kii and Vladimir Khodasevich. Slavic and East European Journal* 62, no. 4 (2018): 643–62.

———. "Two Bloks and One Pasternak: When, How and Why Does One Get into *The Life of Remarkable People*?" Paper presented at AATSEEL Conference. Chicago, 2014.

McQuillen, Colleen. *The Modernist Masquerade: Stylizing Life, Literature, and Costumes in Russia*. Madison: The University of Wisconsin Press, 2013.

Mejlax, M. B., and V. N. Toporov. "Akhmatova i Dante." *International Journal of Slavic Linguistics and Poetics* 15 (1972): 29–75.

Melvill, F. I. "Paradoks Griboedova," in *Na pastbishche mysli blagoi. Sbornik statei k iubileiu I.M. Steblin-Kamenskogo*, edited by M. S. Pelevin. St. Petersburg: Kontrast, 2015.

Melville, Firuza. "Alexander Sergeevich Griboedov: Russian Imperial James Bond *Malgré Lui*." In *Russians in Iran. Diplomacy and Power in the Qajar Era and Beyond*, edited by Rudy Matthee and Elena Andreeva, London and New York: I. P. Tauris, 2014.

Miasnikov, A. S. *A.S. Pushkin*. Moscow: Molodaia Gvardiia, 1940.

Moeller-Sally, Stephen. *Gogol's Afterlife: The Evolution of a Classic in Imperial and Soviet Russia*. Evanston, IL: Northwestern University Press, 2002.

Nabokov, Vladimir. *Nikolai Gogol*. Norfolk, CT: New Directions, 1944.

———. "Philistines and Philistinism." *Lectures on Russian Literature*, 314–29. London: Pan Books (Picador edition), 1983.

Navrotskaya, Anna. "Aleksandr Nevskii: Hagiography and National Biography." *Cahiers du Monde russe* 46, no. 1–2, La Russie vers 1550: Monarchie nationale ou empire en formation? (Jan-June 2003): 297–304.

Nemirovich-Danchenko, V. "Protest Gorkogo. V. Nemirovich-Danchenko o proteste." *Teatral'naia gazeta*, October 6, 1913.

Nepomsniashchaia, T. "Knigi o zamechatel'nykh liudiakh kak tip izdaniia: Seriia ZhZL izdatel'stva "Molodaia gvardiia." Moscow: Fakul'tet zhurnalistiki. Kafedra redaktsionnogo dela i knigovedeniia. Gosudarstvennyi Universitet imeni Lomonosova.

———. "A. M. Gorkii i 'Zhizn' zamechatel'nykh liudei' (K istorii zamysla)." *Vestnik Moskovskogo Universiteta. Seriia XI. Zhurnalistika*, no. 3 (1966): 47–56.
Nesterenko, M. "Uroki 'neopytnoi muzy'," in Anna Bunina. *Neopytnaia muza. Sobranie stikhotvorenii*. 11–25. Moscow: B.S.G.-Press, 2016.
Nickell, William. *The Death of Tolstoy: Russia on the Eve, Astapovo Station, 1910*. Ithaca NY: Cornell University Press, 2010.
Novikov, Vladimir. *Aleksandr Blok*. Moscow: Molodaia gvardiia, 2010.
———. *Pushkin*. Moscow: Molodaia gvardiia, 2014.
———. "*Pushkin*: Opyt dostupnogo povestvovaniia. Fragmenty." *Novyi mir* 3 (2014). https://magazines.gorky.media/novyi_mi/2014/3/pushkin-3.html. Accessed May 7, 2020.
———. "Vyshe Pushkina tol'ko Iisus Khristos." *Vselenaia ZhZL* 3.13 (November 2014): 2.
Orwin, Donna Tussing. "Chronology." in *The Cambridge Companion to Tolstoy*, edited by Donna Tussing Orwin (Cambridge: Cambridge University Press, 2002).
Osovskii, Oleg. "'Literaturnost' protiv documental'nosti kak avtorskaia strategia v sovremennoi biografii (Na materiale poslednikh izdanii serii ZhZL)." *Filologiia i kul'tura* 53, no. 3 (2018): 194–98.
———. "Nou-khau biograficheskogo zhanra." *Voprosy literatury* no. 3 (mai-iun' 2018): 62–83.
Pamuk, Orhan. "Other Countries, Other Shores." *New York Times Magazine*, December 19, 2013.
Pann, Lilia. "A Biography of the Mind," Review of *Joseph Brodsky. A Literary Life* by Lev Loseff. *Russian Studies in Literature* 46, no.1 (Winter 2009–2010): 30–35. English translation of Russian text by Liv Bliss. "Biografiia soznaniia." *Znamia* no. 7 (2006): 212–15.
Paperno, Irina. "Introduction." In *Creating Life: The Aesthetic Utopia of Russian Modernism*. edited by Irina Paperno and Joan Delaney Grossman. Stanford: Stanford University Press, 1994.
Parke, C. N. *Biography: Writing Lives*. New York: Twayne Publishers, 1996.
Pasternak, Boris. "Noch'" (1956). in *Polnoe sobranie stikhotvorenii i poem*. 419–20. St. Petersburg: Gumanitarnoe agentstvo "Akademicheskii proekt," 2003.
Patrusheva, N. G. "F. F. Pavlenkov i tsenzura." in *Knizhnoe delo v Rossii v nachale XIX–XX v*, no. 20 (2019): 63–75.
Piksanov, N. *A. S. Griboedov v vospominaniiakh sovremennikov*. Moscow: Federatsiia, 1929.
Polukhina, Valentina. *Brodsky through the Eyes of His Contemporaries*. Volumes 1 and 2. Revised edition. Boston: Academic Studies Press, 2010.
Pomerantseva, G. E. *Biografiia v potoke vremeni, ZhZL: Zamysly i dostizheniia serii*. Moscow: Kniga, 1987.
———. "K istorii stanovleniia i razvitiia serii 'Zhizn' zamechatel'nykh liudei' (1933–1941)." *Kniga: Issledovaniia i materialy* (Moscow: Kniga), sb. 27 (1973): 92–118.
———. "Seriia 'Zhizn zamechatel'nykh liudei' i zamysel A. M. Gor'kogo." *Kniga: Issledovaniia i materialy* (Moscow: Kniga), sb. 32 (1976): 36–64.

Presto, Jennifer. "The Revolutionary Ecology of Gorky's Italy." *Slavic and East European Journal* 61, no. 3 (2017): 423–44.
Prilepin, Zakhar. "Aleksei Varlamov. Nashemu narodu nado prosit' u Neba ne spravedlivosti a miloserdiia" at http://zaharprilepin.ru/ru/litprocess/intervju-o-literature/aleksej-varlamov-.html.
Pushkin, A. S., *Polnoe sobranie sochinenii*. Leningrad: Nauka. Leningradskoe otdelenie, 1977–1979.
———. "Puteshestvie v Arzrum vo vremia pokhoda 1829 goda." *Polnoe sobranie sochinenii*. 10 t. By A. S. Pushkin. Leningrad: Nauka. Leningr. otd-nie, 1977–1979. T. 6. Khudozhestvennaia proza.—1978. 432–84.
———. *Pis'ma*. Pod red. i s primech. L. B. Modzalevskogo. Moscow-Leningrad: Academiia. T. 3. Pis'ma, 1831–1833. 1935.
Ranchin, Andrei. "A Philological Biography," Review of *Joseph Brodsky: A Literary Life* by Lev Loseff. *Russian Studies in Literature* no.1 (Winter 2009–2010): 36–47.
Rapgof, B. E. *Karolina Pavlova. Materialy dlia izucheniia zhizni i tvorchestva*. Petrograd: Trirema, 1916.
Rassudovskaia, N. *Izdatel' F. F. Pavlenkov (1839–1900). Ocherk zhizni i deiatel'nosti*. Moscow: Izdatel'stvo Vsesoiuznoi knizhnoi palaty, 1960.
Rayfield, Donald. *Anton Chekhov*: A Life. Evanston, IL: Northwestern University Press, 1997.
Reifild, Donal'd. *Zhizn' Antona Chekhova*. Translated by Olga Makarova. Moscow: Nezavisimaia Gazeta, 2005.
Reitblat, A. I. "Russkaia literatura kak sotsial'nyi institut." In *Pisat' poperek*. Moscow: Novoe literaturnoe obozrenie, 2014.
———. "Simvolisty, ikh izdateli i chitateli." In *Ot Bovy k Bal'montu*. Moscow: Novoe Literaturnoe Obozrenie, 2009.
Sandler, Stephanie. Review of *Joseph Brodsky. A Literary Life* by Lev Loseff. *The Slavonic and East European Review* 90, no. 3 (July 2012): 515–16.
Saraskina, Liudmila. *Dostoevskii*. Moscow: Molodaia gvardiia, 2011.
Scammell, Michael. "Pride and Poetry. Review of *Joseph Brodsky. A Literary Life* by Lev Loseff." *The New Republic*, June 7, 2012: 30–34.
Scherr, Barry. "Il'ia Gruzdev—Biograf Gor'kogo." *Revue des Études Slaves* 71, no. 3 (1999): 681–91.
Schuler, Catherine A. *Women in Russian Theatre: The Actress in the Silver Age*. London and New York: Routledge, 1996.
Schwarzband, Samuel. "Les *Carnets* de Derjavine et *La Fille du capitaine* de Pouchkine (Hypothèses)." *Derjavine: un poète russe dans l'Europe des Lumières*. Edited by Anita Davidenkoff. Paris: Institute d'études slaves, 1994. 149–58.
Schweitzer, Viktoria. *Tsvetaeva*. Translated by Robert Chandler, H. T. Willets, Peter Norman. Edited by Angela Livingstone. New York: Farrar, Straus & Giroux, 1993.
Seaman, Donna. Review of *Joseph Brodsky. A Literary Life* by Lev Loseff. *Booklist*, Jan. 1 & 15, 2011.
Seduro, Vladimir. *Dostoevski in Russian Literary Criticism: 1846–1956*. New York: Octagon Books, 1969.
Seleznev, Iurii. *Dostoevskii*. Moscow: Molodaia gvardiia, 1981.

Sergeev, Andrei. "O Brodskom." In *Omnibus*. Moscow: Novoe literaturnoe oboozrenie, 1997.
Shchegolev, P. E. *Duel' i smert' Pushkina*. St. Petersburg: Akademicheskii proekt, 1999.
Shishkova-Shipunova, Svetlana. "'Not Knowing Friend from Foe,' The Reason for Literary Biographies." *Russian Studies in Literature* 46, no.1 (Winter 2009–2010): 68–81.
Shklovskii, V. *Lev Tolstoi*. Zhizn' zamechatel'nykh liudei. Moscow: Molodaia gvardiia, 1963.
Shklovsky, Victor. *Lev Tolstoy*. Translated by Olga Shartse. Moscow: Progress Publishers, 1978.
Shveitser, Viktoriia. *Marina Tsvetaeva*. Moscow, Molodaia gvardiia, 2003. https://www.e-reading.life/chapter.php/95744/3/Shveiicer_-_Marina_Cvetaeva.html [date of access: 1/11/2019].
Siderov, I. S. "O gibeli A.S. Griboedova." *Rossiiskii arkhiv: Istoriia Otechestva v svidetel'stvakh i dokumentakh XVIII-XX vv*. Moscow: Studiia TRITE, 1992.
Simons, Judy. "Secret Exhibitionists: Women and their Diaries." in *Diaries and Journals of Literary Women from Fanny Burney to Virginia Woolf*. London: Palgrave Macmillan, 1990. 1–18.
Skabichevskii, A.M. *A.S. Griboedov, ego zhizn' i literaturnaia deiatel'nost'*. St. Petersburg: P.P. Soikin. 1893, reprinted Moscow: AiKiu Izdatel'skoe reshenie, 2016.
———. *Pushkin. Ego zhizn' i literaturnaia deiatel'nost'*. http://www.litres.ru/pages/biblio_book/?art=175420 Accessed 16 May 2016.
———. "Aleksandr Sergeevich Pushkin. " *Sochineniia A. S. Pushkina: Polnoe sobranie v odnom tome*, ed. A.M. Skabichevskii. St. Petersburg: Izdatel'stvo F. Pavlenkova, 1907. iii–lx.
Skatov, N. "Dvizhenie vpered." *Voprosy literatury* no. 9 (1980): 199–203.
Smirnov, B. *A.M. Skabichevskii –literaturnyi kritik*. Volgograd: Izd. Volgogradskogo universiteta, 1999.
Smirnovskii, P.V. "Biografiia A.S. Pushkina." in *Sochineniia A.S. Pushkina. Polnoe sobranie v odnom tome*. Edited by P.V. Smirnovskii. Moscow: Izdatel'stvo Panafidina, 1900. I–XLVIII.
Smith, Alexandra. "Formirovanie literaturnogo kanona v knige Ariadny Tyrkovoi-Vil'iams *Zhizn' Pushkina*." In *Pushkinskie chteniia v Tartu: 2*, edited by L. Kiseleva, 267–81. Tartu: University of Tartu, 2000.
Smith, G. S., "Going Back (Mainly on Brodsky)." *Canadian American Slavic Studies* 33, nos. 2–4 (1999): 335.
———. "Joseph Brodsky: Summing Up." *Literary Imagination* 7, no. 3 (Fall 2005): 399–410.
Sobolev, Iu. *Chekhov*. Moscow: Zhurnal'no-gazetnoe ob"edinenie, 1929.
———. *Chekhov. Stat'i. Materialy. Bibliografiia*. Moscow: Federatsiia, 1930.
Soloviev, Evgenii. *L. N. Tolstoi. Ego zhizn' i literaturnaia deiatel'nost'*. Zhizn' zamechatel'nykh liudei. St. Petersburg: Biograficheskaia biblioteka F. Pavlenkova, 1894.

Spivak, Monika. *Posmertnaia diagnostika genial'nosti*. Moscow: AGRAF, 2001.
Stone, Jonathan. *The Institutions of Russian Modernism: Conceptualizing, Publishing, and Reading Symbolism*. Evanston, Ill.: Northwestern University Press, 2017.
Sukhikh, I. N. "Chekhov (1960–2010): Novye opyty chteniia." in *A. P. Chekhov: Pro et Contra. Lichnost'* i tvorchestvo A. P. Chekhova v russkoi mysli XX–XXI vekov (1960–2010). Antologiia, vol. 3. St. Petersburg: Izdatel'stvo Russkoi khristianskoi gumanitarnoi akademii. 2016.
Tarkhova, Nadezhda. "K probleme izucheniia biografii Griboedova segodnia." *Voprosy literatyry*, no. 4 (July–August 2013): 130–50. https://voplit.ru/article/k-probleme-izucheniya-biografii-griboedova-segodnya/.
Teasley, Ellendea Proffer. *Brodsky Among Us: A Memoir*. Boston: Academic Studies Press, 2017.
Thomas, Keith. *Changing Conceptions of National Biography: The Oxford DNB in Historical Perspective*. Cambridge: Cambridge University Press, 2005.
Thun-Hohenstein, Franziszka. "V laboratorii sovetskoi biografii: Seriia 'Zhizn' zamechatel'nykh liudei,' 1933–1941." *Sektsiia V, Konstriruvanie chelovecheskoi dushi: Period Stalinizma*.: https://histrf.ru/uploads/media/default/0001/09/78f889e5e7e1a7f1f3fd45fa64d429baf620c8b8.pdf.
Tolstoy, Leo. "And the Light Shineth in Darkness." A Drama in Five Acts [1896–1897, 1900]. Translated by Marvin Kantor with Tanya Tulchinsky. In Leo Tolstoy, *Plays: Volume Three, 1894–1910*. Evanston: Northwestern University Press, 1998. 15–104.
Tomashevsky, Boris. "Literature and Biography." *Readings in Russian Poetics: Formalist and Structuralist Views*. Edited by Ladislav Matejka and Krystyna Pomorska, 47–55. Chicago, IL: Dalkey Archive Press, 2002.
Tosi, Alessandra. "Anna Bunina (1774–1829) and the Origins of Women's Poetry in Russia." *Journal of European Studies* 28, no. 3 (1998): 322–24.
Trigos, Ludmilla A. *The Decembrist Myth in Russian Culture*. New York: Palgrave Macmillan, 2009.
Trigos, Ludmilla A. and Carol Ueland. "Creating a National Biographical Series: F. F. Pavlenkov's 'Lives of Remarkable People,' 1890–1924." *Slavonic and East European Review* 96, vol. 1 (2018): 41–66.
Tsiavlovskaia, T. G., ed. "Ot redaktsii." *Prometei* 10 (1974): 5–11.
Tsimbaeva, Ekaterina. *Griboedov*. Moscow: Molodaia gvardiia, 2003, reprinted 2011.
Tsvetaeva, Anastasiia. "Tomas Karleil' v moei zhizni." in *Neischerpaemoe*. Moscow: Otechestvo, 1992. 208–13.
Tsybul'sky, Vladimir. "Vyzyvaetsia dukh Mikhaila Bulgakova." Gazeta.ru, 14 January 2009, at http://litena.ru/news/item/f00/s01/n0000130/index.shtml.
Turkov, A. M. *Aleksandr Blok*. Zhizn' zamechatel'nykh liudei #475. Moscow: Molodaia gvardiia, 1969.
Tyrkova-Vil'iams, A.V. *Zhizn' Pushkina*. [Two volumes] Moscow: Molodaia gvardiia, 1998.
Ueland, Carol and Trigos, Ludmilla A. "F. F. Pavlenkov's Literacy Project: Popular Serials and Reading Rooms for the Russian Masses." in *The Edinburgh History*

of Reading: Common Readers, volume 3, edited by Jonathan Rose, 157–79. Edinburgh: Edinburgh University Press, 2020.

Ueland, Carol R. and Trigos, Ludmilla A. "Literary Biographies in the *Lives of Remarkable People Series (Zhizn' zamechatel'nykh liudei).*" *Slavic and East European Journal* 60. no.2 (2016): 207–20.

Ungurianu, Dan. *Plotting History: The Russian Historical Novel in the Imperial Age.* Madison: University of Wisconsin Press, 2007.

Varlamov, Alexei. *Bulgakov.* Moscow: Molodaia gvardiia, 2008.

Vdovin, Alexey. "'Dmitry Tolstoy's Classicism'" and the Formation of The Russian Literary Canon in The High School Curriculum." *Ab Imperio* (4/2017): 108–37.

Velikie russkie liudi: sbornik. Moscow: Molodaia gvardiia, 1984.

Veresaev, V. *Pushkin v zhizni.* Moscow: Sovetskii pisatel', 1936.

Vishniakova, Iu. I. "Vospitanie na obraste: 80 let biographicheskoi serii "Zhizn' zamechatel'nikh liudei" izdatel'stva Molodaia gvardiia." *Nashe Nasledie, Vestnik PSTGU, Seriia IV: Pedagogika. Psikhologiia.* Vyp. 53 (2019): 120–32.

Vodovozov, N. V. *Gogol'.* Moscow: Molodaia gvardiia, 1945.

Volkov, Solomon. *Conversations with Joseph Brodsky.* New York: The Free Press, 1998.

Voronskii, A. *Gogol'.* Moscow: Molodaia gvardiia, 2005.

Wachtel, Andrew Baruch. *An Obsession with History: Russian Writers Confront the Past.* Stanford, CA: Stanford University Press, 1994.

———. "The Cult of the Author." *Slavic and East European Journal* 60, no.2 (2016): 280–83.

Weidle, Wladimir. "Petersburg Poetics." In *Nikolai Gumilev. Sobranie sochinenii.* Washington, D.C.: Victor Kamkin, 1968.

Wolfe, Bertram. *The Bridge and the Abyss. The Troubled Friendship of Maxim Gorky and V. I. Lenin.* New York: Stanford University Press, 1967.

Yedlin, Tovah. *Maxim Gorky. A Political Biography.* Westport, CT, and London: Praeger, 1999.

Zaslavskii, David. *F. M. Dostoevskii: Kritikobiograficheskii ocherk.* Moscow: Goslitizdat, 1956.

———. "Literaturnaia gnil'." *Pravda.* January 20, 1935.

———. "Protiv idealizatsii reaktsionnykh vzglyadov Dostoevskovo." *Kultura i zhizn.* December 20, 1947.

Ziolkowski, Margaret. *Hagiography and Modern Russian Literature.* Princeton: Princeton University Press, 1988.

Zolotusskii, Igor'. *Gogol'.* Moscow: Molodaia gvardiia, 1979, 1984, 2009.

———. *Ispoved, Zoila.* Moscow: Sovetskaia Rossiia, 1989.

———. *Nas bylo troe: roman-dokument.* St. Petersburg: "Fond 200-let Nikolaiu Gogoliu," 2011.

Zverev, Aleksei, and Vladimir Tunimanov. *Lev Tolstoi.* Zhizn' zamechatel'nykh liudei. Moscow: Molodaia gvardiia. 2006.

Index

Academia Publishers, 148–49, 169n11
Acmeism, 219
The Adolescent (Dostoevsky), 153, 161, 167
advertisements, 8, 35n45, 63, 239
Akhmadulina, Bella, 295n17
Akhmatova, Anna, 31, 232n15, 233–45, 250, 251; Brodsky, Joseph, and, 241, 275, 276, 277; as martyr, 244, 251, 274; myth of, 242; Tsvetaeva, Marina, and, 233–235, 238, 240, 251
Akimova, Alisa, 1, 32n1
Aksakov, S. T., 9, 93, 279
Aksyonov, Vasily, 273
Aleksandr I (Arkhangel'skii), 41n127
Aleksandrov, Boris, 174
Alexander I (Tsar), 23, 60
Alexander II (Tsar), 11, 36n58
Alexander III (Tsar), 135
Alexei Tolstoy (Varlamov), 26
All-Russian Society for the Dissemination of Political and Scholarly Knowledge, 116n53
All-Union Institute of Experimental Medicine (*VIEM, Vsesoiuznyi Institut Eksperimental'noi Meditsiny*), 193, 194, 215n40
Anastasy, Metropolitan, 61
ancient biography, 3, 4

Andreeva, Maria, 202, 215n39
Andreev, Leonid, 202–3
And the Light Shineth in Darkness (Tolstoy, L.), 139–40
Anna Karenina (Tolstoy, L.), 57, 79, 122, 129, 133
Annenkov, Pavel, 6, 7, 8, 278–79
Annenkov, Yuri, 226, 229
Annenskaya, Alexandra, N., 114n25, 115n32, 115n34; biography of *Gogol*, 93–94, 97–101, 108, 115n36; with primary material, 114n27
Annensky, N. F., 98
Anrep, Boris, 240
anti-Semitism, 282
Apollonio, Carol, 117n64, 169n10
Arap Petra Velikogo (*Moor of Peter the Great*) (Pushkin), 50
Ardis Press, 277, 279
Ardov, Mikhail, 290
Aristotle, 9
Arkhangel'skii, A. N., 41n127
Arndt, Walter, 65n18
Arndt, Yury, 21
arrested books, 11, 36n56
Arzamas, poets and, 50
Aspects of Biography (Maurois), 37n65
"AST" press, 27
The Atlantic Monthly (magazine), 37n65

Auden, W. H., 284
authors: canon formation and cult of, 236–39; forbidden, 119. *See also* writers
autobiography, 50, 64n14, 200
autobiographical novel, Pushkin and, 236, 246
Averintsev, Sergei, 4, 33n14

Babel, Isaac, 209
Baboeuf, Francois-Noel, 16
Backscheider, Paula R., 1, 32n7
Bakhtin, Mikhail, 28–29, 31, 43n160, 146, 154, 161, 169n3, 170n28
Balaganchik (*The Puppet Show*) (Blok, A.), 219, 221, 225
Balmont, Konstantin, 225
Balzac, Honoré de, 114n24
Bantysh-Kamensky, D. N., 5
Barakhov, V. S., 198
Bashkirtseff, Marie, 247–48
Basina, Marianna, 52, 56, 60
Basinsky, Pavel, 30, 44n171, 121, 137–40, 141n6, 142n21, 214n29; Gorky and, 198, 199, 200, 201–7, 213n24; on Silver Age Poetry, 214n34
Basmanova, Marina, 283, 293
Battershill, Claire, 242–44
Batum (Bulgakov, M.), 268
Beg (*Flight*) (Bulgakov, M.), 263–64
Begichev, Stepan, 75, 76
Belaya gvardiya (*The White Guard*) (Bulgakov, M.), 260
Belinsky, Vissarion, 59, 94, 95, 97, 99, 129, 237; Dostoevsky and, 156, 162; Gogol, Nikolai, and, 100, 101, 110, 112n8
Belknap, Robert, 169n10
Belozerskaya, Lyubov E., 255, 260, 261, 263
Bely, Andrei, 93, 101, 103, 222, 226, 228, 232n15
Benton, Michael, 3
Berberova, Nina, 201
Berdnikov, Georgy, 177–80

Berdyaev, Nikolai, 9
Berlin, Isaiah, 240, 241, 285
Bernhardt, Sarah, 248
Bethea, David, 29, 48, 64n15, 249–50
Biografiia i kul'tura (*Biography and Culture*) (Vinokur), 14
Biografiia prodolzhaetsia (*Biography Continues*, ZhZL) subseries, 26
biographers: biographies of, 31; with biography as genre, 46–48, 56; footnotes and sources, 24, 121, 214n29, 256, 282, 284; foreign, 41n123; generalists as, 10, 17; Gorky with, 17, 22; heroes and, 44n172; Loseff as, 279, 296n39; Pavlenkov with, 10–12, 35n46, 36n53, 36n58; purges of, 40n107; with Pushkin, 45, 46–47, 48, 76; role of, 9, 27–32, 32n1, 32n5, 48, 58; Varlamov as, 257–59; women, 3, 35n46, 69, 78–79
biographical legend, 13, 47–48, 96, 241, 276
Biographical Library: in *Lives of Remarkable People* series title of Pavlenkov, 8, 10–11, 31, 33n9, 44n179; 39n97; as series title of other presses, 14, 38n77
biographical novel, 24, 41n132, 55; Griboedov in, 56, 77–78; Grossman on, 57; Tynyanov on, 14, 17, 18, 47, 56, 84, 89n38
biographie romancée, 50, 55, 106
biography, 37n65; ancient, 3, 4; of biographers, 31; as canon, 2, 3, 20; collective, 5, 8, 9, 14, 34n26, 274; commercialization, 238, 239; comparative, 1–2, 32n7, 33n8; compilation approach to, 45, 46–47; functions of, 1–2, 13, 195, 236; as genre, 1, 3, 4, 6, 13–15, 33n8, 45, 56, 57, 93, 95; Gorky and philosophy of, 191–93, 213n18; guidelines, 16, 24; history in Russia, 4–8; life-and-works type of, 47, 49; "new," 12–13, 14, 37nn65–66, 52, 132, 207, 243,

287; philological, 239, 281, 285, 286; poetics of, 2; of political and state actors, 16, 26; popular, 28, 55, 82, 90n50, 115n36, 228; positive role models in, 8, 12, 20, 21, 24, 93, 103, 104, 108, 111; Pushkin and genre of, 45, 48–50; readership, 9–10, 18, 53–54; scholarly, 53, 62, 64n12; "scholarly-popular," 24; talk shows about, 63, 85; theory of, 13–14, 28, 32n7; types of, 5–6, 8, 12, 13–14, 16, 17, 18, 20, 24, 58, 141n2, 191, 237, 256, 263, 277; videos on, 27, 299n85; in wartime, xxx, 19–20, 40n109, 40n111, 65n20, 104–5, 123; of women, 9, 35n46, 234–35; of writers, 11–12, 16, 20, 23–24, 28–29, 46; writing principles, 22. *See also The Lives of Remarkable People*, history of Russian biography in
Biography and Culture (*Biografiia i kul'tura*) (Vinokur), 14
Blok, Alexander, 52, 54, 62, 214n34, 255, 256, 274; death, 225–26; father of, 219–20, 226; modernism and, 217–18, 220–27, 230–31; Novikov, Vladimir on, 218, 224–31; photographs, 224, 226, 227, 229; politics and, 220–22, 229; Russian Symbolism and, 218–19, 222, 226, 227, 230; as Silver Age poet, 223, 228; Turkov, A. M. on, 218, 221–25, 227, 231
Blok, Lyubov, 223, 226
"Blok Volumes" (*Blokovskii sbornik*) series, 223
Bobyshev, Dmitry, 241, 283
Bocharov, Sergei, 62
Bogdanov, Alexander, 199, 212n8
Bogomolov, Nikolai, 30–31
Bojanowska, Edyta, 95, 115n32, 115n39
Bokshanskaya, Olga Sergeevna, 265
Boldyrev, Nikolai, 25, 120, 122
Bonaparte, Napoleon, 18, 157
Bondarenko, Vladimir, 274, 287–93

"Book Bazaar" (*Knizhnoe kazino*) (radio show), 78
books, prohibited, 6, 11; as weapons of propaganda, 20, 40n109
"A Boring Story" (Chekhov), 182
Boris Pasternak (Bykov), 26, 31, 207
Boswell, James, 278
Bourdieu, Pierre, 233–34
brain research, 193–94, 212nn10–11
brand recognition, 9, 21, 26, 27, 62, 238–39
Brintlinger, Angela, 43n160, 90n55, 237, 238–39
British East India Company, 72, 81, 84
Bryusov, Valery, 222, 232n15
Brockhaus and Efron Encyclopedic Dictionary, 34n28
Brodsky, Anna, 285
Brodsky, Joseph: Akhmatova and, 241, 275, 276, 277; biography of, 42n151, 44n171, 48, 239; Bondarenko and, 274, 287–93; critical reactions to Bondarenko biography, 292, 293; critical reactions to Loseff biography, 286–87; death, 293; with hijacking plan, 283; ideological biography and, 289–92; influence, 217, 273, 274; Loseff and, 274, 275, 278, 279, 280, 281–86, 289, 291, 293, 294n2; with Nobel Prize in Literature, 274, 281; personal life and future biographies, 293–94; photographs, 277, 290, 294; publication of *Works* (*Sochineniia*), 279–80; trial of, 283–84; as US Poet Laureate, 274, 293
Brodsky, Maria, 275, 285, 293
Brokhaus and Efron publishing, 14, 34n28
Brooks, Jeffrey, 100
The Brothers Karamazov (Dostoevsky), 148, 153–54, 161, 168
Buckle, Henry Thomas, 128, 142n15
Buddha, 8, 9
Bulgakova, Elena, 255, 260, 264, 265

Bulgakov, Mikhail, 17, 123, 194, 212n12; death, 267–68; Molière and, 265–67, 268, 269; spirituality, 259–61, 268; Stalin and, 263, 264, 265, 268; Tolstoy, Alexei, and, 262; Varlamov on, 255–71; wives of, 255–56, 259, 260–65
Bulgakov, Sergius, 161
Bulgakov, Valentin, 137
Bulgarin, Faddei, 73, 74, 75, 76, 78, 88n23
Bulkina, Inna, 31, 33n8, 239
Bunina, Anna, 234
Bunin, Ivan, 9, 171, 181, 206, 273
Bykov, Dmitry, 26, 30, 31, 44n173, 207–11, 239, 274, 296n34
Byron (Lord), 13, 50, 81, 96
Byt i bytie Mariny Tsvetaevoi (*Everyday Life and Being of Marina Tsvetaeva*) (Shveitser), 245–48

Campfire (*Koster*) (journal), 279
canon: biography as, 2, 3, 20; formation, 236–39; formation and cult of author, 236–39
canonization, 195, 220, 235, 236–37, 244
Captain's Daughter (*Kapitanskaia dochka*) (Pushkin), 50, 57
Carlyle, Thomas, 3, 7, 33n9, 35n47, 237, 252n16
cartoons, 27, 43n154, 81
Catherine II (Catherine the Great, empress of Russia), 34n31, 64n15
Cavafy, C. P., 52–53
celebrity, cult of, 238
Celine, Louis Ferdinand, 27
"The Cemetery" (Gorky), 192–93, 195, 212n7
censorship, 6, 10–11, 17, 22–23, 28, 34n31, 36n55–56, 39n106, 75, 152, 168, 170n25, 180, 239–240, 270, 273
Chaadaev, Pyotr, 60
Chalenko, Alexander, 292
Chavchavadze, Alexander, 71, 86n9

Chavchavadze, Nino, 71, 74, 75, 77, 85, 87n21, 89n34
Chekhov: A Life (Rayfield), 183
Chekhov, Anton, 59, 123, 145, 171–90; Dreyfus affair and, 172, 173; Gorky and, 174–75, 198; inner slave, Chekhov on, 173, 174, 175; letters from, 173, 186, 187; women and, 173, 176, 179, 185, 187
Chekhov: The Life of a Solitary Individual (Kuzicheva), 183–87
Cherkasov, Vladimir, 11
Chernykh, Vadim, 242
Chernyshevsky (Kamenev), 18
Chernyshevsky, Nikolai, 18, 59, 97, 102, 108, 152, 158; arrest, 159; influence, 208, 237
The Cherry Orchard (Chekhov), 176
Chertkov, Vladimir, 138, 139
Childhood ("Detstvo") (Gorky), 200, 214n34
Children's Literature (*Detskaia literatura*), 52, 56
Chiny i liudi (*Ranks and People*) (film), 171–72
Choldin, Marianna Tax, 6
Christian doctrine, 133
Christie, Agatha, 79
Christmas Poems (Brodsky), 288
"*Chto delat'?*" (*What Is to Be Done?*) (Chernyshevsky), 208
Chudakova, Marietta, 258, 261, 264–65
Chukovskaya, Lydia, 240, 245
Chukovsky, Kornei, 17, 18, 37n68, 109, 201, 231n2, 244–45
Clark, Katerina, 15, 220, 262
Clowes, Edith, 205, 215n42
coded language, censorship and, 23, 39n106
Collected Works (Blok, A.), 223, 228
collective biography, 5, 8, 9, 14, 34n26, 274
commercialization, of biography, 238, 239
comparative biography, 1–2, 32n7, 33n8

Index

compilation approach, to biographies, 45, 46–47
Complete Collected Works (Pushkin), 48–49
composers, 1, 9, 40n121, 262
The Confession (Tolstoy, L.), 134
conjecture (*domysel*), 22, 24
Contemporaries (*Sovremenniki*), 244–45
The Contemporary (*Sovremennik*), 152, 158, 159
Cooke, Belinda, 287
The Cossacks (Tolstoy, L.), 57
cover design, 21
Craft (*Remeslo*) (Tsvetaeva, M.), 234
Crime and Punishment (Dostoevsky), 152–53, 155, 158, 161, 165
"Crocodile" (Dostoevsky), 158
Cromwell, Oliver, 127, 142n15
Crowley, Alistair, 27
cults: of heroes and celebrity, 208; of Progress and Gorky, 203, 214n28

Dante, 245, 289
D'Anthès, Georges, 51
Danton, Georges, 16
Da Vinci, Leonardo, 102
The Days of the Turbins (Bulgakov, M.), 263, 264
Dead Souls (Gogol), 99, 100, 104, 105, 113n20
The Death of Vazir Mukhtar (*Smert' Vazir-Mukhtara*) (Tynyanov), 56, 69, 78, 84–85
Decembrist Uprising, 70–71, 74, 75
Deich, A. I., 16–17
Delvig, Anton, 49–50
Demidovs, 9
Demons (Dostoevsky), 147, 148, 149, 153, 159, 165–66, 170n29
Derman, Abram, 172
Derzhavin, Gavriil, 48, 50, 64n14
Desiaterik, Vladimir, 25, 128
de-Stalinization, 22, 105–6
Detskaia literatura (*Children's Literature*), 52, 56

"Detstvo" (*Childhood*) (Gorky), 200, 214n34
Diary Notes (*Zametki iz dnevnika*) (Gorky), 209
Dickens, Charles, 13, 79, 81, 114n24
dictionaries, 5, 8, 13, 34n28, 59
Dictionary of Memorable People of Russia (Bantysh-Kamensky), 5
Diderot, Denis, 32n1, 36n58
Dobrenko, Evgeny, 14, 104, 146, 262
Dobrolyubov, Nikolai, 10, 76, 158–59, 237
Doctor Zhivago (Pasternak), 207
Dolgopolov, Leonid, 228
domysel (conjecture), 22, 24
Donne, John, 291
Dostoevsky: Critical Biographical Sketch (Zaslavsky), 147
Dostoevsky, Fyodor, 24, 43n160, 57, 110, 120, 127, 135, 145–170; biography in Pavlenkov's series, 169n10; exile in Siberia, 120, 147, 152, 156–57, 160, 163, 165; Gorky and, 147–48, 149, 150; ideologue, Dostoevsky as, 147, 150–54; and Pushkin speech, 55, 168; *raznochintsy* and, 161; spirituality and, 157; as writer, 160–68
The Double (Dostoevsky), 156
Dovlatov, Sergey, 273
Dreyfus affair, 172, 173
dualism, 102, 107, 201–2, 205
Dudaev, Dzhokar, 27
Duel and Death of Pushkin (Shchegolev), 41n132, 47, 55–56, 57
"Dve dushi Maksima Gor'kogo" ("The Two Souls of Maxim Gorky") (Chukovsky), 201
Dvenadtsat' (*The Twelve*) (Blok, A.), 220, 226, 229, 230

editorial boards, 257; Academia and Gorky, 169n11; Gorky and, 16, 18, 22, 23, 56; internal notes and workings of, 39n97; members, 16,

18–19, 39n87, 66n37; Pavlenkov and, 16; posthumous publication of Gorky's literary sketches, 37n68; purges and, 18–19; Tikhonov and, 18; Tomashevsky and, 66n37; Tynyanov and, 78, 89n38
editors: Gorky as, 193–95; Pavlenkov and, 11, 19; Pomerantseva as, 12, 36n62, 45, 278–79; and "Russophilia," 42n137; women, 12, 36n62, 45; with writers and censorship, 22–23
education and proper upbringing (*kultur'nost'*), 2
Efron, Ariadna "Alya," 247, 248
Efron, Georgy "Mur," 247, 250
Efron, Irina, 247
Efron, Sergei, 248
Egyptian Nights (Pushkin), 57
Eikhenbaum, Boris, 13–14, 18, 47, 276
Ekho Moskvy (radio station), 78
Elagina, Elena, 250
Eliot, T. S., 284
Emerson, Caryl, 28, 43n160, 61, 113n19, 169n10
émigrés, 46–47, 59–62, 245
encyclopedias, 5, 8, 228
"Enemies" (Chekhov), 176
Encyclopedic Dictionary (*Entsiklopedicheskii slovar'*) (Pavlenkov), 34n28
Epilogue (*Posleslovie*) (Loseff), 280
The Epoch (literary journal), 152
Epuferev, Alexander, 63
Ermilov, Vladimir (General), 70–71, 72, 174–77, 178, 179
Esenin (Lekmanov and Sverdlov), 31
Esenin, Sergei, 31, 249
Essay on Man (Pope), 4
Etkind, Alexander, 244
Etkind, Efim, 279
etymology, of biography, 4
Evening Album (*Vechernii al'bom*) (Tsvetaeva), 247

Everyday Life and Being of Marina Tsvetaeva (*Byt i bytie Mariny Tsvetaevoi*) (Shveitser), 245–46
Evgenii Onegin (Pushkin), 55, 125
Evtushenko, Evgeny, 250 *See also* Yevtushenko, Yevgeny

Facebook, 27, 294, 299n85
Falikov, Ilya, 249–51
Fanger, Donald, 96
Faraday, Michael, 127
Fath-Ali (Shah of Iran), 71, 73, 75, 82–83
Fatherlessness (Chekhov), 181–82
Faust (Goethe), 267
Feinstein, Elaine, 240
Feuerbach, Ludwig, 199
Fiery Revolutionaries series (*Plamennye revoliutsionnery*), 23, 24
Filippov, Aleksei, 82
First Congress of the Union of Soviet Writers, 18, 215n38
Flaubert, Gustav, 126
Flight (*Beg*) (Bulgakov, M.), 263–64
Fomichev, Sergei, 64n12, 69, 71, 80, 82, 86n4
Fontanka.ru, 292
Fonvizina, Natalia, 164
footnotes, 170n25, 296n24; biographers and, 24, 121, 214n29, 256, 282, 284; scholarly audience and, 53
For and Against (Shklovsky), 146
forbidden authors, 119
forbidden books, 6
Formalist biography theory, 13–14, 28
Formalist literary critics, 13. *See also* Eikhenbaum, Boris; Shklovsky, Viktor; Tomashevsky, Boris; Tynyanov, Yuri
Fourierists, 151
Freeborn, Richard, 273–74
Frumkina, Revekka, 246–47
Frunze, Mikhail, 16
Fyodorov, Nikolai, 192, 212n6, 213n14

Gandlevsky, Sergei, 285
Garibaldi, Giuseppe, 13
Gatov, Vasily, 233
genres: of biography and Pushkin, 45, 48–50; biography as, 1, 3, 4, 6, 13–15, 33n8, 45, 56, 57, 93, 95; documentary fictional tales, 52, 56; Pushkin as writer of all, 51 *See also* biographical novel, *biographie romancée*, hagiography, popular biography, scholarly biography, "scholarly-popular" biography, secular biography
Ginsburg, Mirra, 142n11
Ginzburg, Lydia, 28, 29
Gippius, Zinaida, 225
Gireev, Devlet, 258
Gitovich, Irina, 171, 189n22
Givens, John, 269
Gladkov, Alexander, 22
Goethe, Johann Wolfgang von, 181, 267
Gofman, Modest, 61
Gogol (Stepanov), 105–8
Gogol (Voronsky), 101–4, 112n5
Gogol (Zolotussky), 108–11, 237–38
Gogol as a Teacher of Life (popular brochure), 98, 115n30
Gogol: His Life and Literary Activity (Annenskaya), 93–94, 97–101, 108, 115n36
Gogol, Nikolai, 7, 64n3, 93–117, 116n42, 116n55, 126, 135, 140; Annenskaya on, 93–94, 97–101, 108; Belinsky on, 94, Belinsky's letter to, 112n8; biography of, 26, 237; biography in Pavlenkov's series, 97–101; dualism and, 102, 107; as a hick (*khokhol*), 95, 115n32; model for Soviet Russia, 101–4; national identity, 95–96, 113n12; purported psychological disorders and, 94–95; spirituality and, 99–100, 108–11, 117n56; Stepanov on, 105–8; in *Velikie russkie liudi* series, 104–5;

Voronsky on, 101–4; women and, 112n4; Zolotussky on, 108–11
The Golden Calf (*Zolotoi telenok*) (Ilf and Petrov, A.), 209–10
Goncharov, Ivan, 57, 128, 142n15, 237
Gorbachev, Mikhail, 274
Gorbanevskaya, Nataliya, 241
Gorbunov, Iunii, 33n9, 36n52–53
Gordin, Yakov, 275, 280, 295n23
Gore ot uma (*Woe from Wit*) (Griboedov), 69, 70, 74, 75, 76, 79, 81
Gorky (Bykov), 207–10
Gorky, Maxim (A. M. Peshkov), 9, 188n5, 191–216, 262n16, 274; Andreev and, 202–3; Basinsky on, 198; with biographers, 17, 22; biographies, 44n173; biography philosophy of, 191–93, 213n18; brain of, 212n11; Bykov on, 207–11; canonization, 195; "The Cemetery," 192–93, 195; Chekhov and, 174–75, 198; criticism of, 25; with cult of Progress, 203, 214n28; death, 197, 213n14, 213n21; with death of son, 215n40; on Dostoevsky, 147–48, 149, 150; dualism and, 201–2; as editor, 193–95; editorial board and, 16, 18, 22, 23, 56; on editorial board of Academia, 169n11; Fyodorov and, 213n14; folklore and, 215n38; Gruzdev and, 195–98; Koltsov, letter to, 17; legacy, 23; Nepomniashchaia on, 38n78; "new Soviet man" and, 15, 38n80; numbering system, 35n48; "On literature," 84; Overman and, 199, 212n13, 215n40; against petty bourgeois values, 208; Pomerantseva and, 56, 191–92, 193, 212n10; religiosity of, 198, 199, 202, 203–4, 214nn30–33; with "scholarly-popular" biographies, 24; Stalin and, 197, 206, 209; Tikhonov, correspondence, 18, 212n12; Tolstoy, Leo, and, 198, 199, 243,

244; Tynyanov, letter to, 84; *VIEM* and, 193, 194; Wells and Rolland, correspondence, 56; on writers as biographers, 17; and *ZhZL* series, 2, 12–19, 21, 22, 23, 56–57, 69, 122, 237, 238, 265–66
Gosizdat (State Publishing House), 14
Graham DuBois, Shirley, 22, 40n121
great men: dictionaries and encyclopedias of, 5; women with oral histories of, 3; writers as, 7
Great People of the Russian Nation (Velikie liudi russkogo naroda), 20
Great Russian People (Velikie russkie liudi) (Molodaya gvardiya), 20, 40n111, 52, 58, 104–5, 123
Griboedov, Alexander, 14, 64n12, 69–92, 86n8; in biographical novel, 56, 77–78; biographical sources, 74–75; as biographical subject, 70–72, 90n50; biography in Pavlenkov's series, 76–77; Bulgarin and, 88n23; as cultural influence, 86n6; death of, 71–72, 73, 74–75, 77, 87n15, 89n33; Decembrist Uprising and, 70–71, 74, 75; Kyukhelbeker, letter from, 87n13; as martyr, 49; monument to, 87n21, 89n34; Pushkin and, 49, 73, 74–75, 77; Skabichevsky on, 69, 76–77, 88n27, 88n29; Tynyanov on, 77–78, 80, 84–85; *Woe from Wit*, 69, 70, 74, 75, 76, 79, 81
Grigorev, V. N., 74
Grigorovich, Dmitry, 187
Grin, Alexander, 257
Gromov, Mikhail, 180–83, 188n19
Grossman, Leonid, 52, 56, 161; on Dostoevsky, 149, 150–54, 155, 156, 158, 170n23; on Pushkin, 57–58, 59
group biography, 5, 6
Grudzinska-Gross, Irena, 292
Gruzdev, Ilya, 195–98, 213n17
Grzhebin Publishers, 12
Grzhebin, Z., 12
Guber, P. K., 47

Gudzy, Nikolai, 123, 137, 141n9
Guevara, Che, 22
Gumilev, Lev, 241
Gumilev, Nikolai, 232n15, 240
"The Gypsies" (Pushkin), 57

hagiographical biography, 4, 286–87
hagiography, 33n14, 98, 197, 210; post-Soviet, 245–51
Haight, Amanda, 240
Harrington, Alexandra, 241–42
Hasty, Olga, 248, 249
Havel, Vaclav, 292
Haven, Cynthia, 277–78, 287
Hegel, Georg Wilhelm, 59, 127
Heifitz, Mikhail, 279
Heine, Henrich, 16–17
Hellbeck, Jochen, 15
Heller, Leonid, 235
Heraclitus, 278
heroes, 22, 23, 24, 35n47, 44n172, 174–80, 238
"heroization" in Soviet literature, 18
Herzen, Alexander, 10, 132, 158, 273
Historical Dictionary of Russian Writers (Novikov, N. I.), 5
historical fiction, 50, 82
Historical Portraits series (*Istoricheskie portrety*), 14
historico-biographical almanacs, 52
History of the Factories, 14–15
History of the Russian Civil War, 15

The History of Young Men in the Nineteenth Century, 15

Hitler, Adolf, 123
Hodgson, Katharine, 292–93
The House of the Dead (Dostoevsky), 157
How Gogol Worked (Veresaev), 116n43
The Humiliated and Insulted (Dostoevsky), 158, 164

The Idiot (Dostoevsky), 153, 155, 157, 166
Ilchuk, Yuliya, 95, 98, 113n22
Ilf, Ilya, 209–10
Illustrations in biographies, 9, 46, 66n38, 224, 226, 229
Images of Humanity series (*Obrazy chelovechestva*), 14
imperialism, 30, 292
Independent Gazette newspaper (*Nezavisimaya gazeta*), 80
inner life, 24, 34n38, 94, 106, 108, 110, 133, 164, 168, 185, 203, 240
intelligentsia, 2, 10, 18, 32, 132
The Intermediary (*Posrednik*) (Tolstoy, L.), 98
"Italian Verses" (*Italianskie stikhi*) (Blok, A.), 219
Ivan the Terrible, 120, 127, 142n15

Jangfelt, Bengt, 290
John of Kronstadt, 135
Jones, Polly, 23–24, 41n133, 42n138, 106
Jones, W. Gareth, 4, 5, 33n23
Joseph Brodsky: A Literary Life (Loseff), 281–87, 294n2
Joseph Brodsky: Russian Poet (Bondarenko), 287–93
Journey to Arzrum (Pushkin), 49, 73, 74
Joyce, James, 243

Kafka, Franz, 179
Kalma, Anna, 55–56, 66n30, 66n33
Kalugin, Dmitry, 4, 7, 27, 34n38, 35n41, 38n76
Kalyuzhnaya, Lyubov, 239–40
Kamenev, Lev, 17, 18, 19
Kantemir, Antiochus, 5, 33n23, 36n58
Kapuscinska, Zofia, 293
Karamzin, Nikolai, 29, 43n160, 66n28, 128, 129, 142n15
"Karusel" (TV channel), 27
Kataev, Vladimir, 176, 189n22
Katkov, Mikhail, 11, 36n58, 164

Kaverin, Venyamin, 266
Kelly, Laurence, 69, 80, 82, 86n10
Kepler, Johannes, 127
Ketchian, Sonia, 240–41
Khardzhiev, Nikolai, 240
Khodasevich, Vladislav, 47, 48, 212n13, 226
Kholikov, Aleksei, 32, 132, 255–56, 269–70
Khosrow Mirza (Prince), 71
Khrushchev, Nikita, 22, 42n138
Kirov, S. M., 16, 101
Kirpotin, Valery, 146
Kjellberg, Ann, 275
Klim Samgin (Gorky), 196
Kniga Publishers, 23
Knight, Nathaniel, 7
Knipper, Olga, 176, 177, 179, 182, 185
Knizhnoe kazino ("Book Bazaar") (radio show), 78
Kogan, P. V., 172–73, 175
Koltsov, Mikhail, 16, 17, 19
Komarov, G., 280
Korf, Nikolai, 9
Koshelev, V. A., 82
Koteliansky, Samuel, 243
Kovalenko, Svetlana, 239–45, 250
Krieve, Sarah, 244
Krupskaya, Nadezhda K., 59
Krylov, Ivan, 79
Ksenofont, 135
Kudrova, Irma, 246, 250
Kulish, P. A., 7, 97, 98, 113n22, 114n27
kultur'nost' (education and proper upbringing), 2
Kurbatov, Valentin, 132–33
Kurukin, Igor, 30
Kushner, Alexander, 280, 290
Kuzicheva, Alevtina, 183–87
Kuzmin, Mikhail, 225
Kyukhelbeker, Wilhelm, 14, 76, 85, 87n13

Lamont, Rosette, 245–46
"The Landlady" (Dostoevsky), 156, 162

Lappa, Tatyana, 255, 259, 260–62
Last Poets of the Empire (Bondarenko), 287
LaVey, Anton Szandor, 27
Lavrov, Pyotr, 8
Laws of Imitation (Tarde), 33n9
Leary, Timothy, 27
Lebedev, A. A., 69
Lee, Hermione, 11, 75
Leikin, Nikolai, 185
Lekmanov, Oleg, 31, 239
Lenin, Vladimir Ilich, 15, 18, 59, 124, 176, 212n11, 215n39; biography of, 41n123, 42n138; Gorky and, 195; Tolstoy, Leo and, 145
Lentulov, Aristarkh, 226
Lermontov, Mikhail, 20, 76, 126, 135, 140, 145, 210, 236, 287
Lerner, Yakov, 283
Leskov, Nikolai, 9
Lev Tolstoy (Basinsky), 44n173, 121, 137–40
Lev Tolstoy (Zverev and Tunimanov), 121–22, 131–37
Lev Tolstoy (Shklovsky), 124
Lev Tolstoy. Flight from Paradise (Basinsky), 141n6
lichnost' (personhood/unique personality), 7, 15, 23, 27, 35n40, 194, 210
"life creation" (*zhiznetvorchestvo*), 226–27, 228, 230
Life of Mikhail Bulgakov (Chudakova), 258, 264
Life of Pushkin (Basina), 52
Life of Samuel Johnson (Boswell), 278
The Life and Death of Lenin (Payne), 41n123, 42n138
The Life of Klim Samgin (Gorky), 211, 216n41
The Life of Monsieur de Molière (Bulgakov), 142n11, 194, 265–66, 269
The Life of Pushkin (*Zhizn' Pushkina*) (Tyrkova-Williams), 59, 60

life-writing, 4, 13, 15, 23, 27, 29, 49 *See also* autobiography, memoirs, vita/e, *zhiitie*, *zhizneopisanie*
Likhachev, Dmitry, 52, 60
Limonov, Eduard, 27
Literary Gazette (*Literaturnaya gazeta*), 15, 23, 43n169, 109, 147, 148
Literary Heritage series (*Literaturnoe nasledstvo*), 221–22
Literary Issues (*Voprosy literatury*), 23, 41n128, 89n45, 117n63, 132, 237
literary celebrations, 54–55
literary life, 3, 48, 98, 164, 178, 287, 294n2
"Literary Rot" (Zaslavsky), 148–49
"Literature and Biography" ("Literatura i biografiia") (Tomashevsky), 13, 47–48, 124
literature, imports to Russia, 35n45
Little Fire magazine (*Ogonek*), 14, 171–72
Livak, Leonid, 223
Lives of Remarkable Children series ("AST" press), 27
Lives of Remarkable People series (*Zhizn' zamechatel'nykh liudei, ZhZL*), 2, 14, 38n78, 45, 51–54 and passim; *Biografiia prodolzhaetsia* (*Biography Continues*) subseries, 26; history of series, 1–44; categories, 9, 16; consistent elements, 43n169; cover design features, 21; criticism, 30–31; editorial board, 18–19; Gorky and, 2, 12–19, 21, 22, 23, 56–57, 122, 237, 238, 265–66; laboratory of, 17, 23, 39n97, 126; with literary biography reconceived, 27–32; *Literaturnye portrety* (1963, 1967, 1983), 37n68; *Malaia seriia* (*Small series, ZhZL*), 26, 42n151, 44n173, 52, 102, 207; Molodaya gvardiya and, 19, 25–31; numbering system, 35n48; Pavlenkov and, 2, 8–12, 16, 20, 21, 25–26, 31, 35n46, 36n53, 36n58, 49, 53, 54, 56, 76–77, 97,

114n24, 119–20, 122, 237, 238, 239, 268; post-Soviet, 26–27; post war, 21–24; precursors to series by Pavlenkov, 3–10; *Prometei* (*Prometheus*) (journal), 23, 41n122, 52, 54, 59, 65n25; purges and, 18–19, 22, 39n106, 40n107, 103; series title translation, 32n5; wartime series, 19–20
The Lives of Repressed People series ("Ultra.Kultura" press), 27
The Living Pushkin (Miliukov), 62
L. N. Tolstoy (Solovyov, E.), 121, 122, 127–31, 132, 136
Lobachevsky, N. I., 181
Loseff, Lev (Losev, Lev), 42n151, 44n171, 239, 296n30; as biographer, 279, 296n39; Brodsky, Joseph, and, 274, 275, 278, 279, 280, 281–86, 289, 291, 293, 294n2; Bykov on, 296n34; critical reactions to biography of Brodsky, Joseph, 286–87; letter from, 276, 280; as poet, 279, 285–86
Losievsky, Igor, 42n142, 43n158, 43n163, 180
Lotman, Yuri, 28, 31, 43n160, 61, 62, 96, 113n19, 246, 249, 251; on human personality, 29; on Pushkin, 236, 276; on Tolstoy, Leo, 125–26, 127, 131
Lovell, Stephen, 21
The Lower Depths (Gorky), 200, 212n13
Loyola, Ignatius, 8
Ludwig, Emil, 13, 22, 37n65
Lunacharsky, Anatoly, 16, 17, 101, 112n6, 208
"The Lute" (Tsvetaeva, M.), 249
Lutsenko, E., 286

Maguire, Robert, 97, 112n8, 114n28
Makolkin, Anna, 3, 4
Malaia seriia (*Small series*, ZhZL), 26, 42n151, 44n173, 52, 102, 207

Maltsov, Ivan, 73, 76
Mandelstam, Osip, 220–21, 232n15, 240, 274
Mann, Iurii, 101–2, 103
Manson, Charles, 27
Maramzin, Vladimir, 279
Marchenko, Alla, 31
marketing tools, 25, 26–27
martyrs, 4, 8; poets as, 49, 244, 250, 251, 274; writers as, 49, 126, 235
Les Martyrs de la science (Tissandier), 8
Marxism, 146, 147, 172
Marx, Karl, 11, 170n25
Masing-Delic, Irene, 38n80, 232n23
Masonic lodges, 4, 6
Mason, John, 4
The Master and Margarita (*Master i Margarita*) (Bulgakov, M.), 259, 260, 262, 266, 267, 268
Materials for a Biography of Gogol (Shenrok), 98
Materials for the Biography of Pushkin (Annenkov, P.), 6
"*materialy k biografii*" format, 6, 34n35
Matvei (Father), 105, 110
Maurois, André, 12, 13, 22, 24, 37n65, 213n18
Mayakovsky, Vladimir, 13, 20, 57, 201
Mazeppa, Ivan, 78
McLean, Hugh, 103, 115n40
Meandre (Loseff), 286, 297n51
Meilakh, Mikhail, 243
memoirs, 4, 10, 29, 49–50, 74–75, 84, 88n21, 88n29, 97–98, 109, 116n55, 173, 197, 208, 223–24, 228, 231n2, 256, 258, 260 262, 276, 284–86, 295n19, 298n67
memorialization, 49, 220
Mendeleev, Dmitry, 30, 181, 229
Merezhkovsky, Dmitry, 101, 199, 232n15
Meshcheryakov, V. P., 69
Miagkov, Boris, 258
Miasnikov, Alexander S., 52, 58–59
Mickiewicz, Adam, 71

Mikhailovsky, N. K., 33n9
military, books as propaganda weapons of, 20, 40n109
Miliukov, P. N., 62, 67n47
Mill, John Stuart, 120
Milne, Lesley, 258
Milton, John, 128
Mirecki, Alexander, 157
Mirza-Yakub (Chief Eunuch), 71, 83
Mirza, Khosrow (Prince), 71
Mizinova, Lika, 173, 176, 179, 185
modernism: Blok, Alexander, and, 217–18, 220–27, 230–31; with negative connotations, 223
modernist literary experimentation (1910–1920s), 12, 105, 243
Modzalevsky, Boris, 61
Moeller-Sally, Stephen, 95, 116n42
Mokulsky, Stefan, 266
Molière, 17, 123, 142n11, 194, 265–67, 268, 269
Molière (play), 267
Molodaya gvardiya, 19, 22, 23, 25–26, 27, 30, 31; children's series, 43n153; *Great Russian People*, 20, 40n111, 58; with historico-biographical almanacs, 52; as publisher of *ZhZL*, 19, 25–31; Yurkin and, 22, 24–26, 30, 41n125, 279, 283; website, 43n152
montage, type of biography, 18
Montefiore, Simon Sebag, 265
monuments, to Gogol, 111; to Griboedov, 87n21, 89n34; to Pushkin, 54
Moor of Peter the Great (*Arap Petra Velikogo*) (Pushkin), 50
Moralia (Plutarch), 239
Morozov, Savva, 215n39
Moscow Art Theater (*MKhAT*), 147, 148, 177, 182, 263–65, 267–68, 215n39
Moscow Worker newspaper (*Moskovskii rabochii*), 14, 188n5
Moscow Writers Union, 245

Moskovskii rabochii (Moscow Worker), 14, 188n5
Moscow Echo (*Ekho Moskvy*) (radio station), 78
Most Beautiful Lady (*Prekrasnaia Dama*) (Blok, A.), 218, 221
mourning rituals, 3, 89n34
Münster, A. E., 5
My Life (Chekhov), 180
myth of the Soviet reader, 21
mythologization, 73, 125, 142n13

Nabokov, Vladimir, 64n3, 113n12, 208, 273
Naiman, Anatoly, 241, 290, 295n17
Nansen, Fridjtof, 13
Nappelbaum, Moisei, 229
national biography, 5–6, 8
national identity and culture (*narodnost'*), 2, 5–6, 14, 26, 95–96, 113n12, 236, 251, 270, 289
nationalism, 20, 117n63
nauchno-populiarnaia ("popular-scholarly") biographies, 24
Nechaev, Sergey, 153, 159, 163, 170n25
Nechkina, Militsa, 71
Nedobrovo, Nikolai, 240
negative hero, 22
Nekrasov, Nikolai, 76, 208
Nemirovich-Danchenko, Vladimir, 148
Nemirovsky, Igor, 48, 61
Nepomnsiashchaia, Tatiana, 36n62, 38n78
Nesselrode (Count), 73
Nesterenko, Maria, 234
Nevsky, Alexander, 4
"new biography," 12–13, 14, 37nn65–66, 52, 132, 207, 243, 287
New Library of the Poet series (*Novaia literaturnaia biblioteka poeta*), 280, 291
New Literary Observer (*Novoe Literaturnoe Obozrenie*), 80
"new Soviet man," 15, 18, 38n80

New Time (*Novoe vremia*),
  173, 175, 178
New woman, 247–48, as literary
  subjects, 247
Newton, Huey, 27
Nezavisimaya gazeta (*Independent
  Gazette*), 80
Nicholas I (Tsar), 73, 75, 194
Nicholas II (Tsar), 11
Nicolson, Harold, 37n65, 279
Nietzsche, Friedrich, 199, 205, 211
Nikolai Gogol (Nabokov), 64n3
Nikolyukin, Alexander, 239
Nobel Prize, 52, 206, 274, 281
Notes of the Fatherland (*Otechestvennye
  zapiski*), 208
Notes from the House of the Dead
  (Dostoevsky), 135, 165
Notes from the Underground
  (Dostoevsky), 152
novelistic techniques and novelization
  (*belletrizatsiia*), 24, 32, 106, 184
Novikov, Ivan, 47
Novikov, Nikolai I., 5, 7
Novikov, Vladimir, 30, 42n151, 52, 62,
  218, 224–31
Novoe Literaturnoe Obozrenie (*New
  Literary Observer*), 80
Novoe vremia (*New Time*),
  173, 175, 178

Obrazy chelovechestva series (*Images of
  Humanity*), 14
Odoevsky, Alexander, 55
Ogonek (*Little Fire*), 14, 171–72
Okhrannaia gramota (*Safe Conduct*)
  (Pasternak), 209
Okudzhava, Bulat, 274
"The Old Woman and the Little Devils"
  (Blok, A.), 214n34
Olesha, Iurii, 209
On Christian Teaching (Tolstoy, L.), 136
Onegin stanza, Pushkin, 51

*On Heroes, Hero-Worship and The
  Heroic in History* (Carlyle), 3,
  33n9, 252n16
"On literature" (Gorky), 84
On Russia (Blok, A.), 220
On Teaching Russian Literature
  (Stoiunin), 236
"On the Independence of Ukraine"
  (Brodsky), 285
Optina Pustyn monastery, 133, 139
Orlov, V. N., 69, 115n30, 178, 186, 241
Oskolki (journal), 185
Osovsky, Oleg, 31
Otechestvennye zapiski (*Notes from the
  Fatherland*), 208
Overman (Übermensch), 199,
  212n13, 215n40

Pamuk, Orhan, 52–53
Panaev circle, 155, 162
Pann, Lilia, 287
Parallel Lives (Plutarch), 3, 5
Parke, Catherine Neale, 5
Parnok, Sofia, 248
Parus publisher, 12
Parus ("The Sail") (Lermontov), 210
Paskevich (General), 71, 73
Pasternak, Boris, 31, 187, 207,
  209, 240, 274
patriotism, 20, 58, 104, 105,
  154–60, 228
Paul I (Tsar), 78
Paustovsky, Konstantin, 37n68
Pavlenkov, Florenty Fedorovich, 2, 3,
  8–12, 35n47, 141n1; advertisements,
  8, 35n45; with biographers, 10–12,
  35n46, 36n53, 36n58; *Biographical
  Library: Lives of Remarkable People*
  series, 2, 8–11, 16, 20, 21, 25–26,
  31, 33n9, 39n97; 49, 53, 54, 56,
  76–77, 97, 114n24, 119–20, 122,
  237, 238, 239, 268; biography, 25,
  128; censorship, 10–11, 273; with
  editors and editorial board, 11,
  16, 19; legacy, 11–12, 14, 25–26;

numbering system, 35n48; Pisarev, 8, 35n44; precursors to series, 3–10; role models, 8; Solovyov's letter to, 128; with women writers and translators, 9
Pavlova, Karolina, 234
Payne, Robert, 41n123, 42n138
Pearson, Hesketh, 22
Pellico, Silvio, 105, 116n46
PEN American Center, 293
perestroika, 149, 197, 213n20, 244
Pereverzev, Ivan, 103, 170n23
periodicals, émigré, 47
personhood/unique personality. *See lichnost'*
Peshkov, A. M. *See* Gorky, Maxim
Pestalozzi, Johann Heinrich, 19
Peter I (Tsar), 6, 50, 63
Petersburg Censorship Committee, 11
Petrashevsky circle, 151, 162
Petrov, Andrei, 30, 31, 36n62, 78, 209–10
Petrov, S. M., 69
petty bourgeois (*petit bourgeois*) values, 171–74, 175, 177, 186, 187, 208
philological biographies, 239, 281, 285, 286
philosopher, Dostoevsky as, 154–60
Philosophy of the Common Task (Fyodorov), 192
Pikel, R., 264
Pinkevich, A. P., 19
A Pioneer Means Number One (*Pioner—znachit pervyi*), 43n153
Pioneer-Heroes, 42n136
Pisarev (Solovyov), 142n15
Pisarev, Dmitry, 10, 35n44, 128, 142n15, 159
Plamennye revoliutsionnery (*Fiery Revolutionaries*), 23, 24
Platonov, Andrei, 257
Pletnyov, Pyotr, 49, 98
Plutarch, 3, 4, 5, 8, 31, 33n8, 34n24, 239
Plutarch for Youngsters, 237

Pobedonostsev, Konstantin, 138, 170n26
Poema bez geroia ("Poem Without a Hero") (Akhmatova), 241
poetics, of biography, 2
Poet Laureate, US, 274, 293
poets: *Arzamas* and, 50; biographies of, 16, 58, 277; Loseff as, 279, 285–86; as martyrs, 49, 244, 250, 251, 274; *New Library of the Poet* series, 280, 291; Pamuk on, 52–53; Silver Age, 223, 228; women, 234–35. *See also* Akhmatova, Anna; Blok, Alexander; Brodsky, Joseph; Bunina, Anna; Lermontov, Mikhail; Loseff, Lev; Pavlova, Karolina; Pushkin, Alexander; Tsvetaeva, Marina
political actors, 16, 26, 42n138
political storytelling, 233
Pol Pot, 27
Polukhina, Valentina, 275, 278, 282
Pomerantseva, Galina, 36n62, 66n31, 78, 106, 191–92; on censorship and coded language, 39n106; compilation approach and, 45, 46; as editor, 12, 36n62, 45, 278–79; on Gogol, Nikolai, and spirituality, 117n56; Gorky and, 56, 191–92, 193, 212n10; on post-war *ZhZL*, 22; on Pushkin and genre of biography, 45; on readership, 29–30; on Tynyanov, 89n38; on Vinokur, 38n76
Poor Folk (Dostoevsky), 162, 164
Pope, Alexander, 4
Popov, N. A., 69
popular biography, 28, 55, 82, 90n50, 115n36, 228
Portrait Gallery of Russian Personages (Münster), 5
Portrety zamechatel'nykh liudei, 37n68
Poslelovie (*Epilogue*) (Loseff), 280
Pravda (newspaper), 148–49
Prekrasnaia Dama (*Most Beautiful Lady*) (Blok, A.), 218, 221
Prilepin, Zakhar, 257

print runs, 19, 25, 39n90, 42n145, 101, 115n30, 123, 256, 258
Prishvin, Mikhail, 257
Problems of Dostoevsky's Poetics (Bakhtin), 146, 170n28
Proffer, Carl R., 277, 279
Proffer, Ellendea, 258, 277, 279, 284
Progress Publishers, 142n10
Prometei (*Prometheus*) (journal), 23, 41n122, 52, 54, 59, 65n25
proofreading issues, 30, 293
propaganda, 19, 43n155, 237, 245
Protazanov, Yakov, 171–72
psychological essay, 18
Pugachev, Yemelyan, 64n14, 158
Punina, Irina, 241
Punin, Nikolai, 241
The Puppet Show (*Balaganchik*) (Blok, A.), 219, 221, 225
purges, 19, 22, 103, 108: of biographers and writers, 18–19, 40n107; *ZhZL* and, 19, 39n106, 40n107, 103, 284
Pushkin (Skabichevsky), 53–54
Pushkin (Tynyanov), 47
Pushkin, Alexander, 6, 14, 17, 41n132, 45–67, 125, 155, 169n6, 267, 274; autobiographical novel and, 236, 246; biographers on, 45, 46–47, 48, 76; with *biographie romancée*, 50; biographies of, 42n145, 42n151, 52, 53–55, 57–59; creative personality and, 29; canonization, 45–54, 63, 236–37; émigré and post-Soviet views of, 59–62; genre of biography and, 45, 48–50; Griboedov and, 49, 73, 74–75, 77; influence of, 45, 63; as *kammerjunker*, 51, 61; letter of Pletnyov to, 49; Odoevsky's obituary of, 55; Onegin stanza and, 51; pre-revolutionary, 54–56; Skabichevsky on, 11, 52–55; Soviet, 56–58; Tsvetaeva, Marina, on, 249–50, 251; wartime biography, 58–59; women and, 47
Pushkin Fund (*Pushkinskii Fond*), 52

Pushkin in Exile (Novikov, I.), 47
Pushkin in Life (Veresaev), 46, 47
Pushkin's Don Juan List (Guber), 47
Pushkin speech (Dostoevsky), 55, 168
Pushkin's Relationship to Religion and the Orthodox Church (Metropolitan Anastasy), 61
Putin, Vladimir, 26, 30, 131, 238, 240, 270, 291
Pyman, Avril, 232n11

"Queen of Spades" (Pushkin), 51

Radio Mayak, 79, 85, 91n56
Radishchev, A. N., 7, 35n41
Radzinsky, Edvard, 265
Ranchin, Andrei, 286
Ranks and People (*Chiny i liudi*) (film), 171–72
Rapgof, Boris, 234
Raphael, 154
Rasputin, Grigory, 257
Rayfield, Donald, 183, 189n22
raznochintsy, 10, 114n25, 161
Razvedchiki series (*Secret Agents*), 26
reading rooms, 11–12
Realizing Metaphors (Bethea), 48
Red Star (Bogdanov), 212n8
Rein, Evgeny, 287, 290
religion, Gorky and, 198, 199, 202, 203–4, 214nn30–33
Remeslo (*Craft*) (Tsvetaeva), 234
Reminiscences of Leo Nikolayevitch Tolstoy (Gorky), 199
"Reminiscences of the Unforgettable Alexander Sergeevich Griboedov" (Bulgarin), 74
Repin, Ilya, 9, 59
Resurrection (Tolstoy, L.), 134–35
Retribution (*Vozmezdie*) (Blok, A.), 219–20, 229, 255, 256
Revolution Rekindled (Jones, P.), 41n133
Rice, James, 275–76

role models, in biography: heroic, 12; negative hero, 22; positive, 8, 12, 20, 21, 24, 93, 103, 104, 108, 111
Rolland, Romain, 13, 56
Romanov dynasty, 23, 30
Rothschilds, 9, 128, 142n15
Rousseau, Jean-Jacques, 6, 34n24, 124, 129
Rozanov, Vassily, 199, 246
Rozental, N. A., 11
Rubakin, Nikolai, 9–10
Rulers of Rus (Kurukin), 30
Rurik dynasty, 30
Russian Fairytales (Gorky), 209
Russian modernism, 217, 222, 224–25, 227, 230
Russian Orthodox Church, 4, 61, 131–37, 138, 199, 204, 269, 289–90, 293
Russian People, Life Stories of Compatriots Famous in the Fields of Science, Welfare and Social Progress (Volf), 5
Russian Spring (online journal), 292
Russian Symbolism, 218–19, 222, 226, 227, 230
Russophilia, 42n137
Ruzheinikov, Igor, 85
Rybas, Stanislav, 42n138
Ryzhy, Boris, 250

Sabashnikov brothers publishers, 14
Safe Conduct (*Okhrannaia gramota*) (Pasternak), 209
Safer, Morley, 277–78
Sailor in the Saddle (Stone), 41n132
"The Sail" (*Parus*) (Lermontov), 210
Sanaev, Pavel, 63
Sand, George, 35n46, 114n24, 163
Saparov, Mirsaid, 288
Saraskina, Lyudmila, 26, 149, 160–68, 170n29
Sarnov, Benedikt, 262
Saussure, Ferdinand de, 14
Savelyeva, Yevgenia, 283
Savonarola, Girolamo, 8

Scammel, Michael, 290
Scherr, Barry, 195, 280
scholarly biography, 53, 62, 64n12
"scholarly-popular" (*nauchno-populiarnaia*) biographies, 24
Schuler, Catherine, 248
scientists, 8–9, 16, 20, 59, 126–27, 181–82, 193–94, 237
The Seagull (Chekhov), 182
Secret Agents series (*Razvedchiki*), 26
secular biography, 4
Seduro, Vladimir, 146, 147, 169n6
Selected Passages from Correspondence with Friends (Gogol), 94, 97, 100, 102–3, 105, 107, 110
Seleznev, Yuri, 24, 109, 149, 154–60
Self Knowledge (Mason), 4
Sementkovsky, Rostislav, 11, 36n58
Senkovsky, Osip, 127
Sergeyenko, Pyotr, 139
Serov, Valentin, 181
Service, Robert, 265
Setnitsky, Nikolai, 213n14, 215n44
Shakespeare, William, 154, 181, 242, 247
Shakhmatov, Oleg, 283
Shchegolev, Pavel E., 17, 41n132, 47, 52, 55–56, 57, 66n27, 66n28
Sheaf cooperative press (*Kolos*), 14
Shelley, Percy Bysshe, 13
Shenrok, V. I., 98, 114nn27–28
Shevyrov, S. P., 97
Shilovskaya, Elena Sergeevna *See* Bulgakova, Elena
Shilts, Veronica, 293
Shklovsky, Viktor, 17, 31, 62, 122, 123–24, 146
Shliapkin, A. S., 88n29
Shostakovich, Sergei, 71
Shukshin, Vasily, 257
Shulgin, Alexander, 27
Shveitser, Viktoria, 245–51
Silver Age poets, 223, 228
Simic, Charles, 275
Simons, Judy, 247–48

Sinyavsky, Andrei, 246–47
Sinyavsky-Daniel affair, 245
60 Minutes (TV show), 277, 278
Skabichevsky, Alexander, 11, 52–55, 69, 76–77, 82, 88n27, 88n29
Skatov, Nikolai, 237–38
Slavophiles, 24, 98, 205, 285
Slovar' iazyka Pushkina (*Dictionary of Pushkin's Language*), 59
Small series (*Malaia seriia, ZhZL*), 26, 42n151, 44n173, 52, 102, 207
Smelyansky, Anatoly, 258
Smert' Vazir-Mukhtara (*The Death of Vazir Mukhtar*) (Tynyanov), 56, 69, 78, 84–85
Smirnova-Rosset, Alexandra, 98
Smith, Alexandra, 43n160, 60, 292
Smith, Gerald Stanton, 44n171, 274, 279
Snezhnaia maska (*The Snow Mask*) (Blok, A.), 219, 221, 227
Sobchak, Anatoly, 278
Sobolev, Yuri, 173–74, 175, 179
Sochineniia (*Works*) (Brodsky), 279–80
Socialist Realism, 14–15, 103, 195, 207, 228
Socrates, 283
Sokolov, Boris, 258
Sologub, Fyodor, 48, 216n49
Solovyov, Vladimir, 9–10, 232n15
Solovyov, Evgeny, 10, 142n15, 169n10; Tolstoy, Leo, and, 121, 122, 127–31; views on Tolstoy in comparison with other biographers, 132, 136–38, 141n8, 142n18
Solzhenitsyn (Saraskina), 26
Solzhenitsyn, Alexander, 180–81, 197, 258, 273, 274, 278, 285, 291
"Song of the Stormy Petrel" (Gorky), 208
Sorotkina, Irina, 94
Soviet Literature (*Sovetskaia literatura*) (Bykov), 211
Soviet literature, "heroization" in, 18

Soviet Union: collapse, 25, 42n138, 238; "new Soviet man," 15, 18, 38n80
Sovremenniki (*Contemporaries*) (Chukovsky), 231n2, 244–45
Spektor, Alexander, 43n160
Speshnev, Nikolay, 151, 163, 166
spirituality: Bulgakov, Mikhail, 259–61, 268; Dostoevsky and, 157; Gogol, Nikolai, 99–100, 108–11, 117n56; Tolstoy, Leo, and, 131, 133–36, 138
Stalin (Rybas), 42n138
Stalin, Joseph, 14, 16, 58, 102, 176; Bulgakov, Mikhail, and, 263, 264, 265, 268; de-Stalinization, 22, 105–6; Gorky and, 197, 206, 209; legacy, 240; purges, 18–19, 22, 39n106, 40n107, 103, 108
Stanislavsky, Konstantin, 148
Stankevich, Nikolai, 7
State Journal and Newspaper Publishing Collective (*Zhurgaz, Zhurnal'no-gazetnoe ob'edinenie*), 16, 18, 19
State Publishing House (*Gosizdat*), 14
"The Stationmaster" (Pushkin), 57, 169n6
Stepanov, N. L., 94, 105–8, 116n52, 116n54
The Steppe (Chekhov), 182
Stikhi o Prekrasnoi Dame (*Verses on the Most Beautiful Lady*) (Blok, A.), 219
Stirner, Max, 152
Stoiunin, Vladimir, 236
Stone, Irving, 22, 41n122, 41n132
St. Petersburg Academy of Sciences, 5
Strachey, Lytton, 12, 37n65
Strakhov, Nikolai, 98, 131
St. Stephen of Perm, 109, 111
subscriptions, 9, 19, 21, 280
Sumarkin, Alexander, 279
Surat, Irina, 62
Surguchev, I. D., 198
Suvorin, Alexei, 173, 175, 178, 181
Suvorov, Alexander, 59, 237
Sverdlov, Mikhail, 16, 31

sverkhchelovek, 214n27. *See also* Overman (Übermensch)
Sviatopolk-Mirskii, Dmitrii, 44n171

Taras Bulba (Gogol), 104
Tarde, Gabriel, 33n9
Tarkhova, Nadezhda, 70, 71, 90n52
Tarle, E.V., 18
Taubman, William, 42n138
A Theatrical Novel (Bulgakov, M.), 267, 268
There Once was a Slave (Graham DuBois), 40n121
Thomas, Keith, 5, 6
Three of Them (Gorky), 203
The Three Sisters (Chekhov), 176, 182
Thun-Hohenstein, Fransiska, 15, 16, 39n97
Tihanov, Galin, 146
Tikhonov, Alexander N. (Serebrov), 16, 17, 18, 38n78, 194, 212n12, 266
Timenchik, Roman, 241
Tissandier, Gaston, 8
Tiutchev, Fyodor, 279
Tkachev, P. N., 98
Tolstaya, Andreyevna, Sofiya, 131, 133, 134, 137, 138, 140
Tolstoy, Alexei, 9, 26, 31, 105, 107, 257, 258, 261–62
Tolstoy, Dmitry, 237
Tolstoy, Ivan Lvovich "Vanechka," 138
Tolstoy, Leo, 9, 57, 79, 110, 115n30, 119–44, 141n1; on Annenkov, Pavel, 8; biographies, 144n171, 144n173; censorship and, 10, 11; as confessional novelist, 120; and Edict of Separation (1901), 134, 139; frameworks, 124–27; Gorky and, 198, 199, 243, 244; *The Intermediary* and, 98; Lenin and, 145; Lotman and, 125–26, 127; as opponent of Church, 121, 122, 131–37; on resistance, 141n8; in Rzhanov Hospice, 130; sin of pride and 133, 136; spirituality and, 131, 133–36, 138; Tomashevsky and, 124–25; Yasnaya Polyana and, 123, 128, 129, 132, 136
Tomashevsky, Boris, 13, 47–48, 53, 57, 61, 62, 66n34; editorial board and, 66n37; on Gogol, 96; on Tolstoy, 124–25
Toporov, Vladimir, 243
Torquemada, Tomás de, 8
Tosi, Alessandra, 234
Trans-Caucasia Company, 89n41
translators, as biographers, 9, 10, 11, 36n58, 97
Treaty of Turkmanchai (1828), 71, 72
Trigos, Ludmilla, 43n160, 141n1, 265, 266
Trotsky, Leon, 196
Troyat, Henri, 23
Tsiavlovskaia, Tatiana G., 52
Tsimbaeva, Ekaterina, 69, 78–85, 86n1, 89n41–45, 90n55
Tsiolkovsky, K. E., 181
Tsvetaeva, Anastasiia, 252n16
Tsvetaeva, Marina, 232n15, 235, 238, 240, 245–51, 252n16, 274; Akhmatova and, 233–35, 238, 240, 251; biographies as post-Soviet hagiographies, 245–51; as martyr, 250, 274; as mother, 247, 248; Pavlova and, 234; Pushkin and, 249–50, 251
Tunimanov, Vladimir, 121–22, 131–37, 138
Turgenev, I. S., 57, 95, 122, 128, 181
Turkov, A.M., 218, 221–25, 227, 231
The Twelve (*Dvenadtsat'*) (Blok, A.), 220, 226, 229, 230
"The Two Souls of Maxim Gorky" ("Dve dushi Maksima Gor'kogo") (Chukovsky), 201
Tynyanov, Yuri, 13, 48, 62, 66n31, 69, 90n55, 101, 106, 116n54; with biographical novel, 14, 17, 18, 47, 56, 84–85, 89n38; criticism of, 47; editorial board and, 78,

89n38; Gorky's letter to, 84; on Griboedov, 77–78, 80, 84–85; Pomerantseva on, 89n38
Tyrkova-Williams, Ariadna, 42n145, 52, 59–63

Übermensch (Overman), 199, 212n13, 215n40
Ueland, Carol, 43n160, 141n1, 265, 266
Ultra.Kultura press, 27, 43n155
Ulysses (Joyce), 243
Umansky, Alexander, 283
Uncle Tom's Cabin (Stowe), 114n25
universal biography, 5–6, 8
Universal ZhZL (*Vselennaia ZhZL*) (newspaper), 26–27
"The Unknown Woman" (*Neznakomka*) (Blok, A.), 219, 224–26
Untimely Thoughts (*Nesvoevremennye mysli*) (Gorky), 208
Ural (journal), 109
Ural Press, 25
Ushakov, F. V., 7

Varlamov, Alexei, 26; as biographer, 257–59; on Bulgakov, Mikhail, 255–71; criticism of, 269–70; Kholikov on, 255–56
Vasari, Giorgio, 102
Vatsuro, Vadim, 61
Vavilov, Sergei, 16
Vdovin, Alexey, 236
Vechernii al'bom (*Evening Album*) (Tsvetaeva, M.), 247
Velikie liudi russkogo naroda (*Great People of the Russian Nation*), 20
Velikie russkie liudi (*Great Russian People*) (Molodaya gvardiya), 20, 40n111, 52, 104–5, 123
Venclova, Tomas, 277, 290
Vengerov, Semyon, 13
"Venok mertvym" ("Wreath for the Dead") (Akhmatova), 243
Veresaev, Vikenty, 46–47, 48, 56, 64n3, 116n43

Vernadsky, Vladimir, 9
Verses on the Most Beautiful Lady (*Stikhi o Prekrasnoi Dame*) (Blok, A.), 219
Vershinsky, A., 104
Victorian biography, 8, 12
Vielgorskii, Iosif, 105
VIEM (All-Union Institute of Experimental Medicine, *Vsesoiuznyi Institut Eksperimental'noi Meditsiny*), 193, 194, 215n40
Viereck, Peter, 277–78
Vigdorova, Frida, 283
"Vii" (Gogol), 102
Vinogradov, Sergey, 288
Vinokur, Grigory, 14, 28, 38n76
vita/e, 4, 48
Vitberg, Fedor, 98
Vodovozov, N. V., 94, 104–5, 116n45
Volf, M.O, 5
Volkov, Solomon, 277, 287, 288, 295n23
Voloshin, Maximilian, 232n15, 247
Voltaire, 6, 32n1, 124
Voprosy literatury (*Literary Issues*), 23, 41n128, 89n45, 117n62, 132, 237
Vorobieva, Maria (Masha), 293
Voronsky, Alexander, 17, 19, 26, 94; death date, 115n38; on Gogol, Nikolai, 101–4, 107, 111, 112n5
Vorontsova, Eliza, 60
Voskoboinikov, V. M., 43n153
Vozmezdie (*Retribution*) (Blok, A.), 219–20, 255, 256
Voznesensky, Andrey, 274
Vremia (TV channel), 63, 67n54
Vselennaia ZhZL (*Universal ZhZL*) (newspaper), 26–27
Vsesoiuznyi Institut Eksperimental'noi Meditsiny (All-Union Institute of Experimental Medicine, VIEM), 193, 194, 215n40
vymysel (creative invention), 17, 22, 24; *khudozhestvennyi vymysel,* (artistic intuition), 17

Vysotsky, Vladimir, 52, 62, 274

Wachtel, Andrew, 65n16, 235–36
Wadsworth, William, 275
War and Peace (Tolstoy, L.), 57, 129, 137
"Ward No 6" (Chekhov), 175, 182
wartime: books in, 19–20, 40n109, 40n111, 65n20, 104–5, 123
Watts, James, 127
Weidle, Wladimir, 217
Wells, H. G., 13, 56, 104
Western biographical theory, 13–14
Western biography, 17, 24, 191, 256, 263
Westernizers, 24, 285, 292
What Is to Be Done? (*Chto delat'?*) (Chernyshevsky), 208
The White Guard (*Belaya gvardiya*) (Bulgakov, M.), 260, 262–63
Wigzell, Faith, 293
Witte, Sergei, 229
Woe from Wit (*Gore ot uma*) (Griboedov), 69, 70, 74, 75, 76, 79, 81
women: biographers, 3, 35n46, 69, 78–79; biographies of, 9, 35n46, 234–35; Chekhov and, 173, 176, 179, 185, 187; editors, 12, 36n62, 45; Gogol, Nikolai, and, 112n4; New Woman novels, 247; poets, 234–35; Pushkin and, 47; of *raznochintsy*, 114n25; superiority of, 248; translators, 9, 97; "The Unknown Woman," 224–25, 226; wives of Bulgakov, Mikhail, 255–56, 259, 260–65; writers, 9, 40n121, 234, 235
Woolf, Virginia, 12, 13, 243–44
world intelligentsia, 2
World War II, 20–21, 40n109, 56, 58, 265, 289, 298n64
"Wreath for the Dead" ("Venok mertvym") (Akhmatova), 243
Wright, A. C., 258

writers: authors, 27, 236–39; biographies of, 11–12, 16, 20, 23–24, 28–29, 46; Dostoevsky as, 160–68; editors with censorship and, 22–23; exodus of, 273–74, 283; First Congress of the Union of Soviet Writers, 18; Gorky with, 17; as great men, 7; marginalization of women, 235; as martyrs, 49, 126, 235; Moscow Writers Union, 245; poets, 16, 49, 50, 52–53, 58, 228, 234–35, 244, 250, 251, 274, 275, 277, 279, 280, 285–86, 291, 293; as professional producers of good, 126–27; purges of, 18–19; second- and third-rate, 181; sketches of lives of, 5; women, 9, 40n121, 234, 235. *See also* biographers
Writers on Writers (Kniga Publishers), 23

Yagoda, Genrikh, 196
Yakovenko, Valentin, 11, 252n16
Yakubovich, Pyotr, 10
Yanovskaya, Lydia, 258
Yasnaya Polyana, 123, 128, 129, 132, 136
Yedlin, Tovah, 191, 213n20
Yevtushenko, Yevgeny, 250, 274
YouTube, 27, 67n54
Yurkin, Valentin, 22–23, 24, 25–26, 30, 36n62, 41n125, 279, 283

Zametki iz dnevnika (*Diary Notes*) (Gorky), 209
Zamyatin, Evgeny, 259
Zaslavsky, David, 147–149
Zasulich, Vera, 10
Zhdanov, Andrei, 18, 21, 147
Zheliabov (Voronsky), 101
Zhelyabov, Andrei, 16
zhitie, 4, 98
zhizneopisanie, 4
zhiznetvorchestvo ("life creation"), 226–27, 228, 230

Zhizn' Pushkina (*The Life of Pushkin*) (Tyrkova-Williams), 59
Zhizn' zamechatel'nykh liudei. See *The Lives of Remarkable People*
Zhurnal'no-gazetnoe ob'edinenie (*Zhurgaz*, State Journal and Newspaper Publishing Collective), 16, 18, 19
ZhZL. See *The Lives of Remarkable People*
"ZhZLovskii," 26
Zinoviev, Grigory, 17, 19
Zola, Émile, 126
Zolotoi telenok (*The Golden Calf*) (Ilf and Petrov, A.), 209–10
Zolotussky, Igor, 94, 108–11, 115n30, 117n58, 237–38
Zverev, Alexei, 121–22, 131–37, 138, 142n19
Zweig, Stefan, 13, 22

About the Contributors

Angela Brintlinger is professor of Slavic languages and cultures at Ohio State University. She is a teacher, writer, scholar, and translator and has written extensively about biography, including in her monograph *Writing a Usable Past: Russian Literary Culture 1917–1937* (Northwestern UP 2000, reissued 2008).

J. A. E. Curtis is professor emerita of Russian literature and fellow of Wolfson College, University of Oxford. She has written extensively on the Soviet writers Mikhail Bulgakov and Evgeny Zamiatin. Her most recent publications include: *The Englishman from Lebedian'. A Life of Evgeny Zamiatin (1884–1937)* (Boston: Academic Studies Press, 2013); *Mikhail Bulgakov* (London and Chicago: Reaktion Books 'Critical Lives,' 2017); *A Reader's Companion to Mikhail Bulgakov's 'The Master and Margarita'* (Boston, Academic Studies Press, 2019) and an edited volume, *New Drama in Russian: Performance, Politics and Protest, in Russia, Urkaine, and Belarus* (London and New York: Bloomsbury Academic, 2020).

Caryl Emerson is A. Watson Armour III University professor emeritus of Slavic languages and literatures at Princeton University. Her scholarship has focused on the Russian classics (Pushkin, Tolstoy, Dostoevsky), Mikhail Bakhtin, and Russian music, opera, and theater. Current projects include the Russian modernist Sigizmund Krzhizhanovsky, Bakhtin and the performing arts, neo-Thomist aesthetics, and the great Russian novelists approached as religious thinkers.

Radislav Lapushin is associate professor of Russian at the University of North Carolina at Chapel Hill and the author of two books on Chekhov, most recently, *"Dew on the Grass": The Poetics of Inbetweenness in Chekhov* (2010); excerpts from this book are included in the *Norton Critical Edition* of Chekhov's short stories (2014). He coedited *Chekhov's Letters: Biography.*

Context. Poetics. with Carol Apollonio (2018) and is also the author of several volumes of poetry.

Irene Masing-Delic is professor emerita at Ohio State University and is currently affiliated with the department of Germanic and Slavic languages and literatures at the University of North Carolina at Chapel Hill. She has written on Russian and Soviet Utopias (*Abolishing Death*), Turgenev and Dostoevsky, and the Silver Age (some of her articles dealing with these periods are collected in *Exotic Moscow under Western Eyes*). Comparative analysis of Soviet and Russian approaches to presenting *ZhZL* biographies is a long-standing and current research interest. Her most recent publications are articles on Nabokov's Russian novels (*Mary, The Defense, Glory, King Queen, Knave*). Soviet brain research is an emerging area of interest.

Catherine O'Neil is Associate Professor of Russian at the United States Naval Academy. She studied Russian language and literature at the University of Toronto and received her doctorate from the University of Chicago. Her research focuses on Russian romanticism, Pushkin and the reception of English literature in Russia. She has published a monograph *With Shakespeare's Eyes: Pushkin's Creative Appropriation of* Shakespeare, as well as several articles on Russian, Polish and English romanticism.

Alexandra Smith is reader in Russian studies at the University of Edinburgh. She obtained her PhD from the University of London in 1993. Prior to her arrival in Edinburgh, she worked at the University of Essex, University of Bristol, University of Canterbury (New Zealand), and University of Sheffield. Alexandra Smith is the author of *"The Song of the Mockingbird": Pushkin in the Works of Marina Tsvetaeva* (Peter Lang, 1994) and *Montaging Pushkin: Pushkin and Visions of Modernity in Russian Twentieth-Century Poetry* (Rodopi, 2006) as well as numerous articles on Russian literature and culture. Her coedited book, *Twentieth-Century Russian Poetry: Reinventing the Canon* (Cambridge, UK: Open Book Publishers, 2017), was based on the activities of the project of which she was coinvestigator: "Reconfiguring the Canon of Russian Twentieth-Century Poetry, 1991–2008" (funded by the Arts and Humanities Research Council; 2010–2013).

Jonathan Stone is associate professor of Russian and Russian studies and chair of comparative literary studies at Franklin & Marshall College. He studies early Russian modernism, European Decadence, and the print and material culture of the fin de siècle. He is the author of *The Historical Dictionary of Russian Literature* (Scarecrow Press, 2013), *The Institutions of Russian Modernism: Conceptualizing, Publishing, and*

Reading Symbolism (Northwestern University Press, 2017) and *Decadence and Modernism in European and Russian Literature and Culture: Aesthetics and Anxiety in the 1890s* (Palgrave, 2019). He translated Andrei Bely's *Symphonies*, published by Columbia University Press in 2021. He has published articles on Russian symbolism, decadence, the history of the book, and Mikhail Bakhtin in the *PMLA*, *Russian Review*, *Modernism/Modernity*, and *SEEJ*.

Alexander Spektor is associate professor of Russian at University of Georgia Athens. He is the author of *Reader as Accomplice: Narrative Ethics in Dostoevsky and Nabokov* (Northwestern University Press, 2021) as well as articles on Dostoevsky, Bakhtin, Mandelstam, Krzhizhanovsky, and others. At the present time he is working on his second book on the poetics of language in Russian modernist prose. His other projects include preparing a volume of previously untranslated Bakhtin, a volume of translations of Russian contemporary poet Leonid Schwab, and a collection of nonfiction by Sigizmund Krzhizhanovsky.

Ludmilla A. Trigos, independent scholar, received her PhD in Russian literature from Columbia University and has taught at Columbia, Barnard College, Drew University and New York University. Her books include *The Decembrist Myth in Russian Culture* (Palgrave Macmillan, 2009) and *Under the Sky of My Africa: Alexander Pushkin and Blackness* (coedited with Catharine Theimer Nepomnyashchy and Nicole Svobodny, Northwestern University Press, 2006). She has published articles on nineteenth- and twentieth-century Russian literature and print culture, cultural mythologies, violence and terrorism.

Carol Ueland is professor emerita of Russian and directed the Russian studies program at Drew University. Her publications include "Women's Poetry in the Soviet Union," "The Eastern Path of Emigration: Russian Women Writers in China" (coauthored with Olga Bakich), "Joseph Brodsky and Aleksandr Kushner: The Relationship in Verse," "Pseudonyms and Personae of Marianna Kolosova: Creating a New Feminine Voice in Emigration." Book translations include *Apollo in the Snow: Aleksandr Kushner Selected Poems 1962–1988*, with poet Paul Graves, intro. Joseph Brodsky (Farrar, Straus & Giroux, 1991) and *Apollo in the Grass: Aleksandr Kushner Selected Poems*, with poet Robert Carnevale (Farrar, Straus & Giroux, 2015).

www.ingramcontent.com/pod-product-compliance
Lightning Source LLC
Chambersburg PA
CBHW021341300426
44114CB00012B/1035